CALDER'S UNIVERSE

"The underlying sense of form in my work has
been the system of the Universe, or part thereof.
For that is a rather large model to work from."

CALDER'S

A Studio Book

UNIVERSE

JEAN LIPMAN

Ruth Wolfe, editorial director

THE VIKING PRESS, NEW YORK, IN COOPERATION WITH
THE WHITNEY MUSEUM OF AMERICAN ART

This book was in work for two years in a special office—a temporary Calder research department—in the Whitney Museum. The project involved, besides the editorial team and the Viking group which produced the book, the Calders, their family, a number of close friends and many photographers, collectors and dealers.

JEAN LIPMAN
Editorial Director:
RUTH WOLFE
Coordinator: Richard Marshall
Editorial assistant: Hilva Landsman
Viking editor: Barbara Burn
Designer: Bryan Holme
Jean Davidson acted as coordinator between the Whitney's Calder office and the Calders in France.

The publication of the book was the occasion for a major traveling exhibition based on its content: at the Whitney Museum of American Art, New York, October 14, 1976–February 6, 1977; The High Museum of Art, Atlanta, Georgia, March 5–May 1, 1977; Walker Art Center, Minneapolis, Minnesota, June 5–August 14, 1977; Dallas Museum of Fine Arts, Dallas, Texas, September 14–October 30, 1977. The exhibition was presented through the generosity of Champion International Corporation; it was organized by Jean Lipman with Richard Marshall. Charles Forberg Associates designed the installation, and Marcel Breuer acted as consultant. Tom Armstrong, Director of the Whitney Museum, served as consultant and director of the exhibition.

Library of Congress Cataloging in Publication Data
Calder, Alexander, 1898–
    Calder's universe. (A Studio book)
    An exhibition based on this book is scheduled to be held at the Whitney Museum of American Art, Oct. 14, 1976 to Feb. 6, 1977, and at other museums at later dates.
    Bibliography: p.
    Includes index.
    1. Calder, Alexander, 1898–   . I. Lipman, Jean. II. Whitney Museum of American Art, New York. III. Title.
N6537.C33L56   709′.2′4 [B]   76–28232
ISBN 0–670–19966–4

Note on the Captions

Dimensions: height precedes width; for three-dimensional objects the largest dimension is given; measurements are in inches up to 6 feet and thereafter in feet and inches.

The artist has been consulted for various caption data; sizes or dates listed as approximate are based on his recollection.

Titles of works, in English or French, appear as approved by the artist.

Contents

Preface 6

Introduction 10

Toys 44

The Circus 56

Drawings 80

Oil Paintings 110

Gouaches 118

Graphic Work 132

Tapestries and Rugs 156

Theatrical Productions 170

Innovative Projects 182

Household Objects 198

Jewelry 206

Bronzes 216

Wood Sculpture 220

Wire Sculpture 232

Mechanized Sculpture 252

Mobiles 260

Stabiles 304

Calder's Calendar 329

Author's Bookshelf 341

Who's Who in Calder's World 346

Acknowledgments 349

Preface

This book is intended to be a distillation of Alexander Calder's life and achievement, presenting the outstanding examples of the many kinds of art which he has originated or developed in a personal way. In preparing this critical selection from fifty years of Calder's work, the Whitney Museum's editorial team has spent two years discussing the project with the dealers, museum directors and curators, collectors and critics who have been most directly involved with his career; with members of his family; and, of course, with Sandy Calder himself. The final choice was made much as a museum might have formed an ideal Calder collection, had all his work been available for acquisition. The examples reproduced here were chosen by elimination—a difficult project—after scrutiny of several thousand examples. Quality was the determinant rather than an attempt to cover every variety of work. Even with this puristic approach, no significant category of his oeuvre has been omitted, for such is Calder's virtuosity that he has created outstanding series of works in almost every art medium.

An exhibition based on the content of the book has been organized by the Whitney Museum of American Art and will open in October 1976, in New York. It will then travel to The High Museum of Art in Atlanta, the Walker Art Center in Minneapolis and the Dallas Museum of Fine Arts.

Because I've been so bold as to qualify myself as author of this critical book on Calder, it seems sensible to mention my qualifications. My husband, Howard, and I have known the Calders for about forty years. We met at a party in New York, and I recall that Sandy asked us where we lived. We told him Wilton, Connecticut, and he said he was in Roxbury, not far from us, and why not drive over and visit sometime. He seemed jolly and friendly, and we greatly admired his sculpture, so one day when we were on our way somewhere we stopped at the old Roxbury house. There were about a dozen people outside, a few playing croquet, others watching and drinking draft beer from a good-sized barrel. Sandy ambled by and, I remember distinctly, just said, "Hello, what color do you want?" and I said, "Red?" and he handed me a red mallet and ball and another set to Howard. We joined the croquet game, then drank beer and ate something and left—and I recall thinking that it was like a party out of *Alice in Wonderland*. Since that day we have made many trips to Roxbury (and the Calders to us) and to Waterbury with Sandy to see work in progress at Segre's Iron Works. In later years we visited the Calders in Saché whenever we were anywhere in France, and I don't think we have missed any of his annual New York exhibitions since he joined the Perls Galleries in the mid-fifties. Calder events have often determined the focus of our leisure time. We have planned trips to include major exhibitions and dedications of recent stabiles; the most memorable, in 1973, was the maiden voyage of *Flying Colors*, a jet plane painted with Calder's design.

As collectors, my husband and I have acquired Calder sculpture of all kinds, from large stabiles to a three-inch mobile that Sandy gave us as his *smallest* work. We have quite a few pieces of his jewelry, and gouaches—many of them gifts to us when we visited Saché. We also have examples of oils, lithographs, illustrated books, posters, toys and household implements—and a rug he designed for Howard to make. Most important, as far as we are concerned, are *Le Guichet*, the splendid stabile that we acquired for Lincoln Center in New York, and the great early works from his personal collection that Sandy released for us to give the Whitney Museum. After many pleas, he also consented to have his famous Circus installed at the Whitney on extended loan.

During the thirty years that I was editor of *Art in America*, Sandy was incredibly generous, making covers and illustrations, helping with a portfolio of his circus drawings, creating a special *Art in America* lithograph and a poster—and also patiently, if reluctantly, submitting to long interviews for several major articles about him. While I was editor of publications for the Whitney Museum, I prepared *Calder's Circus*, with lots of help from Sandy; it was published as a paperback with a correlated Whitney show and poster. I should also mention the delightful "Save Our Wildlife" poster that Sandy contributed to my "Save Our Planet" poster series sponsored by Olivetti for the benefit of UNICEF. For the Archives of American Art (a bureau of the Smithsonian Institution) Sandy, his son-in-law Jean Davidson and I collaborated in producing a portfolio of his zoo drawings, which he had rediscovered, after almost fifty years, in his Roxbury studio.

Sandy's generosity has extended in all directions, and I'm afraid both my husband and I have been shameless in our requests. A few years ago Howard, then secretary of the Archives, asked him for some of his papers and photographs for microfilming. Sandy was recalcitrant in this instance (we think he disliked thinking of himself as part of an archive), but in the end he said, "Howard, I don't want to sort through all this stuff, I have it in a suitcase in Roxbury, so just tell them to come and get it." Thus the Archives acquired a great collection of Calder letters, photographs, press clippings and marked catalogues—all of which are also on microfilm in five regional offices. This material is an important element in our book. When I was rereading Calder's autobiography, I noticed a sentence which startled me: "In those days, for the Circus, I always had printed invitations, which I did myself with a linoleum cut. I wish I had some of these left." There were four in the Archives suitcase!

Although there are numerous books, booklets and catalogue essays on Calder, each of them is specialized in some way or presents a sampling of rather casually selected work. There is none with our stated purpose: a highly selective presentation of Calder's work based on esthetic merit rather than an all-inclusive survey of his prolific oeuvre.

In addition to presenting the best of his work, I hope also to sum up something of Calder the man, whose extraordinary presence and personality cannot be communicated through his work alone.

Critical scrutiny and evaluation of Calder's art have interested me for a long time, and the formation of this ideal collection has been evolving gradually in my mind; now I am getting it into print with a team of three co-workers. Ruth Wolfe, who was executive editor of *Art in America* for several years when I was editor, has worked along with me since the early planning stages of the book, compiling a chronology and bibliography, consulting with me on the text and photographs, and acting as editorial director of what became a complex Whitney Museum project. For the past two years we have worked out of a special Calder office, with Richard Marshall serving as coordinator for the Whitney exhibition. Hilva Landsman was our editorial assistant and, with Ruth and Richard, participated in the research for the book.

The introductions to each chapter will briefly present and comment on the various categories of Calder's work. While major objects separate reasonably into chapters, there are some that could fit just as comfortably in one category as another; for example, the decision to assign the Dallas–Fort Worth Airport motorized mobile to "Mobiles" rather than "Mechanized Sculpture" was somewhat arbitrary (in this case, the mobile aspect of the work seemed more important than the fact that it is mechanized). Calder has also made a great many unique, unclassifiable works which we have grouped in the chapter titled "Innovative Projects." I should add that while the sequence of the chapters is somewhat chronological, Calder's series of productions overlap years and decades. Calder worked as a toymaker in the twenties, but he continues to make toys to this day. Every category of his work has been in constant evolution, a continuous, complex weave of subjects and styles. His circus subjects are prominent from the mid-twenties through the present, executed as wire sculptures, woodcarvings, bronzes, drawings, watercolors, oils and gouaches. For example, the Circus seals were followed by the *Performing Seal* mobile (c.1950), a seal abstracted for an untitled lithograph (1962) and the seal with green ball in a 1971 tapestry. The universe, with its infinite space and the majestic movement of the sun, moon, stars and planets, has also been a consistent source of inspiration and imagery for the artist. Indeed, as we explored his work and his statements, it seemed so pervasive a theme that *Calder's Universe* presented itself as an appropriate title for the book.

We have planned this book to allow Calder primarily to speak for himself, adding a wide range of comments by the people who have been most perceptive about his intentions and achievements. We are particularly grateful to his friends and professional associates who contributed statements and drawings, done especially for this book, which appear in the Introduction.

After years of exposure to Sandy, to his work and to critical writing about him, I have come to one of many possible conclusions about a basic reason for his stature in the international art world. His genius seems to be, in part at least, that everything he attempts starts fresh, with the happy anticipation of a stimulating experiment brought to a successful conclusion. Even when a project is inspired by another artist or by one of his earlier creations, the elements are rearranged into new patterns in such a way that the work is re-created. Calder's life work is notable for its originality, vitality, grace and power. It is based on an extraordinary blend of practical technology and creative imagination, of lightheartedness combined with unlimited appetite for sober work; and this great artist's personal and professional simplicity is distilled from the most sophisticated sources.

I fully realize the pitfalls in the task we have set ourselves: to make a critical selection from Calder's prodigious body of work. We can only hope that our best editorial efforts will clarify rather than compress Calder's monumental achievement.

J. L.
January 1976

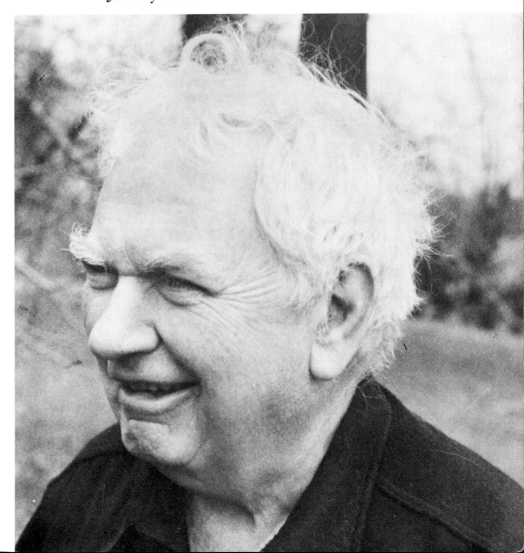

Alexander Calder.

Introduction

The Calder family is virtually unique in the history of American art, having produced—so far—four generations of artists, with promising talent in the fifth. Alexander Milne Calder was born in Scotland in 1846, the son of an Aberdeen stonecutter. This first Alexander Calder worked with his father as a carver of marble tombstones. Aberdeen was a thriving port and fishing center on the North Sea and an important trading outlet for Scottish textiles. Young Alexander is said to have loved the wharves and ships, and to have dreamed of a sea journey to the United States. Scotch and practical, he planned to work at his trade in order to reach America. He went to Edinburgh, and then to London, where he was given a job on the Albert Memorial, which portrayed the late husband of Queen Victoria. Then, aged twenty-two, with meager savings and a young wife, he sailed to America. He settled in Philadelphia in 1868, and two years later a son, Alexander Stirling Calder, was born.

Alexander Milne had studied at the Royal Institute in Edinburgh and the South Kensington School in London; in Philadelphia he studied under Thomas Eakins, Thomas Anshutz and other established artists at the Pennsylvania Academy of the Fine Arts. He produced a number of monumental bronze sculptures, including an equestrian statue of General Meade for Fairmount Park, and four huge eagles and four figure groups that are still in place on the Philadelphia City Hall tower, which is capped by his famous thirty-seven-foot statue of William Penn. This huge project engaged his energies for more than twenty years.

At the time of his father's death, in 1923 at the age of seventy-six, Alexander Stirling Calder (1870–1945) was a highly successful sculptor and a prominent member of the National Academy. The second Calder had studied at the Pennsylvania Academy in the 1880s and at the Académie Julian and the École des Beaux-Arts in Paris from 1890 to 1892. On his return he became an instructor at the Pennsylvania Museum School of Industrial Art and later at the National Academy of Design and the Art Students League in New York. His monumental sculptures were commissioned for numerous city sites—among them Philadelphia, New York, Pasadena, San Francisco, Detroit, Indianapolis, Jefferson City and even Reykjavík, Iceland. Like his father, Alexander Stirling devoted his life to classical sculpture: notable examples are the figure of Washington on the Washington Square Memorial Arch in New York and the elaborate Swann Fountain in Logan Square, Philadelphia, which can be seen with his father's William Penn atop City Hall in the distance. (Situated on the same axis with City Hall and Logan Square is the Philadelphia Museum; since a huge white Calder mobile, *Ghost*, was installed in the stairwell, Philadelphians have been heard to refer to their first family of sculptors as "Father, Son and Holy Ghost.")

Alexander Stirling's wife, Nanette Lederer (1866–1960), was a fellow student at the Pennsylvania Academy when they met; she became a professional portrait painter. Their daughter, Margaret (Peggy), was born in Paris during her parents' stay there in

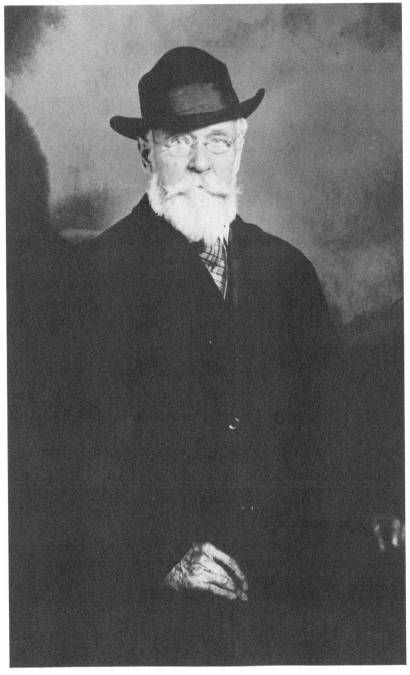

Alexander Milne Calder (1846–1923).

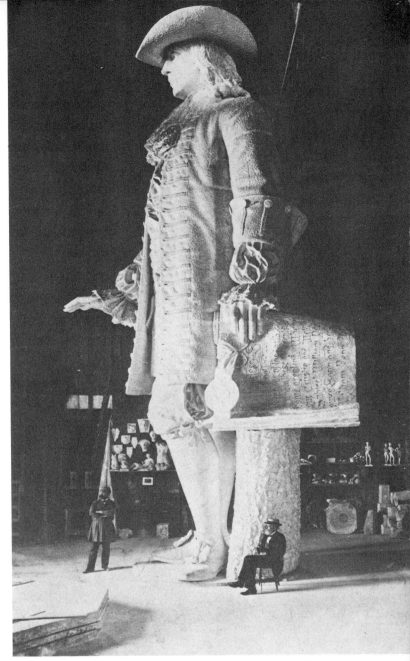

Model for *William Penn*, 1894, Philadelphia City Hall.

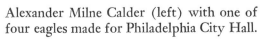

Alexander Milne Calder (left) with one of four eagles made for Philadelphia City Hall.

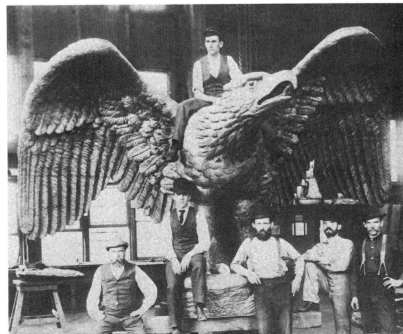

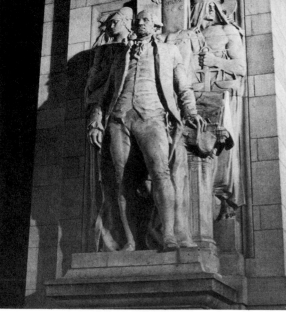

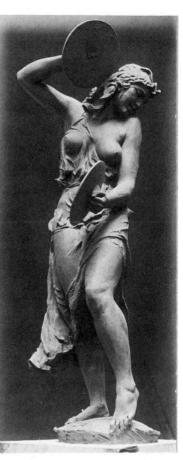

LEFT: *George Washington*, 1918, Washington Square Memorial Arch, New York.

RIGHT: *Dancing Naiad*, 1915, Depew Fountain, Indianapolis, Indiana.

BELOW: *Laughing Boy*, 1910, Jane de Tomasi, Cold Spring Harbor, New York (twelve-year-old Sandy).

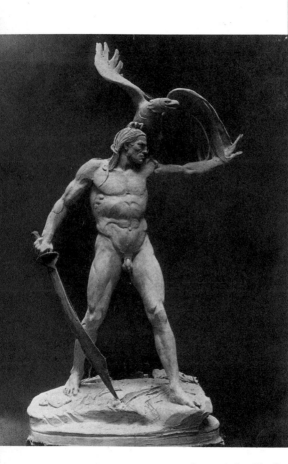

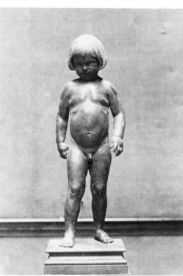

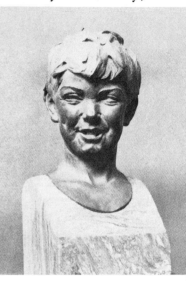

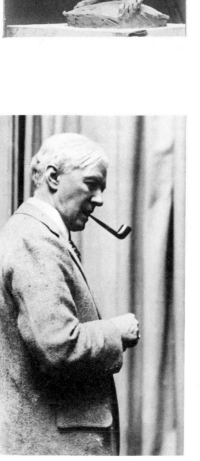

ABOVE, LEFT: *Son of the Eagle*, c. 1913, present location unknown.

ABOVE, RIGHT: *Man Cub*, 1902, Pennsylvania Academy of the Fine Arts (four-year-old Sandy served as model).

RIGHT: *Leif Ericson*, 1931, Reykjavík, Iceland.

12

Alexander Stirling Calder (1870–1945).

1896; their son, Alexander, the third Alexander Calder, was born July 22, 1898, in Lawnton, now part of Philadelphia. Sandy weighed eleven pounds at birth, and when as a four-year-old he posed for his father's sculpture titled *Man Cub*, and later for his mother's oil portraits, it was evident that he was on his way toward the now-famous Calder bulk. The Calder family moved west in 1906 because the climate was recommended for the father's heart disease, a recovery project made possible by a gift of $10,000 from John Lambert, a well-to-do painter friend. The Calders lived in Arizona and then in Pasadena, California, until 1910, when they came to New York State, first settling in Croton-on-Hudson and then in Spuyten Duyvil. In 1913 they returned to California, living in San Francisco and then Berkeley, where Margaret Calder Hayes now lives. In 1915 the family moved again, to New York City, and Sandy entered Stevens Institute of Technology in Hoboken, New Jersey, to study engineering.

The most important events and achievements of his career are listed in the chronology, "Calder's Calendar," and the many people who played a part in his rich life are indexed and identified in "Who's Who in Calder's World." Something more needs to be said about the members of his immediate family, to whom Calder is deeply attached and who have been an integral part of his life and work. In 1931 Sandy married Louisa Cushing James (the philosopher William James and novelist Henry James were her great-uncles) at her family home in Concord, Massachusetts. Their two daughters, Sandra and Mary, were born in 1935 and 1939. In 1955 Sandra married Jean Davidson, son of sculptor Jo Davidson; he is a free-lance writer and a former White House correspondent, and especially important for Calder history because he acted as picture editor and "Boswell" for Calder's autobiography, taking down Calder's comments during long dictation sessions in 1965–66. Sandra, born "amidst blooming mobiles and the first ripple of success," as Jean has described it, is a fourth-generation Calder artist. Her illustrations for children's books are remarkable for their gay content, bold color and strong line—comparable to but in no way derived from her father's drawings and gouaches. The Davidson family—Sandra, Jean and their two children, Shawn, born in 1956, and Andrea, born in 1961—live in Saché, France, where Sandy and Louisa now spend most of each year. Shawn—Willy to his family—is well on his way to becoming a fifth-generation Calder artist. He recently began studying art in New York and shows marked talent as a cartoonist. Mary married Howard Rower in 1961; they live in New York with their two sons, Holton and Alexander, born in 1962 and 1963. Alexander the fourth, called Sandy like his grandfather, can be seen in the following pages with Grandpa trying to look like the baby, and a couple of years later at Lincoln Center while his grandfather supervises the installation of *Le Guichet*.

It is important to consider, in a general way, some of the influences that came early in Calder's fifty active years as an artist. Young Sandy grew up in an art environment; homes were studios, and most of his parents' friends were artists. (One thinks of Louis

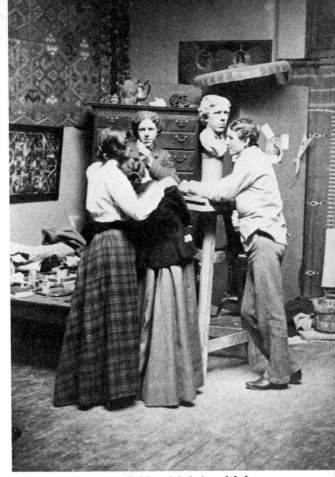

Alexander Stirling Calder (right), with bust of his brother Walter (left), Nanette Calder in plaid skirt, Paris, 1895.

Sandy Calder with mother and father, 1914.

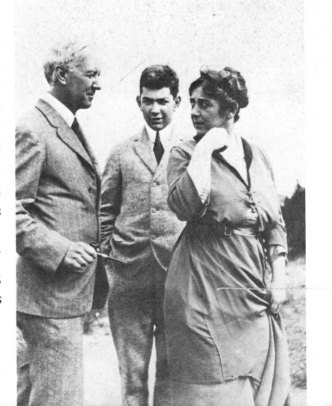

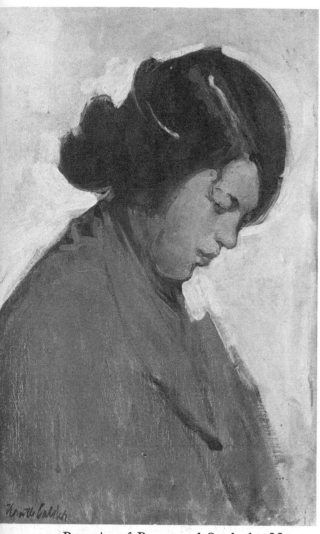

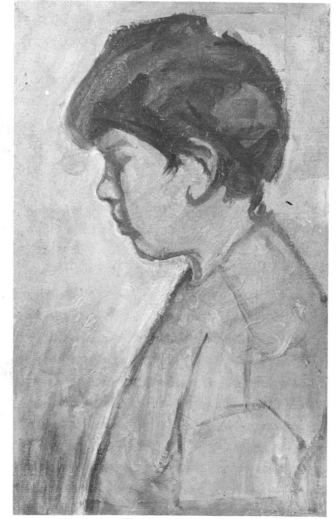

Portraits of Peggy and Sandy by Nanette Calder, painted in 1910 at Croton-on-Hudson, New York, Margaret Calder Hayes, Berkeley, California.

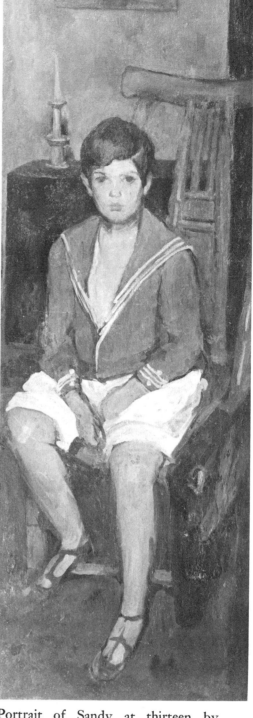

Portrait of Sandy at thirteen by Nanette Calder, private collection, New York.

14

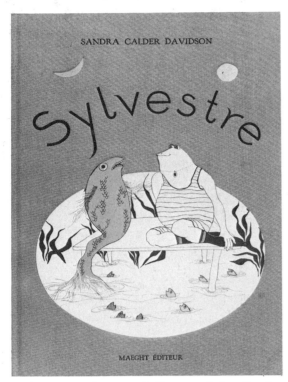

Sylvestre, written and illustrated by Sandra Calder Davidson, 1962.

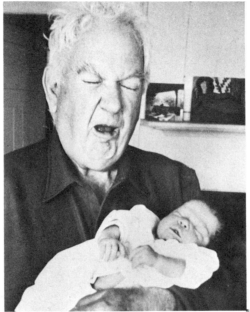

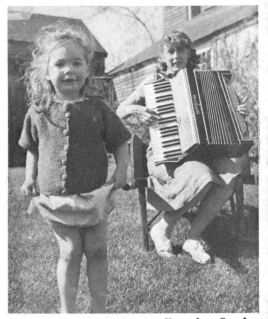

Louisa playing the accordion for Sandra, Roxbury, 1936.

Sandy as a baby, with grandson Sandy Rower, 1961. BELOW: With grandson Sandy during installation of *Le Guichet*, Lincoln Center, New York, 1965.

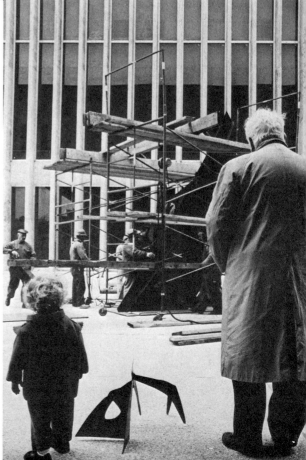

Pasteur's remark, that discovery comes to the prepared mind.) Calder's career might be said to have started at the age of five when, he recalls, he was making little wood and wire figures; at eight he made jewelry for his sister's doll, Thomasine, using bits of copper wire collected from spliced cables left in the streets. Among his childhood creations that have survived is an inch-square piece of copper with two of its corners twisted in opposite directions, so that it spins when one holds it between two fingers and blows on it. Sometimes he and Peggy collaborated; she still has a hat and saddle they made for a small doll and toy horse. Sandy constructed the frame for the hat and provided stirrups and a ring of sheet brass for the saddle; Peggy covered both with chamois.

Before he was ten Sandy had his first workshop. Peggy gave him his first pair of pliers, saving up her weekly allowance of five cents to buy him the seventy-cent tool. From that time on he always had a workshop. When he was in the fourth grade in Pasadena, it was a tent with a wooden floor; later in Croton he was given a cellar room; after the move to Spuyten Duyvil he again had a cellar workshop well equipped with tools. He mentions in his autobiography that he was respected by his playmates for the things he made out of wood, leather, corks, nails and pieces of copper wire, and that his parents always liked and encouraged homemade things.

During his high-school years in San Francisco, Calder tells us, "father had the skylight and I the workshop in the cellar." When he became a practicing sculptor his workshops were of central importance: in Paris from 1926 to 1932 he had studios at 22 rue Daguerre, 7 rue Cels, 7 Villa Brune and 14 rue de la Colonie. His studio in Roxbury and the first and then the second huge one in Saché have been frequently photographed and written about. John Canaday described the Roxbury house with its adjacent workshop as "the loft studio and Greenwich Village pad raised to a celestial level," and the content of the workshop as "an organized clutter. The clutter is apparent to anybody; the organization exists only in Calder's head. He can put his hand on any tool or any bit of wire or metal even when it is buried in what looks like a mound of scrap awaiting removal."

When Selden Rodman saw the studio in Roxbury, he found an interesting parallel between the artist and the Wright brothers:

This was no studio such as sculptors had traditionally worked in throughout the ages. No casts, no marble, no plaster, no armatures. Not a bicycle shop, to be sure, but cer-

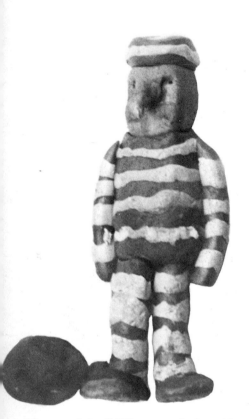

Clay model of Nixon made by Alexander Rower for his grandparents.

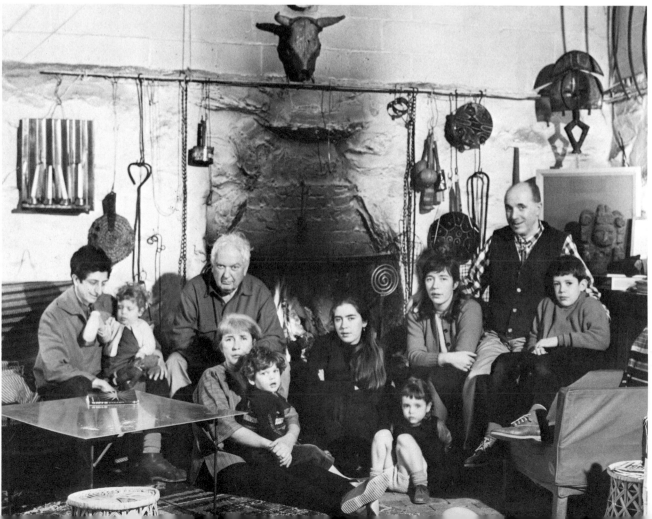

Christmas in Roxbury, 1964. FROM LEFT: Howard Rower holding son Alexander, Sandy Calder, Louisa holding Holton Rower, Mary Calder Rower, Andrea Davidson, Sandra Calder Davidson, Jean Davidson with son Shawn.

16

tainly a machine shop. The floor was deep in steel shavings, wire, nuts and bolts, punched sheet metal. . . . The air was busy with dangling "contraptions," as the brothers in Dayton used to call their experimental warped airfoils and rudimentary engines. But more significantly, I thought, the Wrights too were in love with simplicity, with perfection of motion and economy of means.

The origins of some of Calder's basic ideas and materials can be traced to his boyhood. He mentions that Germantown Academy's athletic rival, Penn Charter, had red, blue and black for their insignia, which, he says, "I always found an amusing combination of colors. I still like it today." The boy who was fascinated by the machinery and movement of San Francisco's gaily painted cable cars eventually made sculpture that moved. His wire sculpture and jewelry go back to the days of Thomasine and other of his sister's dolls. It is also interesting to hear about some gauntlets with wire rings that went with a three-inch helmet he made of overlapping sections of sheet brass put together with wire rivets. His satisfaction in making handy household implements might have originated in the fourth grade at Garfield School in Pasadena. He remembers that he made "a blotting pad out of wood, with a blotter tacked on the bottom and a wire hook to hang it on the side of the desk." He also thought up such things as a two-pronged fork made of wire with a trigger ejector to demolish garden slugs.

In 1922, as fireman on the passenger ship *H. F. Alexander*, he invented several practical devices, including a baffle to direct breezes into the overheated boiler room where he worked. Calder's fascination with the universe, evident in many of his works, originated on this sea voyage. In one of the most vivid passages of his autobiography he recalls:

It was early one morning on a calm sea, off Guatemala, when over my couch—a coil of rope—I saw the beginning of a fiery red sunrise on one side and the moon looking like a silver coin on the other. Of the whole trip this impressed me most of all; it left me with a lasting sensation of the solar system.

Of his many "firsts," perhaps the most important is Calder's concept of the universe as the main subject of an artist's work. In his autobiography, published statements and interviews he has repeatedly stated that the universe is his basic theme, and he has emphasized it frequently in his work with the symbol-shapes of sun, moon and stars. He once told a *Life* reporter: "The first inspiration I ever had was the cosmos, the planetary system. My mother used to say to me, 'But you don't know anything about the stars.' I'd say, 'No, I don't, but you can have an idea what they're like without knowing all about them and shaking hands with them.'" To another interviewer he explained: "In 1932, a wooden globe gave me the idea of making a Universe, something like the solar

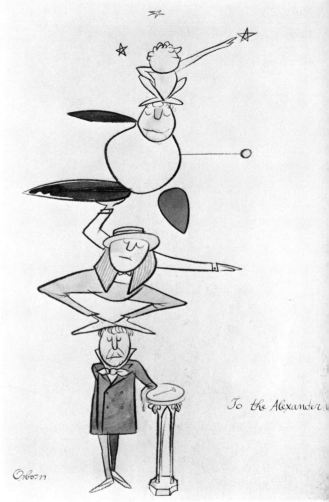

To the Alexanders, drawing by Robert Osborn for Howard and Mary Calder Rower.

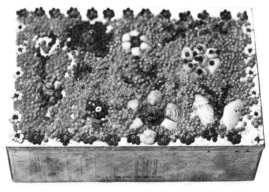

Decorated box made by Andrea Davidson for her grandparents.

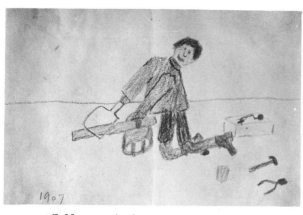
Self-portrait done at age nine.

system. That's where the whole thing came from." He told the critic Katharine Kuh: "The basis of everything for me is the universe. The simplest forms in the universe are the sphere and the circle. I represent them by discs and then I vary them." For a catalogue of a Caracas exhibition he wrote: "From the beginnings of my abstract work, even when it might not have seemed so, I felt there was no better model for me to choose than the Universe. . . . Spheres of different sizes, densities, colors and volumes, floating in space, traversing clouds, sprays of water, currents of air, viscosities and odors—of the greatest variety and disparity." In 1951, for an artists' symposium on "What Abstract Art Means to Me," he stated that "the underlying sense of form in my work has been the system of the Universe, or part thereof. For that is a rather large model to work from." In 1973 he reiterated this: "I work from a large live model."

Calder's cosmic imagery was appreciated by his earliest critics. When he first exhibited mobiles in New York in 1932, art critic Edward Alden Jewell's review was headlined:

Alexander Calder's "Mobiles," at the Julien Levy Gallery,
Suggest Majestic Swing through Space.

Henry McBride's review spoke of "the Saturns and Jupiters, if that is what they are, that move so lazily on their orbits."

Undoubtedly the most specific influence on Calder's art stems from his study and practice of engineering. He graduated from Stevens Institute of Technology with a degree in Mechanical Engineering in 1919, and for the next four years had a string of jobs related to various aspects of his studies. One involved automotive engineering in Rutherford, New Jersey; there was drafting work for New York Edison; map-coloring for a hydraulic engineer in Bridgeport, Connecticut; field work in Youngstown, Ohio. He worked as an accountant in the head office of a Manhattan firm of efficiency engineers, as a department-store systems analyst, and as an agricultural-machinery demonstrator in West Virginia. He also did lettering for a New York firm of machinery designers—and this is only a partial list.

The general engineering course at Stevens had as its expressed aim the balance of theory and practice; students were taught that they must be able to *do* as well as to *know*. It is significant that during Calder's four years of study, the courses in which he excelled were Mechanical Drawing, Descriptive Geometry, Drafting, Mechanical Engineering Laboratory, and Applied Kinetics. The kinetics course, as outlined in the Stevens catalogue issued in his senior year, is of particular interest in connection with his future work as a sculptor: "Discussion of the laws governing the plane motions of rigid bodies, with applications to machines, compound and torsion pendulums, translating and rotating bodies. . . . Discussion of work and energy, with simple applications to machines."

The Stevens Yearbook presented a vivid personal description of the young Calder:

ALEXANDER CALDER
"A blithe heart makes a blooming visage."

This thesis partly concerns the facial contortions which exist at the time of joy, happiness and like emotions. There are three forms—the laugh, grin and smile. The second is most perfectly exhibited in the case of Sandy Calder. Sandy is evidently always happy, or perhaps up to some joke, for his face is always wrapped up in that same mischievous, juvenile grin. This is certainly the index to the man's character in this case, for he is one of the best natured fellows there is.

The man is father to the child. Billy Drew [William B. F. Drew, a close friend at Stevens and best man at Calder's wedding] has stepped in as self-appointed Professor of "Ways and Means in Public" to Sandy-child, and the latter is, as a result, becoming quite sophisticated.

Our request to Mr. Drew for a fuller picture of Sandy in the Stevens days brought a letter, informative and amusing:

What struck one at the very start was a very quiet, warm person, physically solid and ready to roughhouse at any moment just for fun. He also played football and lacrosse just for sheer physical pleasure; and as for dancing, nobody whirled the girls more rapidly.

Puns, puns, puns by the ton. He loved them and always accompanied them by that amusing giggle.

Then the other side. The clearest mind it has been my pleasure to know. Descriptive geometry, passing of planes through cones, etc. Prof. Knapp would advise the class to close their eyes so they could concentrate better because the subject was supposedly so difficult. Sandy would look at the sheet with the problem, sketch the answer on it and put it in his inside pocket and wonder why they had to bother teaching such a simple subject. He was never a "grind" because he didn't have to be. 10:00 o'clock, lights out and into bed. He couldn't teach many of the boys who needed help because to him the solution would be done in two or three steps that took the average boy six or seven to arrive at the same answer.

Prof. Hazeltine, the famous radio and mathematical genius, was explaining in detail on the blackboard a complicated electrical problem. The part that fascinated Sandy was that Hazy drew a perfect circle freehand.

So you see how early was that fascination with free, balanced work, the clear mind, the mathematical perception, but always that fascination with new forms.

His direct approach to problems was refreshing. If anyone lacked studs for a formal affair's stiff white shirt, Sandy suggested brass fasteners that we used to clip the lab reports together. If a visible hole appeared in a black sock for some formal affair, Sandy used black India ink to cover the flesh.

I never heard him say an unkind or derogatory word about anyone. I don't know if it ever occurred to him that people did those things. His very rare display of anger only occurred if there was an injustice to a student or professor.

What a delightful companion. You mention the matter of the Yearbook and "Sandy-child." Perhaps it was that we were mutually attracted because we had various

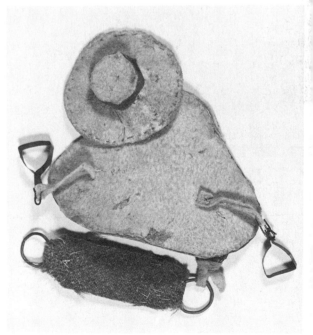

Toy saddle and hat made by Sandy and Peggy Calder, 1907.

19

interests in common, but the ones each of us had beyond that extended the interests of the other. So who was bringing sophistication to whom?

Although Calder attended the Art Students League (1923–26), studying under Kenneth Hayes Miller, George Luks, Guy Pène du Bois, Boardman Robinson and John Sloan, the academic approach never made much of an impression. He has always been an inventive craftsman rather than a conventional fine-arts practitioner. In 1925 in New York he lived in a long, narrow bedroom on Fourteenth Street, one wall of which he painted floor to ceiling with a circus scene. On the other, he recalls that he did "some bit of a tropical scene . . . with real bananas and oranges in wire rings sticking out of the painted plaster"; this sounds like both a progenitor of mixed-media constructions and an ancestor of Calder's Towers and Constellations. A year later, in Paris, he noticed a little island in the Seine on which there were "birds with long slender tails and a red disc about two inches in diameter on the end—this was right up my alley." His *Only Only Bird* and other members of this unique tin-can flock may be related to these Parisian birds.

Calder's famous miniature Circus and series of circus drawings originated from his 1925 sketches of Ringling Bros. and Barnum & Bailey Circus performances for the *National Police Gazette*. His fame, and his career as a sculptor, began fifty years ago with his Circus, which was the point of departure for all his future production. His Circus performances attracted the Paris art world; it was through the Circus that he met the most advanced artists of the time and was exposed to their work.

In 1931—the year of his first exhibition of abstract sculpture—Calder told an interviewer: "Why do I live in Paris? Because in Paris it's a compliment to be called crazy." Calder's decision to live and work in that city—then the creative center of the art world—had far-reaching effects on his development as an artist. When he arrived there at the age of twenty-eight, he was a talented illustrator, the maker of clever and humorous toys. The stimulation of the Paris avant-garde transformed him into a serious abstract artist and, ultimately, into an artist of international stature. It is doubtful that he could have achieved this within the provincial confines of American artistic life at that time, when modern art was, indeed, considered "crazy" by the majority of his fellow countrymen.

Calder's early works—especially the wire portraits and book illustrations—have a noticeable connection with advanced art as it developed in Paris in the early decades of this century. The influence of the so-called primitivism of African tribal art, which appealed to artists and collectors of the time, is reflected in a general way in much of Calder's jewelry and in some of his gouaches and drawings. As for influences by other artists, Alfred Barr in his 1936 book *Cubism and Abstract Art* noted Mondrian, Gabo, Arp and Miró as the most important for Calder. To these, Calder's dealer Klaus Perls says he would add Léger, a close friend in the early years and one with whom

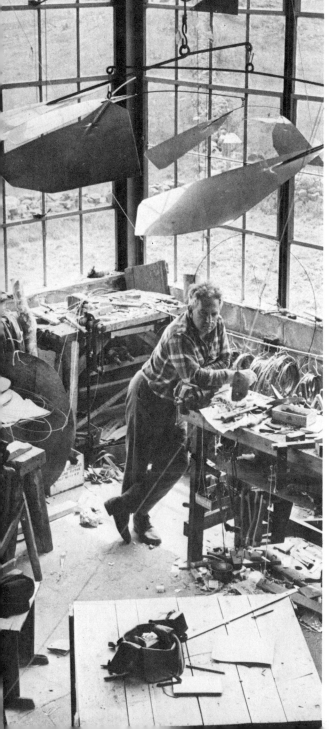

In the Roxbury studio.

Calder shared many common interests—from a fascination with machinery to a fondness for Paris cafés.

As a member of the Abstraction-Création group in Paris in the early thirties, Calder was in close contact with fellow members Arp, Mondrian, Pevsner (Gabo's brother and with him an exponent of Constructivism) and other pioneers of the modern movement. Miró was, and still is, a close personal friend; a stylistic relationship between the two is especially evident in some of Calder's gouaches, and in his sculptural inventions called Constellations after Miró's paintings of the same name. Many Mirós hang on Calder's walls, along with works by Mondrian, Léger, Tamayo, Toulouse-Lautrec, Tanguy, Ernst, Salemme and other artists he admires.

After the Abstraction-Création days, Calder never allied himself with movements or groups of artists. Yet by virtue of friendship with key figures he has maintained his interest in all the most important aspects of modern art. He participated in several important Surrealist exhibitions and contributed two sequences to Hans Richter's Surrealist film *Dreams That Money Can Buy*. As Calder's most perceptive critic, James Johnson Sweeney, has pointed out, the spirit of Calder's art has many affinities with Dada. Marcel Duchamp was a good friend, both in France and in the United States; it was he who originated the name "mobiles" and with Sweeney helped name the Constellations. Like Duchamp, Calder has always enjoyed bilingual puns and *double entendres*. Whereas Duchamp's puns tended to be cerebral and somewhat enigmatic, Calder's humor is of the earthy variety, intended to amuse, not embarrass. He likes titles such as *Peau Rouge, Indiana*, which he gave to a large red stabile made for the University of Indiana, and *The Jealous Husband*, a rare instance of titled jewelry, which certainly calls to mind a chastity belt! He is also amused by dogs lifting their legs gracefully high as they urinate, a subject he likes to draw, and he has had some simple fun with sex anatomy in his drawings and book illustrations.

Calder has described often and in detail his 1930 visit to Piet Mondrian's studio and his subsequent conversion to abstract art (see "Oil Paintings"). Mondrian is one of the few direct influences he acknowledges; what is interesting about his relationship with the painter is that Mondrian served only as a point of departure—"a shock that started things"—and that Calder went on to find his own solutions to the problems of making abstract art. Calder's work is based less on that of other artists than on his own experiences: the wire he had played with as a child; his facility in caricature, which is, after all, a form of abstraction; his training as an engineer.

Concerned about the political situation in Europe, Calder and his family returned to the United States in 1933. They continued to maintain close contacts with many of the important artists of the time, especially European artists-in-exile. Scores of artists have been among his friends, but relatively few have affected his work. Beginning with his American years, outside influences diminished rapidly and a fresh style took over in each of the media that Calder developed in his freewheeling way.

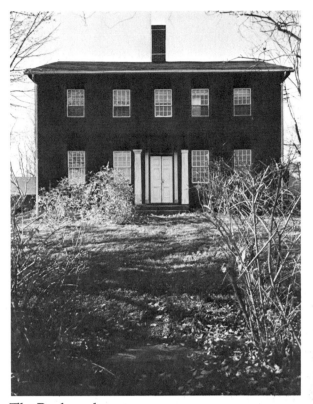

The Roxbury house.

21

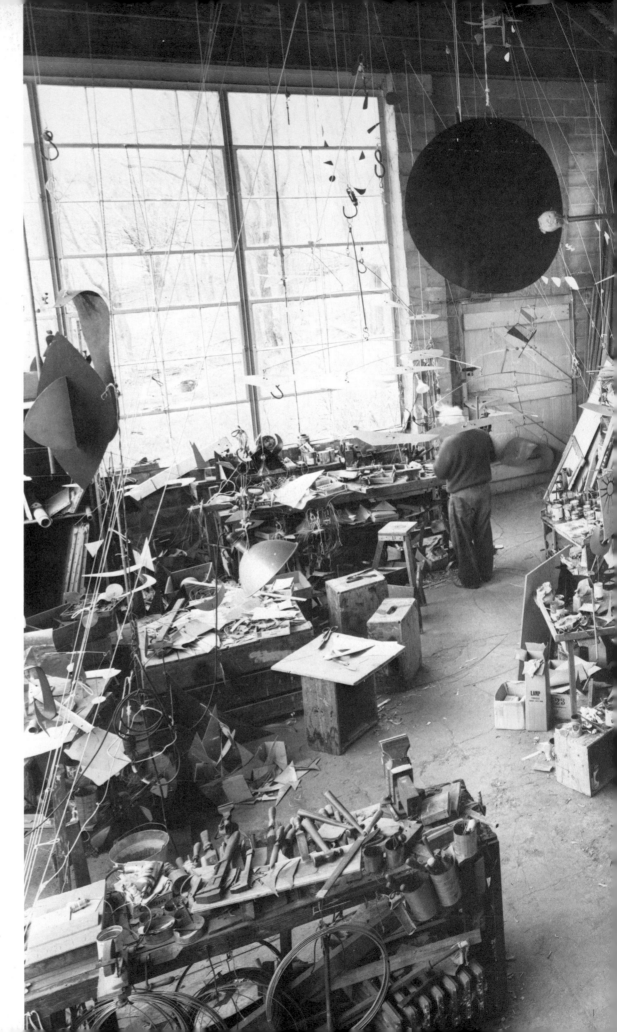

The Roxbury studio.

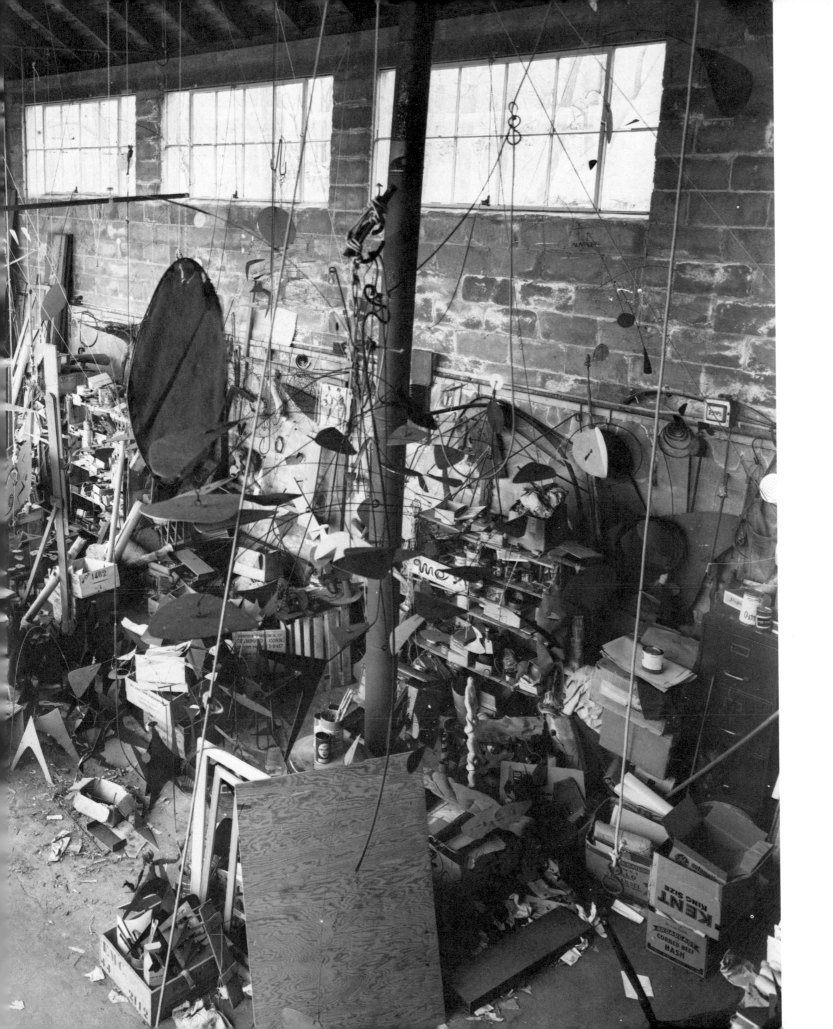

23

Sandy's friends say . . .

We thought that the most valid way to focus on the special quality of Calder's life and work might be to ask some of the people who know him best to tell us what they would like to say about him at this time.

Sandy the man, the friend, has a heart as big as Niagara. Calder the artist has the force of the ocean. I salute you, Sandy.
                                                                    —JOAN MIRÓ

Forty years ago Sandy Calder cleared our eyes and minds to receive a totally new kind of sculpture. He is one of the great innovators in the history of art.

—DOROTHY C. MILLER

Sandy Calder—an artist who combines philosophy and fun, precision and abandon, vagaries and permanence in his own personal brand of sculpture. Who else has given us so much delight with so little pomposity? Who else can make snowflakes tremble and an acoustic ceiling float in cloud-like majesty? No other American artist has so brilliantly mirrored the optimism and sly humor of our country.   —KATHARINE KUH

Sandy Calder from the very beginning had a style, and my greatest admiration for him is that he continued maturing and at the present time has done his best work. He is one of our great sculptors. I don't like to limit him to America as an American sculptor, but consider him a world figure.   —LOUISE NEVELSON

Sandy Calder's sculptures are often linear, floating, made of thin metal sheets and wire, delicately gamboling, turning. Their paths are traceless. Their relations to things around escape definition, proportion, rules. They are formed by the hidden breeze, by the pull of gravity. This is true of his mobiles in a very direct sense, and in a broader sense of his stabiles, constellations, household implements and various improvisations as well. A world of delicate and unsophisticated inventions of which the basic concept is transparency.

These very qualities of Calder's work make it so much at home in and between our buildings—a good neighbor and interconnected part of architecture and the geometric space. Opposites to the extreme, but good friends.

And there is Sandy himself, a slow-moving, big presence, spreading his considerable volume with no visible concentration or direction. Still, we know that Sandy is very much there, alert and observing: the creative craftsman, the artist, humorous and human. He does not say much, does not explain or apologize; his moods flow directly into doing.

—MARCEL BREUER

If anybody could understand what Sandy Calder was saying, I would have cast him as God. As it is, I take him on faith.   —ARTHUR MILLER

Calder's power is based on his understanding of the universe through its most elementary and direct principles. His love of simple forms, the play of pure colors and the relations of various forces in equilibrium infuse his art with an astonishing vitality. The diverse elements of his sculptures are united or separated by color, they are related to the world around them—that is, space—and the intermediary is none other than a persistent good humor. —Daniel Lelong

I've followed Calder's career for forty years—and more—both as an artist and a friend. His mobiles and stabiles are known and loved all over the world, but even they do not reveal the style of his extraordinary personality. —Alfred H. Barr, Jr.

Just over fifty years ago A. Stirling Calder wished one thing above all for modern sculpture: that it should be "not a specimen, but an actor in the life of the day." Calder's own son, Alexander, was only a young man at the time; but before long he fulfilled his father's hopes a hundred times over. He brought sculpture to the consciousness of millions of people who would never have thought about it at all; and he spoke in his work for a world in which everything is possible and nothing need be taken at its own valuation.

The World Trade Center, for instance: Is there a more ridiculous set of buildings on the face of the earth? No, there isn't. But when we turn the corner and come upon the crab-red Calder which cuts the cant out of the whole enterprise, we say to ourselves, "A free man was here"; and straightaway we feel better. Public sculpture was a stuffed-shirt's paradise till Calder came along; or, if not that, a source of heartbreak to the big men, from Rodin onwards, who tangled with officialdom. Calder changed all this.

But he and Louisa have also shown us how to live, as citizens and as responsible individuals. We shall never forget how they took a full-page ad in *The New York Times* in 1966 to support the peace movement, reminding us that "reason is not treason." We needed to read those words in that place at that time, and no one else came forward to say them. Calder is the greatest fun to be with, as everyone knows; no one was ever less of a frock-coated Great Man. But you don't get to do what he has done, or to be what he is, without an inner intransigence. In the man, as in the work, iron is the metal. —John Russell

My first acquaintance with Sandy Calder's work was in 1931 or 1932 during a visit to my home city of Barcelona. I was on my way to a small club that fellow members of the GATCPAC [Group of Architects and Technicians from Catalonia for the Progress of Contemporary Architecture] had just opened on the main promenade, the Paseo de Gracia. To my amazement I saw a small crowd gathered around one of the display windows, and the object of their admiration was a new contraption—a "mobile"—the work of an American sculptor, Calder. The people there, like many others around the world, were attracted by a sculpture that was animated and alive.

It was not until 1933 that I met the artist himself, I think in Paul Nelson's house in

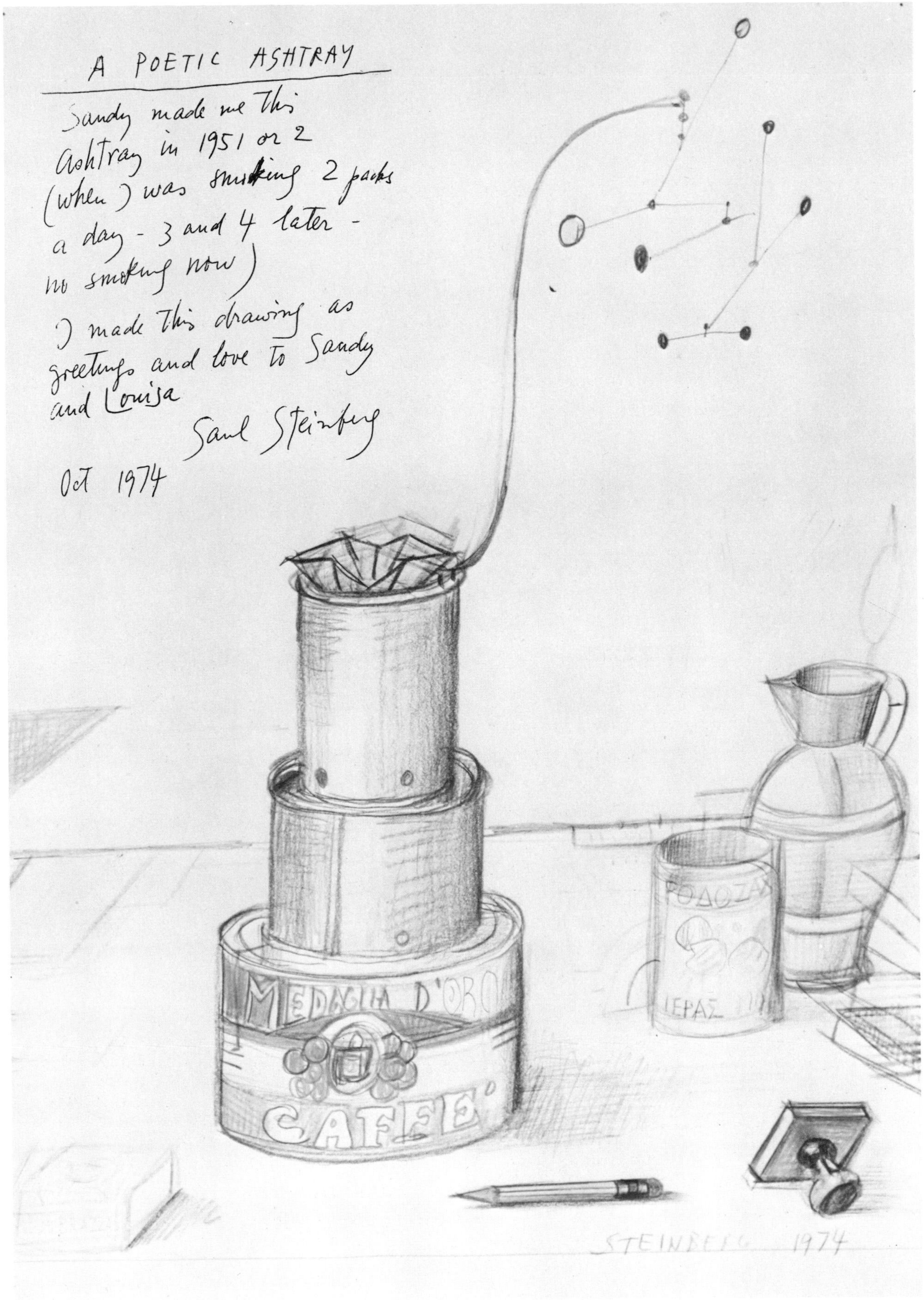

A POETIC ASHTRAY

Sandy made me this
ashtray in 1951 or 2
(when I was smoking 2 packs
a day - 3 and 4 later -
no smoking now)

I made this drawing as
greetings and love to Sandy
and Louisa
                    Saul Steinberg

Oct 1974

STEINBERG   1974

Paris. He and his wife Louisa were surrounded by their five valises containing their Circus show, and Louisa was playing some *bal-musette* tunes on her accordion.

I saw Sandy, Joan Miró and other mutual friends frequently in the Café de Flore, or the Select in Montparnasse. On Sundays we often went to visit Jean Arp and Nelly van Doesburg in Meudon-Val-Fleury, and had long walks and talks in the Forêt de Meudon.

In 1937, while the Civil War continued in Spain, the Spanish Republic built a pavilion for the International World's Fair in Paris. Picasso, Miró, Gonzalez and Alberto were commissioned to provide murals and sculptures. The Spanish Government asked Commissioner José Gaos to place a mercury fountain there too, as the mercury mines in Almadén had been occupied by the rebel troops. Such a fountain had been built for the World's Fair in Seville in 1929—and it was a masterpiece of unimaginative design that made mercury look like water. My own outspoken views were that we could not possibly place such a fountain in front of Picasso's *Guernica,* whereupon Gaos asked me to find a Spanish artist to produce a new design. I told him I knew of no one in Spain who could meet those requirements, but that a remarkable American sculptor named Calder could produce something striking and unique.

Sandy got the commission. A few days later he requested some mercury for a demonstration model and was told that it would be much too expensive. Undaunted, Sandy made his model in wire and tin and used lead shot instead of mercury to prove that this machine would move. It did move and it was approved. On my way home to Montparnasse, I saw a small group of bystanders gathered on the sidewalks opposite the Café du Dôme. Curious to see what the attraction was, I joined them—only to find Sandy kneeling on the sidewalk demonstrating his moving mercury fountain! The completed fountain was a tremendous success, with silver-like mercury cascading in the black tar-painted metal forms.

Following my arrival in New York in 1939, I saw Sandy and Louisa often. During my first visit to their Roxbury, Connecticut, home, he gave me a special mobile. At that time I was living in a New York hotel, with scarcely enough room to move around myself, let alone a mobile—but he had made a demonstration piece that could fit in my only valise! It is beautiful in my house in Cambridge and has traveled with me for thirty-five years!

Christmas in Roxbury was something to remember—everyone received the most unexpected and unusual gifts. The Calder house became a gathering place on weekends for Léger, the Tamayos, André Masson, the Josephsons, etc. Sandy and Louisa have always maintained close contact with old friends, regardless of their friends' successes or difficulties. During the war years Sandy also promoted café gatherings in The Jumble

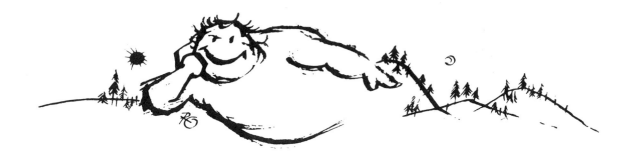

"We can't compress Sandy into a few words./ Too much of him!.... too large... and his qualities are too varied & contradictory. Engineer-Artist. /Capricious yet totally logical. A serious Santa Claus. /Mobile as a dream.. ..stabile as the very earth, & sometimes both./ A lover of fun, full of wit & play, but confronted by things evil he is as grim a battler as one could ask for. /He is that rare combination of delight & POWERS with which he has blessed us all.

Robert Osborn

Shop in Greenwich Village on Fridays, where all new arrivals from occupied Europe came to join the regular group. Léger, Masson, Breton, Chagall, Lipchitz, Tanguy, Marion Oswald met the local artists, those of us who had preceded them. One evening Sandy, in a friendly mood, wanted to pull all the tables together, but Marion Oswald wisely told him that he couldn't do that: "People enjoy cafés because those at one table can say nasty things about their 'friends' at other tables—if you put them all together, the fun is finished!"

Sandy has remained unchanged through the years. He continues to get great pleasure out of his work, and that pleasure is contagious to the spectator. At a recent dinner honoring his great friend Miró at the Moulin de la Galette, Sandy spontaneously painted the paper napkins around the room, much to everyone's amusement. (Unfortunately, one of the guests, more greedy than amused, was caught trying to take some home.)

—Josep Lluis Sert

Back in 1958, writing about Calder for the first time, I managed to squeeze out of the typewriter a paragraph to the effect that "the idea of spatial movement, materialized in static forms in Futuristic sculpture, is given specialized expression in the mobile, invented by Alexander Calder. As sculpture, the mobile is also closely related to the theories of Constructivism, but differs in that it assumes a sequence of identities in space rather than revealing its total identity at one time."

Since then, Sandy, whom I had never met, has become a friend, and although I'll stick by the essential accuracy of that polysyllabic comment as far as it goes, I realize that it misses about three-quarters of the point. Surely there has never been another artist whose creative life has given him as much sheer fun as Sandy Calder has taken in his. And that same quality of fun, along with elegance and vigor, is captured in everything he does. It's all there in plain sight, and although I've written several pieces on Calder's art since that first one, I've always been conscious that he, of all major twentieth-century artists, is the one who is least in need of explanation. All you have to do is look, and enjoy.

—John Canaday

Eighteen years of collaborating with Sandy Calder have unfolded a web of intricate insights into the maze of this great person. I have known him as a man of genius whose intellectual curiosity soars to the beyond and then concretizes itself in his work. A true craftsman, Sandy has welded practical knowledge with principles of engineering—and a keen sensitivity to the intangible dimension—to create a new happening in each of his artistic pursuits. I have grown to love Sandy as a true friend—unassuming, congenial, informal—who has drawn me into his work in a way that has completely transformed my life-style. Happiness is indeed working with Sandy, experiencing mutual anticipation and expectation of the finished product, conversing casually, uplifted by his wit and lively humor. Indefatigable, determined, a gentleman of firm convictions, Sandy's each attempt evolves in optimism. His great love and enthusiasm for life is communicated directly through his talent and skill, a lasting heritage for all humanity, for all times.

—CARMEN SEGRE

At the very beginning Sandy came to see me in my office with an eight-inch model he had made. With a mischievous look he said, "I want the final object to be forty-five feet high." Our research department immediately set to work, conciliating the technical imperatives of the problem with the form and lines of the model. For the larger sculptures we even run wind-tunnel tests to check our estimates (wind resistance, mooring, warping).

During the building process, Sandy visits our foundry nearly every day, participating in the birth of his new object; then we discuss the outline and thickness of the gussets and bracing required—according to the size of the object.

This long cooperation, in which I played a modest role, has allowed me to measure how completely Sandy masters space and balance; he envisions the finished object before we have even begun to assemble it.

Behind his rough and massive appearance, his friends discover and appreciate the warm humanity, the simple kindness, of this great genius.   —JACQUES BAZILLON

Coincidence, or predestination? In 1954, we moved our gallery from its cramped Fifty-eighth Street quarters up to our present seven-story house on Madison Avenue. The building was just one yawning emptiness.

At exactly that moment our friend Curt Valentin died suddenly, leaving behind his gallery's group of modern sculptors—the most creative in the world. Of them all, Calder was the only one both of us agreed we hoped to represent.

We wrote him, he came, he saw, he said, "I'll fill the place for you." And he did, not just with hundreds upon hundreds of objects, but with the generous spirit of his boundless goodwill. Later, he even added a sculpture garden in the back of the house, with its own Calder murals, and designed our sidewalk which became the first and so far only such original work of art in New York.

He was both surprised and delighted when we suggested the spring for his first exhibition with us. No more December shows with implications of Christmas presents and tree decorations! Here his art would be taken totally seriously. He left all the financial and exhibition management to us, and, miraculously, never undersold the gallery from his studio. His always perfect behavior in the normally high-strung artist-dealer relationship has put us, throughout these twenty years, on *our* best behavior, too, and so complete mutual trust was solidly established. What a rare pleasure in our small art world!

—DOLLY AND KLAUS PERLS

Sandy says . . .

Sandy has always had a remarkably uncomplicated view of himself, his work, life and family, and a way of succinctly stating his values—though he repeatedly makes it clear that he just wants to work, not talk about it. His autobiography contains the sum of what he has wanted to say. Just as we have made a selection from his vast body of work, so we have extracted what seemed to be the most enlightening comments from interviews and statements and, above all, from *Autobiography with Pictures*. This marvelously entertaining document is the basis of the text of this book, as it will be for any future publication on Calder.

Sandy has said that he had "a big advantage" in that he was "inclined to be happy by nature." Indeed, from his earliest years, his life has been filled with a series of pleasant events and people. The names of the famous crop up again and again in his life story; a random sampling of those people who have been part of his life, many as close friends, would include Piet Mondrian, Joan Miró, Henri Matisse, Arshile Gorky, Pavel Tchelitchew, Meret Oppenheim, Loren MacIver, John Piper, Kay Sage, Peter Blume, William Einstein, Ben Shahn, Everett Shinn, Henry Varnum Poor, Jean Tinguely, Niki de Saint Phalle, Alberto Giacometti, Barbara Hepworth, Marcel Breuer, Peggy Guggenheim, Jo Mielziner, Virgil Thomson, Jean-Paul Sartre, John Dos Passos, Arthur Miller, Marya Mannes, Edward Steichen, Henri Cartier-Bresson, James Thrall Soby, Kenneth Clark, Daniel Catton Rich, John Walker, Lincoln Kirstein and scores of others (listed in "Who's Who in Calder's World"). He has gotten along well with just about everyone —Picasso, Hemingway and Dali are notable exceptions. Asked by a *Life* reporter if he ever experienced sadness, he answered, "No. I don't have the time. When I think I might start to, I fall asleep. I conserve energy that way." His life work, in all media, has a core of pure joy—in the concept, the execution, the color—all of which directly communicates pleasure to the viewer.

About his wife: "I do all right with Louisa"—a fine marriage splendidly understated in six words. "Louisa took all my new objects and my work without demur. She seemed to accept them, and it did not occur to me or to her to discuss it."

About taste: In his autobiography he describes the three-story house in the rue de la Colonie that he and Louisa rented in 1931, where they whitewashed all the walls and painted the woodwork a shiny black. They bought a stack of dishes on a trip to Palma, "simple, white, with either blue or red circles around the rim"—Calder colors. He tells how, at that time, Louisa had gone to buy a *broc* and a washbasin for their cook, and continues: "Now, a *broc* is a beautiful thing of conical shape, tall and slender—and instead she had bought a pitcher, fat and dumpy. She said, 'You won't see these things anyway, because they'll be in the cook's room.' But I was furious, and took the two objects down to the cellar and drove a spike through each. I feel that if one accepts things which one does not approve of, it is the beginning of the end, and by and by you get more things of a similar nature. This is akin to the stunt of giving objects away which you don't like. Then the people think you do like that sort of thing, and pretty soon they'll give you back something of a similar nature. Bad taste always boomerangs." (The art critic John Russell, after visiting the Calders in Saché in 1967, described their house as "a place where the priorities have been got right once and for all.")

About his work: "I feel an artist should go about his work simply with great respect for his materials . . . simplicity of equipment and an adventurous spirit are essential in attacking the unfamiliar and unknown. . . . Disparity in form, color, size, weight, motion, is what makes a composition. . . . It is the apparent accident to regularity which the artist actually controls by which he makes or mars a work."

"I have chiefly limited myself to the use of black and white as being the most disparate colors. Red is the color most opposed to these, and then, finally, the other primaries."

"You should know how to get the best out of leisure; it's a stimulating atmosphere for invention."

"I have a cardboard visor. I put it down and look for it when I arrive in the shop. That ties in with what I was doing yesterday."

"Sometimes I intend to destroy one of my works, but then I improve it." "If I don't like a piece, it's no good. That's my only criterion. . . ." "I have developed an attitude of indifference to the reception of my work, which allows me to go about my business."

Calder deliberately uses the word "work" instead of "art," and he usually calls individual pieces "objects" because "then a guy can't come along and say, no, those aren't sculptures. It washes my hands of having to defend them." In early catalogues there are few titles; Calder was inclined to use the generic term mobile, and over the years he has invented other general titles, such as Towers, Gongs, Totems, Crags, for series of related works. Specific titles can be convenient, he admits: "A title is just like the license plate on the back of a car. You use it to say which one you're talking about." "Sometimes it's the whole thing that suggests a title to me, sometimes it's just a detail." Often his titles are purely descriptive (*Red, Black and Blue*), but many refer to animals or other natural phenomena (*The Crab, Snow Flurry*). The title of his great mobile for Kennedy Airport, *.125* (the thickness of the metal from which the elements were made), reflects his background in engineering. Calder always loves puns or a play on words (he named the stabile *Gwenfritz* for the woman who commissioned it, Gwendolyn Cafritz, much to her dismay).

Talking to a reporter about a mobile fourteen feet across made for the lobby of the Terrace Hilton in Cincinnati, Calder remarked, amused rather than annoyed, "I understand that people there now say, 'I'll meet you under that thing.'" He is blithely in-

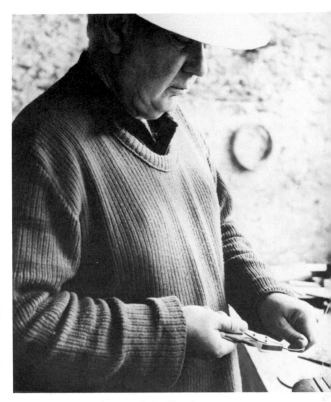

At work in Roxbury.

33

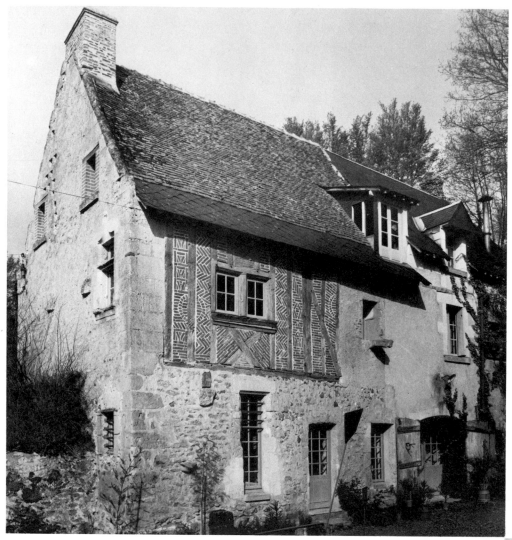

"François Premier," Calder's Saché house.

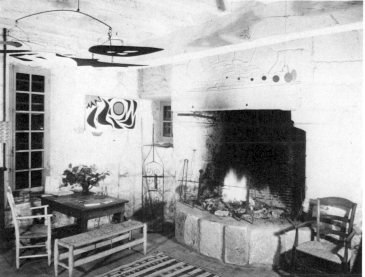

different also to patrons' ideas for commissioned work if they don't coincide with his. When the architect Wallace K. Harrison commissioned a discreet corner sculpture for his dining room, Calder made an object that not only filled the entire corner but trailed across the ceiling, taking over the entire room. Told that Calder was designing a big black mobile for the Guggenheim Museum, the architect Frank Lloyd Wright sent word that he wanted it made out of gold. Calder sent back his answer: "All right, I'll make it of gold, but I'll paint it black." He told Geoffrey Hellman, for a *New Yorker* article, that his Pittsburgh airport mobile had been painted green and gold, the county colors, without consulting him. "I wrote them that it ought to be painted red," he said, "and sent them four cans of red paint and I hear it's red now." A large stabile made for the Princeton campus was tried out in orange and black at alumnus Alfred Barr's suggestion. Calder said "no" to that; it's now Calder black instead of Princeton orange and black.

Calder's personal declaration of independence is frequently reiterated. Describing his project for *Man*, the huge stainless-steel stabile made for Montreal, he recalls that at first a sculpture sixty-four feet tall was discussed: "They asked me to stretch it to sixty-seven feet because it was 1967. But I told them that was like giving me the commission because I was sixty-seven years old. I happened to be sixty-seven then." He was once commissioned to do a stabile, preferably suggesting a horse, for a Texas town. When it was finished the Texans said it didn't look like a horse. "Well, it probably isn't a horse," Sandy said.

Calder never wastes words; his answers to Whitney Museum questionnaires about his pieces in the collection are typical. The questionnaire item reads "method of execution (give full details)." His answers for three pieces are as follows: For *Double Cat*—"chisel & mallet, rasp"; for *Old Bull*—"cut & bent"; for *Indian Feathers*—"I made a

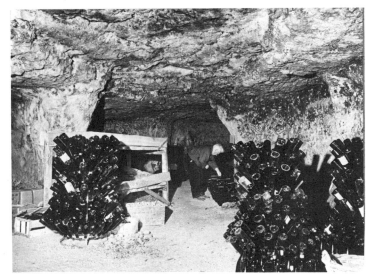

In the wine cellar.

35

model & took it to Etab. Biémont in Tours." When asked pontifical questions about his work, Calder typically replies as he did to an artists' questionnaire for a 1958 exhibition, *Nature in Abstraction:*

Do you feel that nature has any serious relation to your own work?
"Everything is natural. If you can imagine it, you can make it. . . ."
If so, is it a conscious or a predominantly subconscious one on your part?
"I just don't think about it."
Presuming that you as an abstract artist are drawn to nature by certain eternal qualities or forces sensed there, would you say that your work is a predominantly subjective expression of your personal relation to these qualities and forces?
"I just do the best I can."

To one interviewer Calder said, "Don't ask me any questions if you can find the answers in books." Another time, when he was being interviewed for a major piece in *The New York Times Magazine*, the writer began asking questions about his "concerns" and his "accomplishments"—at which point Sandy, who had a minor throat infection, abruptly ended the interview with, "Excuse me, I've got to do my gargling." Such answers provide fair warning to future interviewers: tackle Calder at your own risk!

Humor is an essential ingredient of Calder's art. Verbal wit is an equally prominent aspect of his personality, and many examples, as I write now, come freshly to mind. One time we were going to the Segre foundry to see a stabile in process of construction. As we left the Calder driveway, my husband asked Louisa whom the large barn with the shiny metal roof belonged to (not knowing that the Arthur Millers—Miller was then married to Marilyn Monroe—lived next door). Sandy, who had just closed his eyes for a catnap, muttered, "That's Marilyn's hot tin roof."

Another year, this time in Saché, I told Sandy about David Smith's statement in *Art News* that a certain painted sculpture was worth only its weight of sixty pounds of scrap steel, because the collector who bought it had the paint removed. Smith obviously wanted it known that he no longer considered it his work. (I knew Sandy would be interested, for, though he didn't exactly consider David a rival, he wasn't too enthusiastic about the occasional mention of Smith as America's most important sculptor.) Sandy asked, "*What* was it that collector did to David's piece?" and I said, "I told you, he stripped off all the paint." Sandy: "And then it fell apart?"

Sculptor Isamu Noguchi was a close friend in the early days, when he ran the victrola for Sandy's Circus performances, but since then their relationship has cooled. Isamu didn't appreciate Sandy's published explanation for his request to have his mobile for the Paris UNESCO Headquarters removed from the area of Noguchi's

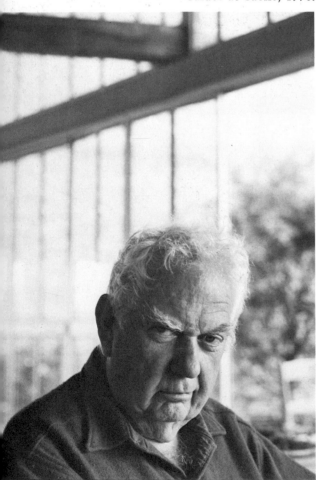

Calder at Saché, 1970.

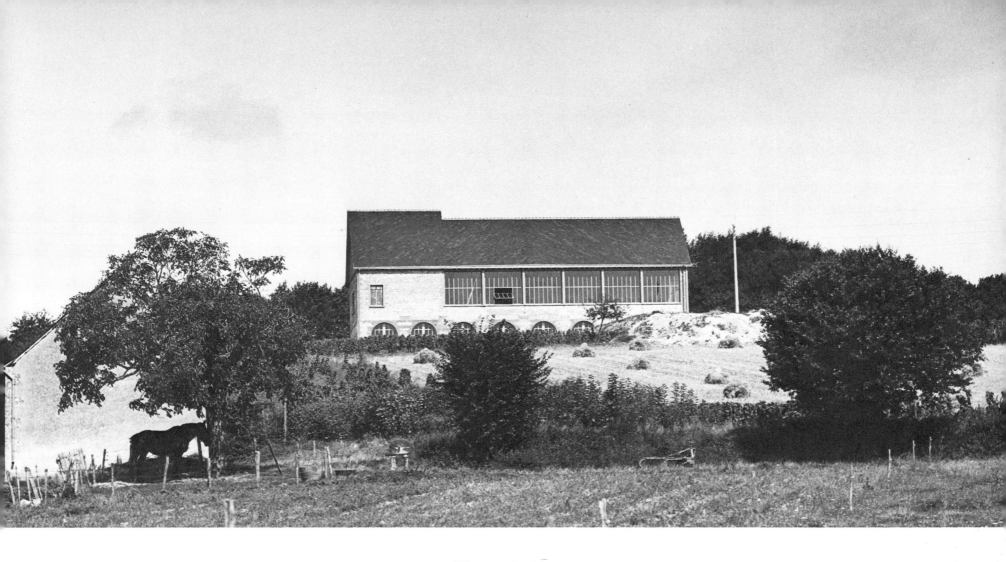

The new Saché studio.

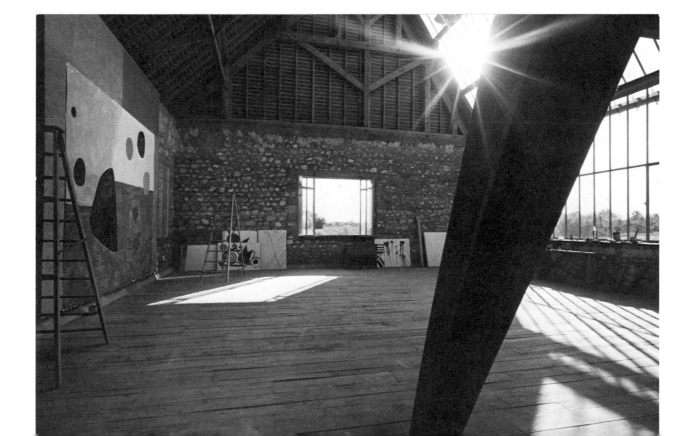

Japanese garden. *Spirale* had a pyramidal base, and Calder explained that Noguchi "would probably cover the base with powdered sugar and call it Fujiyama. They moved it around the corner. . . ." Undoubtedly Noguchi didn't find the story about Calder's misplaced case of black paint for *Spirale* as amusing as Sandy did: "There was some confusion when they unpacked it in Paris. It was called JAPALAC, and they thought it must be for Noguchi." Sandy obviously loved this; he retold the tale in his auto-biography, and again, with an improved finale, for an *Art in America* interview: the painter "had put all the Japalac in the Jap, alack, rock garden."

Sandy's wit can be barbed, but he is extraordinarily sensitive to the feelings of his friends and colleagues. Klaus Perls describes him as "a man of one hundred per cent goodwill." However, it is a mistake to picture Calder as a happy-go-lucky man who lives in isolated villages in France and Connecticut, interested only in his art and a select art circle. On the contrary, he and Louisa have always been concerned with social and political issues. He has contributed many posters, editions of lithographs (including *Contour Plowing* for the Whitney), other works of art and money for cultural, social and political causes. In 1967, when New York City sponsored a show of outdoor sculpture, each of the invited artists was asked to choose a site for his work. Calder picked Harlem, saying he "would like to make a gesture of friendship, if they would accept it." He also said, "I suppose everybody has had that idea." (No one else had.) He offered to give the two stabiles "if the people of Harlem show interest in having them." (They did not.)

The Calders were early and vigorous opponents of American involvement in Vietnam. In 1965, as chairman of "Artists for SANE" (the Committee for a Sane Nuclear Policy), he led a group to Washington to protest the escalating war. With Louisa he took a full-page ad in *The New York Times* to wish his countrymen a happy 1966 and urge them to dedicate the New Year to peace. And in 1972, long before the Watergate impeachment furor, Sandy and Louisa—again in a *Times* ad—joined with other sponsors to call for Richard Nixon's removal from office on the grounds that his conduct of the Vietnam War was unconstitutional.

Sandy is never willing to compromise with any situation he considers unacceptable (rare as these are in his view), whether it involves his work, as we have seen, or politics, or even social niceties. One example of the latter: Some time ago we and the Calders were lunching in Connecticut at the Lester Bealls'. (Lester, a prominent graphics designer, had just acquired a mobile for his house in Brookfield Center.) After lunch Lester took us to see his new studio. It was all white with partitioned open shelves stacked with varicolored papers—a handsome Mondrian-like interior. Sandy was fascinated with the large sheets of bright paper and asked Lester if he had a pair of scissors. Lester promptly produced them, and Sandy picked out several sheets of red, yellow, blue and orange. Lester seated him at a long white table and as Sandy began to snip, Lester's thought, if it

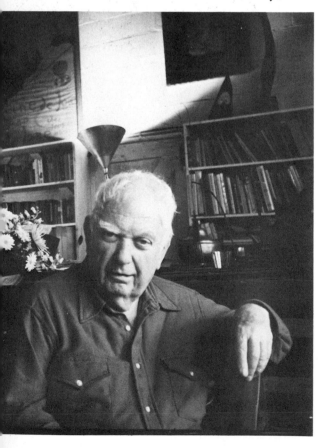

Calder at Roxbury, 1975.

could have been cartooned with a bubble-caption, would have read, "A Calder collage!" Sandy continued cutting and Lester asked if he wanted paste or anything. Sandy looked up with his sweet, lopsided smile and went on snipping, now cutting the paper into smaller bits. Lester looked worried. Sandy put all the pieces of paper together, cut them neatly into confetti-size bits, said, "I'm finished," and gaily tossed them all into the air. Sad for Lester, but Sandy likes giving things when *he* wants to.

In minor as well as major matters, Calder leads his life exactly as he wishes, as illustrated by his special style of dress. Today he habitually wears baggy work pants and a red flannel shirt from L. L. Bean; for formal occasions he changes into a well-worn gray suit—but retains the red shirt. In his youth he was renowned for his unconventional attire. He recalls in his autobiography that when he first went to Paris he took along a custom-tailored suit made of "racy tweed cloth . . . orange with a yellow stripe," and a straw hat with his old fraternity ribbon around it—an outfit that earned him the designation "the cantaloupe with the straw hat." In 1929 a reporter covering a fashionable New York party was fascinated by Calder's handmade jewelry:

He was a nice young man, quietly mirthful, distinguished from among the other white-shirt-fronted gentlemen of the party by a curiously wrought ornament which seemed to be a bee or dragonfly of gold filaments, perched where a shirt-stud should be. . . . The dragonfly (or bee) was not gold—it was brass wire.

Frances Hawkins remembers a much less elegant Calder, whom she met when she was Martha Graham's manager:

Sandy Calder arrived on campus [Bennington College, Vermont, where he came in 1935 to do sets for Graham's *Panorama*] driving an old-fashioned touring car which also contained a very shaggy dog named Feathers. Sandy was wearing a shirt with the sleeves torn out, bedroom slippers with purple pompoms on them and no pants—only undershorts. I was asked if I would take him into town to get some proper clothes, and we located a clothing store in the then small village. Sandy said to the storekeeper, "I need a pair of pants." The storekeeper, a typical Vermonter, looked Sandy up and down and said, "You sure do."

As Sweeney has pointed out, Calder's indifference to conventional dress is more significant than one might think:

Calder in a lumberjack's shirt, wearing a necktie he has embroidered for his own pleasure, and in baggy trousers, is comfortable, alive; Calder in a dinner jacket is stilted, limited, confined. Calder's undress has all the seriousness of the dress of a dandy, with all the dandy's playfulness and fantasy; the solemnity of the conventional constricts him personally and spiritually. And this holds for his art as well.

New York Times ad, January 2, 1966.

39

The critics say . . .

Calder will have a lasting place in the history of art for his innovative work with motion in sculpture, specifically for his development of the mobile as a new art form. Although David Smith and Louise Nevelson are sometimes mentioned as America's greatest sculptors, most critics agree, I think, that Calder comes first—and there are many who believe him to be the most important living sculptor in any country. He has lived at the peak of a great art epoch, but he created a whole range of personal peaks. Almost any category of his work (see contents page) would have won him recognition as an outstanding artist; together they add up dramatically to validate his fame. No other American artist has had a greater impact on the art of his time. He, alone of our major artists, is an international figure—literally as much at home in France as in America and actually considered a French artist by the French. His work is to be seen in almost every nation. This enormous oeuvre, encompassing an amazing range of subjects, media, scale and style, can perhaps best be compared to Picasso's. Barbara Rose has commented that Calder is in many ways like Picasso—that whatever he touches comes alive, infused with joyous verve and formal inventiveness, and that, like Picasso, he is "the eternal child, the *naïf* whose vision never goes stale, who brings to each experience the ingenuousness of the innocent eye."

Calder's childlike, playful qualities have been commented on by many observers. "This giant child" is the way the French critic Michel Seuphor described Calder in a book on contemporary sculpture. Seuphor also wrote a novel, *Douce Province*, about Parisian life in the thirties; it presents a vivid description of Calder's house and a Circus performance with the Paris art world in attendance. "*C'est un enfant, ce Calder . . . c'est l'enfant en l'homme . . . tout le mystère de l'enfance.*" Sweeney began his article "Alexander Calder: Work and Play" by saying: "Calder has always played his art as he plays his life. But play with Calder is never frivolous. It is serious, but never solemn. Play is a necessity for Calder which he has to respect, to treat seriously." In another essay Sweeney makes the point that although Calder is a nonconformist whose art is full of humor, he has never directed his humor against art. Never one of the anti-art artists, he has always been a positive creator.

Léger once pronounced Calder "a hundred per cent American." In his *Conversations with Artists*, Selden Rodman agreed:

He is the embodiment of such characteristic American traits as canniness, geniality . . . energy, inventiveness, pragmatism. His distaste for theory and concept is American, and so is his dry humor. He has the advantage of having been an American so long through his heritage—both his father and his grandfather were American sculptors—that he can live in France a good part of every year without any sense of expatriate guilt and without becoming in the least bit French. And the fact that he didn't have to make a living was in his case an advantage too: the material ends and pecuniary rewards never meant anything to him. He could, and did, make things solely for the satisfaction of making them. If they were cleanly cut, cleverly arranged and ingeniously related, that was enough. They had to "work."

In the introduction to his definitive catalogue for the 1943 Calder retrospective at the Museum of Modern Art (revised for a 1951 reprint), Sweeney brilliantly summarized the Calder style:

Exuberance, buoyancy, vigor . . . humor . . . dignity. . . . All these are features of Alexander Calder's work, together with a sensibility to materials that induces new forms and an insatiable interest in fresh patterns of order.
    . . . The most conspicuous characteristics of his art are those which have been attributed to America's frontier heritage—"that coarseness and strength combined with acuteness and inquisitiveness; that practical, inventive turn of mind, quick to find expedients; that masterful grasp of material things . . . that restless, nervous energy . . . that buoyancy and exuberance which come with freedom." But Calder is a child of his own time. His vernacular is the vernacular of his age in America—an age in which the frontiers of science, engineering and mechanics have dominated the popular imagination in the same way that the national frontier dominated it a century ago.
    . . . Calder's mature work is the marriage of an internationally educated sensibility with a native American ingenuity. Through the individuality of his work he has an established place in contemporary art both here and abroad.

A decade ago Barbara Rose epitomized Calder's consistently joyous oeuvre, and her comment seems even more to the point now than when she wrote it:

Calder's copious production, extending from the miniature wire Circus . . . to the monumental stabiles . . . stands as a monument to the highest kind of creative endeavor, a testimony of affirmation during a period when an optimistic stance grows increasingly difficult to sustain.

Jacques Prévert described Calder's magic in six words: "He gives pleasure, that's his secret."

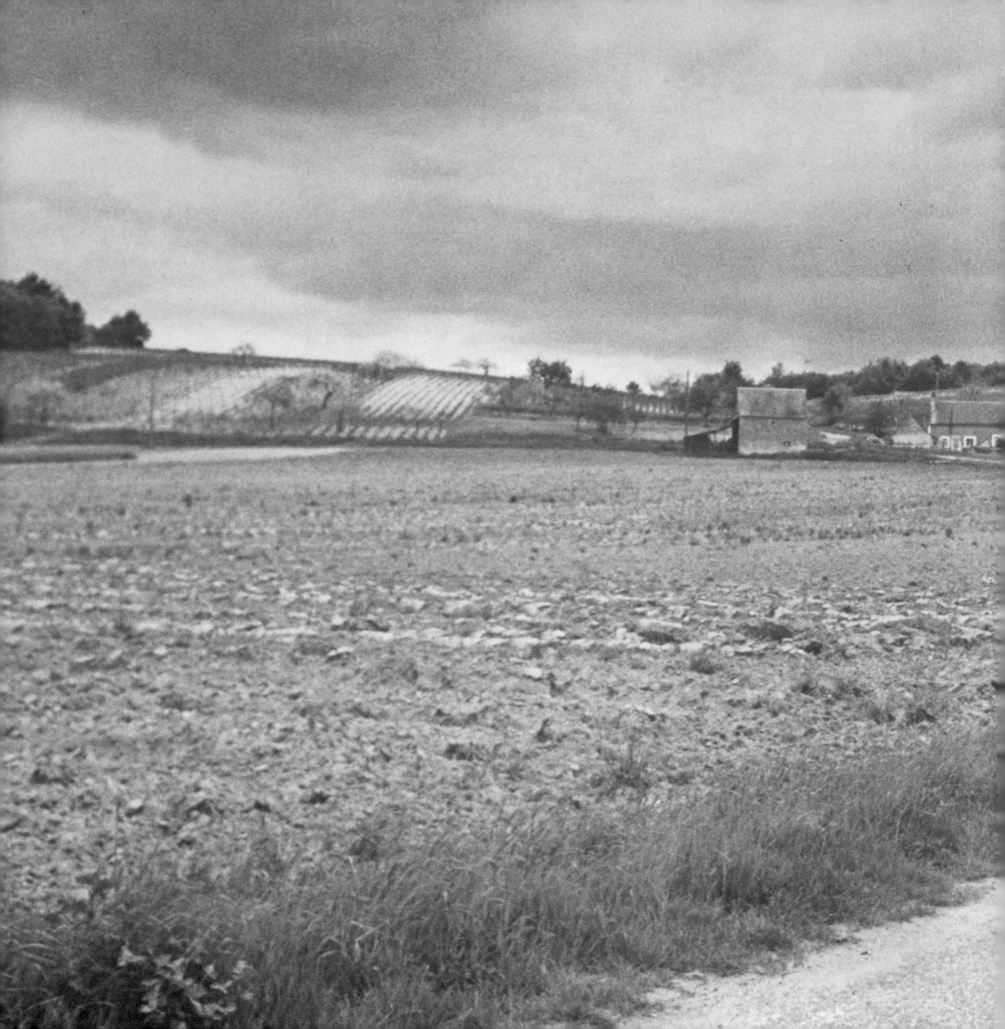

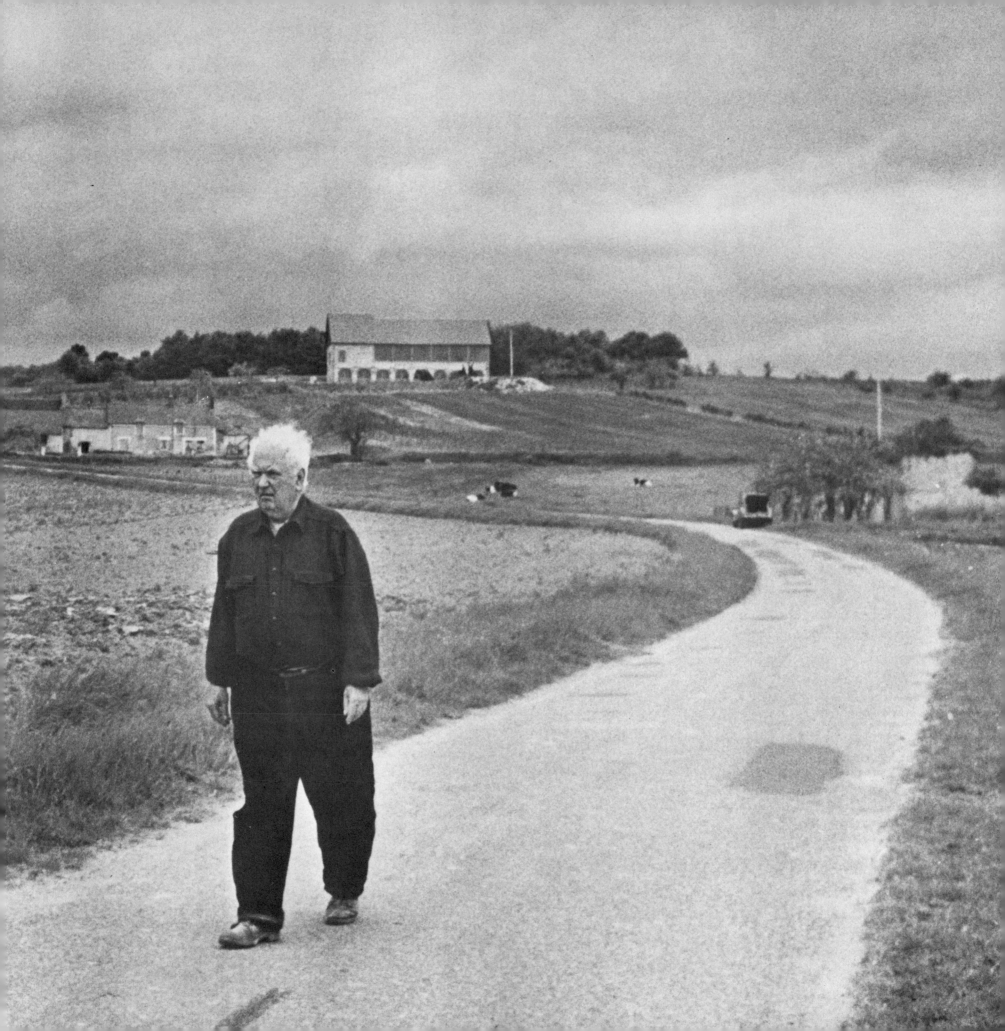

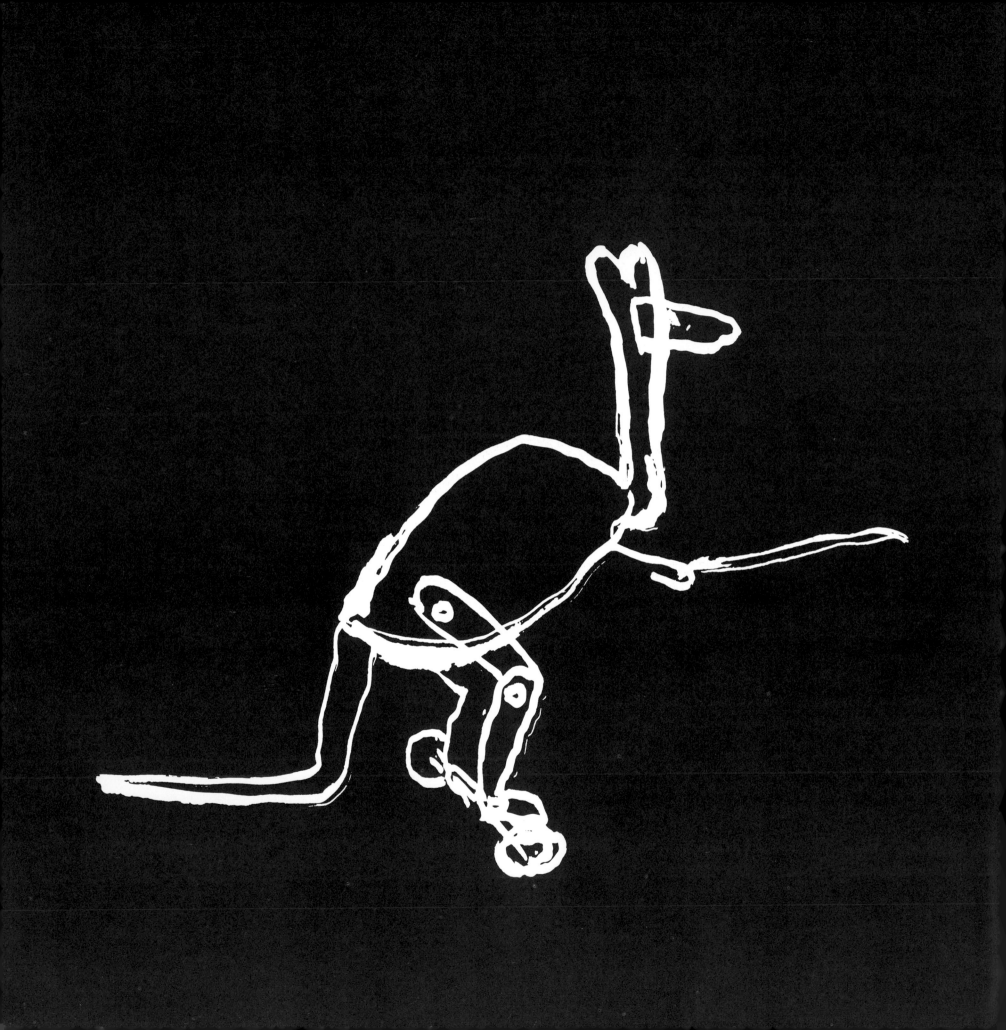

They call me a "playboy," you know. I want to make things that are fun to look at, that have no propaganda value whatsoever.

James Johnson Sweeney, Calder's long-time friend and foremost critic, was the first to recognize the importance of toys and play in Calder's life work. He recalls that Brancusi, at the age of eighty, said: "To keep one's art young, one must imitate young animals. What do they do? They play." A love of play—serious, creative play—is fundamental to the art of Brancusi, Miró and Calder himself. According to Sweeney, Calder's originality lies "in his determination to respect the role of play . . . exploiting this element for esthetic ends." When Calder was beginning to experiment with movement in sculpture, Sweeney notes, "Toys pointed the way"—with their unfamiliar rhythms, provocative surprises and condensed resemblance to natural movement. "All the lyricism of Calder's work, all the poetry, has its source in play." "In the world of play he is most truly himself, there he lives to the fullest; and he plays with forms, colors, lines, movements, figures."

As children, Sandy and his sister, Peggy, were very close and shared an unusual interest in making and manipulating imaginative toys. Peggy described for us some of the toy animals and the puzzles and games they made; Sandy was the innovator, she his assistant. They especially liked animals, had several Noah's Arks of different sizes, and used to invent activities for the Ark animals. One of Sandy's first toy creations was a group of carved wood chickens that wobbled back and forth on wire legs. Peggy still has these and other toys, including a plow that Sandy made out of lead for a toy horse. She recalls with special pleasure a small cannon that used the inch-long Chinese firecrackers called lady-fingers as ammunition.

Growing up did not put an end to toymaking. Calder recalls that he once took a few figures from a popular toy called the Humpty-Dumpty Circus and animated them to perform tricks for children. "There was an elephant and a mule. They could be made to stand on their hind quarters, front quarters, or heads. Then there were clowns with slots in their feet and claws in their hands; they could balance on a ladder on one foot or one hand. I had once articulated these things with strings, so the clown would end up on the back of the elephant." Calder used these and many similar devices in the animal toys and the miniature Circus which he began making shortly after his arrival in Paris in 1926.

The following year some of Calder's toys were exhibited at the Salon des Humoristes. Waverly Root, a friend from the days when Calder occupied a tiny studio-room in the rue Daguerre, has described him working on a toy bird which pulled a worm out of the ground. The stubborn yanking of the bird and the resistance of the worm were, according to Root, "at the same time excruciatingly funny and remarkably beautiful."

Toys

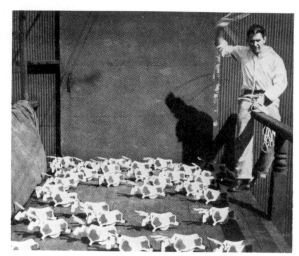

Calder with herd of Gould Company bulls, 1930.

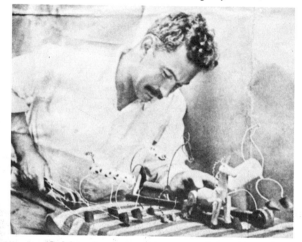

Calder demonstrating toys in action, 1928.

In 1927 Root wrote a prophetic article—never published—suggesting that Calder was catching in his toys an essence of humor and animal motion that might well develop into a significant sculpture of motion.

In Paris a Serb who was in the toy business told Calder he could earn a living making articulated toys. He was interested, because, as he puts it, "The base of my subsistence was still seventy-five dollars a month provided by mother, and my ingenuity. I made my own workbench, for instance, and whatever furniture was needed, with planks and old cases. So I immediately set to work and made some articulated toys with wire, wood, tin and leather. When I looked for my Serb, he had disappeared, but I continued making toys in this way."

A second attempt was more successful. Calder, back in the United States, was recommended to the head of the Gould Manufacturing Company of Oshkosh, Wisconsin, which had a "Toddler Toys" division. Calder made working models and supervised the manufacture of the Gould toys, which were quite similar to some he had been making for his two small nephews. As Sandy describes the firm: "They were door manufacturers, using plywood and thicker chunks of wood. I took their scraps and made various toys—a rowboat, a kangaroo, a bucking cow, ducks, a skating bear. I was given a very modest royalty, which was augmented much later when there was a notice about me in *The New Yorker*, mentioning the Oshkosh toys." The company's advertising leaflet describes the new "action toys" designed by "Alexander Calder of New York and Paris." The items are listed by number: "No 23R wiggles like a swimming fish. No 17R has the action of a scared duckling. No 18R has the slow, gentle motion of a feeding pelican. . . . No 16R has a regular kangaroo hop. . . . No 22R is a goring bull."

Calder's early toys culminated in his famous Circus, to which the following chapter is devoted. Not only did Calder's Circus introduce him to the advanced art world of his time, but it became the foundation of all his mature work. Through the years, toymaking has continued to be one of Calder's favorite pastimes. In line with his mother's conviction that the homemade is superior to the store-bought, Calder has provided all the children in his family—nephews, daughters, grandchildren—with playthings ingeniously contrived from cast-off tin cans, wire, film canisters, whatever was close at hand. His daughters remember with particular delight a multi-storied dollhouse with working elevator and resident dolls.

Children are not the only beneficiaries of Calder's inventions. He once made a mobile of red and blue balls for a friend's cat to bat around, and for his own cat there was a mask that transformed the surprised feline into a furry cow. Calder's friends have often been the delighted recipients of such adult toys as the birth-announcement kangaroo, the tin-can birds or the "bullfighter-trainer," a black, red-horned iron bull named

Carreta, who was a house gift from Calder to his host during a stay in Caracas. *Carreta* is an enlarged version of the "goring bull" designed years earlier for Gould. When moved toward an imaginary bullfighter, its head, which is attached to an eccentric disc on the wheels, lunges repeatedly up and down and forward and back, quite like a ferocious bull. Seeing him at work is a wildly funny, exciting happening (here he appears quietly grazing on his present owner's ranch in Missouri).

Calder's toys are miniature monuments to his love of play. The shorthand rhythms of his little toys are not basically different from those of the major mobiles. Léger said of Calder's early work, "It's serious without appearing so." As Pierre Guéguen sees it, "Calder was not just playing a little game, he was playing a great game that had a great future, not only for his own mobiles, but also for the development of sculpture." Sweeney sums it up: "Calder's art is eternally young. He plays, he amuses himself, and in so doing invests his art with life and force . . . he has discovered, in playing, a new world."

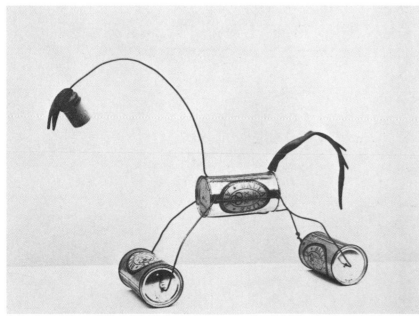

Canasson Kodak, 1960. Film canister, tin cans, wire, leather, 13½″ h. Shawn Davidson, Saché, France.

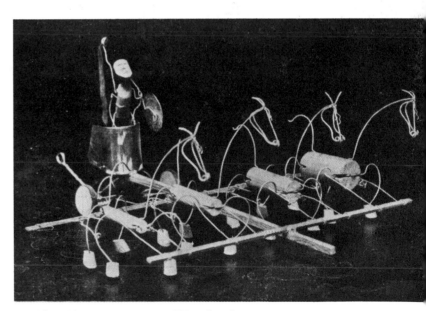

Le Char Romain, c. 1928. Wood, wire, metal, approx. 14″ w. Present location unknown.

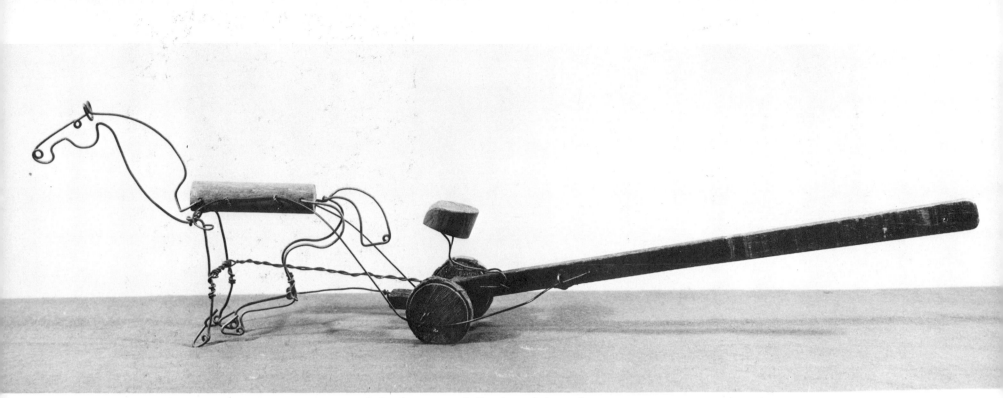

Toy Horse, 1926–27. Wood, wire, 31″ w. Collection of the author.

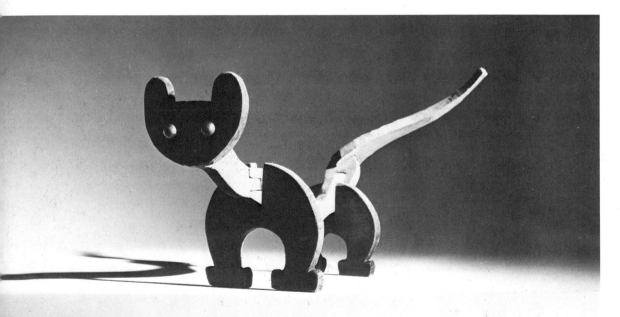

Kitten, 1927–28. Wood, 18″ w. Present location unknown.

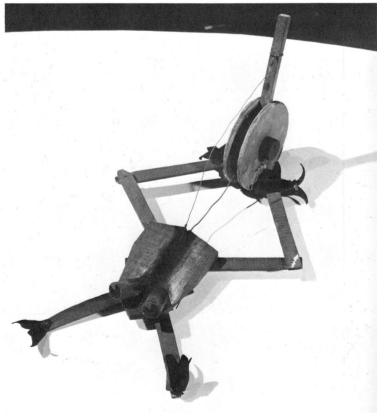

Frog, 1927–28. Wood, wire, 19″ w. Present location unknown.

48

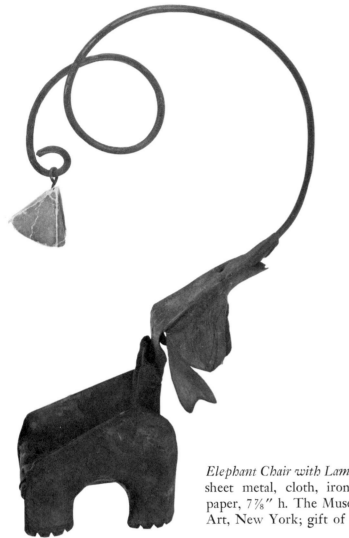

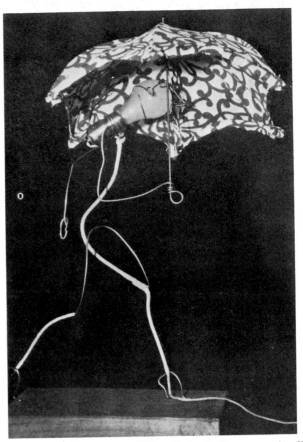

Elephant Chair with Lamp, 1928. Painted sheet metal, cloth, iron wire, painted paper, 7⅞″ h. The Museum of Modern Art, New York; gift of the artist.

Umbrella Lamp, 1928. Wire, light bulb, toy umbrella, approx. 24″ h. Present location unknown.

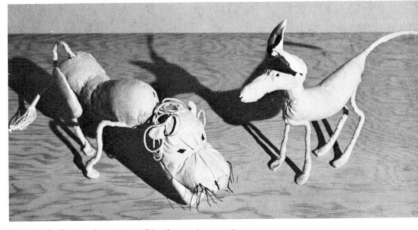

Stuffed Animals, 1927. Cloth, string, wire, approx. 6″ h. Present location unknown.

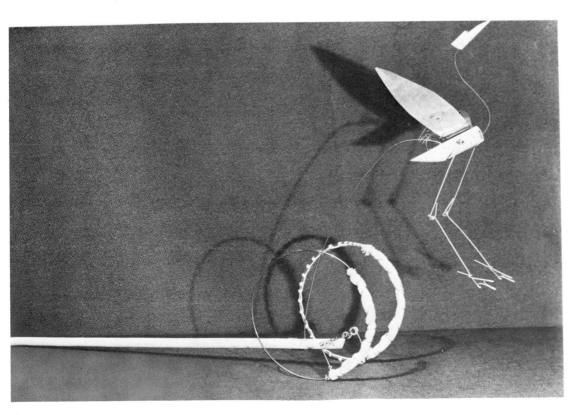

LEFT: *Bird Toy*, c. 1928. Tin, wire, 30″ h. Present location unknown.

Fish Pull-toy, c. 1960. Wood, wire, approx.
10″ h. Sandra Davidson, Saché, France.

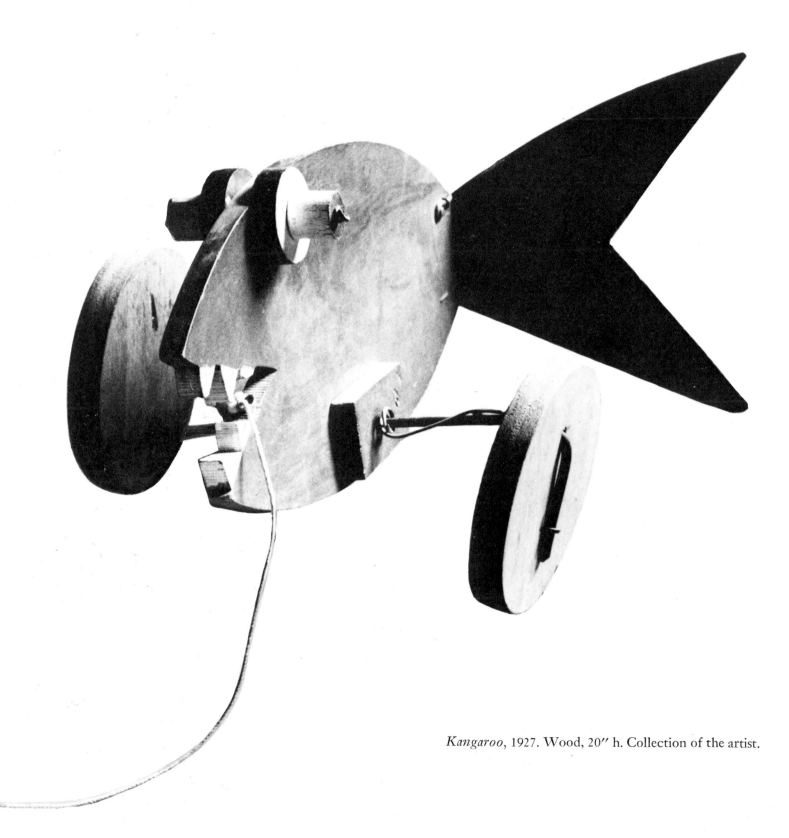

Kangaroo, 1927. Wood, 20″ h. Collection of the artist.

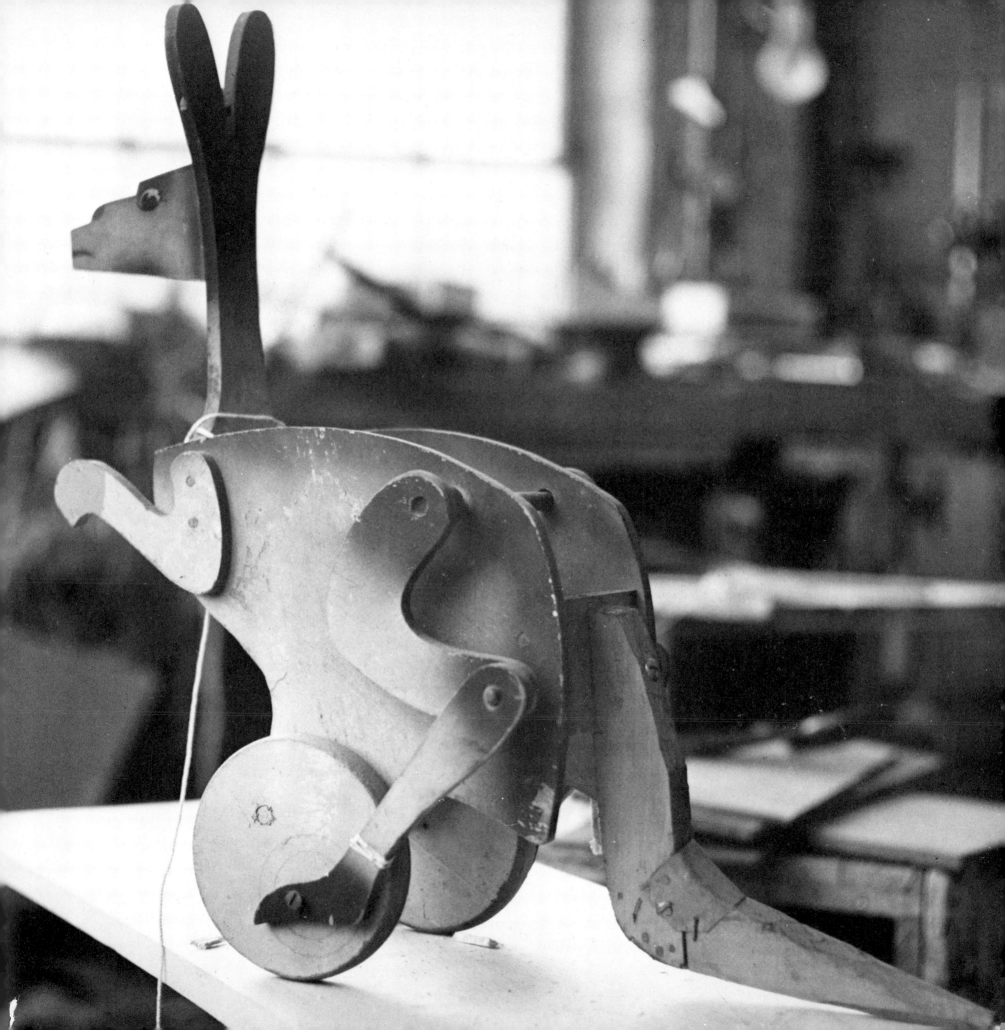

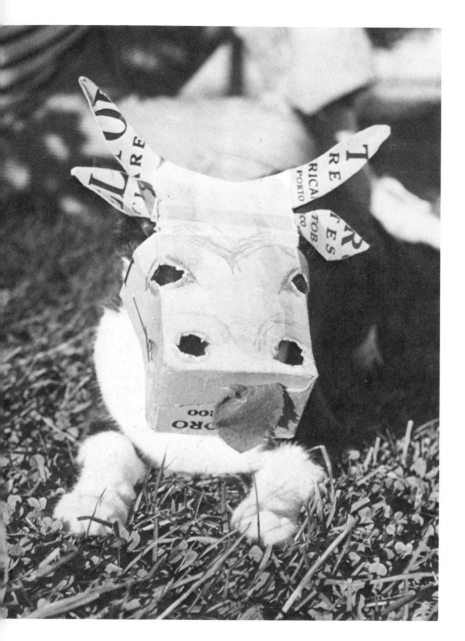

Calder's cat as a cow, 1950.

BELOW: *Birth-announcement Kangaroo*, 1959 (two views). Paper, 6″ h. Mr. and Mrs. Cleve Gray, Cornwall Bridge, Connecticut.

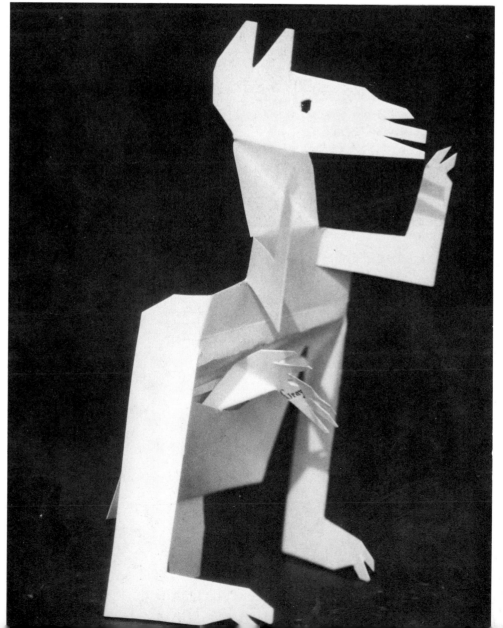

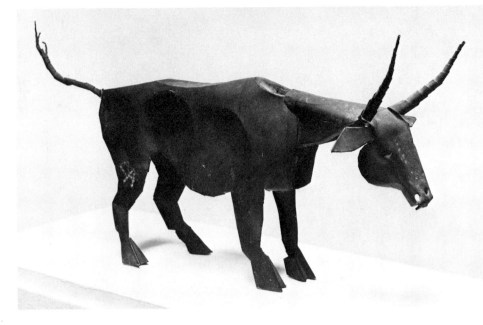

Old Bull, 1930. Sheet brass, 18″ w. Whitney Museum of American Art, New York; gift of the Howard and Jean Lipman Foundation.

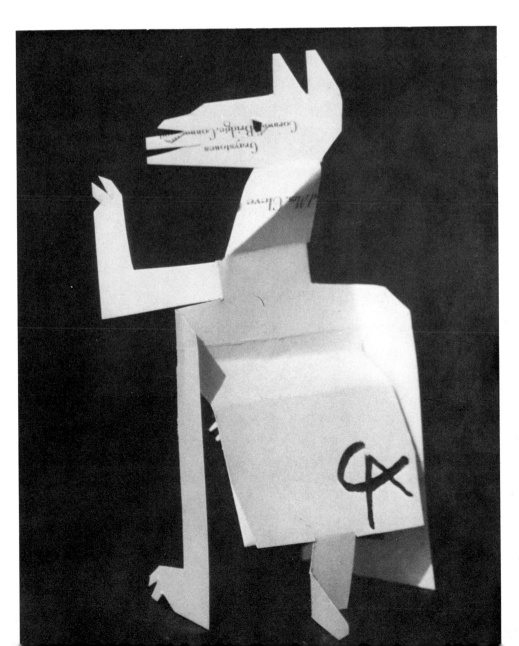

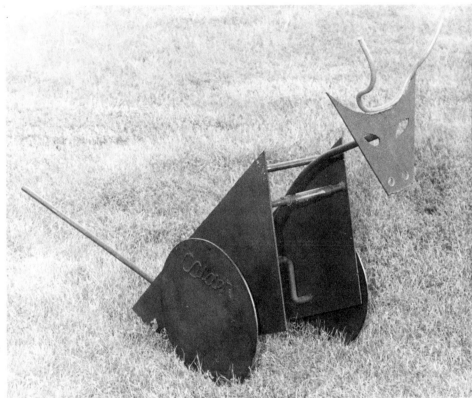

Carreta, 1955. Painted steel, 6′3½″ w. Mr. and Mrs. Leonard J. Horwich, Chicago.

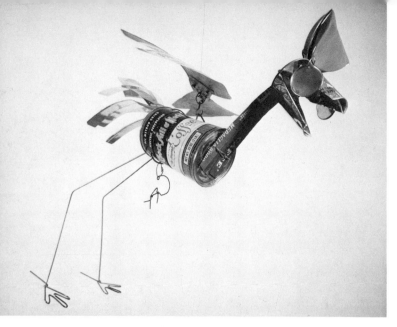

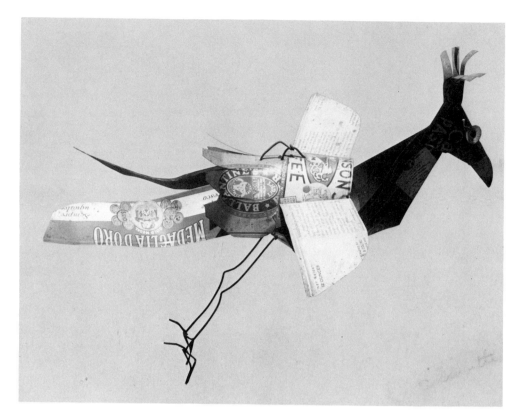

Chock, 1972. Tin can, wire, 28″ w. Whitney Museum of American Art, New York; gift of the artist.

RIGHT: *The Only Only Bird*, c. 1950. Tin can, wire, 22″ w. Collection of the artist.

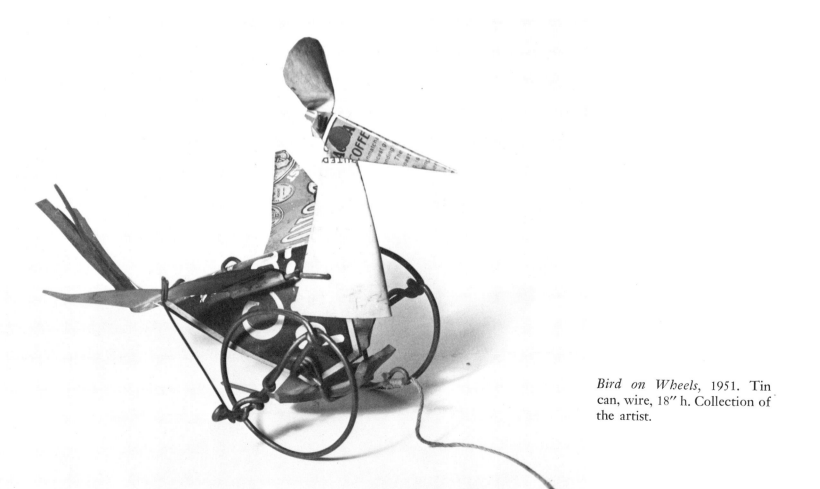

Bird on Wheels, 1951. Tin can, wire, 18″ h. Collection of the artist.

54

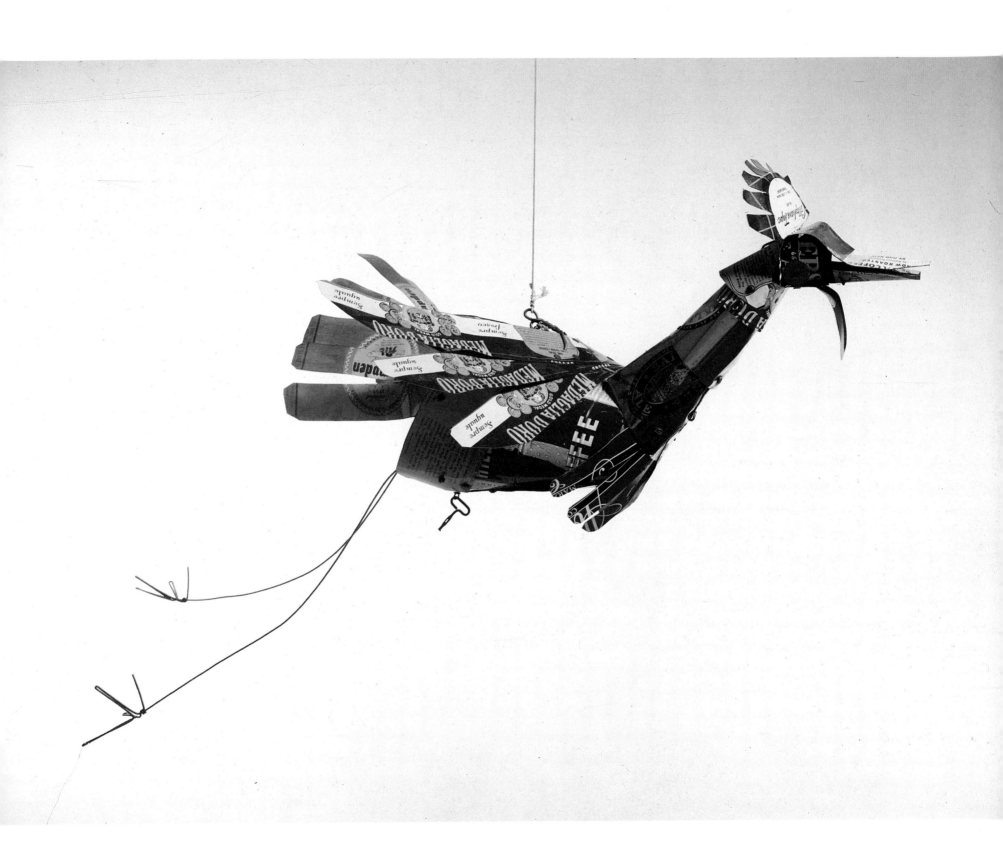

Le Coq de Saché, 1965. Tin can, wire, 32″ h. Jean and Sandra Davidson, Saché, France.

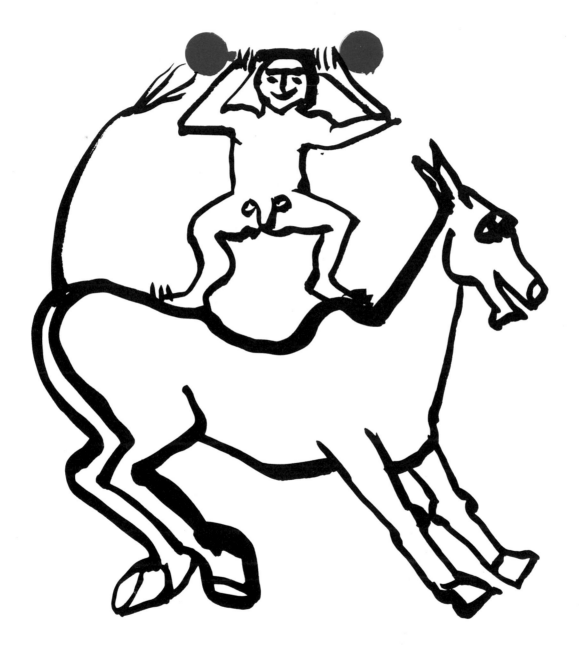

I've always been delighted by the way things are hooked together. . . . It's just like a diagram of force. I love the mechanics of the thing—and the vast space—and the spotlight.

Calder made this statement when asked about his interest in the circus. He was recalling his first visit, in the year 1925, when he worked as a free-lance artist for the *National Police Gazette* in New York. "I went to the circus, Ringling Bros. and Barnum & Bailey. I spent two full weeks there practically every day and night. I could tell by the music what act was getting on and used to rush to some vantage point. Some acts were better seen from above and others from below. At the end of these two weeks, I took a half-page layout to the *Police Gazette*." The drawing appeared in the May 23 issue, and Calder was paid his standard rate—twenty dollars.

"I always loved the circus . . . so I decided to make a circus just for the fun of it." Calder's own miniature Circus, now on extended loan to the Whitney Museum and on permanent display there, was begun in Paris in the mid-twenties with just a few figures. He enlarged the Circus over half a dozen years into a full performance with a troupe of dozens of people and animals. During the next thirty years, he gave performances for friends and for special audiences in Europe and the United States. Most often it was just "for fun," but as his fame grew, Calder often performed in conjunction with his exhibitions; occasionally he "hired out"; and there were also benefit performances such as the one held in Washington during World War II to aid Free France. Press clippings, expressing enthusiasm in many languages, occupy an astonishing number of pages in Calder's scrapbook.

The Circus as a performance is a delightful event. Sweeney has vividly described one of those evenings in Paris in the late twenties:

The circus was given in Calder's narrow room; the guests would crowd onto the low studio bed; the performance would take place on the floor in front of them. A bit of green carpet was unrolled; a ring was laid out; poles were erected to support the trapeze for the aerial act and wing indicators of the "big top"; a spotlight was thrown on the ring; an appropriate record placed on a small portable phonograph; "Mesdames et Messieurs, je vous présente—," and the performance began.

For those not lucky enough to have seen a live show, there is the film *Calder's Circus*, photographed in color by Carlos Vilardebo at Calder's home in Saché in 1961. Ringmaster Calder is puppeteer and sound-effects man; victrola circus music is managed by his wife. In the following pages the stars of the Circus are presented in photographs by Marvin Schwartz; when one looks at the individual performers, it becomes evident that each one is a marvelously vital, humorous and original figurative sculpture.

The Circus

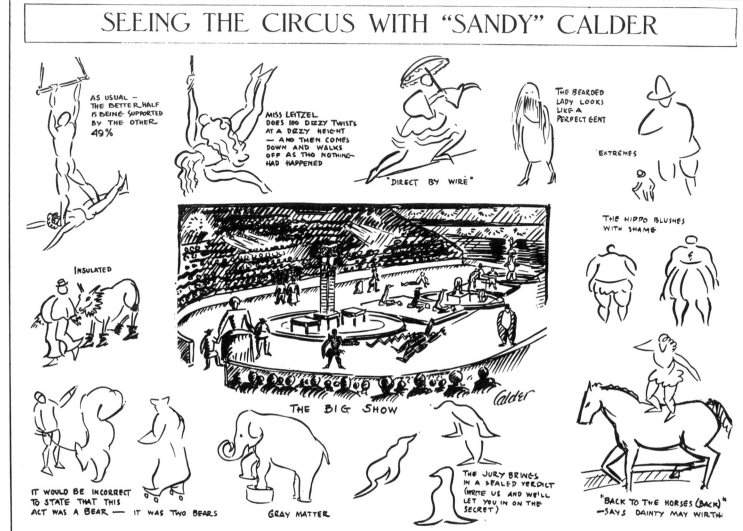

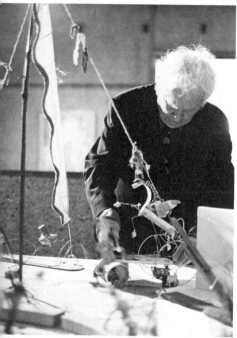

Reinstalling the Circus, Whitney Museum of American Art, 1975.

Calder has described his Circus activities in various parts of his autobiography:

Before my return to New York, in the early fall of 1927, I wanted to take my circus with me, and I had to submit the two suitcases which held the show then—it has grown to five since—to the Douane Centrale in Paris. All the artists were stamped with a rubber stamp on the buttocks. Some still carry traces of this branding.

Finally, Louisa and I got married on the seventeenth of January, 1931. I took the circus to the James house in Concord, Massachusetts, and ran it the night before the wedding.

The reverend who married us apologized for having missed the circus the night before. So I said:

"But you are here for the circus, today."

I was making the most of the [Paris] studio being so close to our living quarters, working for hours every day, but feeling free to knock off if something worth while came along. Once in a while I would pull the workbenches around, link them with planks, make the bleachers for the circus, and we would have it three nights running. Sometimes, we had nearly a hundred people. There were regular aficionados and occasionally some new people; others were bringing someone along. In the front row, there was always a place reserved for Louisa's great-aunt, Mrs. Alice Cuyler, who was quite elderly but enthusiastic.

I met a fellow who ran a weekly called *Le Boulevardier*, somewhat similar to *The New Yorker*. He gave me some things to do and their artistic adviser, Marc Réal, became

Circus performance, 1929.

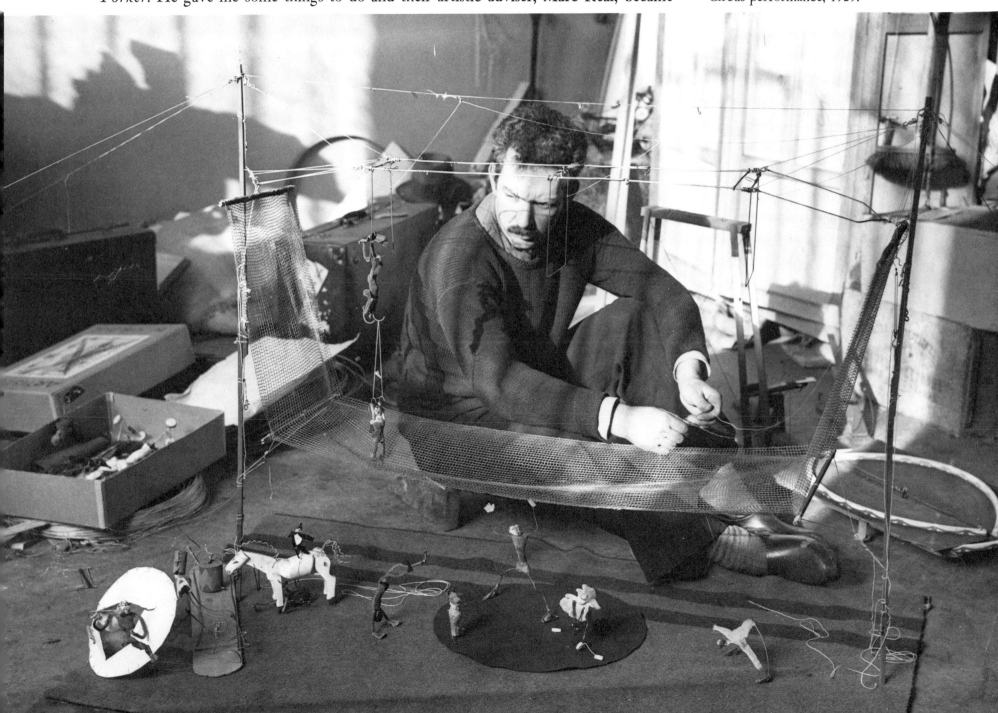

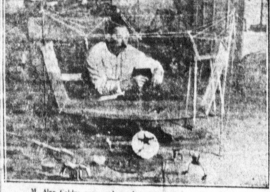

Paris newspaper clipping, 1931, from Calder's scrapbook.

quite a friend because when I said I had a small circus, his face brightened up and he said, "Let's see it."

One time Réal brought in Paul Fratellini [the circus performer] and he took a fancy to the dog in my circus show. It was made of rubber tubing and he got me to enlarge it for his brother Albert, who always dragged a dog around with him. Before that he had had a stuffed dog. Mine trotted and its tail wagged around. However, they just ignored the fact that I had made it and never announced it in their act—it remained a gift.

Shortly before sailing, I insisted on trying to show Sweeney how to dance and managed to fall backward. His forehead hit my Adam's apple and my voice disappeared. It was rather lugubrious. I recovered my voice later on, but have never quite managed to make the old noise of the seal in my circus.

I had taken my circus along to Chicago, and gave several performances, and I think one evening I hired out to a Mrs. Brewster. She had an elegant black-and-white marble floor into which I could not nail. So we got a storm door and nailed a stick onto it at each corner to moor my guy lines. To add strength to the sticks, we piled a few logs of firewood on each. Mrs. Brewster, who had rented me out for fifty dollars instead of the hundred I asked, thought that this firewood was rather shabby, so she had some cyclamens brought in to stand in front of it.

I got rid of these.

Mrs. Aline Bernstein said that if she got a job she was hoping for, in theatrical production, she would buy this object and would I please call her up on a given day. I called her up and she did not have the job. I said, "I would like to invite you to my circus, but I don't know just where I am going to run it."

She said, "You can run it here, very soon—it is often a circus here, anyhow—and by the way, we are having a party this evening, why don't you join us?"

So, Louisa and I went. There were lots of people and lots of fancy food and liquor. The sky was the limit.

In those days, for the circus, I always had printed invitations, which I did myself with a linoleum cut. I wish I had some of these left. Mrs. Aline Bernstein set the date and asked me to invite some of my friends—she would invite some of hers. So I promptly sent her a batch of invitations, which were green and white, and she must have remembered that I had a few friends too.

The evening set, I arrived . . . with my five valises and a very small gramophone. One entered on Park Avenue, but the place was really—at the end of a long corridor—on Madison. I was greeted by Mrs. Bernstein. There seemed to be four or five people around. The room was somewhat oblong. I pushed sofas back against the wall, then I removed a bust from a table behind me at a far corner. I recognized the bust as Noguchi's. The bust lady wore a monocle—she was the daughter of the house.

My hostess said, "That's a young Japanese sculptor." I said, "Yes, he's coming tonight." (I'd asked him to come and run the victrola for me.)

Her guests seemed to be dressed negligently or in negligees. My guests arrived and occupied the shorter of the two bleachers. They included Louisa, Bob and Jane Josephy, Millie and Sandy Knox, Val Dudensing and his wife, and Lee Simonson and others.

Millie Knox had a white fur coat, and Mrs. Bernstein's sister, who was in the clothing business, kept eyeing this coat—with I don't know what.

By and by Noguchi arrived and I had set up the masts, the various cords, and the curtains. As I spent most of the time on my knees when performing the circus, I had bought a pair of basketball kneepads and was trying to break these in.

Well, I performed the circus.

I remember Lee Simonson, who was right in front of me, being very careful to pick up his peanut shells and put them in a container to spare the "lovely" blond wall-to-wall carpet.

Finally the chariot race, the last act, came off and my friends went home. It was always a long job packing things afterward—like in the real circus—and I always did it myself, having the knack and the memory.

Mrs. Bernstein said, "It's a lot of work."

That was her only comment.

As I was packing up, I revealed a Bergdorf Goodman suit box—purple figures walking across a white field. Mrs. Bernstein's sister (who worked for Bergdorf Goodman) asked me, "Where did you get that box?"

It was her only comment.

I told her that Josephy, the friend with whom I was staying, had received it from his bootlegger with a load of liquor.

I was never aware that the great Wolfe—that is, Thomas Wolfe, the writer—was present at my circus performance. He did not have the good sense to present himself and I only heard from him much later—some nasty remarks on my performance, included in a long-winded book [*You Can't Go Home Again*].

In a letter Noguchi reminisced about this 1929 performance, and others:

The occasion of Sandy's circus at Aline Bernstein's was a very memorable one. That was the time I first met Thomas Wolfe sprawled huge over a bed. Aline, I had known previously because of our mutual interest in the theater, and later we did become involved in developing a fashion museum which is now housed in the Metropolitan. At that time New York was a much more intimate place, it seems to me. I had been involved in Sandy's circus in Paris from the very beginning when he started to collect the various characters—Master of Ceremonies, sword swallower, hoochy-koochy dancers, Japanese jugglers. And he had more or less put me in charge of the crank-up phonograph mainly with the record "Ramona." It is part of my memory of Paris during 1927–28 of all the wire figures of Sandy balancing in the air. And the circus was a natural outburst into the

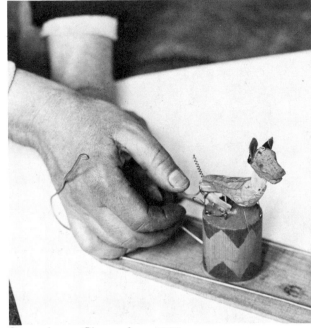

Operating a Circus dog, 1929.

Invitation to Circus performance, 1929.

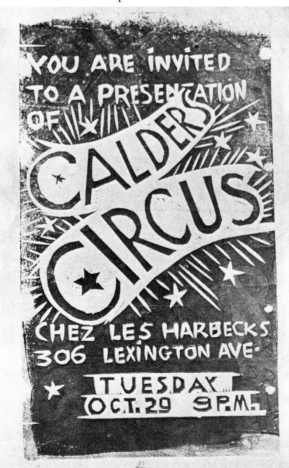

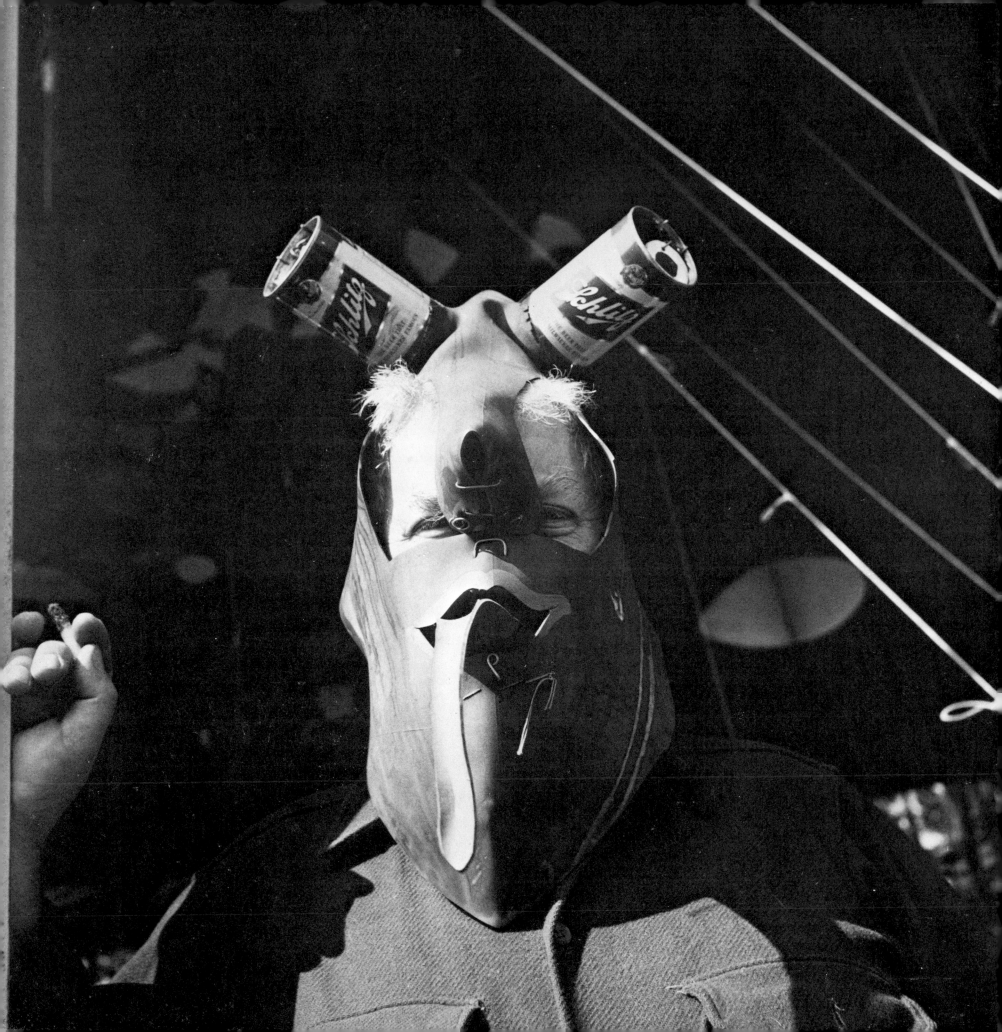

particular situation of life we call the circus. And each of these characters took on a very definite personality as they emerged once more to the tune of "Ramona."

Sandy was of course a great aficionado of the circus and had made a dog of wheel-spokes for legs which the Fratellini would drag around at the Cirque Medrano. I remember once going with Sandy and James Johnson Sweeney to a circus where I pulled a lion's tail which was sticking out through the cage, from which exploit I have derived great honor over the years, at least with Mr. Sweeney.

The early part of this century was the period of the great vogue of circuses. Many artists were interested in the circus as a popular art and were attracted to Calder's performances. His Circus brought him into early contact with the leaders of the Paris art world—Mondrian, Miró, Cocteau, Van Doesburg, Kiesler, Man Ray, Pascin, Léger, Foujita, Pevsner, Arp—many of whom had an effect on his development as an artist.

Sweeney has pointed out that Calder's miniature circus "was to serve as a laboratory in which some of the most original features of his later work were to be developed." It is interesting to compare the figures shown here with works in the following chapters. The wire, wood and bronze sculpture, the jewelry, drawings, gouaches, and even the great mobiles and stabiles and the gay Animobiles evolved from the Circus. As a theme, the circus continues to fascinate him; in 1975, exactly fifty years after he sold his first circus drawing to the *National Police Gazette*, Calder's exhibition at the Perls Galleries was *Recent Mobiles and Circus Gouaches*. He has shown a constant partiality for animal sculpture in almost all media and often uses specific circus subjects and titles; one of his monumental stabiles is named after the Circus ringmaster, Monsieur Loyal. Most important, the basic qualities of Calder's major works have developed as abstractions of his early Circus troupe. This is especially evident in the mobiles, with their precision engineering, their tightrope tension and balance, and their lively acrobatic motion. As if to illustrate this point, Peter Bellew, in his recent book on Calder, juxtaposes photographs of actual circus tightrope acts with mobiles, and performing circus elephants with large stabiles. The circus esthetic—a combination of suspense, surprise, spontaneity, humor, gaiety, playfulness—is at the heart of all Calder's work.

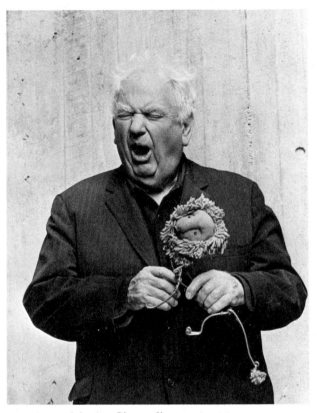

Roaring with the Circus lion, 1971.

Calder as a clown, 1950.

OVERLEAF: *The Circus*, 1926–31. Wood, metal, cloth, paper, leather, wire, string, rubber tubing, cork, buttons, sequins, nuts, bolts, bottle caps. Figures 2–14″ h. Collection of the artist, on extended loan to the Whitney Museum of American Art, New York.

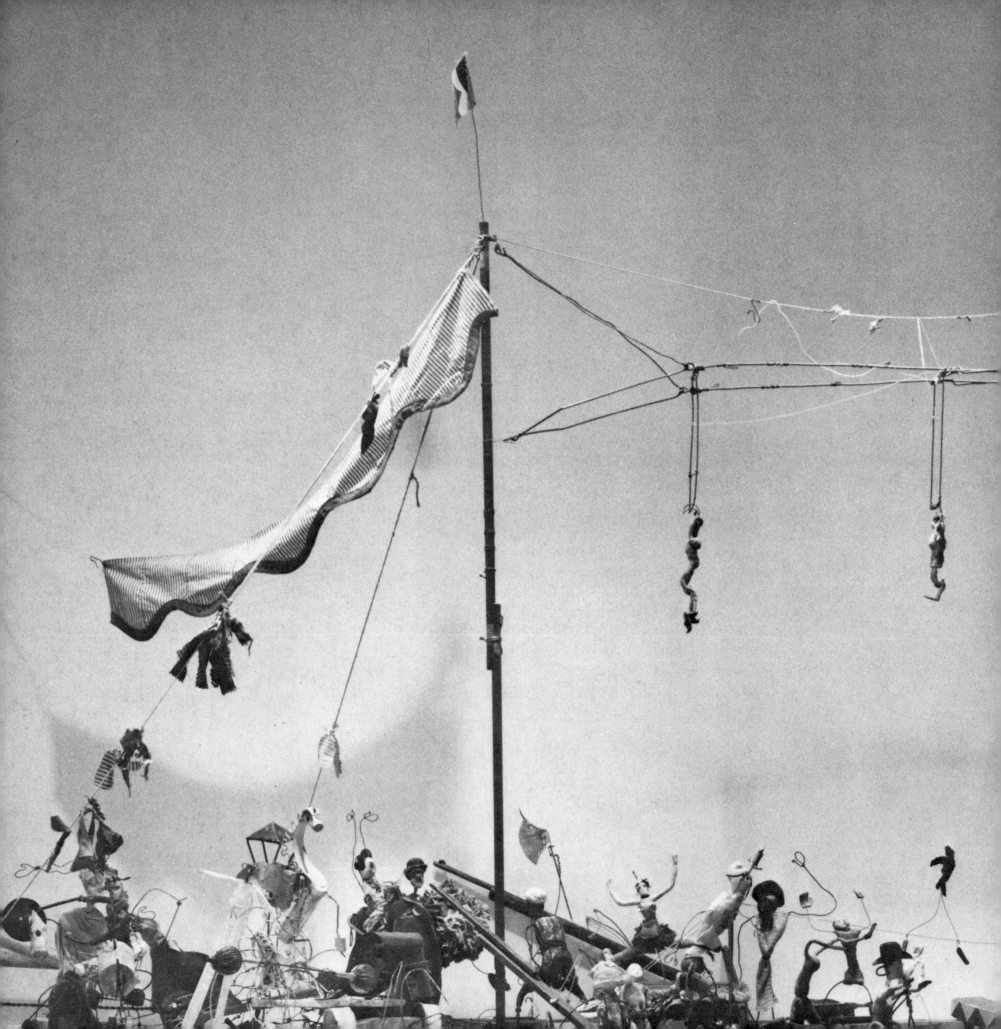

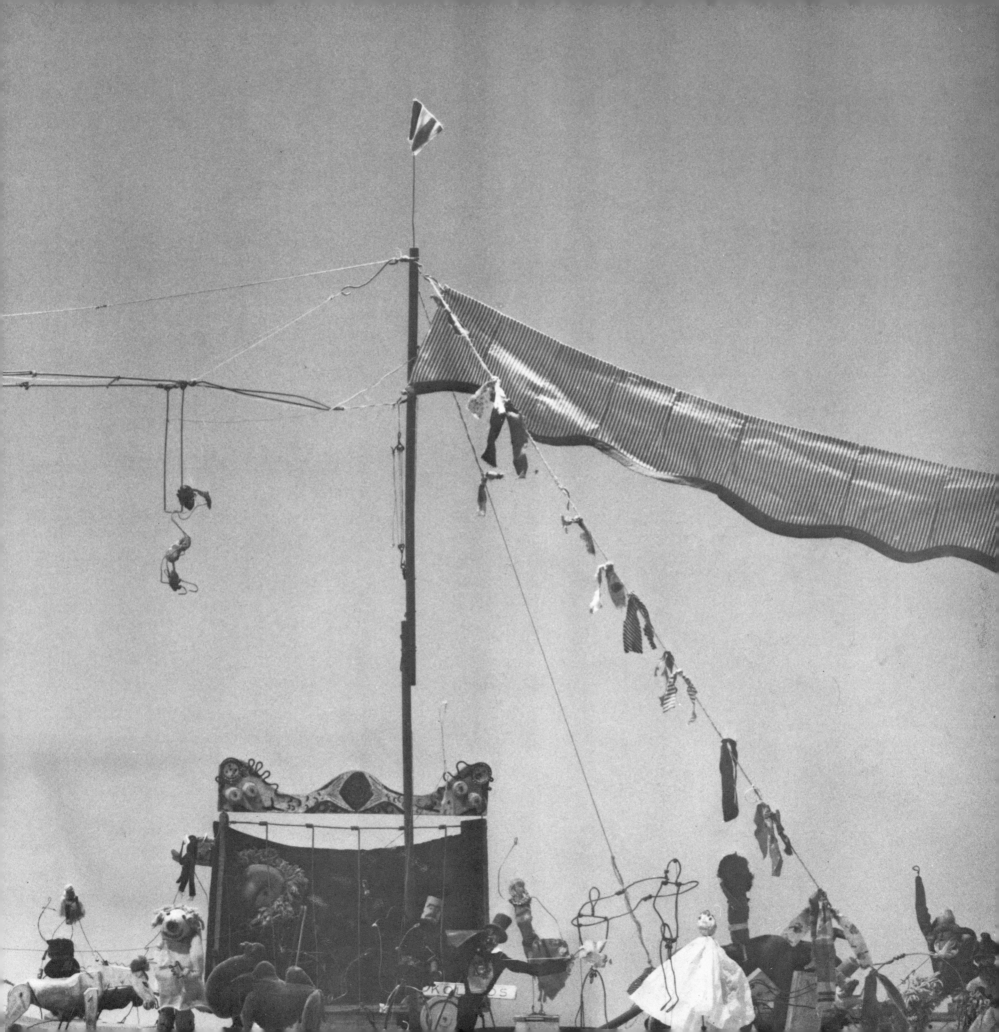

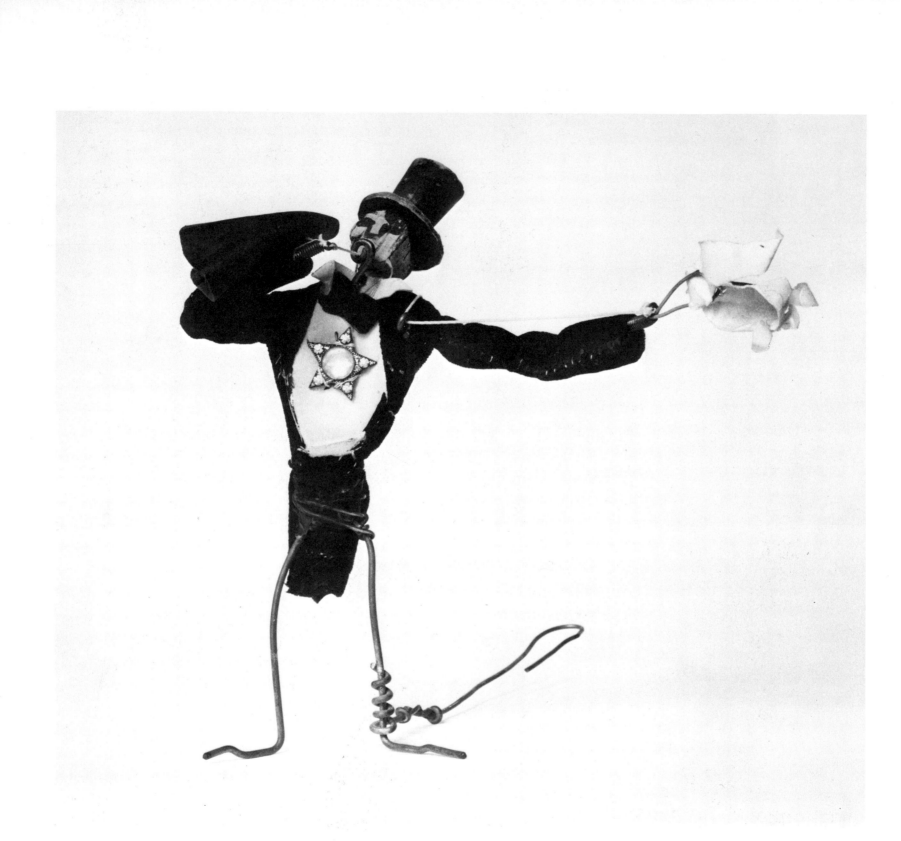

Monsieur Loyal, Ringmaster.

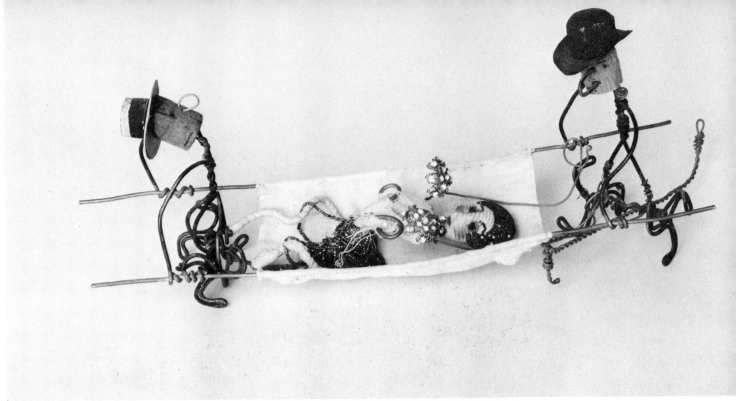

Stretcher Bearers.

Spear Thrower and Exotic Dancer.

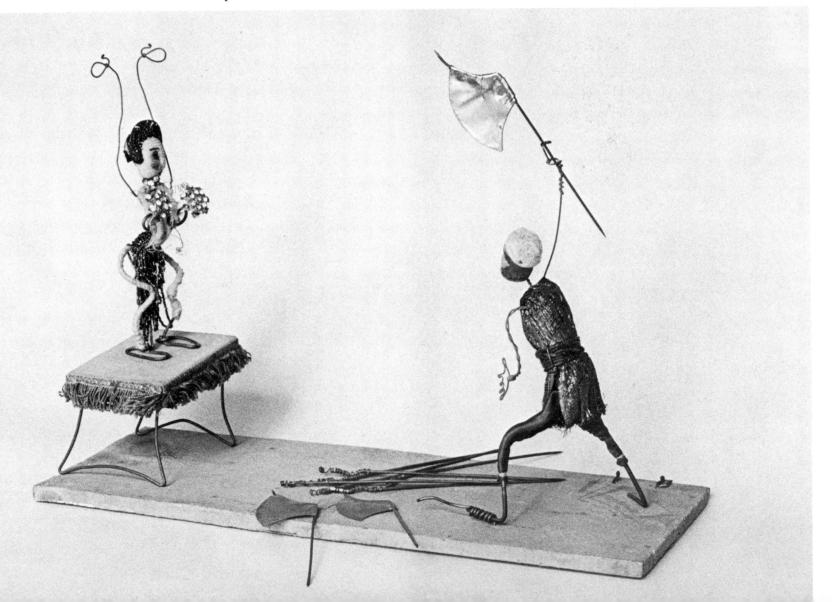

67

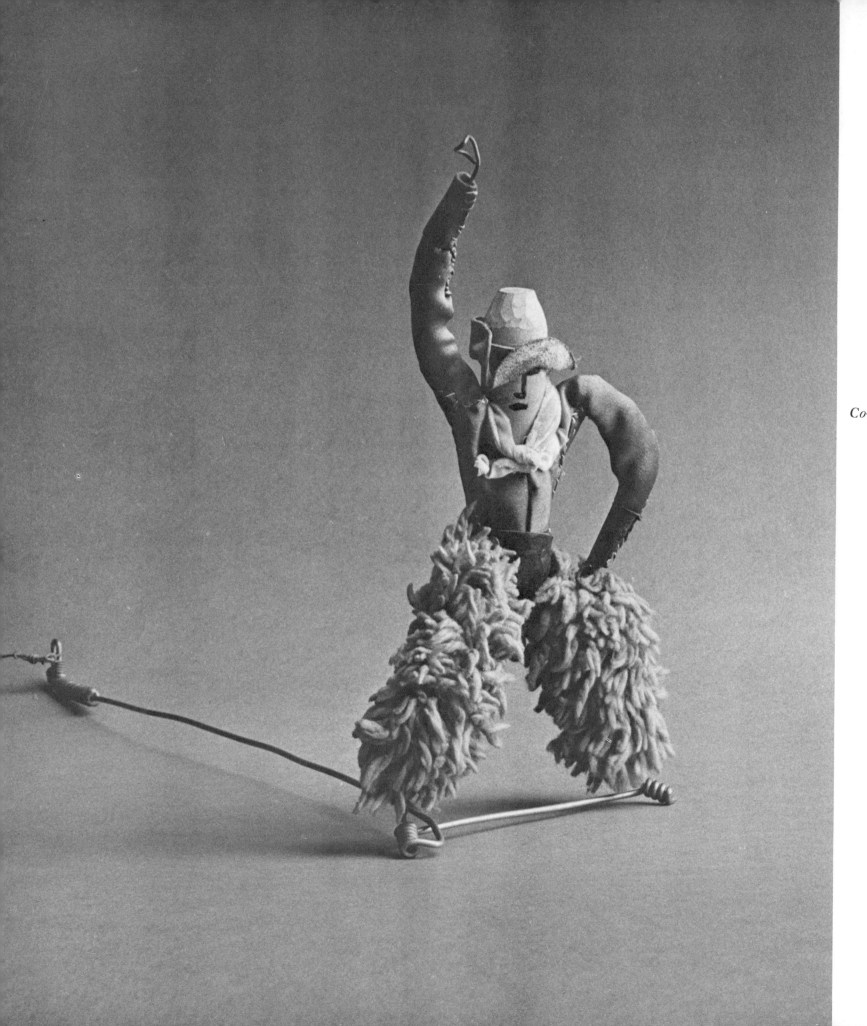

Cowboy.

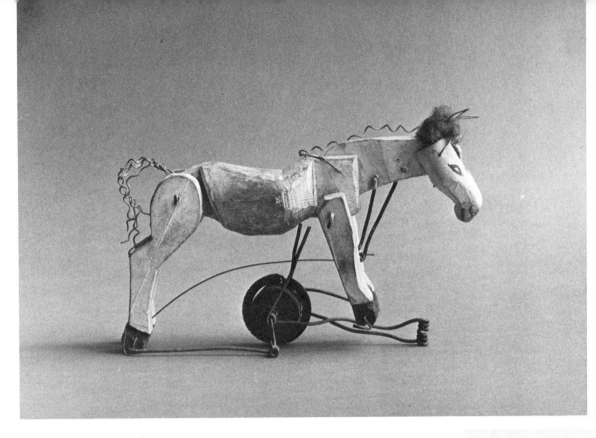

Horse.

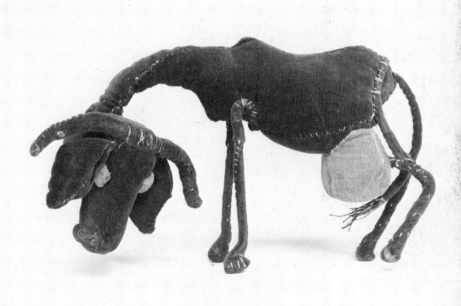

Cow.

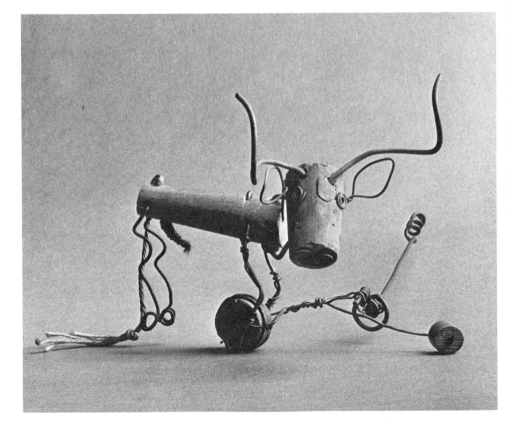

Bull.

69

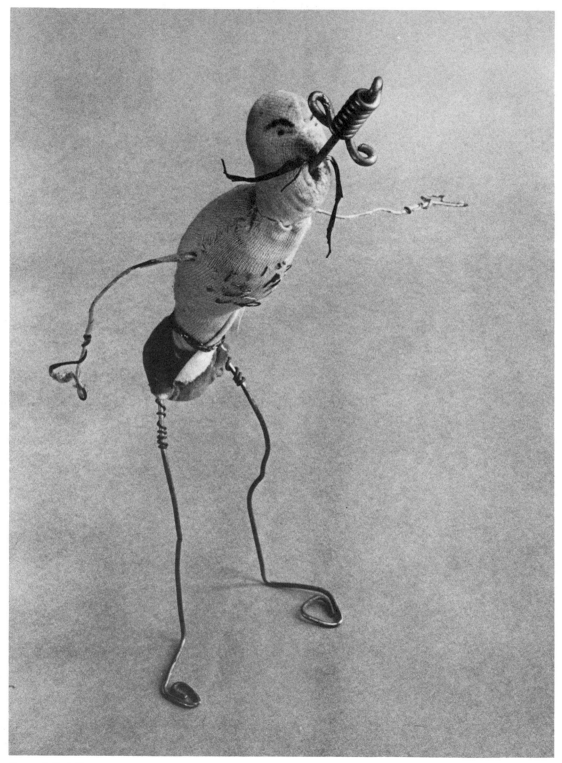

Sword Swallower.

Negress.

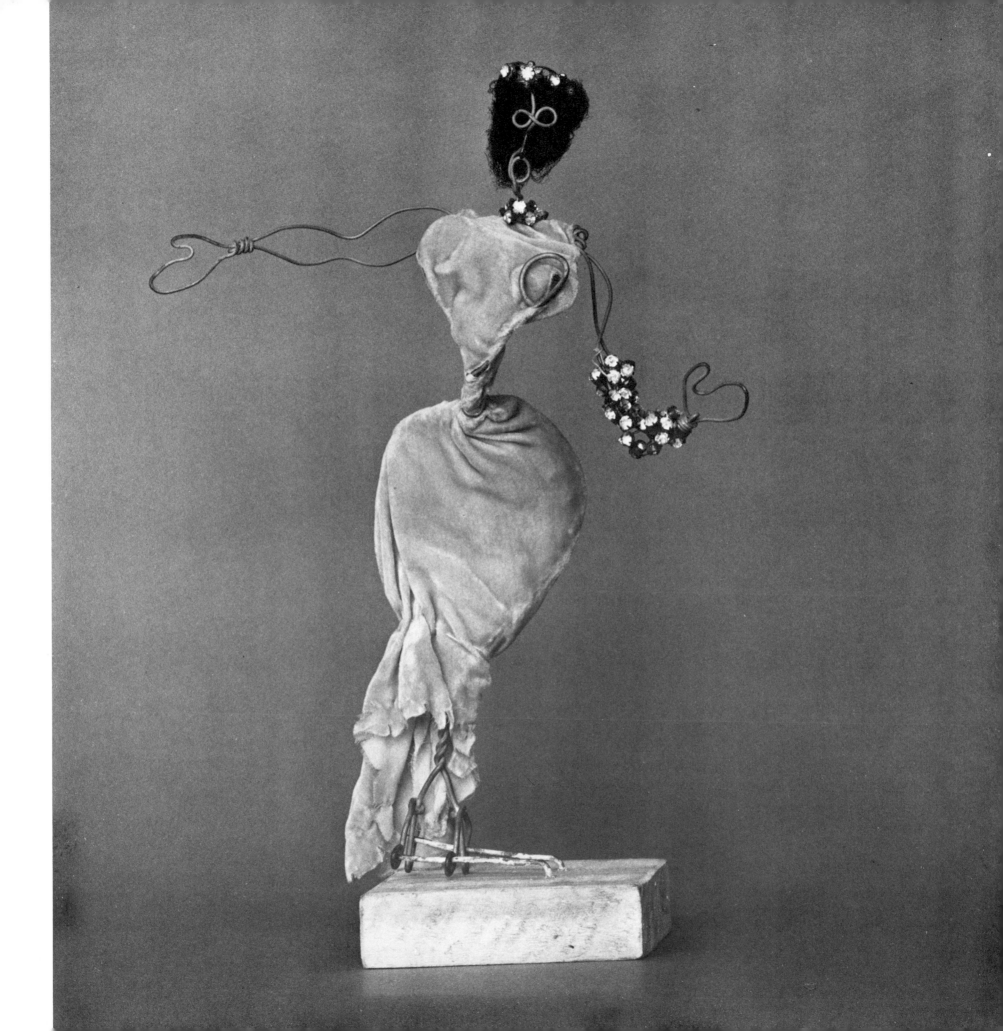

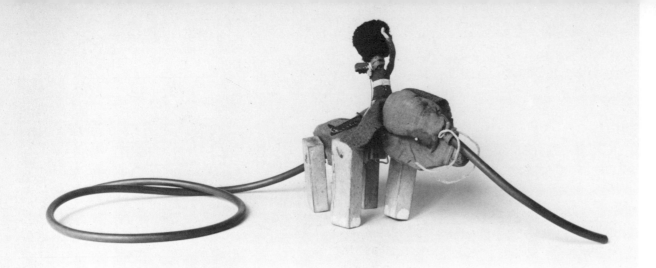

Elephant and Trainer.

Bearded Lady.

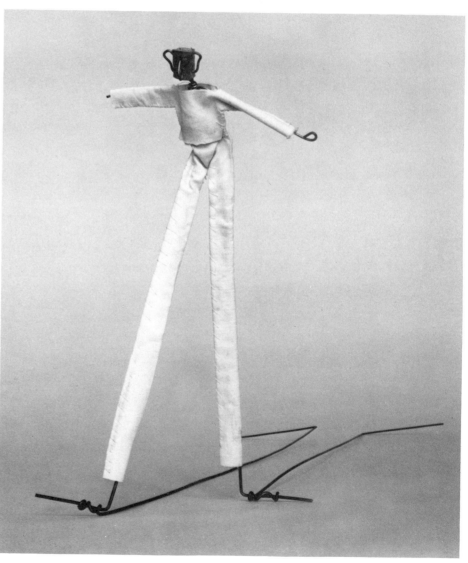

Man on Stilts.

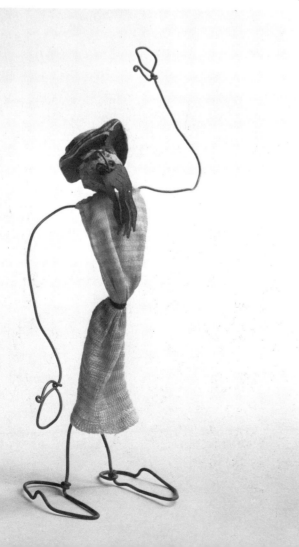

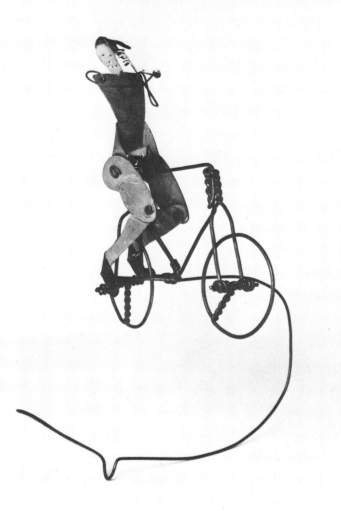

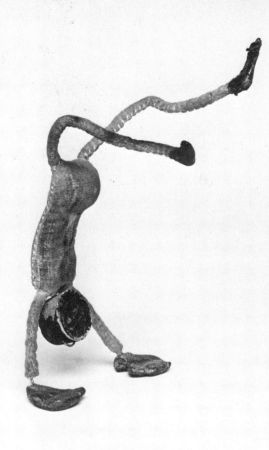

Acrobat.

Cyclist.

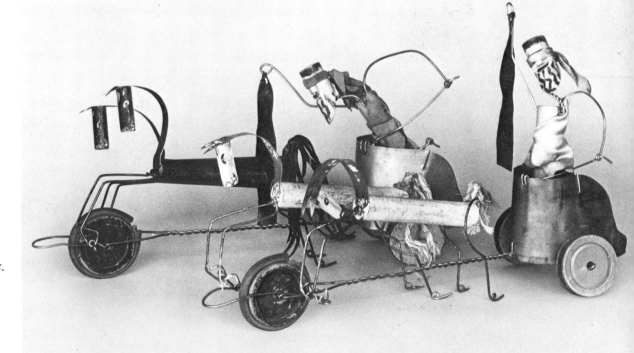

Charioteers.

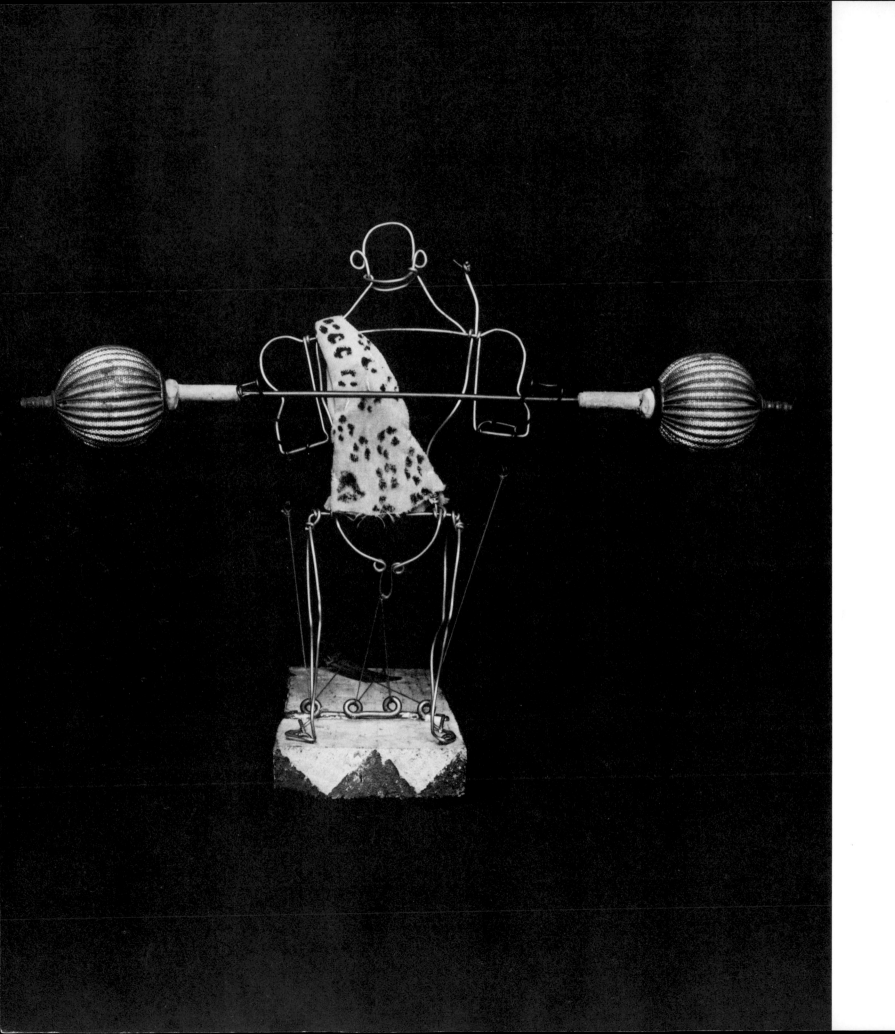

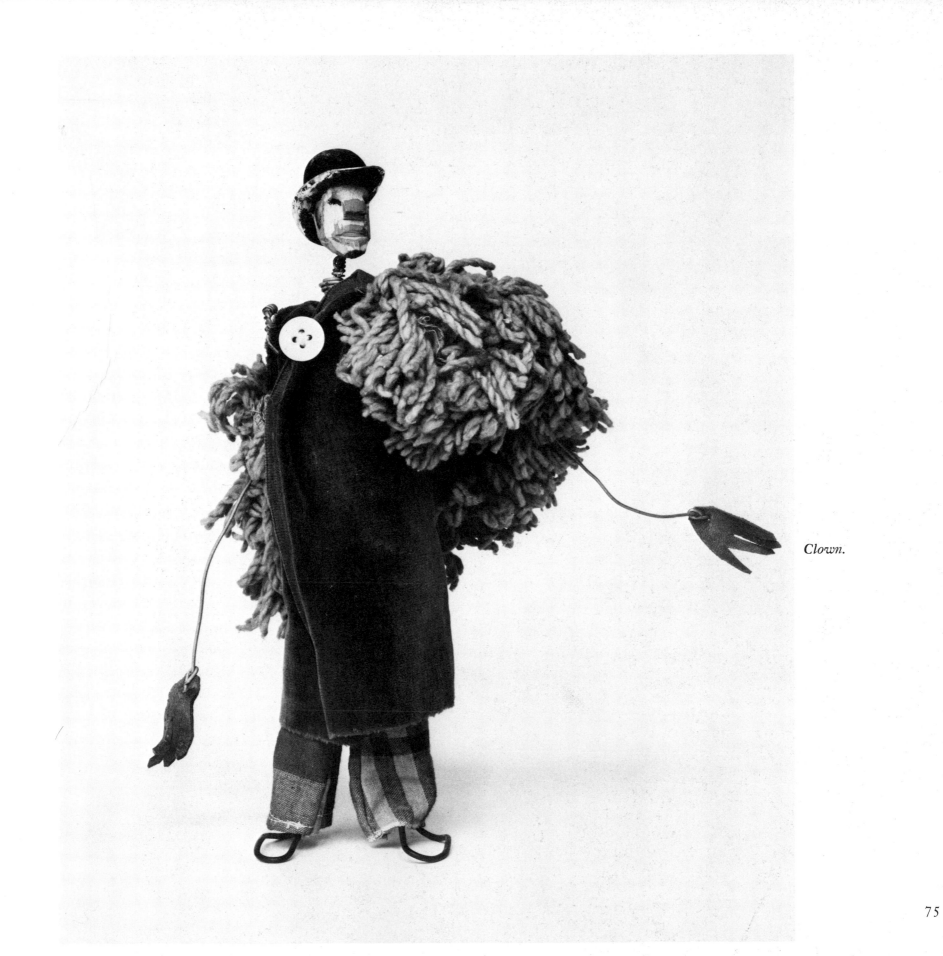

Clown.

Rigoulot, the Weight Lifter.

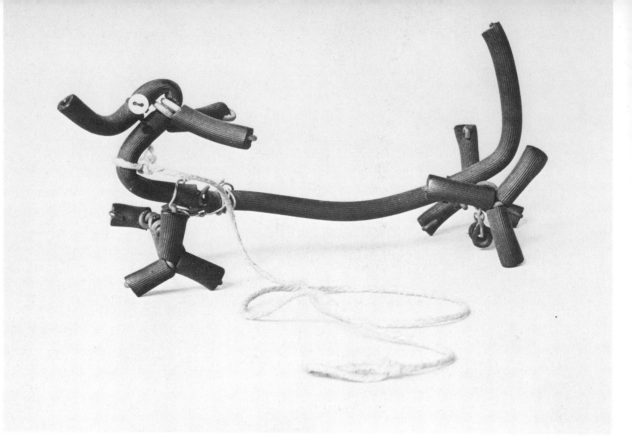

Miss Tamara the Dachshund.

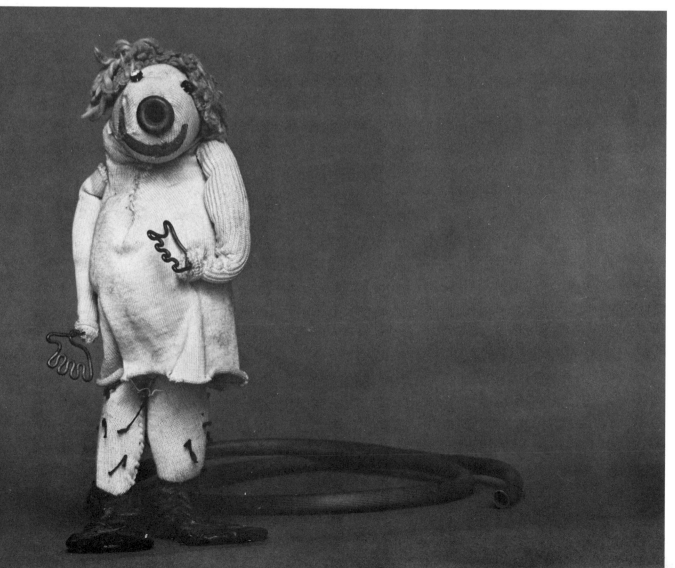

Little Clown, the Trumpeter.

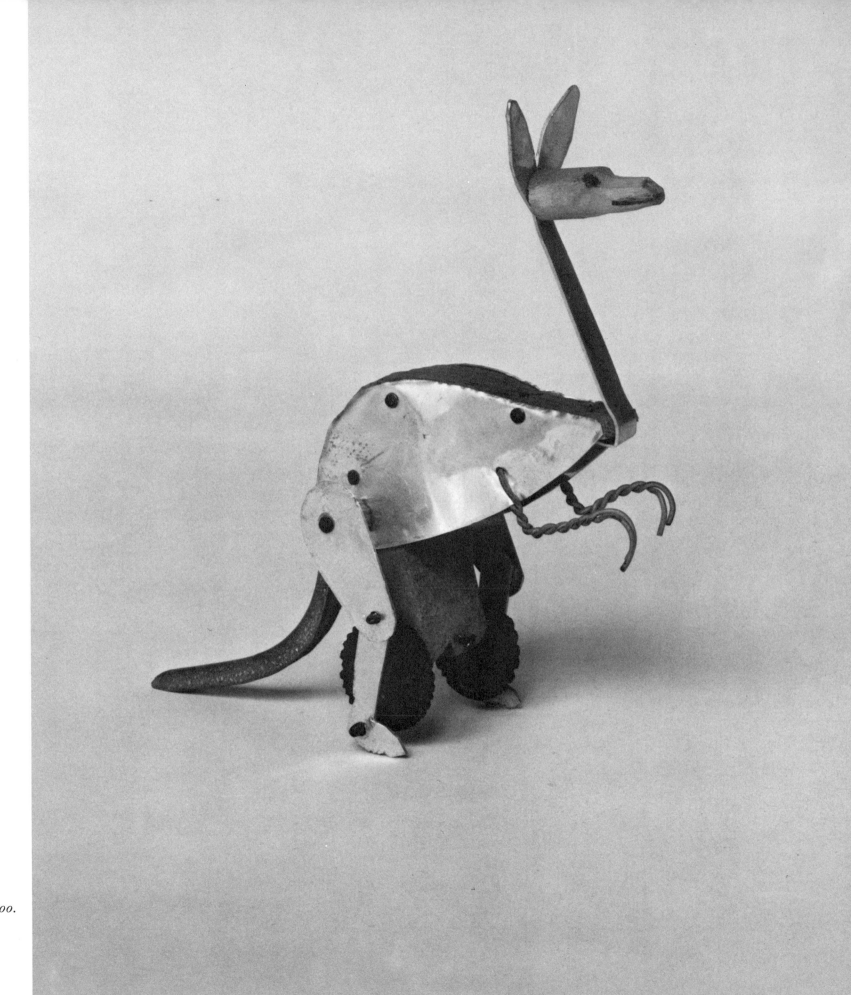

Kangaroo.

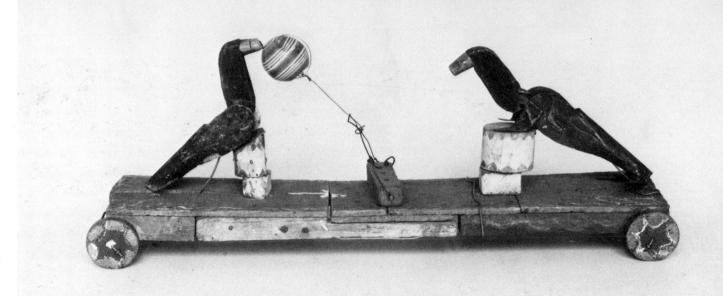

Seals.

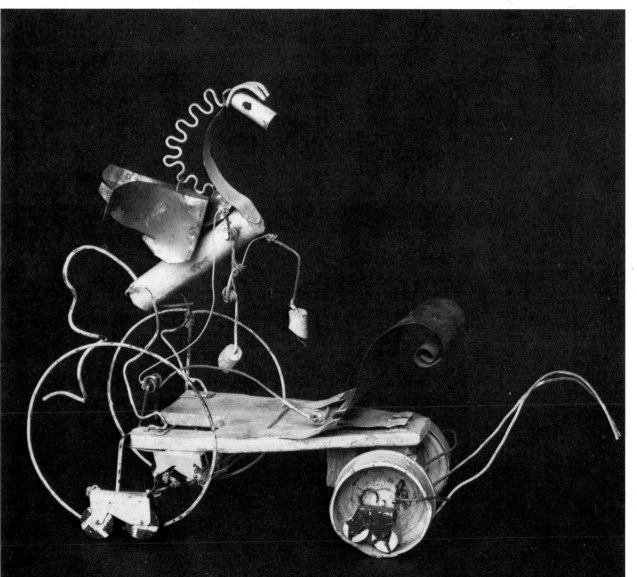

Pegasus.

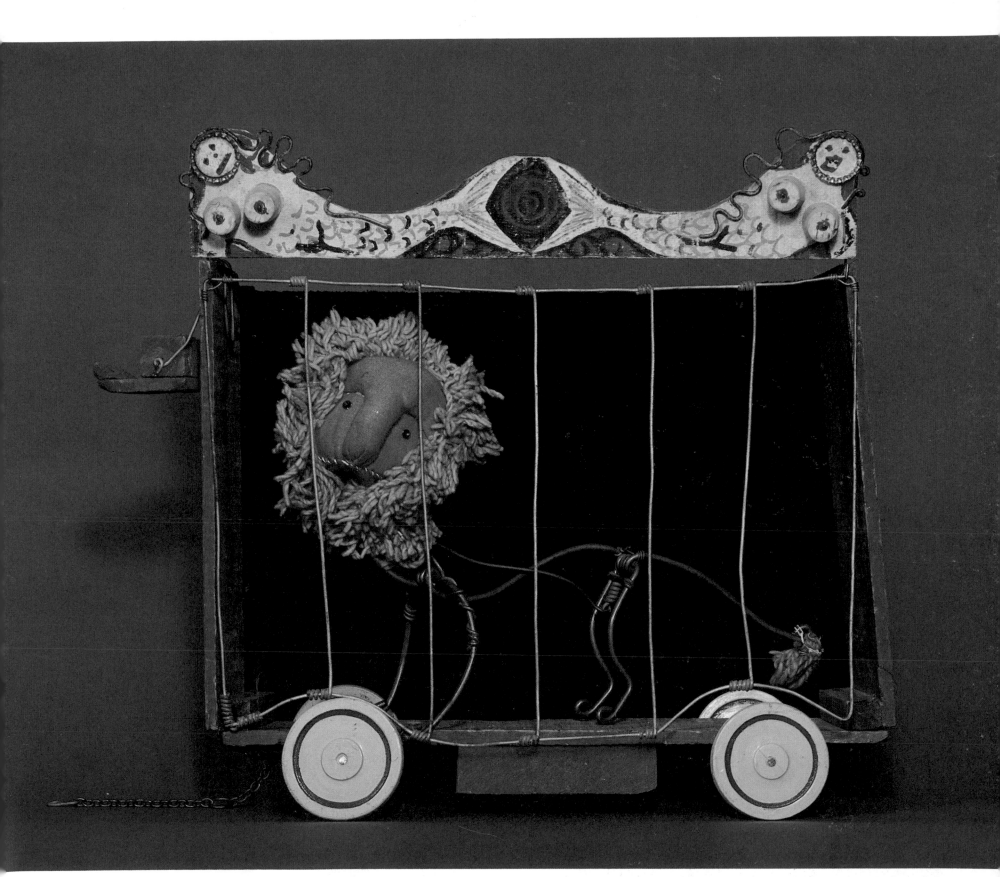

Lion.

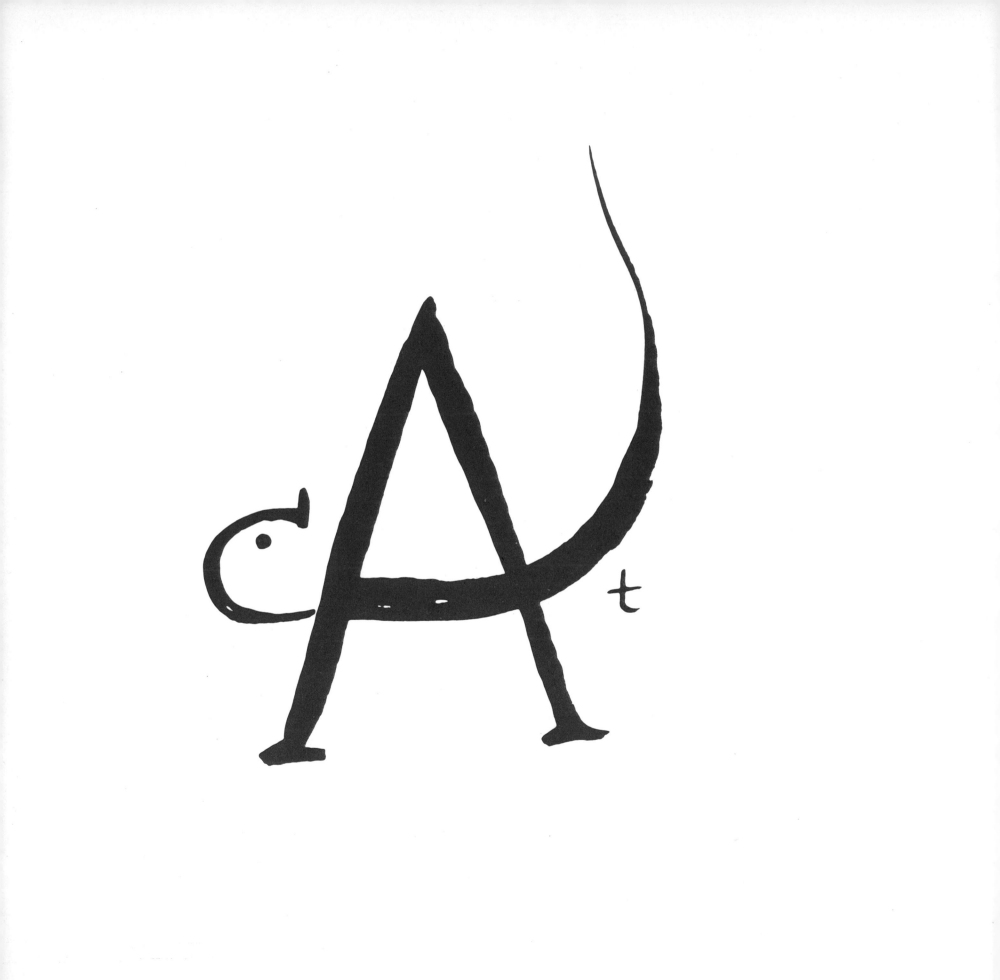

When you have no workshop you can always draw.

After graduating from Stevens Institute of Technology in 1919, Calder worked at various kinds of engineering jobs. In 1921, while doing drafting work in an engineer's office, he became interested in drawing and shortly after that began to draw regularly at a public night school on East 42nd Street in New York. It was an elementary charcoal-drawing class, but he rarely missed a night. Later, after he entered the Art Students League, drawing became a passion. Calder tells in his autobiography how he and a group of students had friendly competitions: "There were short pauses in the class. We would draw very rapidly and the first who finished would show off his drawing." He discovered a certain wrapping paper that was good for drawing: "You folded a sheet into eight rectangles and it would fit in your pocket. With this we used to pass our time drawing people in the subway on our way to and fro."

Calder has produced an enormous number of drawings, many of them made specifically as book illustrations (these are shown in the chapter devoted to his graphic work). Almost all the drawings selected for reproduction here are executed in ink. Calder has also experimented with watercolors and colored crayons, but most of the works in these media lack the originality and virtuosity of the simple ink drawings. Especially noteworthy are three series done in the early years, then packed away and rediscovered recently: the zoo drawings, the circus series and the "space" drawings.

The earliest group was the result of sketching trips to New York's Central Park Zoo and the Bronx Zoo in 1925 and 1926, during Calder's Art Students League days. These, along with a number of oil paintings of the same period, were the first serious art work he had attempted. The drawings—248 in all—were virtually forgotten until 1972 when they were discovered in the artist's studio in Roxbury. When Dolly and Klaus Perls showed them to me, I immediately recognized the sketches as the source of Calder's 1926 book *Animal Sketching*, which I had come across while researching my book on his Circus. At my suggestion, a number of the sketches were published as a gift for the members of the Archives of American Art; they appear here, much as they did in the Archives portfolio. Calder provided a sketch showing exactly how he had made the drawings. In order to make on-the-spot observations, he set up a drawing board of cardboard to which he tacked a piece of paper the size of a typewriter page; he clipped a bottle of India ink to the right of the cardboard and used a brush to draw. In a letter accompanying the Archives portfolio, his son-in-law Jean Davidson described this procedure and offered further information:

Looking over these old drawings, Calder said recently, "I also chased a Dalmatian—they often had one around in the old fire stations—till I caught one in a good urinating attitude." This direct approach was more important to him than any theory of art, and helps us understand why he remains [now in his late seventies] the great Adventurer of shapes to come.

Drawings

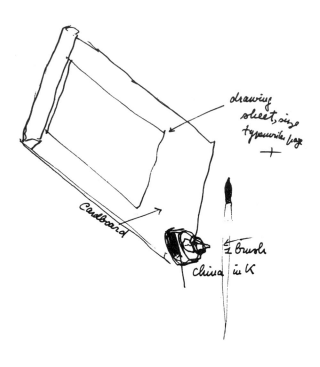

Calder's sketch of materials used for 1925–26 zoo drawings.

In the zoo drawings Calder's bold, original draftsmanship makes its first appearance. "I seemed to have the knack of doing it with a single line," he noted in his autobiography. His rapid, shorthand technique was closely related to caricature, which evidently interested Calder because he included a section on it in *Animal Sketching*. "A caricature," he wrote, "emphasizes the characteristic features, whatever they may be, without regard to the variety of the model." Calder's skill in grasping the essentials of his subject and in rendering them with economy and flair is already apparent in the zoo drawings; this reductive technique would prove useful to him in his later experiments with abstraction.

The zoo drawings are also the earliest evidence of Calder's constant interest in animal subjects. Whether he drew animals, or represented them in wire, wood, bronze or sheet metal, he always directly conveyed the essentials of shape and, most important, movement. "ANIMALS—ACTION. These two words go hand in hand in art . . . there is always a feeling of perpetual motion about animals and to draw them successfully this must be borne in mind." This is another passage from *Animal Sketching*, which was intended as an informal instruction book for beginners like himself. It is full of acute observations: "Remember that 'action' in a drawing is not necessarily comparable to physical action. A cat asleep has intense action." And advice: "When an animal is in rapid motion . . . keep rapidly transmitting your impressions of the animal's movements, and enjoy what you are drawing." (Calder seems to have followed this happy dictum in all his work.)

After he went to Paris in 1926, Calder continued to draw, attending classes at the Académie de la Grande Chaumière. It was at this time that he began to work with wire. His pen-and-ink drawings, which followed the first wire sculptures, are unique. They are actually based on the sculpture: Calder used lines exactly as if they were pieces of thin wire, drawing nothing that could not have been twisted out of wire. Each of these drawings can be looked at as if it were a wire sculpture flattened out on the page. Calder's portrait line drawings are splendid examples of this approach; and the masterpieces in this style are the large circus drawings made in France in 1931 and 1932, just at the time when Calder had completed his Circus troupe and was becoming celebrated for his performances.

The large circus drawings came to light about ten years ago in Roxbury when I asked Sandy to locate a lithograph. He hunted, and discovered instead a dusty parcel. It was labeled "Circus Drawings—1931." After he carefully brushed it off and opened it, my husband and I exclaimed how marvelous the dozens of drawings were and asked Sandy how he liked them now. "I'm astounded!" he said. This was the first time in more than thirty years he had seen them. Subsequently he found other packages of drawings in the Roxbury and Saché workshops and incidentally located some forgotten wood and wire sculptures, too, several of which are illustrated in later chapters.

The casual way in which he tucks away and often misplaces things offers an insight into Sandy's attitude toward his work. Once he has finished something, he is no longer concerned, and often forgets it, because his interest is always in the *next* project. It is the experience of making it, not the object itself, that has the greatest value for him. However, he has total recall about his work when asked; he has given us precise information to identify photographs of pieces made decades ago. Typical examples: When shown an old photograph by Herbert Matter of a cat toy, Sandy said he made it in Paris in 1927 or 1928; it was wood, dovetailed so that the parts could move, about eighteen inches long head to tail; he didn't know where it was now, probably thrown away long ago. Recently I asked him about a remarkable pin set with a large ivory whale, which I had seen a woman wearing about twenty years ago at a benefit gala. I knew it had to be one of Sandy's; he remembered it, said he had made it for a Mrs. Albert Milton who lived on Painter Ridge in Washington, Connecticut. (She is still there, and had her pin photographed for the chapter on jewelry.)

Another package of early drawings was "lost" in the Museum of Modern Art in New York for almost forty years. Calder describes how it happened:

I think it was in December of 1930, when I came over to marry Louisa, that I brought some drawings with me. The Museum of Modern Art was located in the Heckscher Bldg. and there was a very pleasant young man there, Pat Codyre. As I was to be in New York only a short time I confided my drawings to Pat in the hopes that he might sell one or two for me. I never saw Pat again, and when, in Chicago I saw a drawing or two, by me, I thought I was on his traces. But last fall [1966] Alfred Barr unearthed these drawings, and they must be the ones I left with Pat.

The entire contents of this package were exhibited at the Perls Galleries in New York in the fall of 1967; among them were *Louisa*, *Three-ring Circus* and *In Perspective*, shown here.

In Perspective was one of Calder's earliest "space" drawings. Between 1930 and 1932 Calder made a series of pen-and-ink drawings in this style, anticipating the work of our current Minimal artists by three decades. Begun after his visit to Mondrian's studio (described in the next chapter), the "space" drawings reveal the impact of the Dutch painter's austere abstractions on young Calder, whose work, up to that time, had been exclusively representational. These marvelously pure compositions graphically represent Calder's constant interest in the solar system and other heavenly bodies—"The basis of everything for me is the universe," he once said—and they coincide with his earliest abstract wire compositions, some of which he titled *Universe*.

The precision, clarity and elegance of Calder's draftsmanship carries over into his three-dimensional work. Sometimes Calder actually begins a sculpture by drawing its outlines on a sheet of metal. The relationship between the single-line drawings and the wire sculptures has already been noted, and draftsmanship is an important element of the mobiles and stabiles as well. A mobile in motion draws complex patterns in space; and the bold contours of the great stabiles, silhouetted against bright sky or steel and glass façades, may be read as monumental drawings in the modern cityscape.

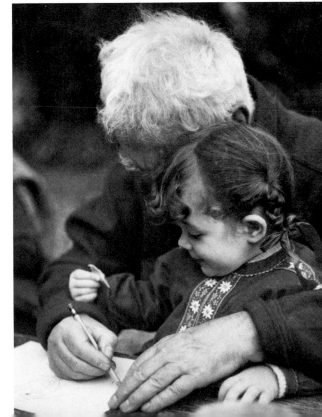

With granddaughter Andrea Davidson, Saché, 1964.

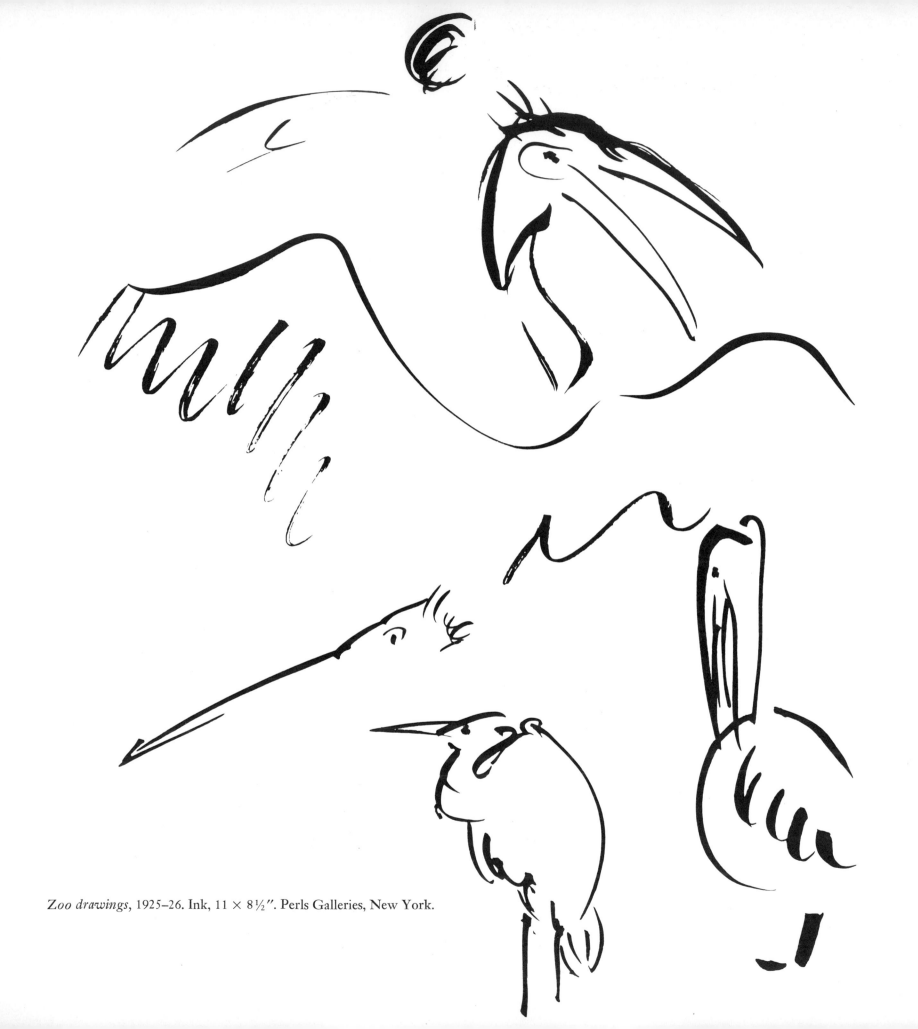

Zoo drawings, 1925–26. Ink, 11 × 8½″. Perls Galleries, New York.

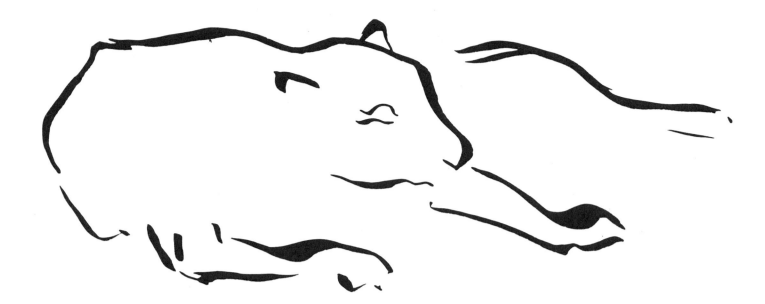
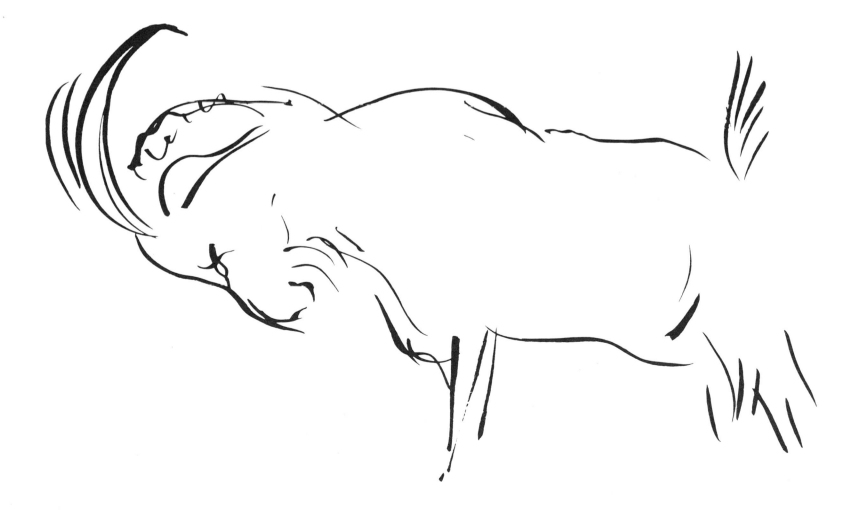

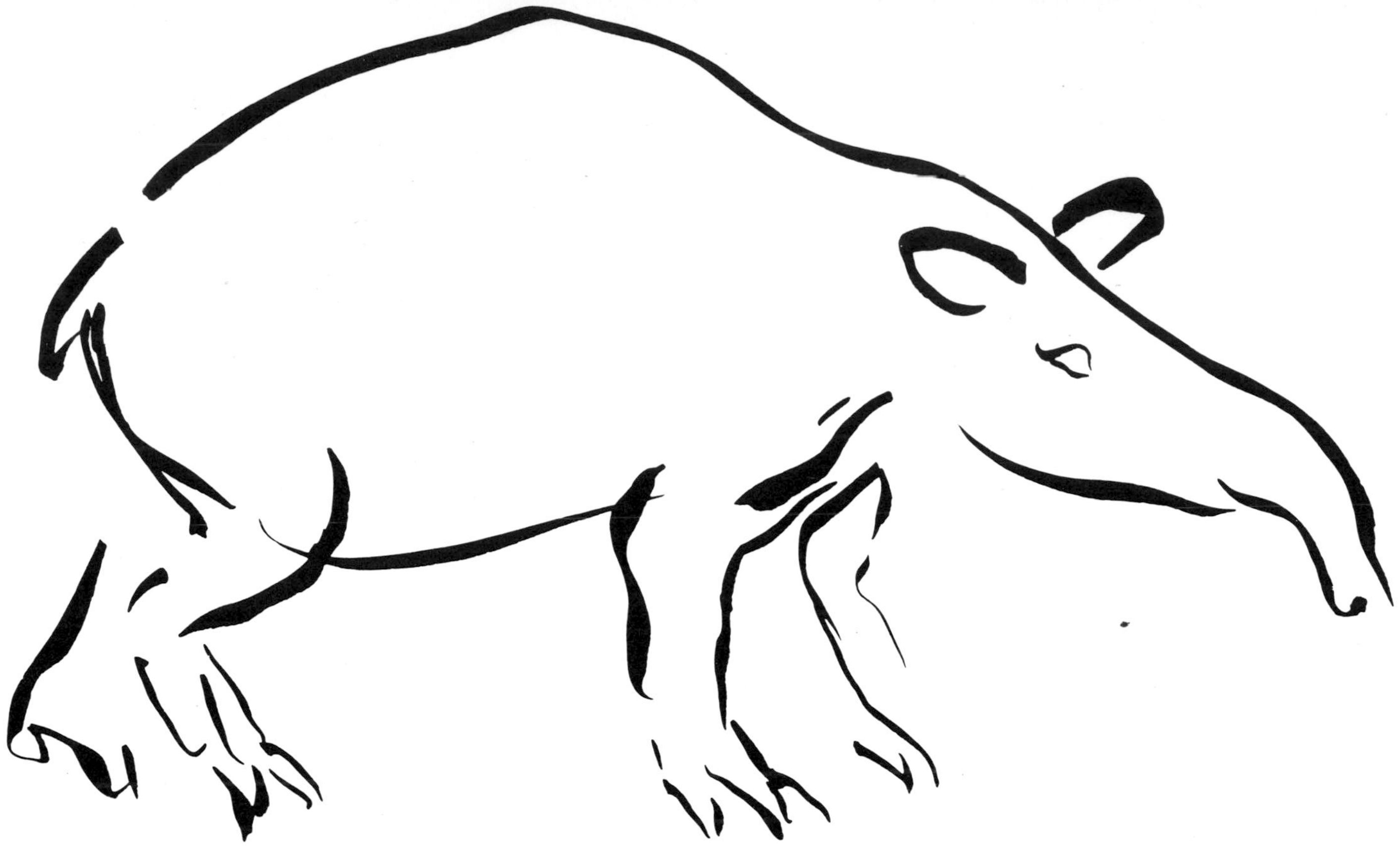

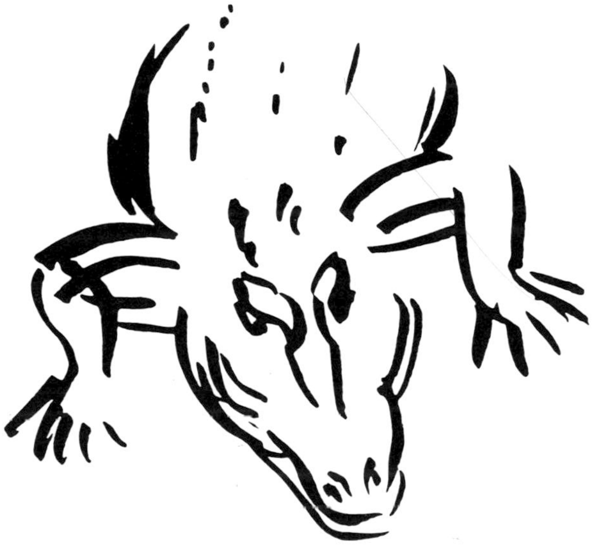

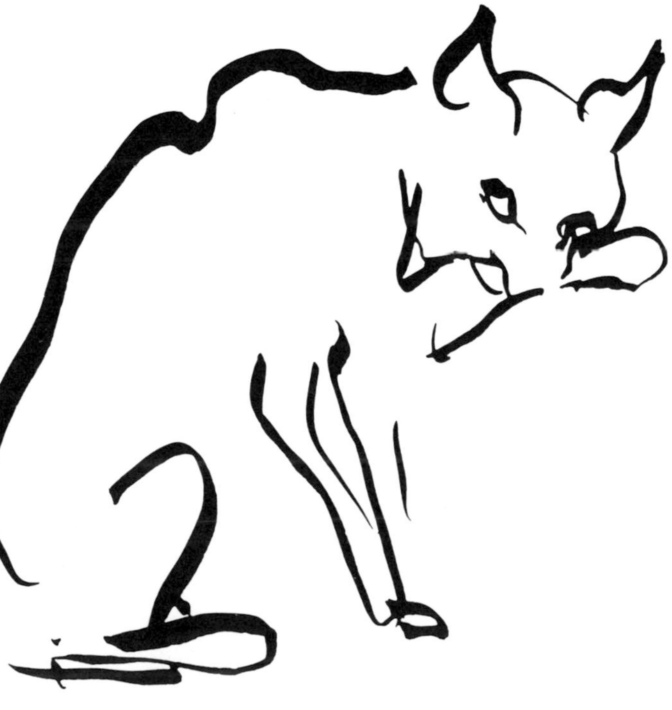

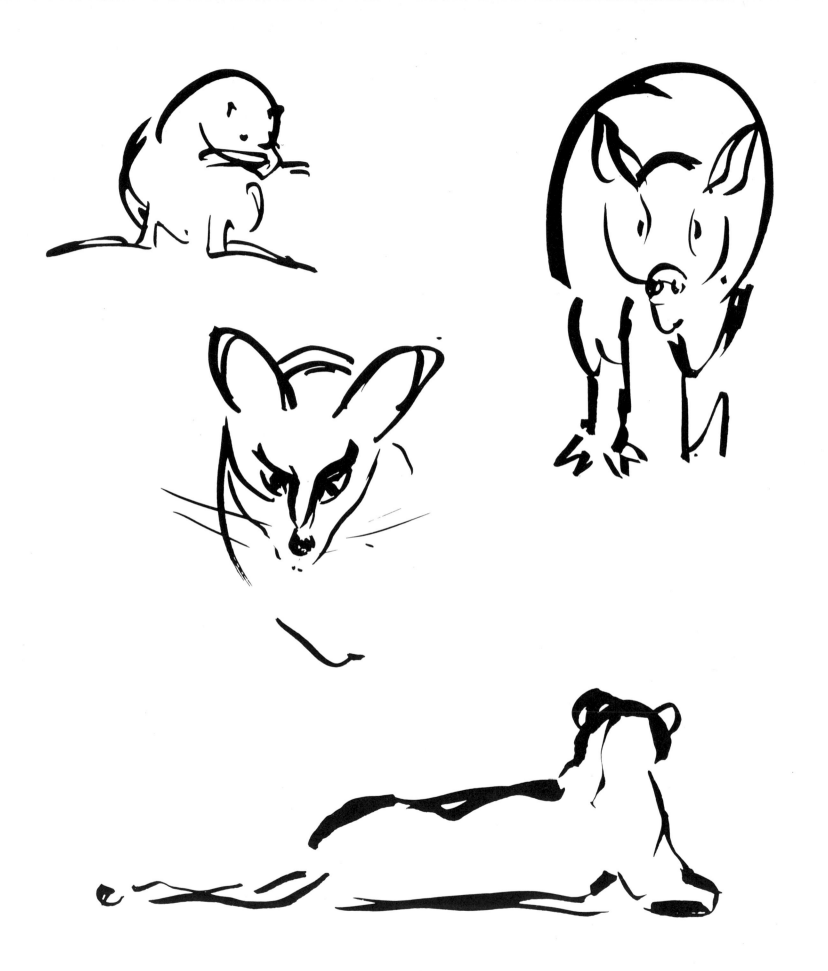

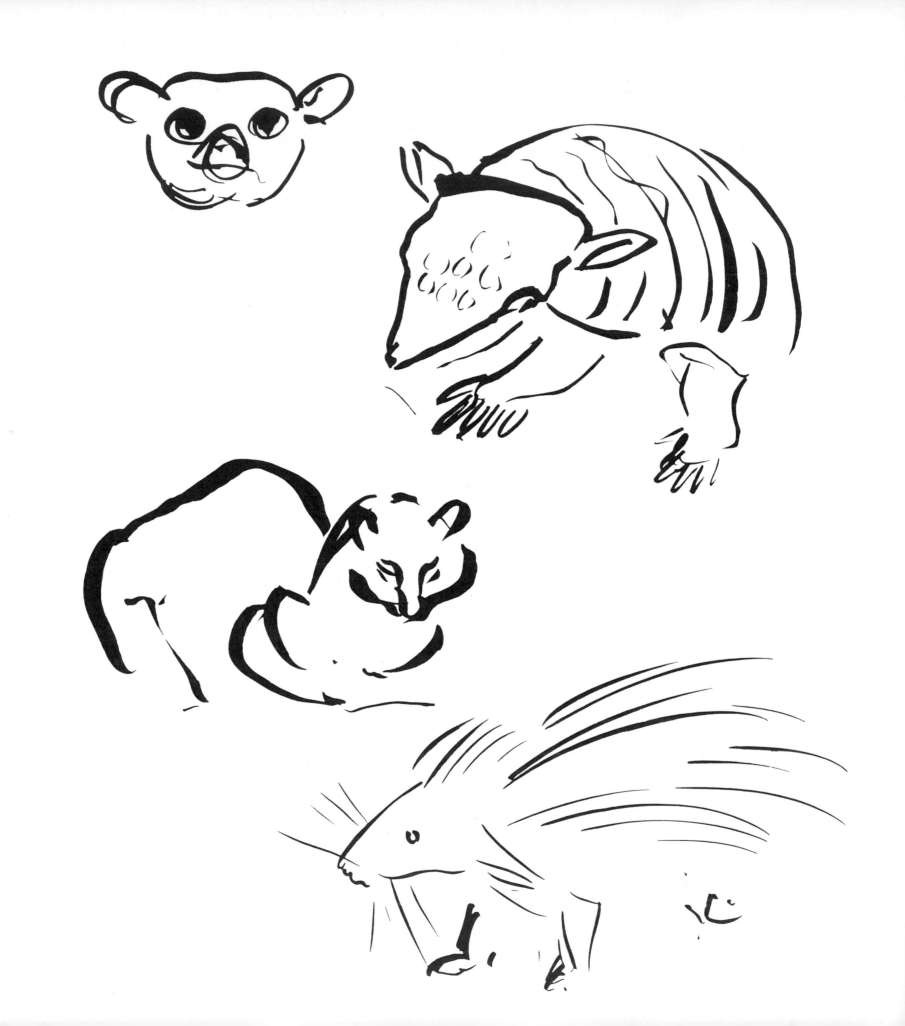

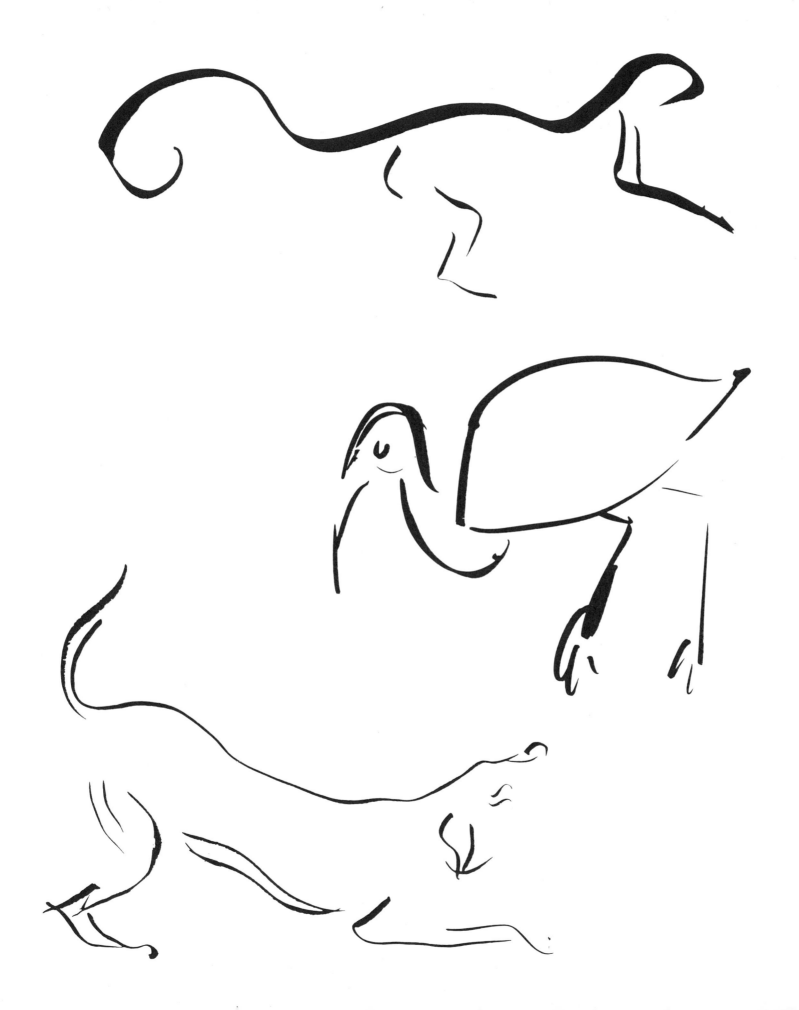

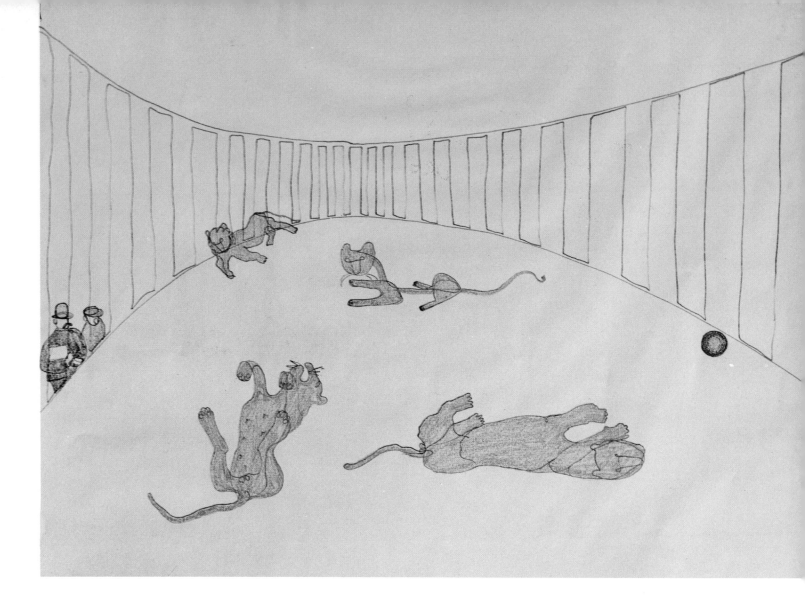

Lion Cage, c. 1931. Ink, crayon, 22¾ × 30¾″. Mr. and Mrs. William B. F. Drew, New York.

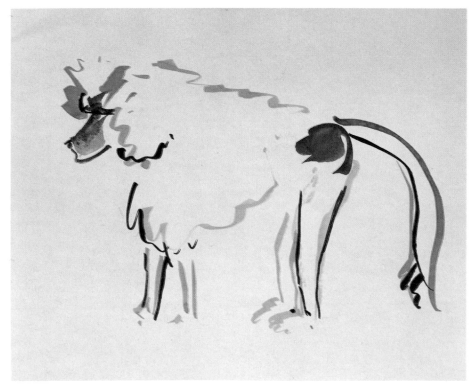

LEFT: *Baboon*, c. 1924. Ink, watercolor, 10⅛ × 15⅛″. Perls Galleries, New York.

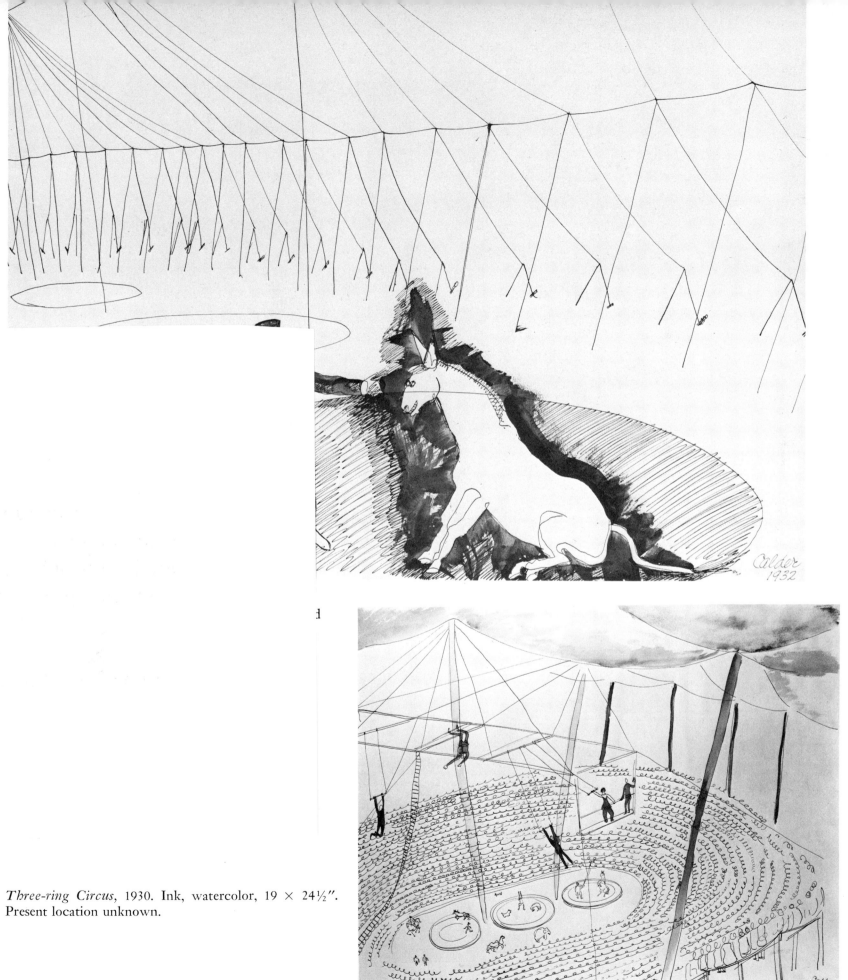

Three-ring Circus, 1930. Ink, watercolor, 19 × 24½″.
Present location unknown.

91

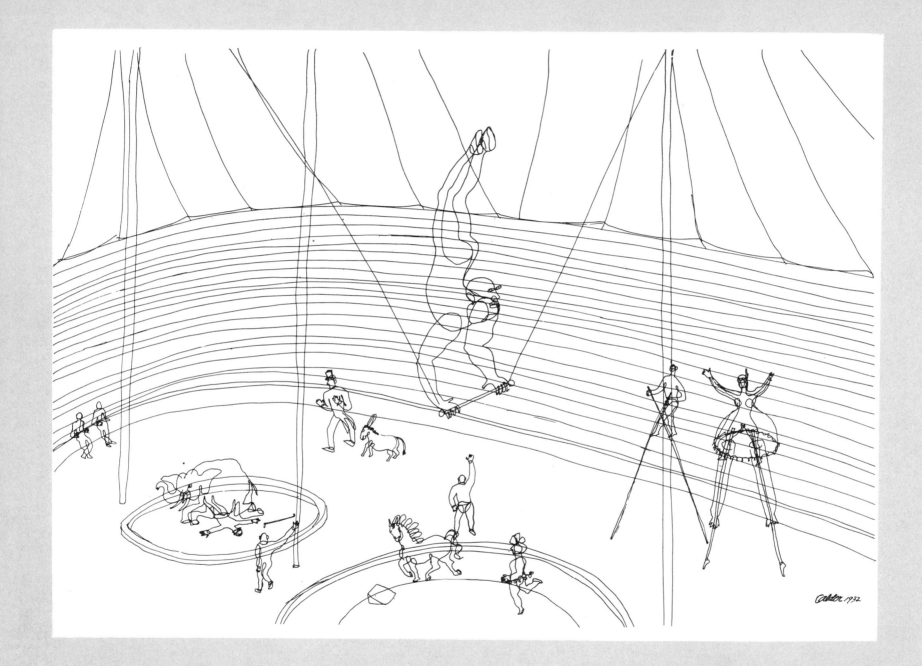

The Circus, 1932. Ink, 20¼ × 29¼″. Mr. and Mrs. Klaus G. Perls, New York.

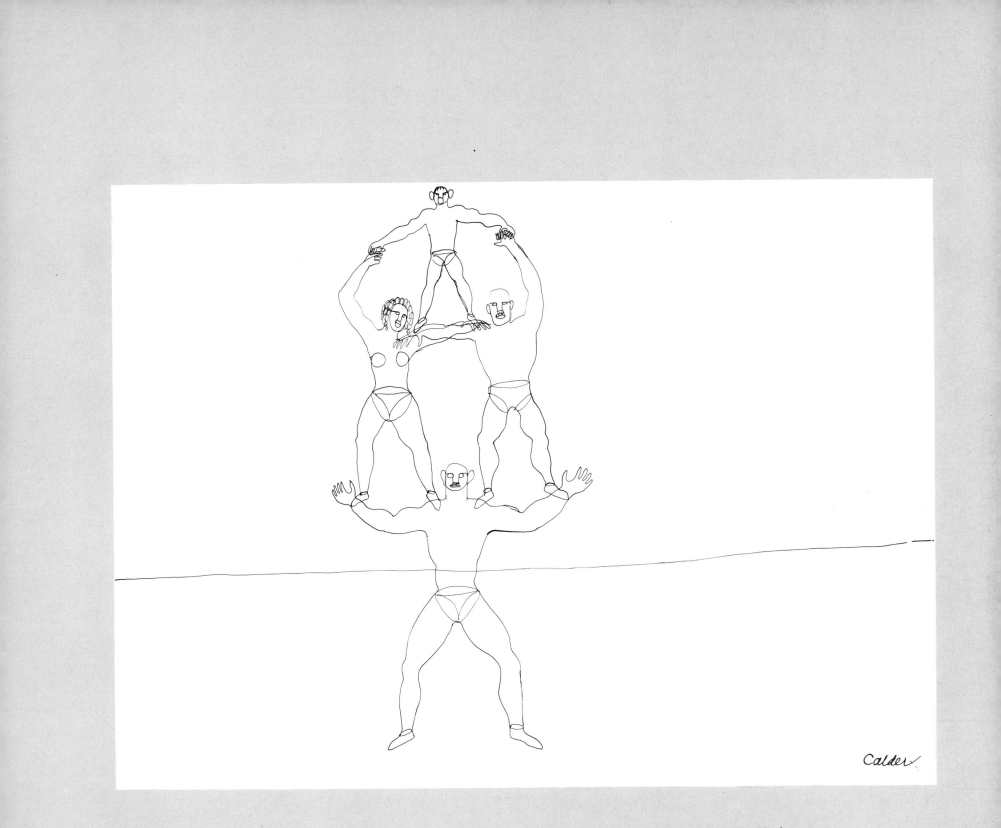

Tumbling Family, 1931. Ink, 22¾ × 30¾″. Mr. and Mrs. Alvin S. Lane, Riverdale, New York.

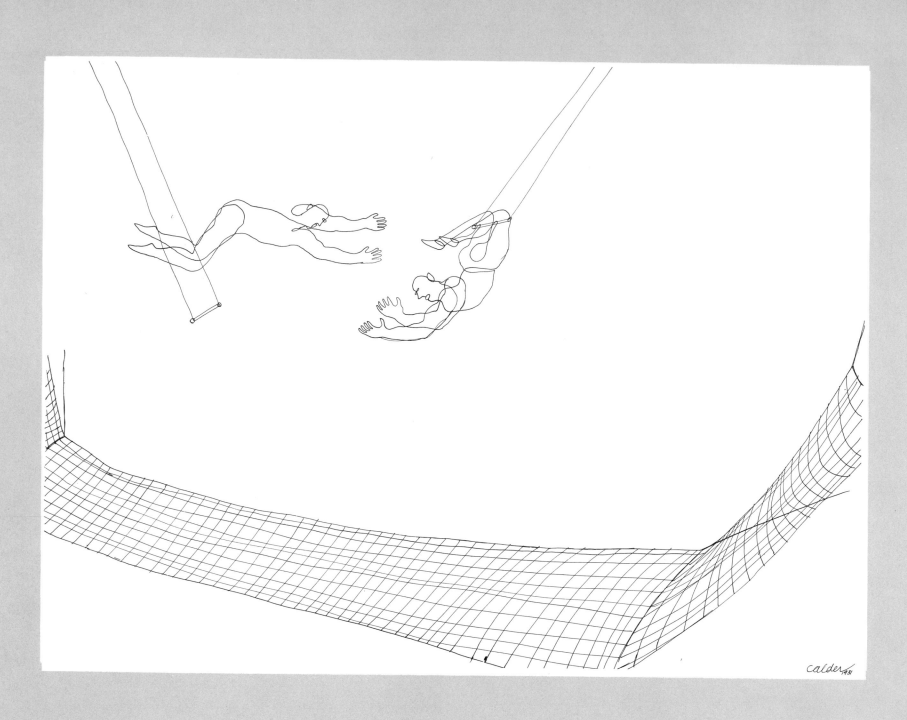

The Catch, 1931. Ink, 22¾ × 30¾″. Dr. and Mrs. Arthur E. Kahn, New York.

On the High Wire, 1932. Ink, 20½ × 24⅞″. Collection of the author.

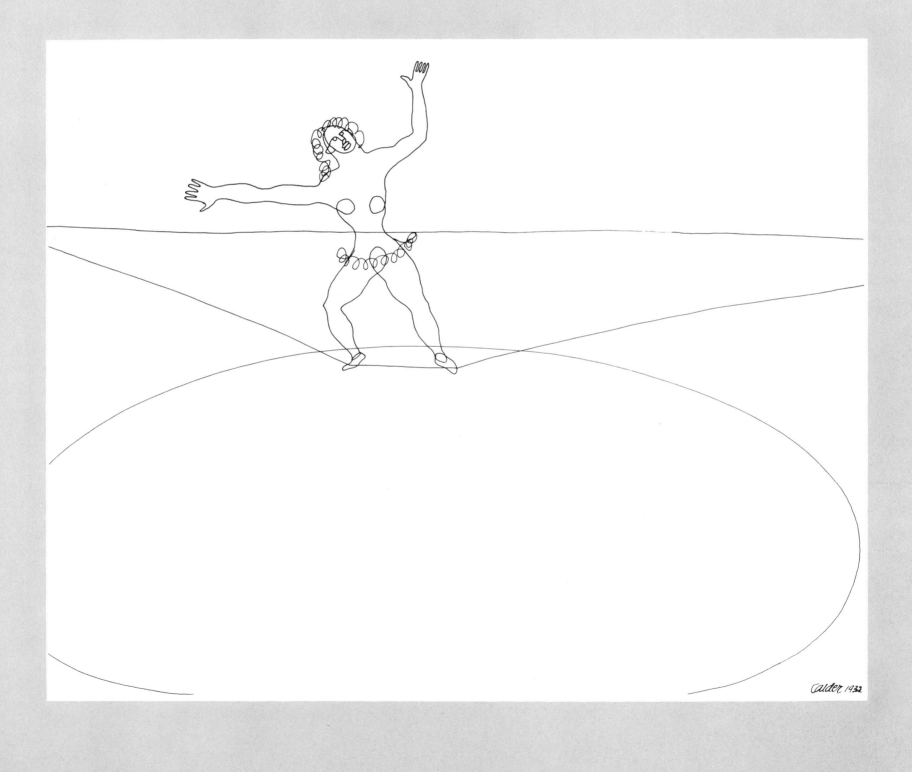

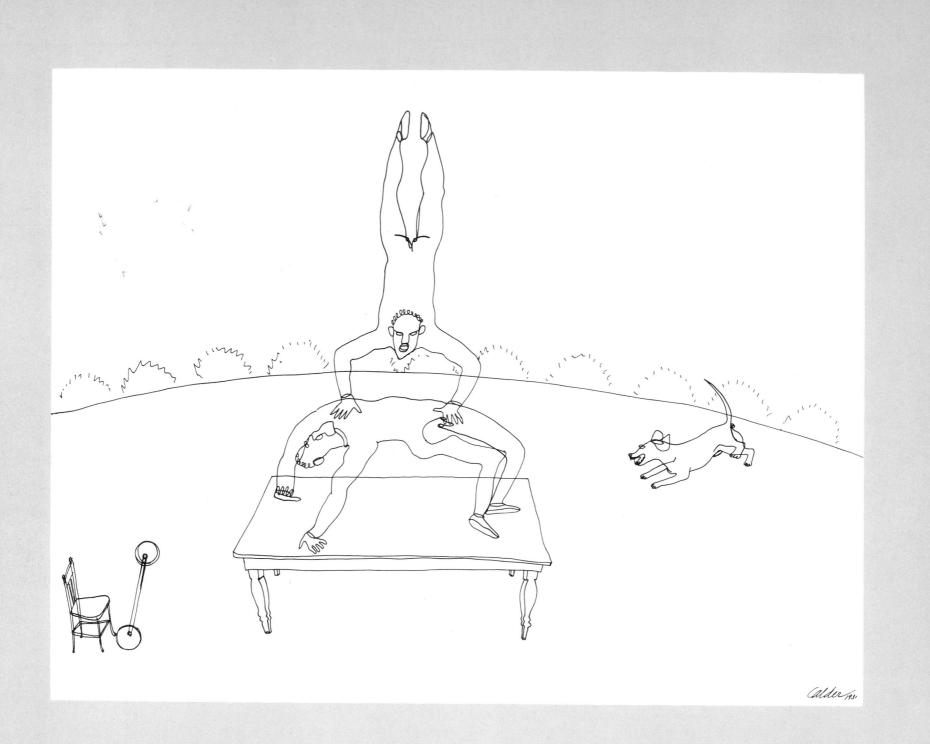

Handstand on the Table, 1931. Ink, 22¾ × 30¾″. Mr. and Mrs. Philip A. Straus, New York.

Juggler with Ball, 1931. Ink, 22¾ × 30¾". Collection of the author.

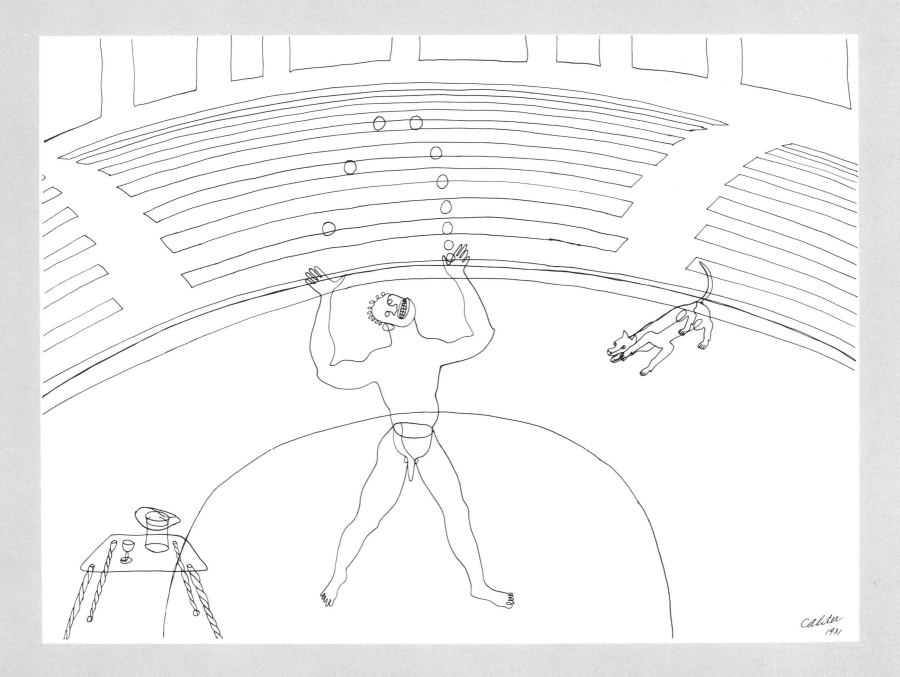

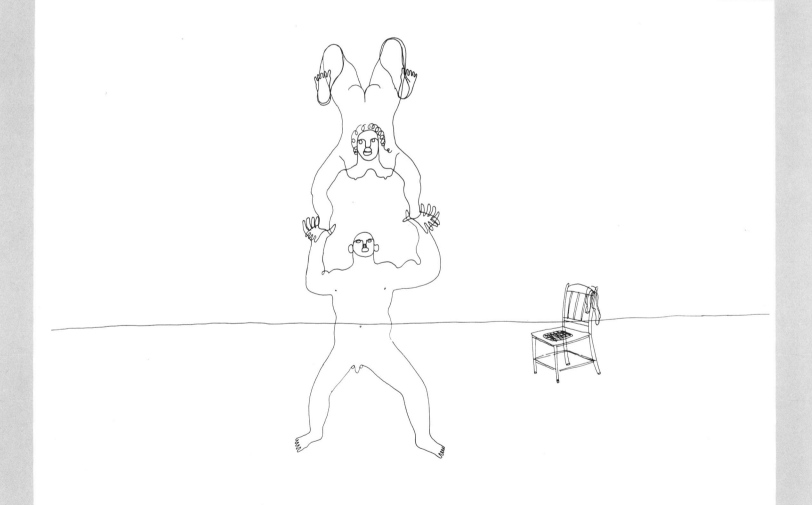

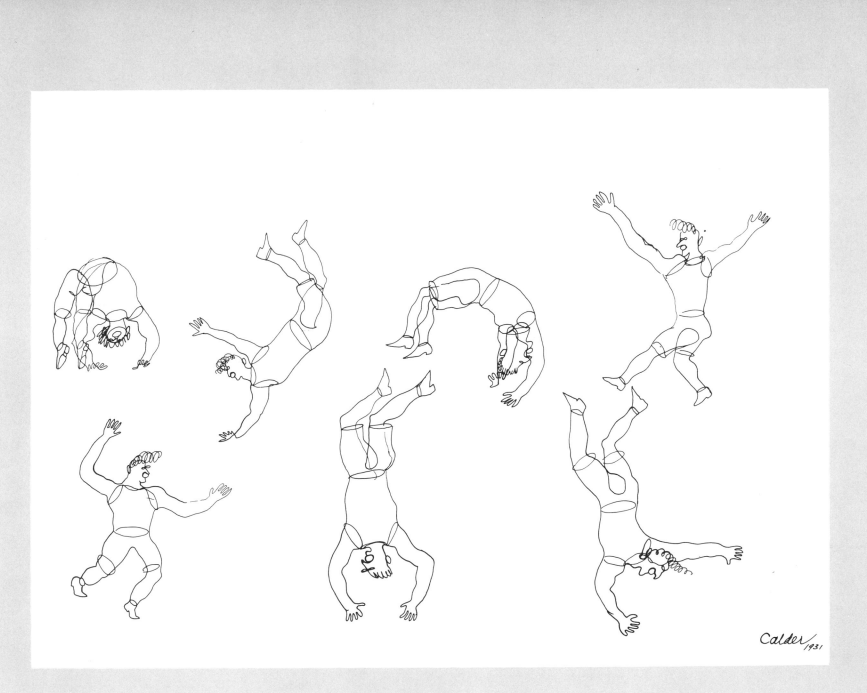

Somersaulters, 1931. Ink, 22¾ × 30¾″. Mr. and Mrs. Alvin S. Lane, Riverdale, New York.

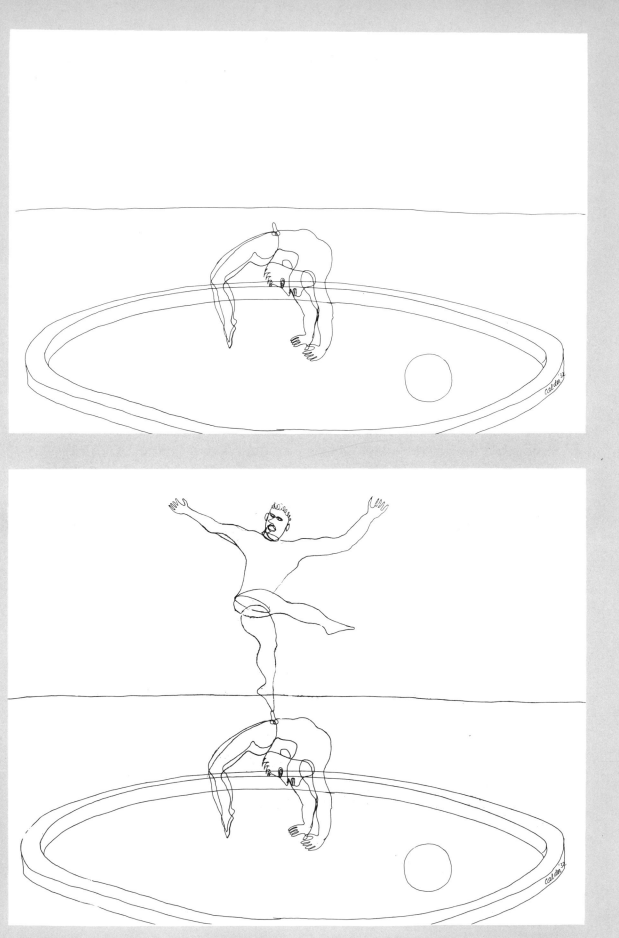

Two Acrobats, 1932. ABOVE: Front of drawing. BELOW: Backlit to reveal figure drawn on reverse. Ink, 21½ × 29½″. Collection of the author.

100

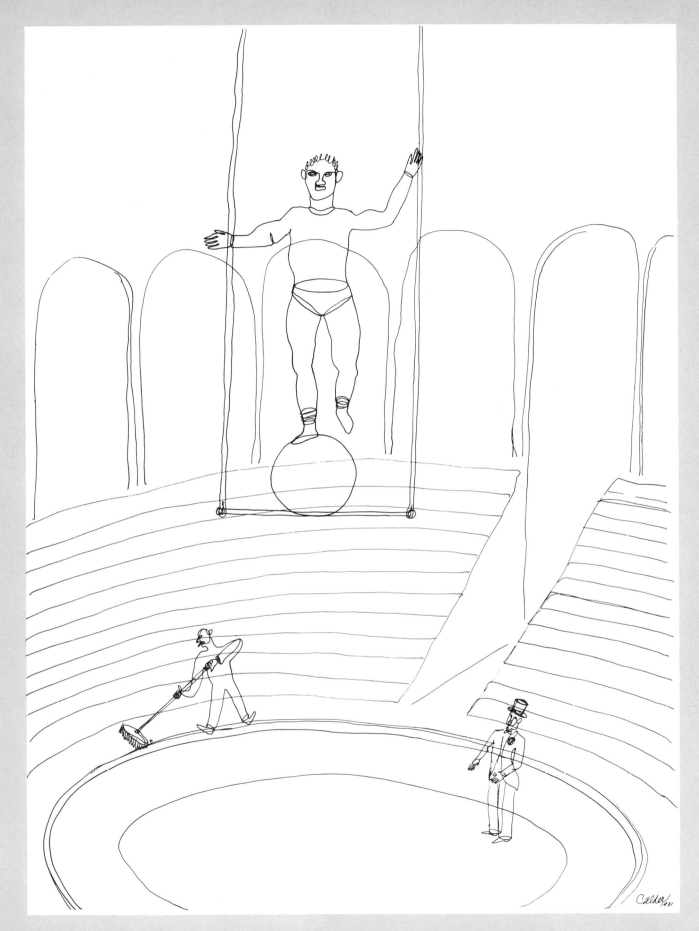

101

Tumbler on Swing, 1931. Ink, 30¾ × 22¾″. Collection of the author.

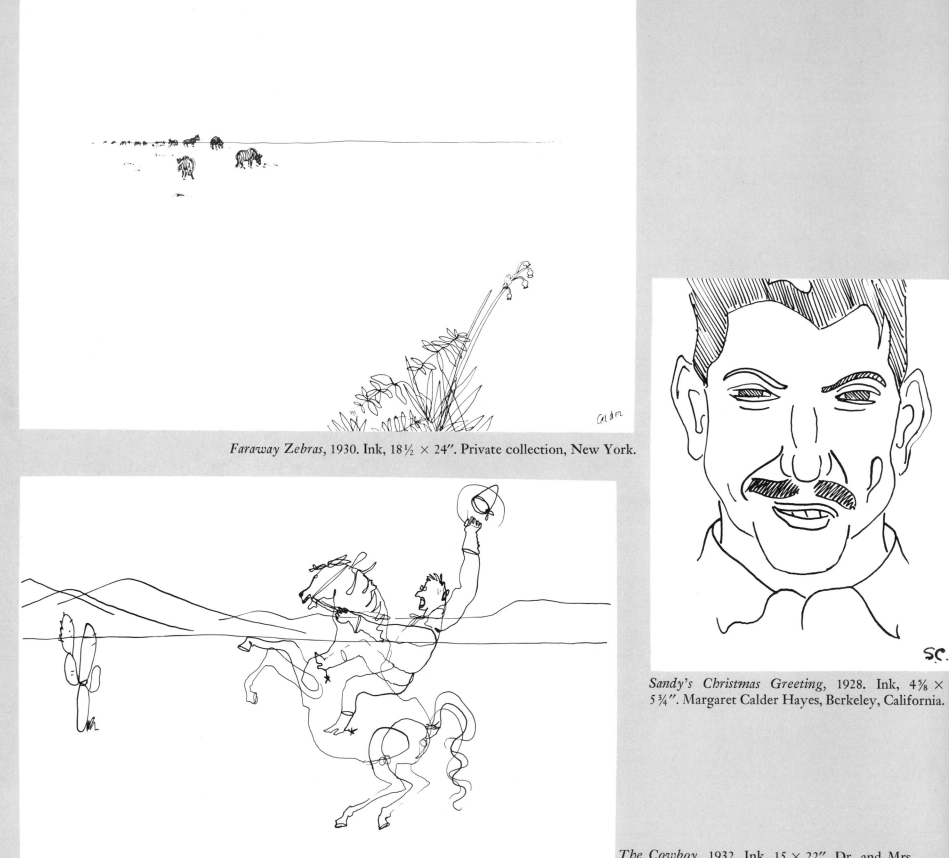

Faraway Zebras, 1930. Ink, 18½ × 24″. Private collection, New York.

Sandy's Christmas Greeting, 1928. Ink, 4⅞ × 5¾″. Margaret Calder Hayes, Berkeley, California.

102

The Cowboy, 1932. Ink, 15 × 22″. Dr. and Mrs. Irving F. Burton, Huntington Woods, Michigan.

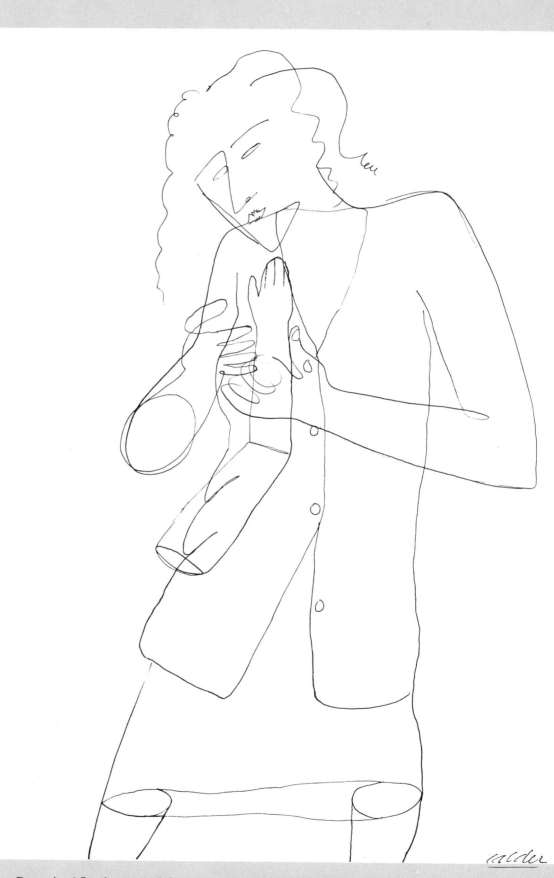

Portrait of Louisa, 1931. Ink, 24½ × 19″. Private collection, New York.

103

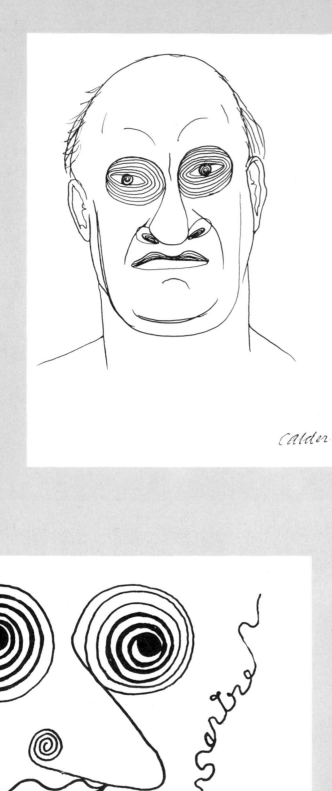

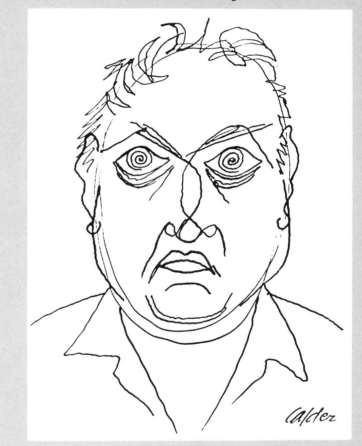

Curt Valentin, 1944. Ink, 11¼ × 10⅜″. Mr. and Mrs. Klaus G. Perls, New York.

Self-portrait, c. 1940. Ink, 14½ × 11⁷⁄₁₆″. Mr. and Mrs. R. Wallace Bowman, Los Angeles.

Sartre with Cigarette, 1947. Ink, 6 × 4½″. Formerly collection of Charles Alan, New York.

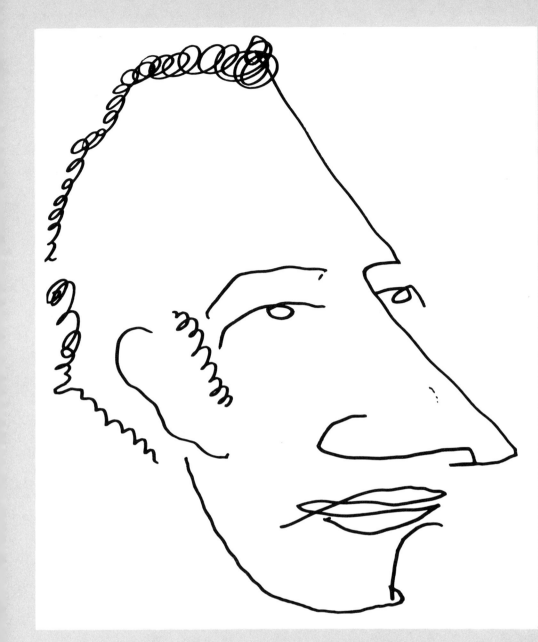

Klaus Perls, 1969. Ink, 11 × 8½″. Mr. and Mrs. Klaus G. Perls, New York.

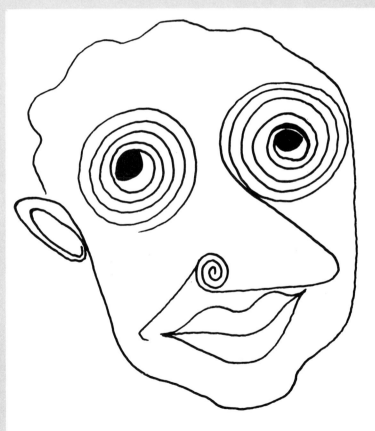

Sartre, 1944. Ink, 7 × 5½″. Mr. and Mrs. Klaus G. Perls, New York.

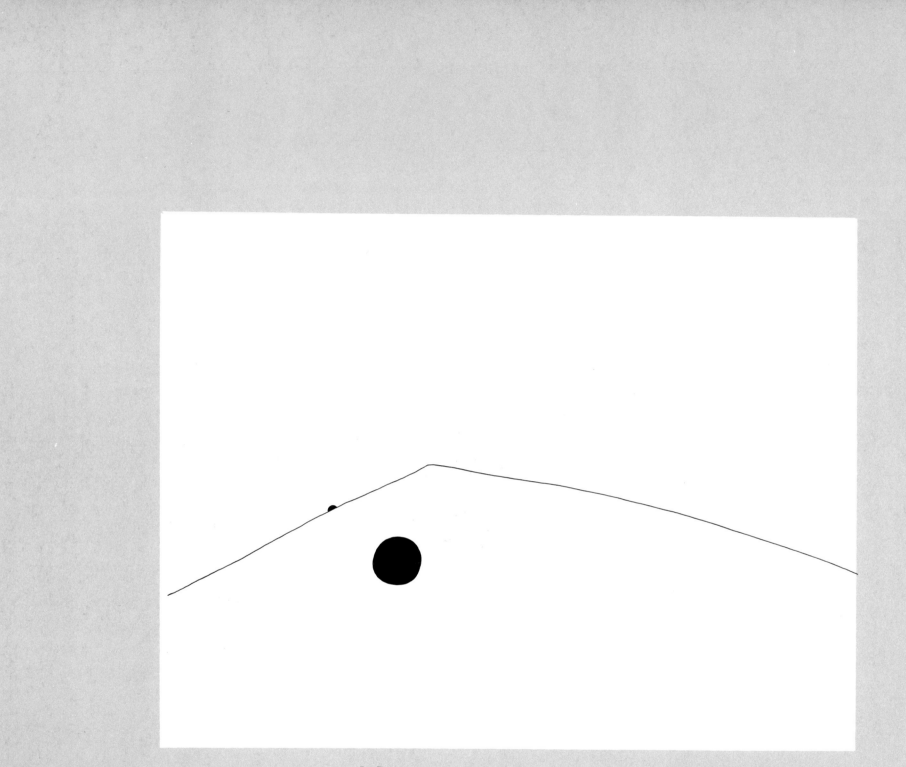

In Perspective, c. 1930. Ink, 19 × 24¾″. Jean and Sandra Davidson, Saché, France.

OPPOSITE: *Two in the Center*, 1931. Ink, 30¾ × 22¾″. Thomas P. Whitney, Washington, Connecticut.

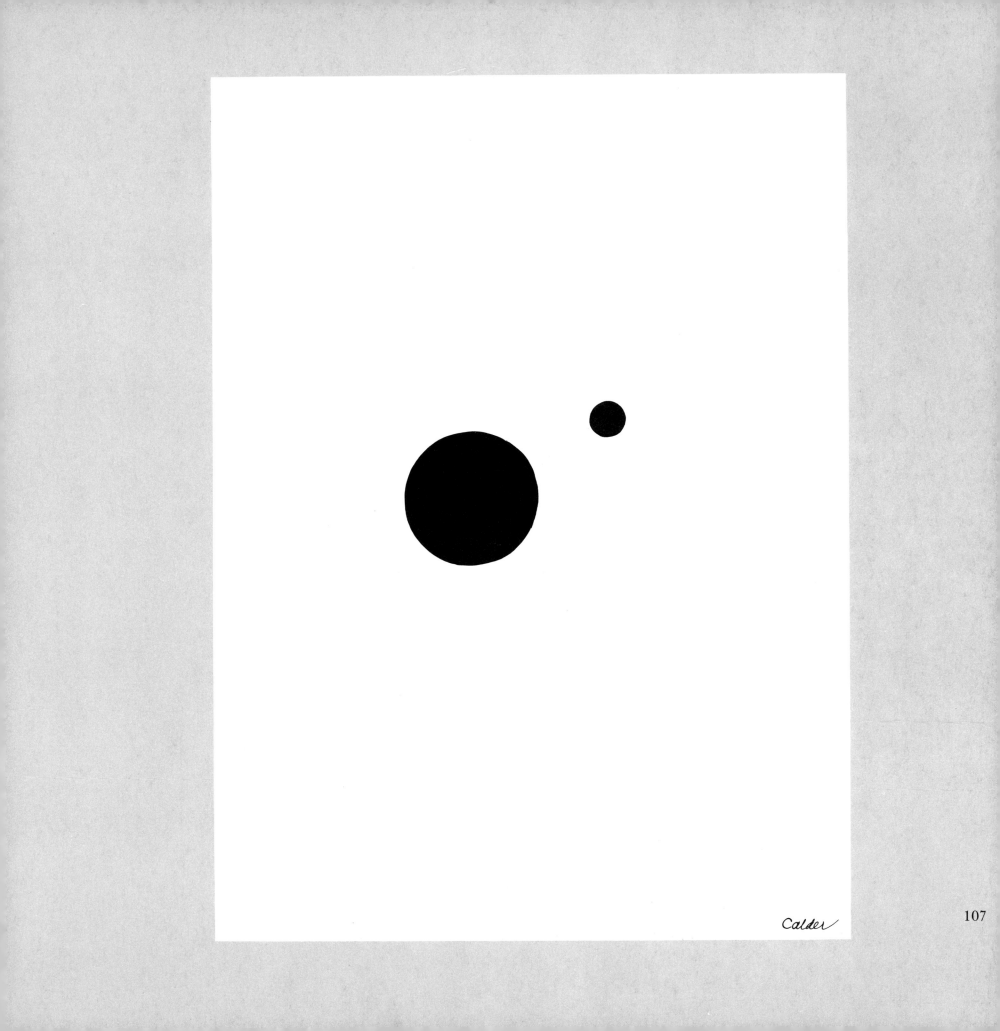

Calder

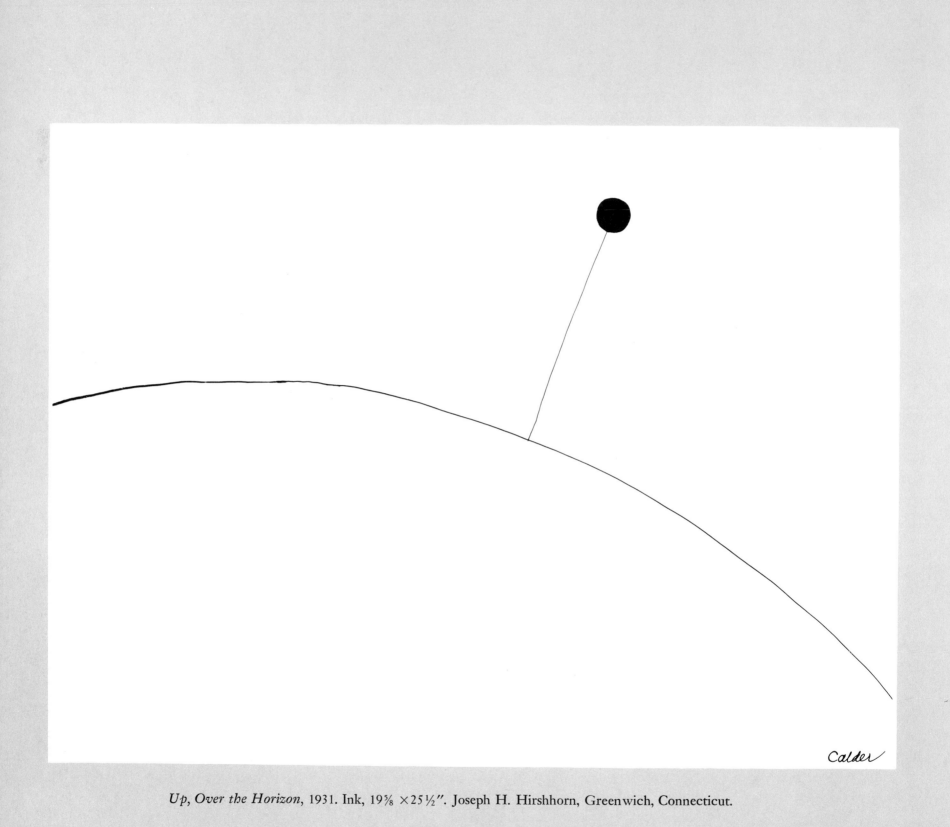

Up, Over the Horizon, 1931. Ink, 19⅝ ×25½″. Joseph H. Hirshhorn, Greenwich, Connecticut.

Many, 1931. Ink, 19⅝ × 25½″. The Museum of Modern Art, New York; gift of Mr. and Mrs. Klaus G. Perls.

109

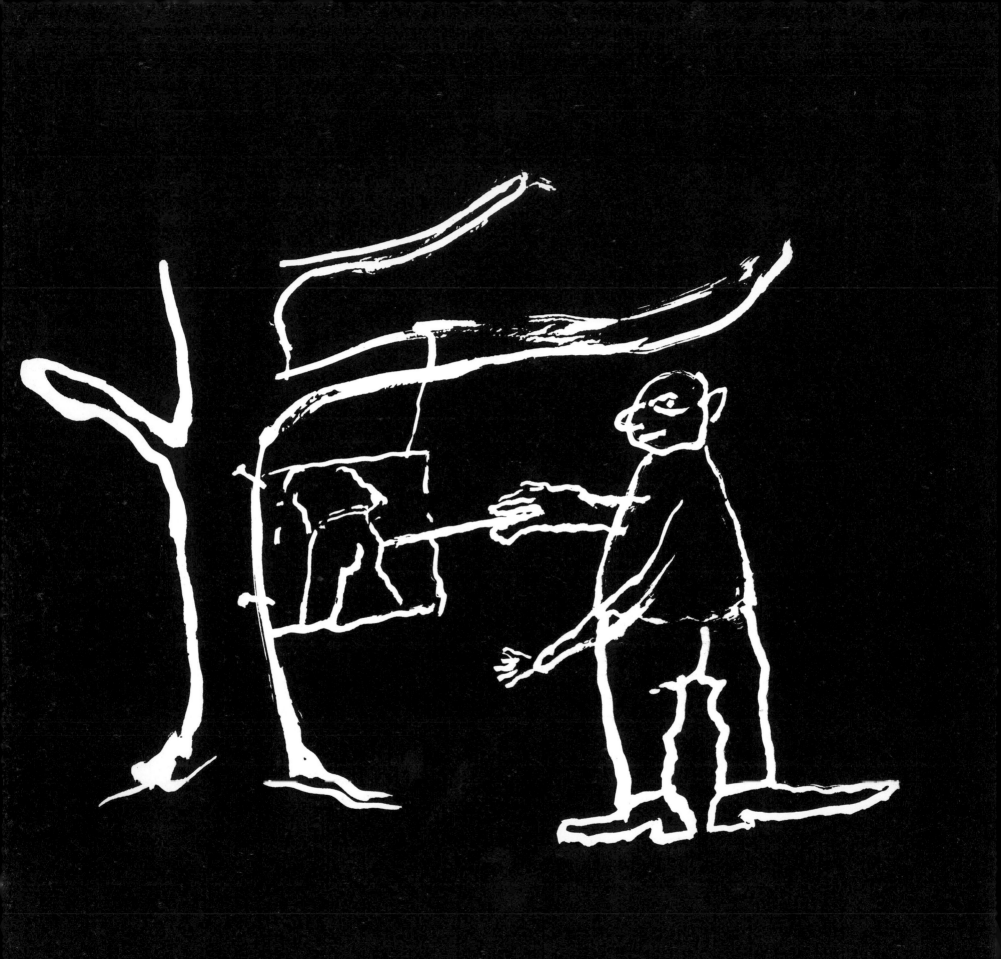

When I met Mondrian I went home and tried to paint.

Calder entered the Art Students League in New York in 1923, at the age of twenty-five. He studied under George Luks, Kenneth Hayes Miller, Guy Pène du Bois and Boardman Robinson, "drew a bit" in Thomas Hart Benton's class, and went evenings to John Sloan's classes. Calder's critical comments on his teachers' methods, culled from his autobiography, reveal that what he most appreciated was technical guidance, with freedom to work out his own approach.

Sloan was a good instructor, not trying to make you do it his way but urging you to develop capabilities of your own.

Miller's technique was to have his students draw a life-class figure which could be a nude sitting on a stool; then the student, to show his imagination, was supposed to invent the drapes, the shelves, little windows, fruits and flowers, and an assortment of shadows, as background.

Oil Paintings

In his class, Luks would take a large varnish brush and dip it in the probably brown or gray residue of yesterday to smear a whole new canvas with the mixture. Then with another brush he would put a pink egg for a head, blue eye-dots, red lips, climaxing with the fine art of putting in the shadows and highlights—everybody else trying to do the same thing.

Boardman Robinson . . . was an excellent teacher. I guess it was he who taught me to draw with a pen in a single line.

Benton's motto was, "Even if it's wrong you make it definite"—it might have been his *malheur;* his paintings reminded one of plasteline figures.

I took a liking to the painting of Guy Pène du Bois. I felt his girls looked like woodcarvings, even somewhat like toys. He had a stunt of painting everything black with blue on one side and orange or red on the other. I was interested in what I thought was a certain solidity in the result, though others feel they look like candy-box designs.

All Calder's teachers painted in oil. Calder's early efforts in this medium were creditable, but it was not until he began painting in gouache that he found a technique perfectly suited to his high-spirited, rapid, spontaneous expression. He has produced scores of bold, splendid gouaches, whereas his work in oil diminished after the 1940s. It is relatively difficult to find Calder oils that one can admire. However, we should record his first critical notice, by Murdock Pemberton in *The New Yorker*, following his first exhibition of oils held at The Artists' Gallery in New York: "A. Calder is also a good bet."

Between the Art Students League and the Saché *gouacherie* came the Paris years. Calder began modestly, as a student at La Grande Chaumière, and eventually found him-

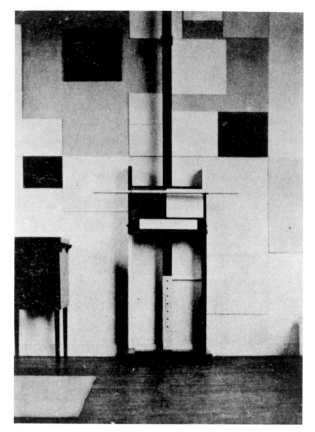

Mondrian's studio, rue du Départ, Paris.

self in the company of many of the most advanced French artists of the time. One who influenced the style of his paintings—and later, though less directly, his gouaches—was the artist who was to become a close friend, Miró; an interest in cosmic imagery—sun, moon and stars—is apparent in the works of both artists. When Calder first visited Miró's studio in 1928, he saw collages that startled him:

One of them was a big sheet of heavy gray cardboard with a feather, a cork and a picture postcard glued to it. There were probably a few dotted lines, but I have forgotten. I was nonplussed; it did not look like art to me.

Two years later, in 1930, Calder paid a visit to another artist's studio:

Mondrian lived at 26 rue du Départ. (That building has been demolished since, to make more room for the Gare Montparnasse.) It was a very exciting room. Light came in from the left and from the right, and on the solid wall between the windows there were experimental stunts with colored rectangles of cardboard tacked on. Even the victrola, which had been some muddy color, was painted red.
I suggested to Mondrian that perhaps it would be fun to make these rectangles oscillate. And he, with a very serious countenance, said:
"No, it is not necessary, my painting is already very fast."
This visit gave me a shock. A bigger shock, even, than eight years earlier, when off Guatemala I saw the beginning of a fiery red sunrise on one side and the moon looking like a silver coin on the other.
This one visit gave me a shock that started things.
Though I had heard the word "modern" before, I did not consciously know or feel the term "abstract." So now, at thirty-two, I wanted to paint and work in the abstract. And for two weeks or so, I painted very modest abstractions. At the end of this, I reverted to plastic work which was still abstract.

Some of the "modest abstractions" of 1930 are reproduced here; it is interesting to find that *The Pistil* (see "Wire Sculpture"), which Calder made the following year, has a black-and-white painted base almost identical to his Mondrian-like oils. Calder went on to apply the lessons learned in those few weeks of painting to his later sculpture, adopting Mondrian's limited but brilliant palette—the primary colors plus black and white. These were also the favorite colors of Calder's friends Miró and Léger, and they are, incidentally, the most popular colors in France, where workmen's blue coveralls and bright children's clothing still make a lively blue-red-yellow pattern on city streets. Today the rich blue, vermilion and yellow of Calder's work have become so closely identified with him that they are sometimes spoken of as "Calder colors."
Although he soon lost interest in painting on canvas, Calder began to apply flat paint to his new abstract sculpture. Painted sculpture is a commonplace today, but in the early thirties it was certainly a departure from the gleaming marble and bronze that had been the accepted media of virtually all sculpture since the Renaissance. Sweeney

recently pointed out that color is only one of the characteristics that link Calder's early efforts in painting with his sculpture. Other characteristics—less obvious but nonetheless directly related to his painting and drawing—are the emphasis on line and the two-dimensionality of most of the individual elements of the mobiles and the stabiles.

In numerous statements Calder has acknowledged his debt to Mondrian. By his own testimony it is clear that the visit to Mondrian's studio was the point of departure for his mobiles and was crucial in determining the general direction of his future work, which in turn has determined the course of much of twentieth-century sculpture.

Circus, 1926. Oil on burlap, 69 × 83″. Margaret Calder Hayes, Berkeley, California.

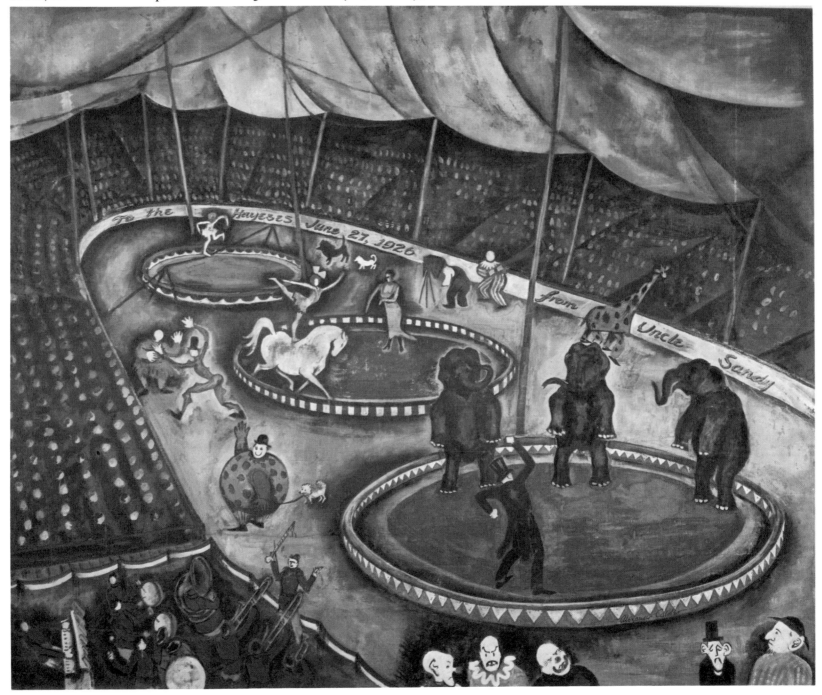

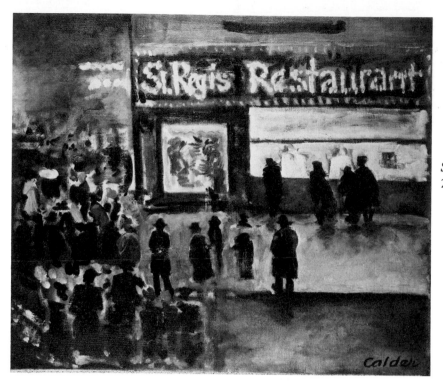

St. Regis Restaurant, 1925. Oil on canvas,
25¼ × 30″. Perls Galleries, New York.

Untitled, 1930. Oil on canvas, 32 ×
25½″. Jean and Sandra Davidson,
Saché, France.

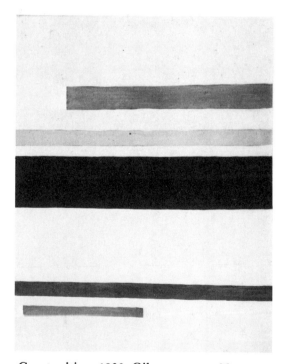

Composition, 1930. Oil on canvas, 22 ×
19″. Collection of the artist.

114

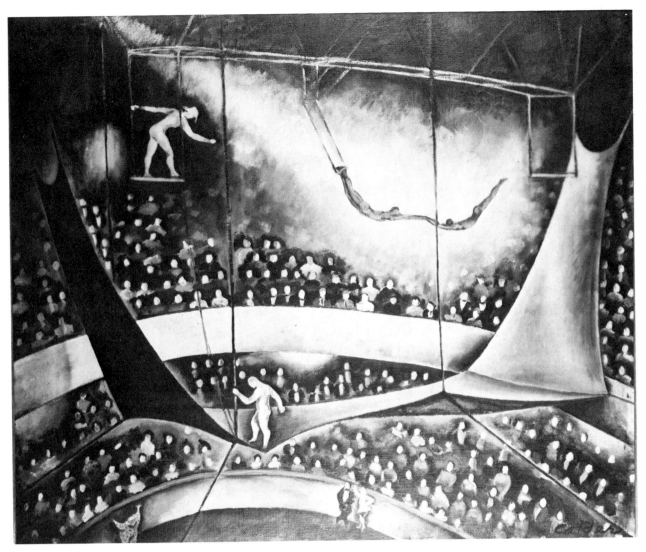

The Flying Trapeze, c. 1925. Oil on canvas, 36 × 42″. Perls Galleries, New York.

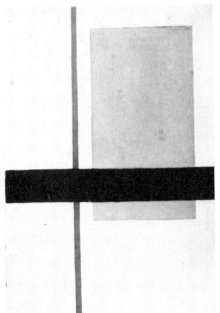

Composition, 1930. Oil on canvas, approx. 19 × 18″. Present location unknown.

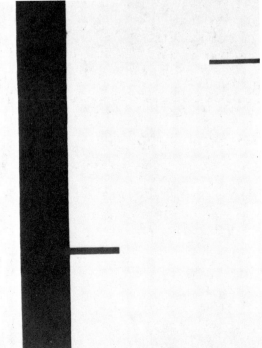

Composition, 1930. Oil on canvas, approx. 19 × 17″. Present location unknown.

115

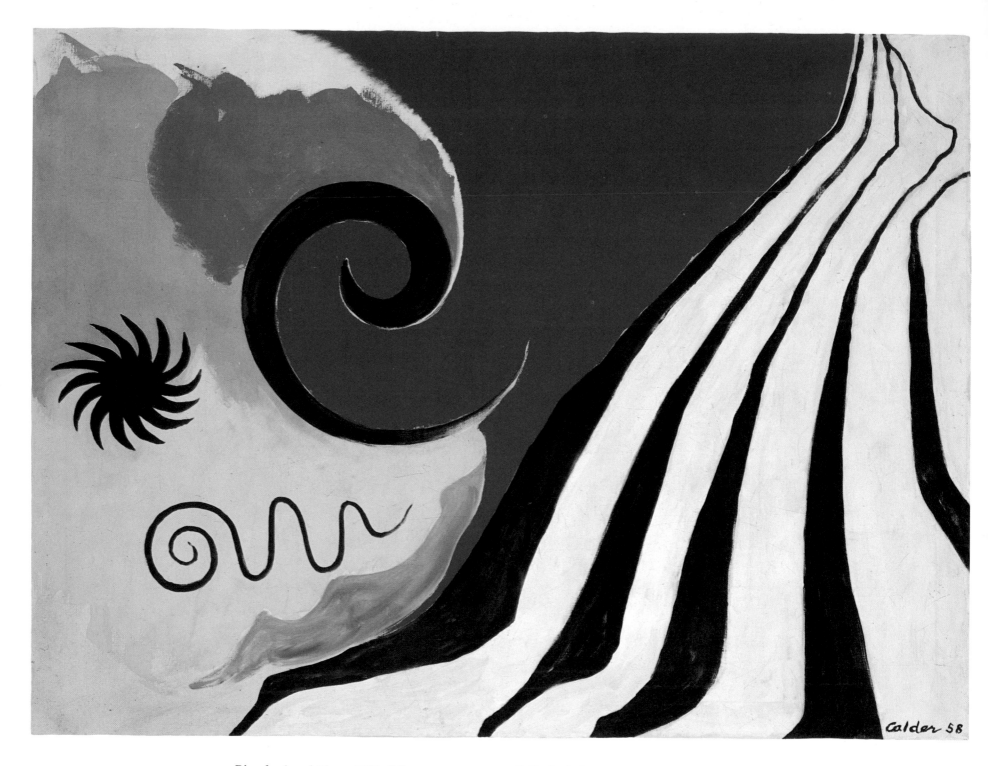

Pinwheel and Flow, 1958. Oil on canvas, 30 × 40″. Perls Galleries, New York.

Composition, 1930. Oil on canvas, 18 × 27″. Collection of the artist.

A Manhattan, 1944. Oil on canvas, 24½ × 29½″. Mr. and Mrs. William B. F. Drew, New York.

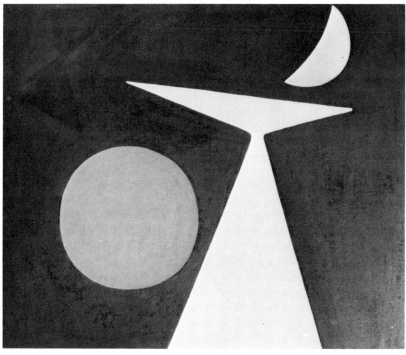

The Canvas Rhombus, 1945. Oil on canvas, 12¾ × 6½″. Perls Galleries, New York.

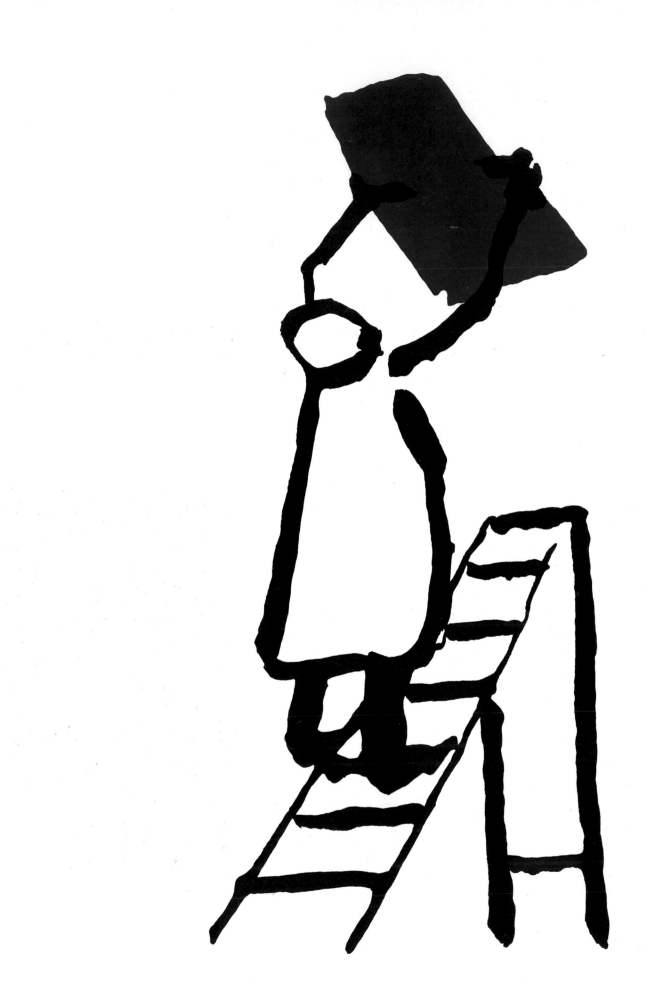

I very much like making gouaches. It goes fast and one can surprise oneself.

Calder began painting in gouache in the thirties, but it was not until the mid-forties that he achieved a bold breakthrough in this medium—opaque watercolors that are better suited to his temperament than either transparent watercolors (too pale) or oils (too slow): "With oils you have to wait too long for the stuff to dry."

In 1953 the Calders rented a charming little house, "Mas des Roches," near Aix-en-Provence, but as it was without electricity or piped water they moved to "a rather pretentious three-story yellow stucco building with red shutters, and quite handsome in spite of it all." In both places Sandy set up studios especially for painting. At "Mas des Roches": "I used the carriage shed as a studio. It was like a big one-car garage with an open door. I put in a little table and did gouaches there—many of them. . . . I would moisten the paper with a flow of water and wait till it dried a bit but not too much; then I would draw on it with a brush full of China ink—this would develop clouds and trees and fungi and things of that nature. In addition to the watery variety, I did some large human heads with crosshatched stripes."

In the yellow house: "I found a very funny room on the third floor, with giddy flowery paper, which I used to continue my '*gouacheries*.' I had made gouaches before, but here I was practically doing nothing but gouaches and concentrating on them. I seemed to develop something new."

The following year the Calders bought a house in Saché, a small village near Tours. One of the first things he did was set up a workshop in a nearby shed and what he calls his *gouacherie* in a tiny, vine-draped stone cottage directly across the road from the house. Calder whitewashed the walls and sealed off the windows facing the road—his favorite way of fitting out a studio—creating a hermetic environment where he paints by artificial light. Jean Davidson has suggested that Calder's penchant for working in windowless rooms dates back to his childhood, when his parents invariably gave him the cellar for his workshop. Calder has recently built a new house and studio on a hilltop overlooking Saché, but he still prefers the old workshop and usually spends a part of each day in the *gouacherie*.

In Calder's autobiography there are many passing references to scenery that particularly impressed him. These descriptions often recall some aspect of his work which he has abstracted from nature, and one is particularly reminded of the gouaches. On a trip to Brazil in 1948: "When we crossed the Amazon River, the moon shone in spots from overhead on the river and cut out great black islands of different shapes; this was not always very distinct, but when you could grasp it, it was stunning." In India in 1954: "We went several times to the calico factory of the Sarabhais, in the middle of Ahmedabad, over a high bridge, in the heart of the town. Standing on the bridge, we could look

Gouaches

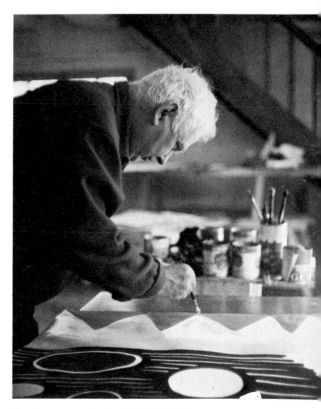

In the *gouacherie*, Saché, 1964.

119

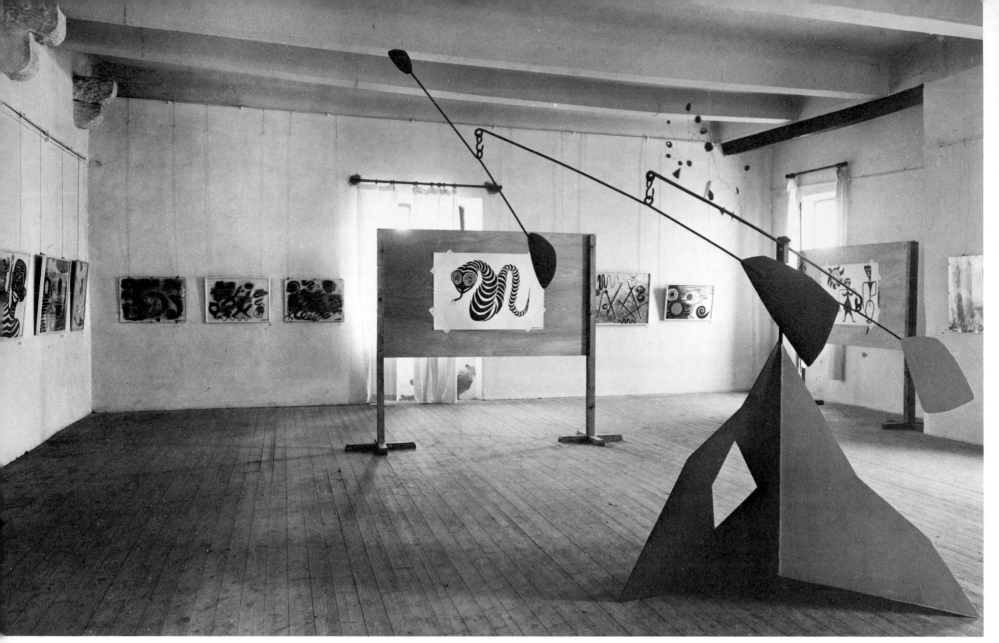

Exhibition at Musée Grimaldi, Antibes, 1956.

down at the calico that had been freshly dyed, great varicolored bands, over six feet wide, spread out on the gravel over the dried-out river bed. It made quite a wonderful pattern of stripes."

Calder's gouaches, seemingly simple, are infinitely inventive works that only a masterly painter could produce. Some are based on natural forms; some are abstract designs. The best ones, joyously conceived, firmly structured, brilliantly colored, add up to one of the most remarkable bodies of work in our time. In recent years he has produced stupendous numbers of gouaches, doing some almost daily the way other people do morning exercises. Inevitably there are a great many below top quality, and it is unfortunate that these have been exhibited and sold. However, Calder's work in this medium must be judged by the splendid examples, of which there are many.

Exhibition at Perls Galleries, New York, 1963.

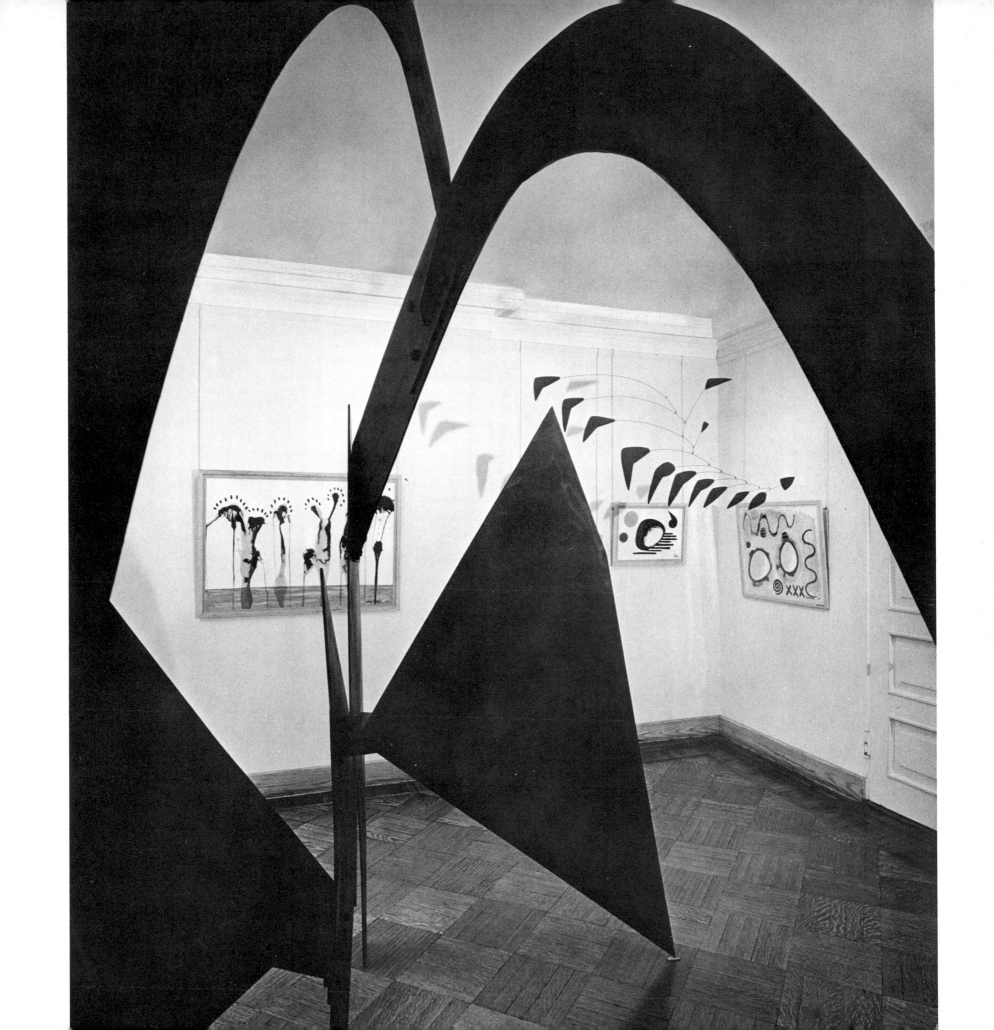

Aix, 1953. Gouache, 29 × 43″. Jean
and Sandra Davidson, Saché, France.

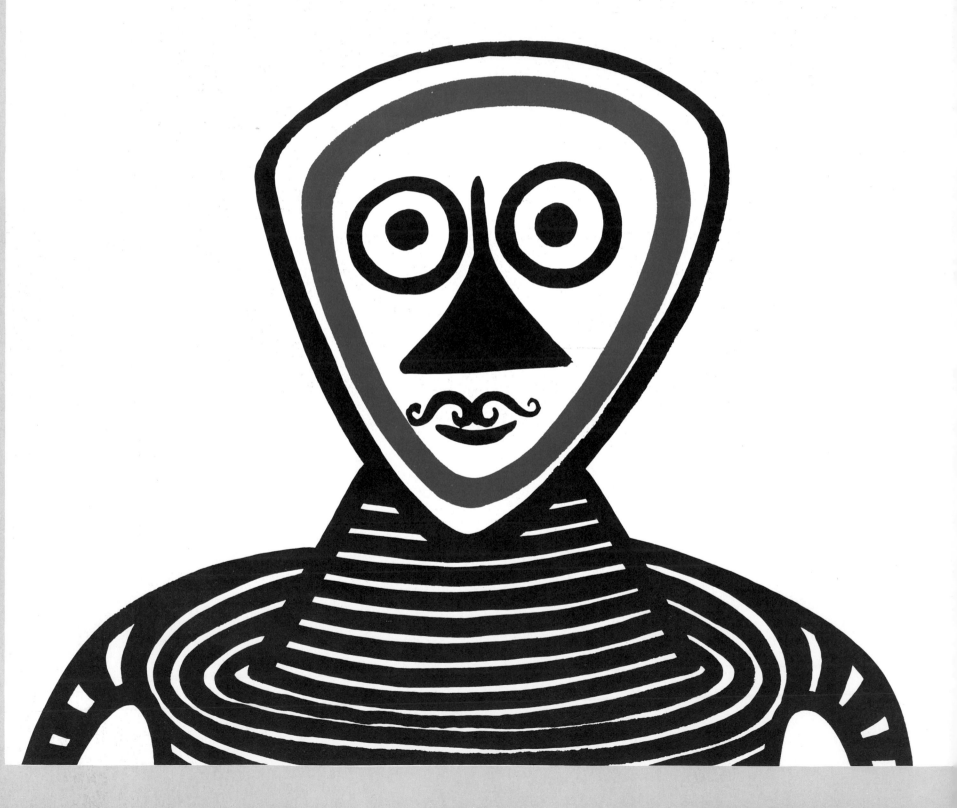

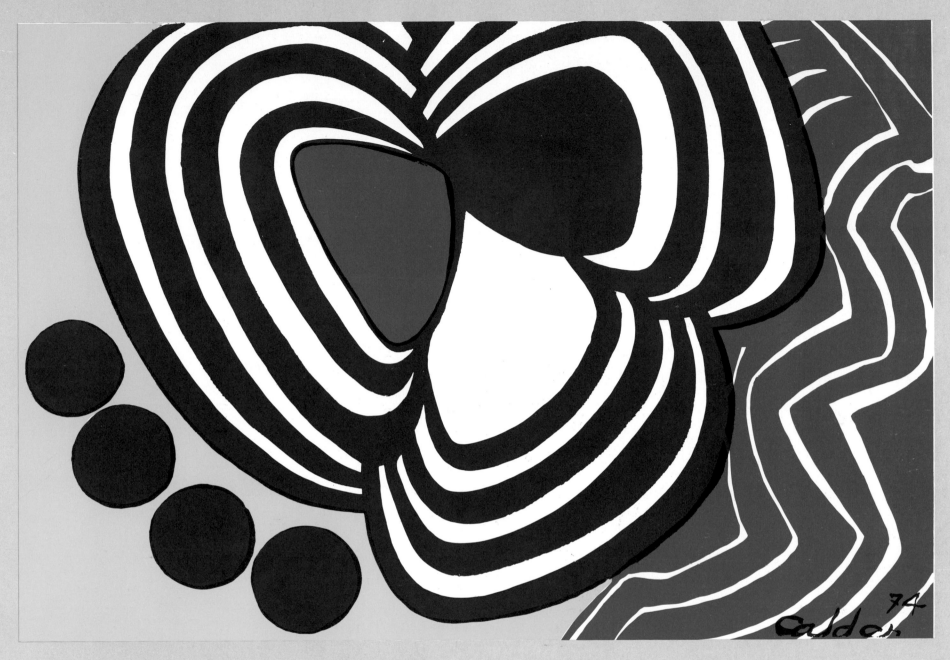

Four Black Dots, 1974. Gouache, 29 × 43″. Whitney Museum of American Art, New York; gift of the Howard and Jean Lipman Foundation.

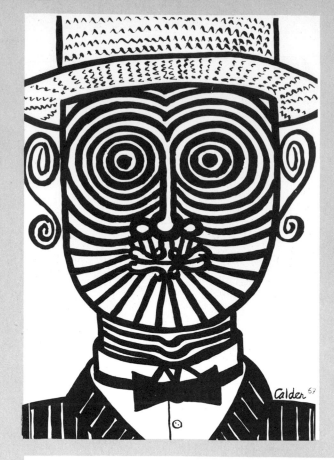

Le Buveur d'Eau, 1967. Gouache, 43 × 29".
Private collection, New York.

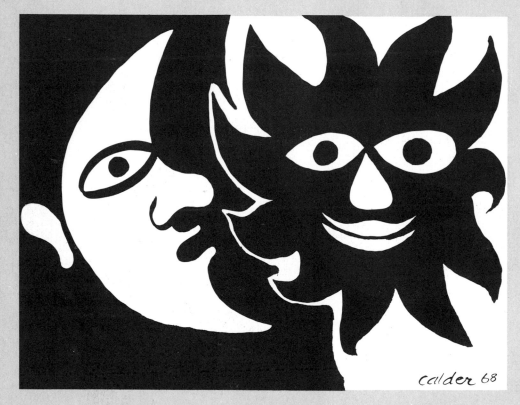

Black Sun, White Moon, 1968. Gouache,
22⅞ × 30⅝". David H. Treherne-Thomas,
New York.

Woman and Dog, 1944. Gouache, 31 ×
22½". Mr. and Mrs. Robert Melamed, Way-
zata, Minnesota.

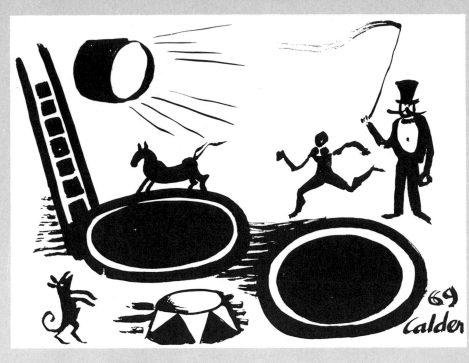

The Spotlight, 1969. Gouache, 22½ × 30½″. Private collection, New York.

Yellow Equestrienne, 1975. Gouache, 23 × 30⅝″. Mr. and Mrs. A. R. Landsman, New York.

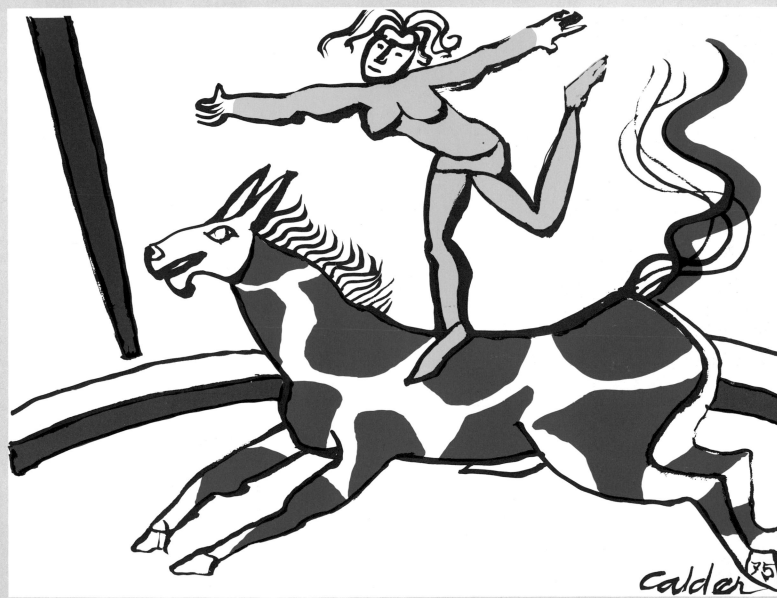

125

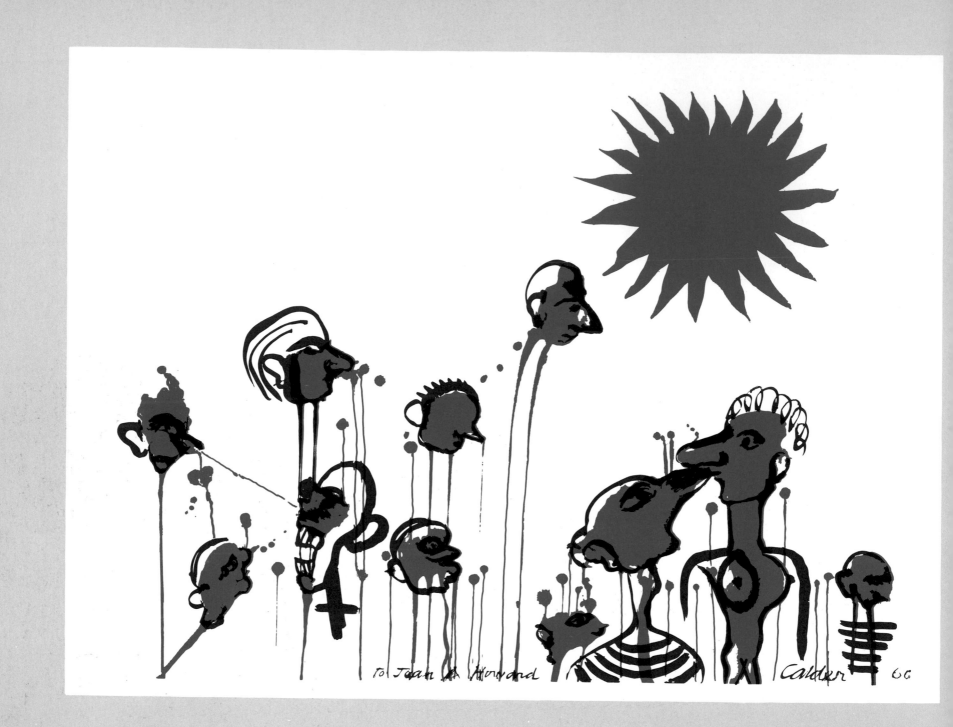

French Revolution, 1966. Gouache,
29 × 43″. Collection of the author.

Big Bug, 1970. Gouache, 29 × 43″. Collection of the author.

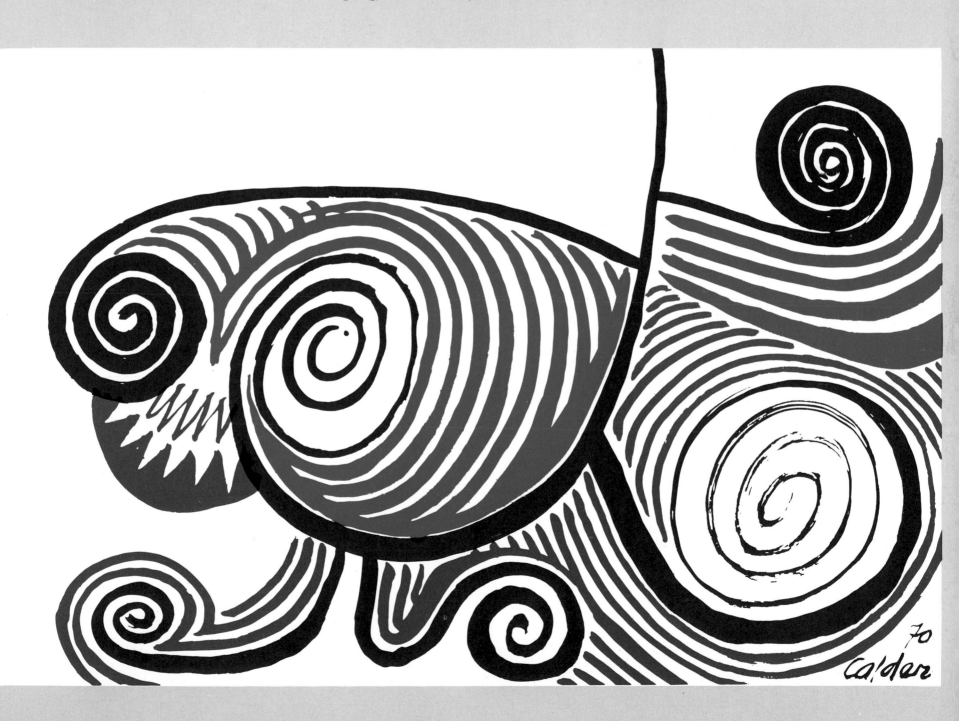

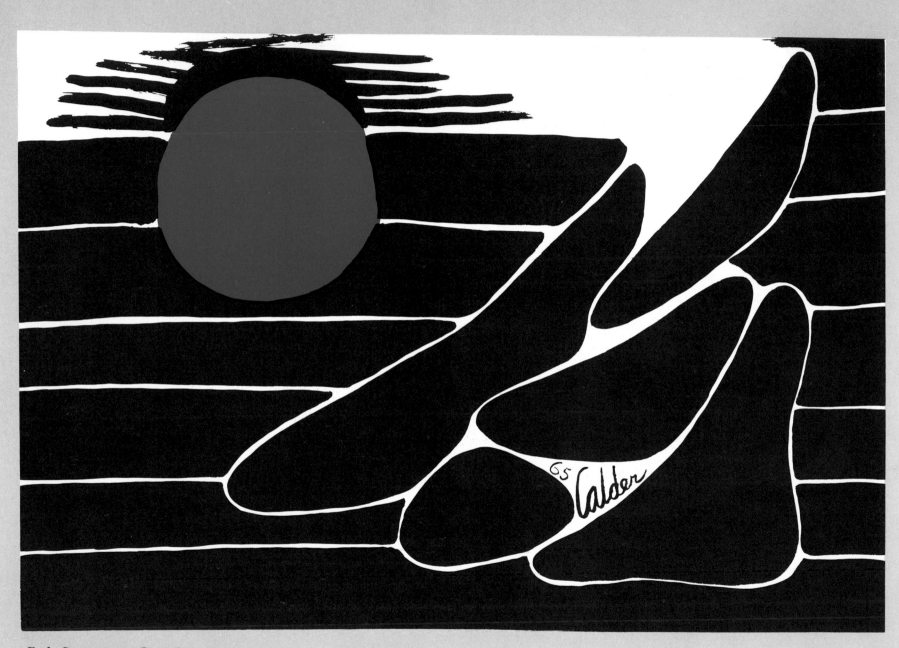

Red Sun, 1965. Gouache, 29 ×
42″. George Schiller, New York.

OPPOSITE: *Flying Saucers*, 1969. Gouache, 46 × 32″. Jean and Sandra Davidson, Saché, France.

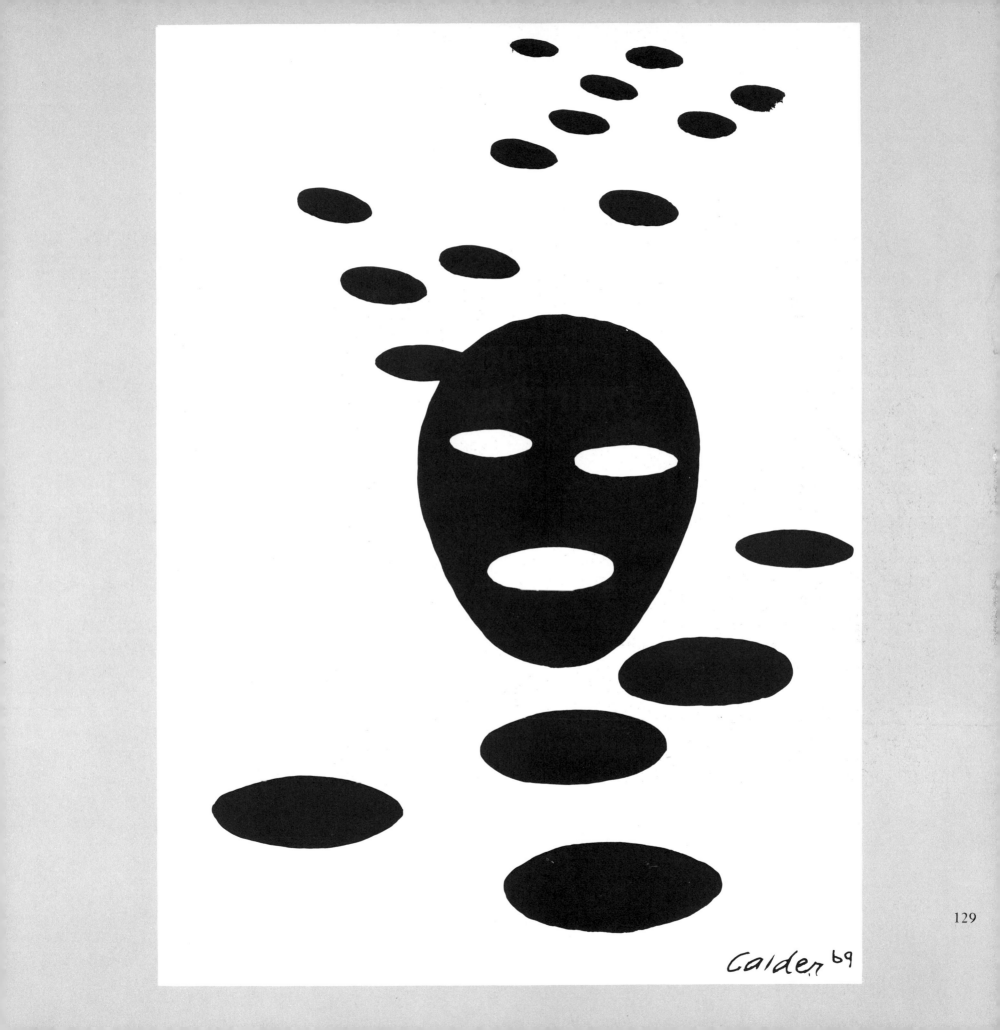

129

Calder 69

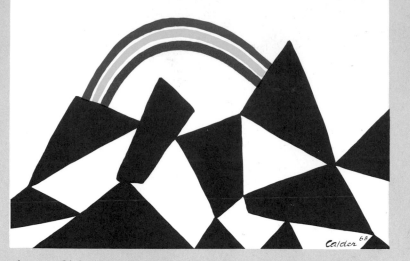

Arc en Ciel, 1965. Gouache, 29 × 43″.
Present location unknown.

OPPOSITE: *Untitled*, 1972. Gouache, 43 × 29″. Mr. and
Mrs. John I. H. Baur, Katonah, New York.

Red Saucer, Black Cloud, 1969. Gouache, 29 × 43″.
Mr. and Mrs. Stuart Caplin, New York.

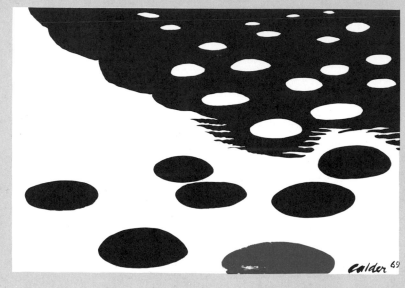

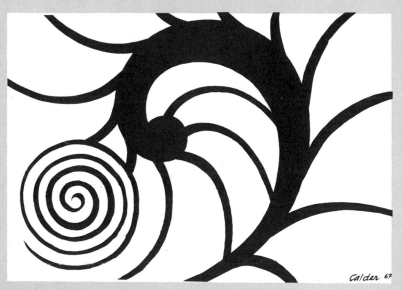

Black-and-white Nautilus, 1967. Gouache,
29 × 43″. Present location unknown.

Target and Crag, 1972. Gouache, 29 × 43″.
Present location unknown.

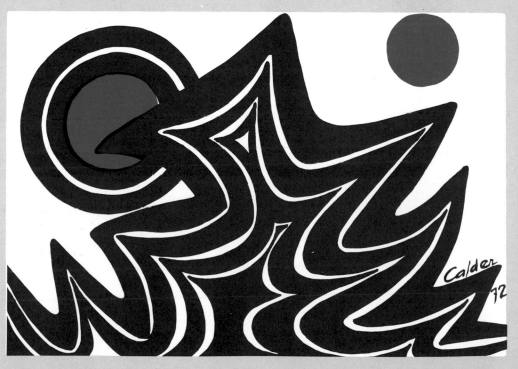

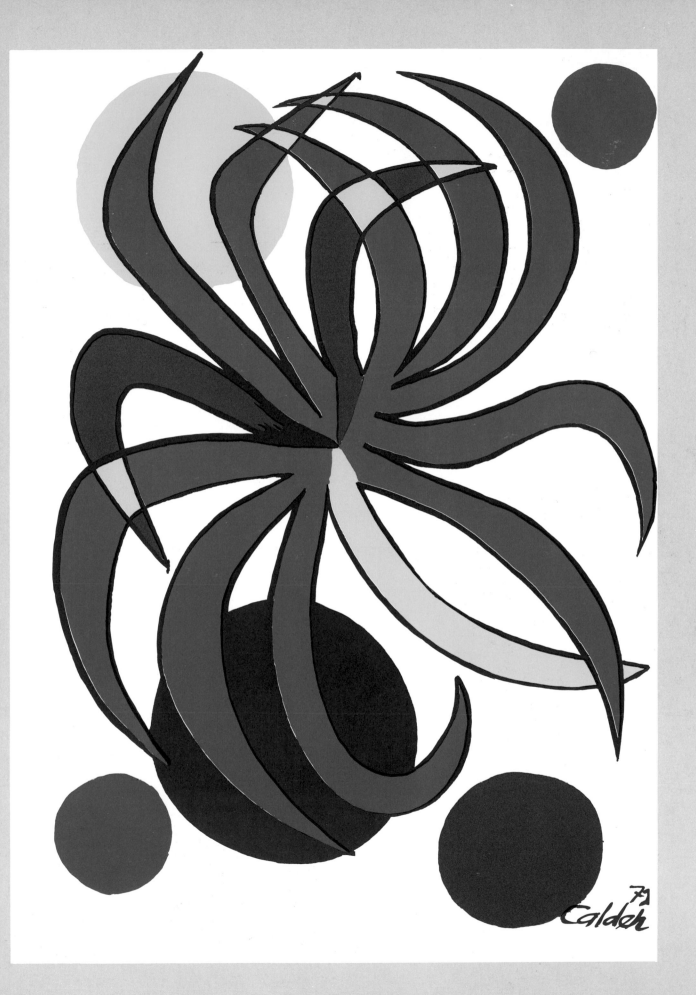

131

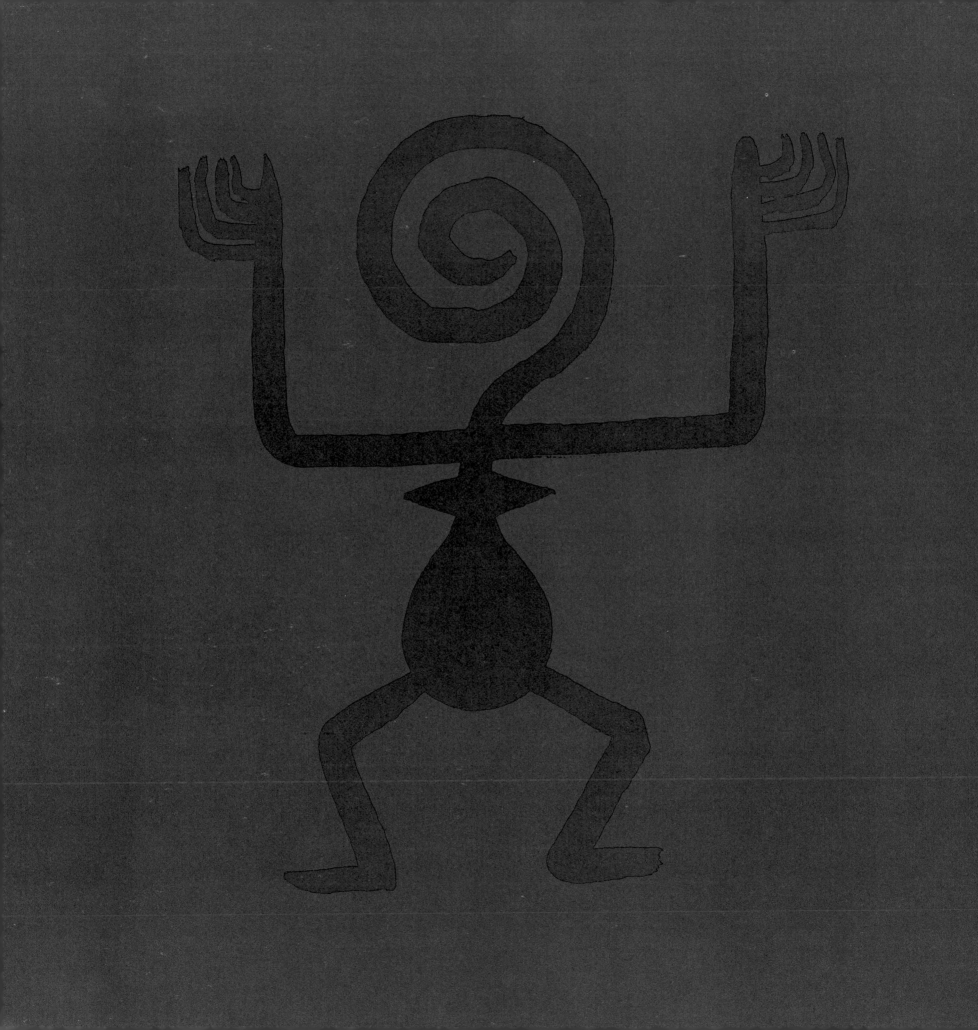

It's a far cry back to my first visit to Paris, in 1926, and a séance in the sketch class of the Académie de la Grande Chaumière. A young lady from one of the Southern States entered the room, and cried out, "I don't know which it is, but I want to etch or sketch." Most of the time ever since I've felt pretty sure that I knew what I wanted to do—but for the past few weeks I've been rather in the predicament of the above young lady.

Graphic Work

Calder ended this comment on his quandary as a novice etcher with the conclusion that, despite all the problems of itchy acid burns, "the stickiness of everything," the mess of dirty rags and lots of other annoyances, "I have quite enjoyed the whole thing."

Calder has practiced all the major forms of printmaking, producing numerous etchings, woodcuts, linoleum cuts and lithographs. He worked with the great print-maker Stanley William Hayter and his Atelier 17 group, experimenting with various kinds of prints and, as one might expect, devising unconventional techniques. Hayter described one of these in his contribution to *Homage to Alexander Calder*, published to honor the artist's seventy-fifth birthday. Rather than cutting away parts of the wood-block, Calder hammered a wire sculpture into the block, and the resulting indentation appeared in the print as a white line on a black wood-grained background. In the late forties he worked with Rudolph Charles von Ripper in New York to learn the technique of drawing through a soft ground onto zinc plates for his illustrations for an edition of La Fontaine's fables. These etchings are identical in style with the pen-and-ink line drawings from which the illustrations for Calder's other early books were reproduced.

Calder's early illustrated books are among the most remarkable of his achievements; pages from all six volumes, dating from 1926 to 1955, are reproduced here. In 1950 he was chosen by *The New York Times* as one of the ten best illustrators of children's books of the past fifty years. We certainly would not quarrel with the "best illustrator" part of the award, but *children's* books they are not (for that honor we would nominate Sandra Calder Davidson). There is no point in heaping up adjectives to describe the content and style of Calder's line illustrations. Every one of the books, three of which have now been reprinted in paperback, must be seen by anyone interested in Calder and his work.

Three limited-edition albums have been published in recent years, with original etchings made by Calder for each publication. They are: *La Proue de la table* by Yves Elléouët, *Santa Claus* by e e cummings and *Fêtes* by Jacques Prévert.

La Proue de la table is an imaginary eight-page newspaper—issue "N°. O"—in an edition of fifty-five, with line illustrations and seven black-and-white signed and numbered etchings, including a self-portrait. This publication is of relatively minor interest.

Santa Claus, measuring twenty-eight by twenty-two inches, is a volume in keeping with Calder's current interest in monumental works. Increased scale does not mean increased labor on his graphics any more than on his sculpture. The publisher prepared huge waxed plates, and Calder incised them with a rough tool, he says, in a few hours. The nine etchings, with their shaggy outlines, are related in style to the illustrations in his earliest books, but the former are far more original.

Fêtes is a delightful forty-eight-page prose-poem homage to Calder accompanied by his brilliantly colored embossed etchings. Sandy described how these were done: he made an exact drawing in color, and then cut out the abstract shapes from sheet metal a bit heavier than the aluminum he uses for mobiles. These shapes were laid out in the open press, arranged according to the drawing, and the specified colors were brushed on. The paper was run through the press, and the metal pieces produced a subtle embossed effect in the finished print. This process is as unconventional and personal as the hammered-wire woodblocks he made years ago, and the etchings relate directly to his mobiles, just as the woodblock prints relate to his early wire sculpture.

Poet Jacques Prévert's writing is as exciting as Calder's prints; many writers seem to have been inspired to think, feel and communicate at their best when Calder is their subject. His text begins:

> Mobile en haut
> Stabile en bas
> Telle est la tour
> Eiffel
> Calder est come elle.

Prévert's title is explained in a few words: "Calder fait des fêtes pour la vie" ("Calder makes festivals for life"). He describes Sandy as "that ogre with fairy fingers," likening him to a dolphin—splendid, joyful, playful. The Larousse dictionary definition of "statue," he declares, makes him understand why Calder never made statues: "A statue is a cold personage, without energy, without action, without movement."

Calder does a large number of just about everything he attempts, so a list of all his magazine illustrations and covers would be a long one. In the preface I mentioned Calder's contributions to *Art in America*, and I should add here that the heading for Cleve Gray's article "Calder's Circus" was actually twisted out of wire. When Cleve asked him to letter a special headpiece, Sandy picked up a length of heavy silver wire and his pliers and made the foot-long CIRCUS in a few minutes.

In the forties he designed one cover each for the magazines *Vertical, View, Interiors* and *Style en France*. Since he joined the Galerie Maeght in Paris in 1950, he has done many covers, pages and special decorations for its publication *Derrière Le Miroir*.

Donald Karshan, print collector and critic, wrote a few years ago in *Art in America* about Calder as a graphic artist. He pointed out that there is a natural continuity between Calder's brightly polychromed sculpture and his colorful lithographs. A simple process for executing Calder's color lithographs was developed some time ago by Fernand Mourlot, the distinguished Paris lithographer, and some are now being made in Paris and New York by the lithographer George Goodstadt in the same way. For these lithographs Calder does not work directly on the stone. Rather, he paints a gouache which functions as a maquette; then the design is redrawn by a *chromiste-designateur* on zinc plates—a separate plate for each color, plus an additional plate that prints a thin, transparent rose over areas of the flat colors to give them a range of tone. The print is executed according to Calder's exact directions. Papers for the prints are the same that Calder uses for the gouaches—almost invariably paper manufactured by the French firm Arches. The original gouache is a maquette for a lithograph in the same sense that a metal maquette is a scale model for a sculpture fabricated in a foundry. Unlike the photomechanical offset reproduction, made for printed illustrations, the direct-lithography print is not intended to be an exact replica but rather a graphic interpretation of the artist's work by master craftsmen. Calder lithographs are, in fact, outstanding examples of the "multiples" developed during the last decade when artists as well as dealers have welcomed the opportunity to make works of art available to a wide public.

Calder's art is perfectly suited to poster design. His simple, hard-edge images and limited range of pure colors add up to bold, eye-catching visual statements. Some posters, like the lithographs, are based on gouaches; others refer to a specific theme and bear a

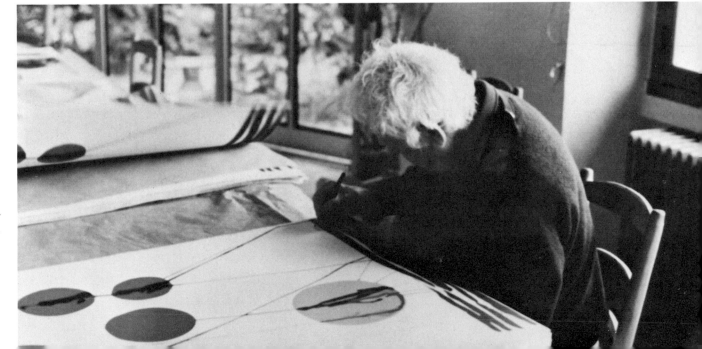

Signing Nicaraguan earthquake-relief lithographs, Saché, 1973.

message, in Calder's distinctive handwriting, that is an integral part of the overall design. For his exhibitions Calder has always designed posters with great facility (and often catalogue illustrations and invitations as well). In recent years he has contributed numerous poster designs to the peace and environmental movements and other humanitarian causes. A close friend has said that the artist is not overly optimistic about the success of these causes, but that he would rather join them to do what he can than stand back and do nothing. The best of his posters have come out of his feeling of commitment. *Pour le Viet Nam*, executed in an exceptional range of soft, somber hues, is a powerful image, explicit in its reference to the crucified Christ. The *Humanité* poster, with its witty H-man, is both funny and serious; it ranks among the great posters of our century.

Some of Calder's etchings and woodcuts and a few early lithographs are interesting, but laboring over a process intermediary to the final result has never set well with Calder. Even the informal linoleum cuts which he made in the early days for Circus invitations, exhibition catalogues and personal cards seem to lack the typical Calder sparkle. It is the late lithographs—a virtual cloning of the best gouaches—that are without question the most exciting Calder prints. These lithographs, and the posters as well, are great multiples that have vastly extended the impact, influence and pleasure of Calder's work.

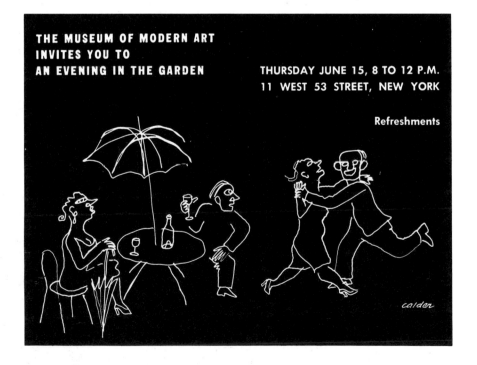

Party invitation, 1944. Lithograph, 6½ × 8″. The Museum of Modern Art, New York.

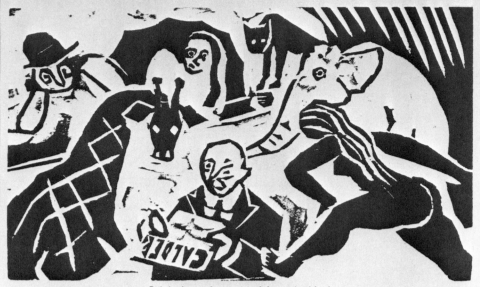

Original woodcut printed from the block

YOU ARE INVITED TO AN EXHIBITION OF WOOD CARVINGS BY
ALEXANDER CALDER
AT THE WEYHE GALLERY · 794 LEXINGTON AVE · N.Y.
FEBRUARY 4TH TO 23RD 1929

Weyhe Gallery invitation, 1929. Woodcut, 5 × 5¾". Archives of American Art, Smithsonian Institution, Washington, D.C.

Christmas card, 1927. Linoleum cut, 7¾ × 8⅜". Margaret Calder Hayes, Berkeley, California.

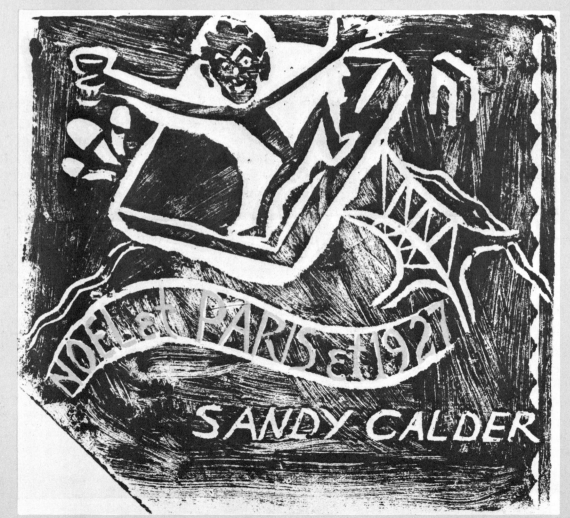

CONTENTS

Introduction 7
Action 9
Rhythm—Seals . . . 11
Cats 13
Dogs 15
The Elephant . . . 21
Birds 23
Monkeys 29
The Deer Family . . . 31
Horses 39
Caricature . . . 43
Pose 45
Cows 47
Animal Instinct . . 53
The Lion 57

Illustrations from *Animal Sketching*, 1926.

138

✦ ACTION ✦

Animals—Action. These two words go hand in hand in art. Our interest in animals is connected with their habits, their food, the animals they prey upon or that prey on them, their habitats and protective coloring. Their lives are of necessity active and their activities are reflected in an alert grace of line even when they are in repose or asleep. Indeed, because of their markings many animals appear to be awake when they are sleeping, and many mammals sleep so lightly that even when apparently asleep they will move their ears in the direction of a sound that is inaudible to us. A deer sometimes will move each ear in a different direction, catching two warning sounds. So there is always a feeling of perpetual motion about animals and to draw them successfully this must be borne in mind.

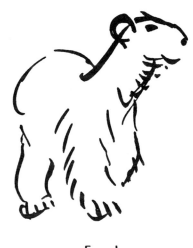

[9]

◝ POSE ◜

The pose, or rather, lack of pose of the animal will often prove a disturbing element. Sometimes the beast will be reclining, probably asleep. Then, unless he is in the throes of a nightmare, it will be easy sailing, provided you can get a good vantage point. However, if he is on the move there may still be two possibilities. The animal may be repeating a certain cycle of motions, as a caged lion paces back and forth, or it may perform the action only once, as a dog may yawn. In the first case it is possible to wait and observe and study the action, thus building up one's knowledge by repeated views of the same thing. In the second instance, memory and "impressionableness" come into play very strongly, as well as ease and speed of execution.

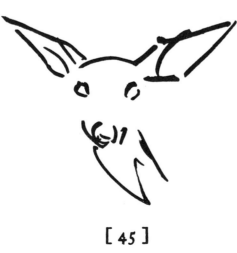

[45]

[62]

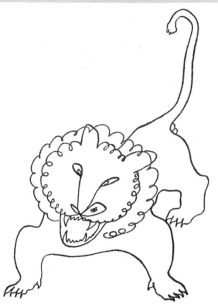

A GNAT CHALLENGES A LYON

AS a lyon was blustering in the forrest, up comes a gnat to his very beard, and enters into an expostulation with him upon the points of honour and courage. What do I value your teeth, or your claws, says the gnat, that are but the arms of every bedlam slut? As to the matter of resolution; I defy ye to put that point immediately to an issue. So the trumpet sounded and the combatants enter'd the lists. The gnat charged into the nostrils of the lyon, and there twing'd him, till he made him tear

13

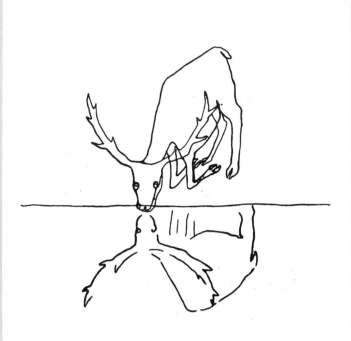

A STAG DRINKING

AS a stag was drinking upon the bank of a clear stream, he saw his image in the water, and entered into this contemplation upon't. Well! says he, if these pityful shanks of mine

1

Illustrations from *Fables of Aesop*, 1931.

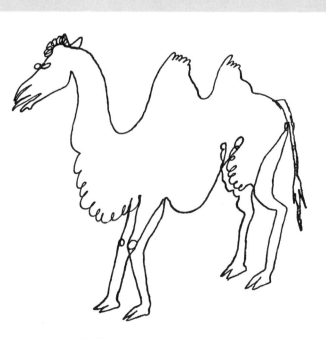

A CAMEL AT FIRST SIGHT

UPON the first sight of a camel, all people ran away from't, in amazement at so monstrous a bulk. Upon the second sight, finding that it did them no hurt, they took heart upon't, went up to't, and view'd it. But when they came, upon further experience, to take notice, how stupid a beast it was, they ty'd it up, bridled it, loaded it with packs and burdens; set boys upon the back on't, and treated it with the last degree of contempt.

46

A MAN AND TWO WIVES

IT was now cuckow-time, and a certain middle ag'd man, that was half-gray, half-brown, took a fancy to marry two wives, of an age one under another, and happy was the woman that

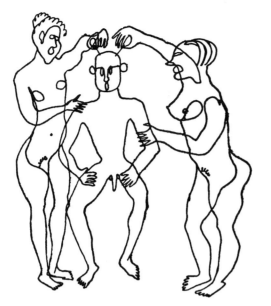

could please him best. They took mighty care of him to all manner of purposes, and still as they were combing the good

86

A BOAR AND A HORSE

A BOAR happen'd to be wallowing in the water where a horse was going to drink, and there grew a quarrel upon't. The horse went presently to a man, to assist him in his revenge. They agreed upon the conditions, and the man immediately arm'd

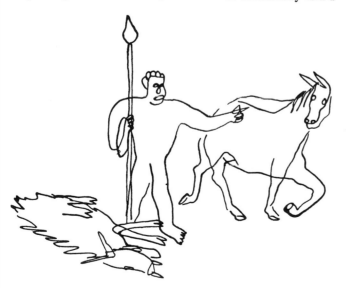

himself, and mounted the horse, who carry'd him to the boare, and had the satisfaction of seeing his enemy kill'd before his face. The horse thank'd the cavalier for his kindness, but as he was

90

A WOLF AND A CRANE

A WOLF had got a bone in's throat, and could think of no better instrument

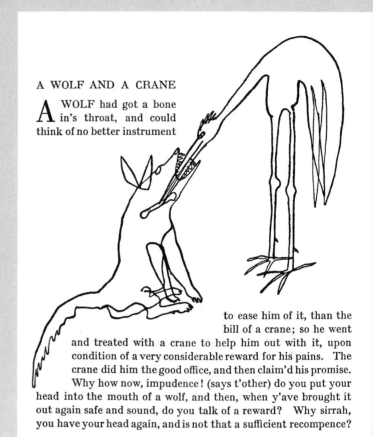

to ease him of it, than the bill of a crane; so he went and treated with a crane to help him out with it, upon condition of a very considerable reward for his pains. The crane did him the good office, and then claim'd his promise. Why how now, impudence! (says t'other) do you put your head into the mouth of a wolf, and then, when y'ave brought it out again safe and sound, do you talk of a reward? Why sirrah, you have your head again, and is not that a sufficient recompence?

THE MORAL

One good turn, they say, requires another: but yet he that has to do with wild beasts (as some men are no better) and comes off with a whole skin, let him expect no other reward.

93

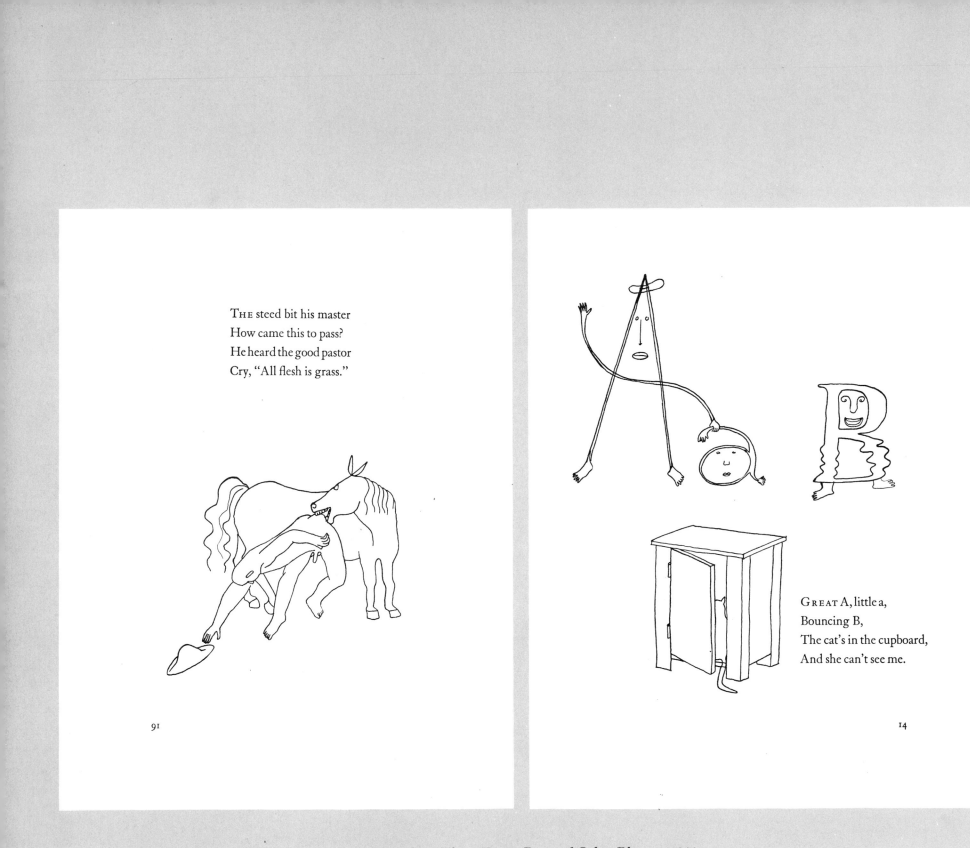

THE steed bit his master
How came this to pass?
He heard the good pastor
Cry, "All flesh is grass."

91

GREAT A, little a,
Bouncing B,
The cat's in the cupboard,
And she can't see me.

14

Illustrations from *Three Young Rats and Other Rhymes*, 1944.

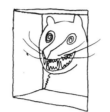

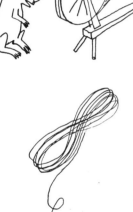

THREE little mice sat down to spin.
Pussy passed by and she peeped in.
"What are you at, my fine little men?"
"Making coats for gentlemen."
"Shall I come in and cut off your threads?"
"Oh no, Mistress Pussy, you'd bite off our heads!"

49

THE dogs of the monks
    Of St. Bernard go,
To help little children
    Out of the snow.

Each has a rum-bottle
    Under his chin,
Tied with a little bit
    Of bobbin.

37

143

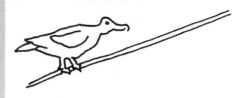

"God save thee, ancient Mariner!
From the fiends, that plague thee thus!—
Why look'st thou so?"—With my cross-
bow
I shot the ALBATROSS.

The ancient Mariner inhospitably killeth the pious bird of good omen.

Illustrations from *The Rime of the Ancient Mariner*, 1946.

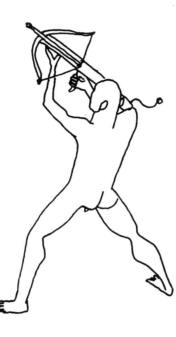

12

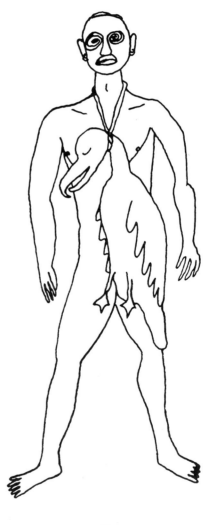

23

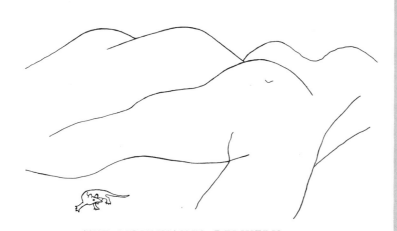

THE MOUNTAIN'S DELIVERY

A mountain having labor
With clamor rent the air.
The neighbors who came running
Predicted she would bear
A city broad as Paris
Or at least a manor house,
But at the crucial moment
The mountain dropped a mouse.

*

How like so many authors
Who say they'll set to paper
A vast Promethean epic
But all that comes is vapor.

23

Etchings from La Fontaine's *Selected Fables*, 1948.

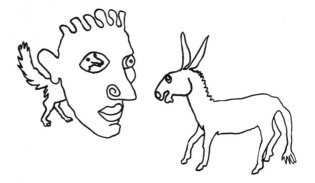

THE FOX AND THE MASK

Fame's the most specious of integuments,
No deeper than the make-up of a mime
Which the idolatrous public, time after time,
Will raise to pinnacles of prominence.
The average ass reacts by outward sense;
The fox, on the other hand, will peer and sniff
Behind the mask, and turn it round, and if
He thereby finds sufficient evidence
That the great figure's an inane facade,
He will repeat the verdict he let fall
Upon a hero's huge and hollow bust.
He praised the art and added: "A splendid head!
Pity it has no brains." A test we all
Might use for masks in whom we place our trust.

47

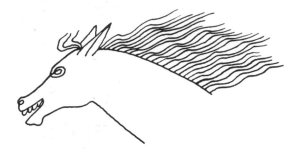

Hast thou given the horse strength? hast thou clothed his
   neck with thunder?
Canst thou make him afraid as a grasshopper? the glory of
   his nostrils is terrible.
He paweth in the valley, and rejoiceth in his strength: he
   goeth on to meet the armed men.
He mocketh at fear, and is not affrighted; neither turneth
   he back from the sword.
The quiver rattleth against him, the glittering spear and
   the shield.
He swalloweth the ground with fierceness and rage: neither
   believeth he that it is the sound of the trumpet.
He saith among the trumpets, Ha, ha; and he smelleth the battle
   afar off, the thunder of the captains, and the shouting.

Job

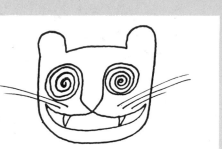

Rousseau. Do you like Cats?
Boswell. No.
Rousseau. I was sure of that. It is my test of character. There you have the despotic
   instinct of men. They do not like cats because the cat is free, and will never consent to
   become a slave. He will do nothing to your order, as the other animals do.
Boswell. Nor a Chicken, either.
Rousseau. A Chicken would obey your orders if you could make them intelligible to it.
   But a cat will understand you perfectly, and not obey them.
Boswell. But a Cat is ungrateful and treacherous.
Rousseau. No. That's all untrue. A Cat is an animal that can be very attached to you; he
   will do anything you please out of friendship. I have a Cat here . . .

James Boswell, *Dialogue with Rousseau*

   Inhabits woods of *Europe* and *Asia*: domesticated everywhere; when tranquil purrs,
moving the tail; when irritated is very active, climbs, spits, emits a fetid odour; eyes shine
at night, the pupil in the day a perpendicular line, by night, large, round; walks with its claws
drawn in; drinks sparingly; urine of the male corrosive; breath fetid; buries its excrements;
makes a horrid mewling in its amours; mews after and plays with its kittens; wags its tail
when looking after prey; the lion of mice, birds, and the smaller quadrupeds; peaceful among
its tribe; eats flesh and fish, refuses hot or salted things, and vegetables; washes behind its
ears before a storm; back electric in the dark; when thrown up, falls on its feet; is not infested
with fleas; gravid 63 days, brings 3-9 young, blind 9 days; delights in marum, cat-mint and
valerian.

Carl Linnaeus, *System of Nature*

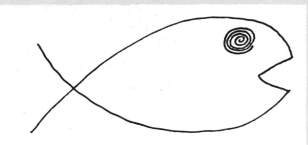

THE FISH

I looked into his eyes
which were far larger than mine
but shallower, and yellowed,
the irises backed and packed
with tarnished tinfoil
seen through the lenses
of old scratched isinglass.
They shifted a little, but not
to return my stare.
— It was more like the tipping
of an object toward the light.

Elizabeth Bishop
from "The Fish"

   The fishes in the waters under the earth represent the inhabitants of hell. The waters
in Scripture is represented as the place of the dead, the Rephaim, the destroyers; and whales
and sea monsters that swim in the great deep are used in Scripture as emblems of devils and
the wrath of God, and the miseries of death and God's wrath are there compared to the sea,
to the deeps, to floods and billows and the like.

Jonathan Edwards, *Images or Shadows*

Illustrations from *A Bestiary*, 1955.

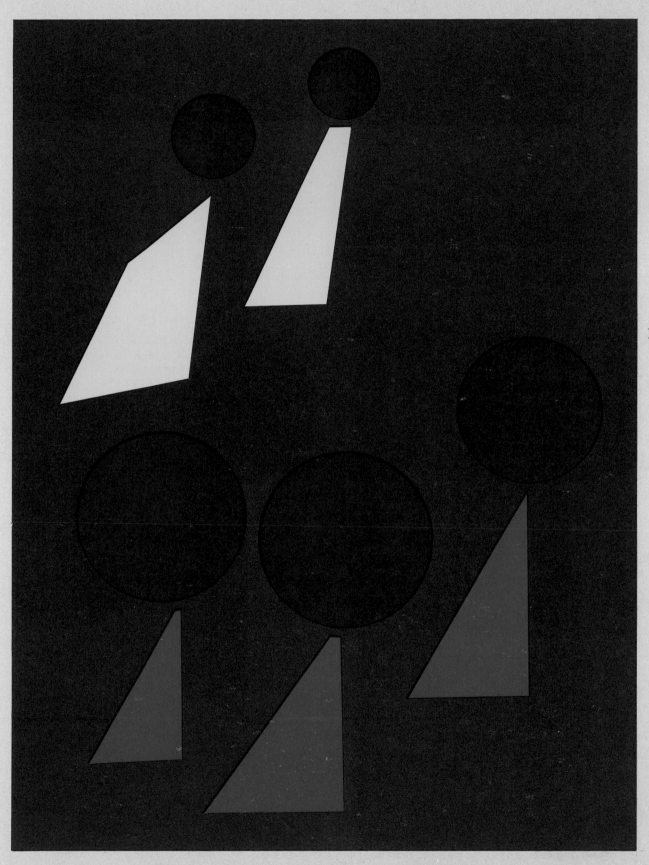

Frontispiece of *Fêtes*, 1971. Embossed etching, 19 × 14⅛″. Whitney Museum of American Art, New York; gift of the Howard and Jean Lipman Foundation.

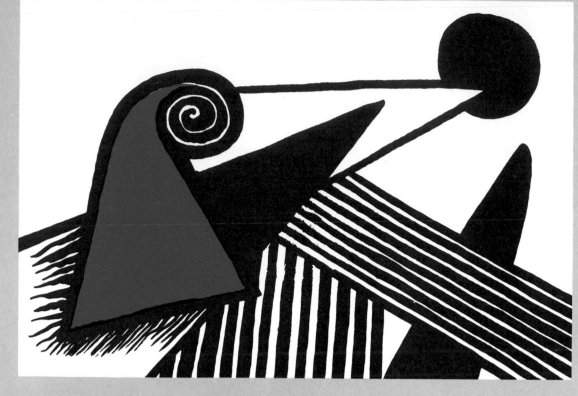

Phrysien et Fer, 1969. Color lithograph, 43 × 29″. John F. Kennedy International Airport, The Port Authority of New York and New Jersey.

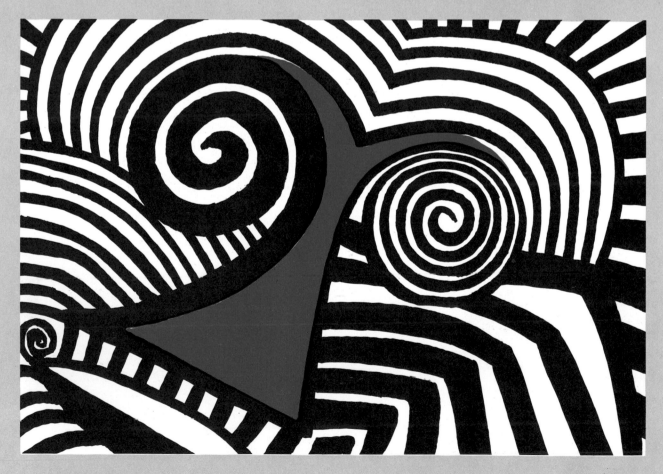

The Red Nose, 1969. Color lithograph, 29⅜ × 42⅝″. Weintraub Gallery, New York.

148

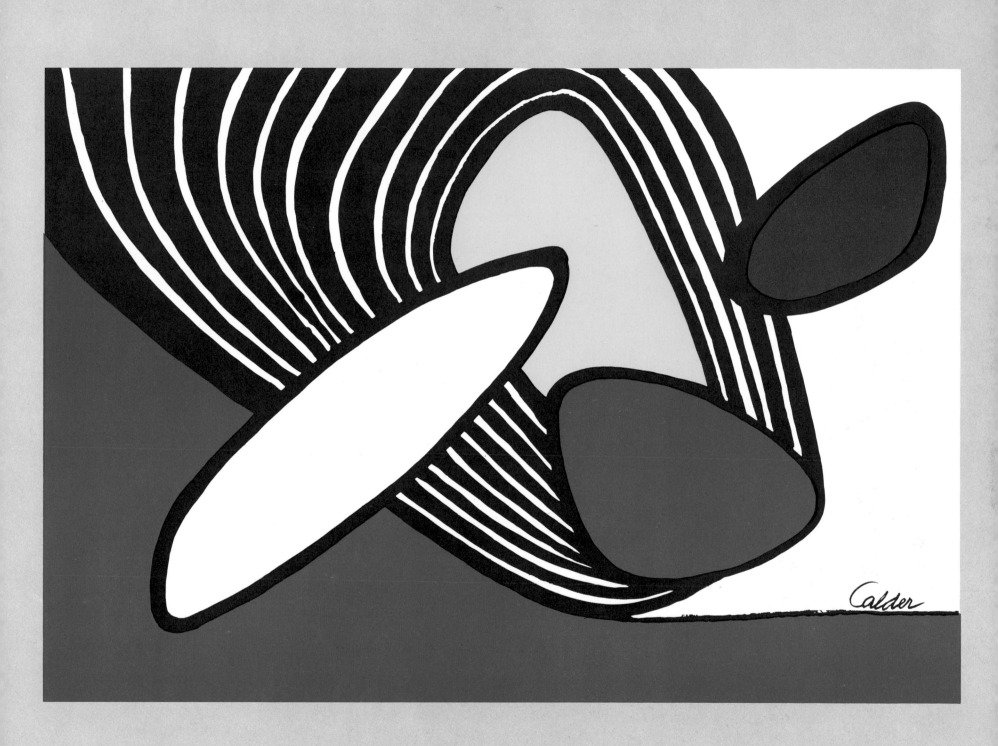

Contour Plowing, 1976. Color lithograph, 26⅜ × 38″. Whitney Museum of American Art, New York.

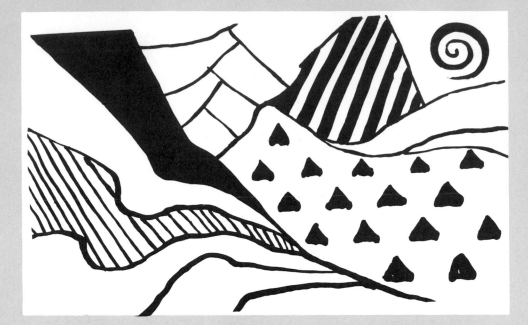

La Récolte, 1962. Etching, 24⅞ × 35⅞″. Galerie Maeght, Paris.

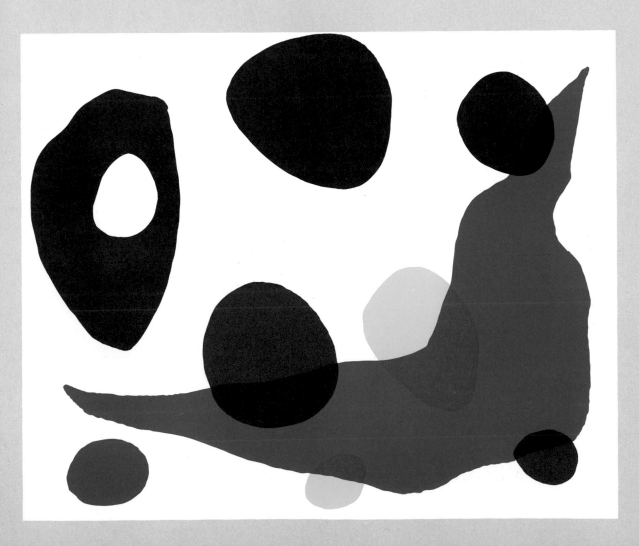

Untitled, 1962. Color lithograph, 17½ × 22″. Collection of the author.

OPPOSITE: *Untitled*, 1965. Color lithograph, 33 × 24¾″. Los Angeles County Museum of Art; gift of Mr. and Mrs. Felix Juda.

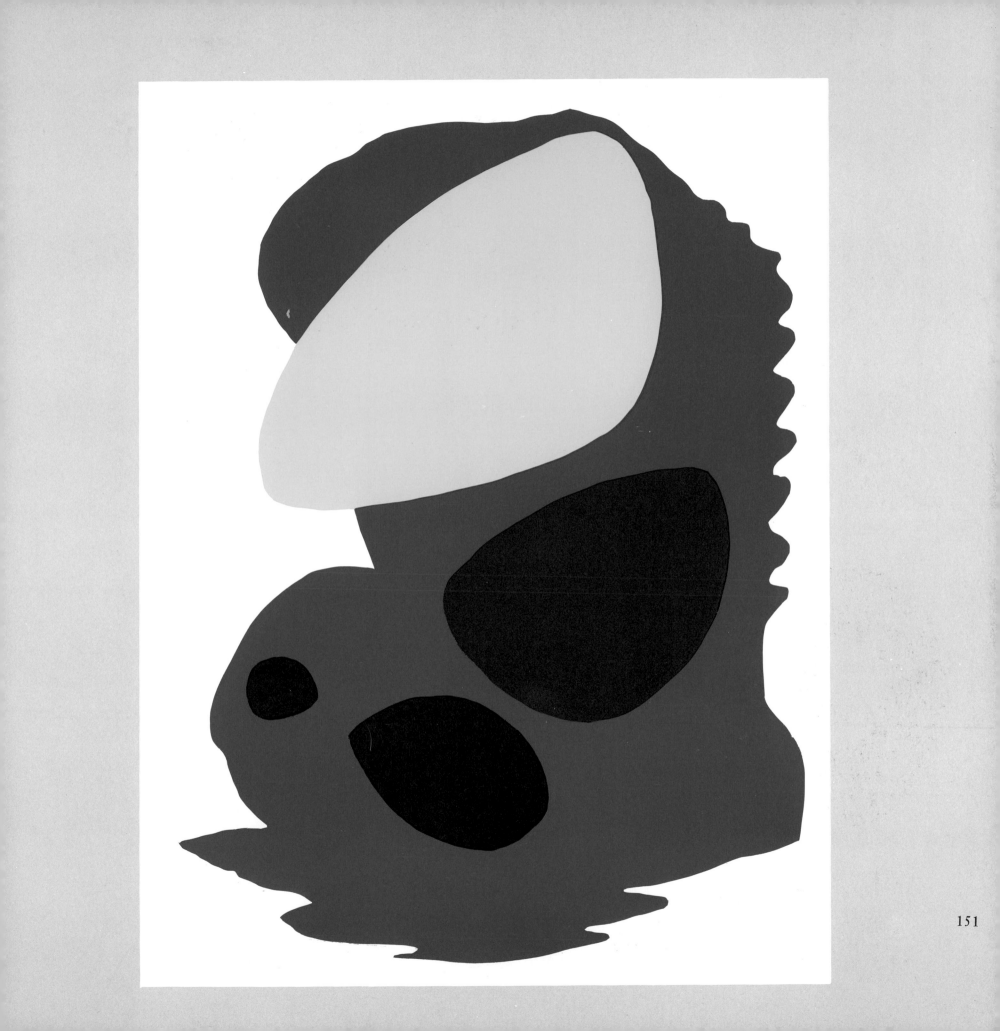

151

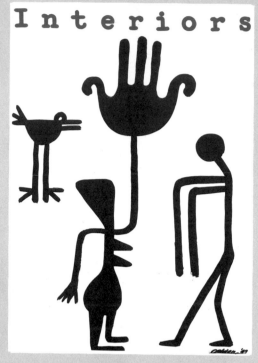

Cover for *Interiors*, December 1949.

BELOW: Book jacket for *What Is American in American Art*, 1963.

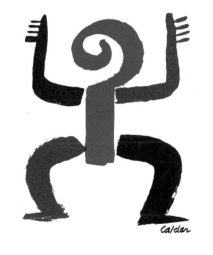

WHAT IS AMERICAN
IN AMERICAN ART

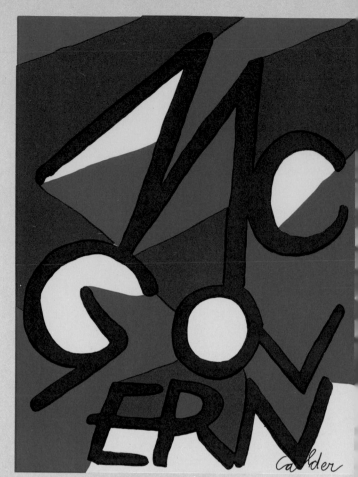

McGovern, 1972. Color lithograph, 29 × 22″. Collection of the artist.

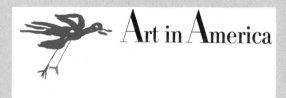

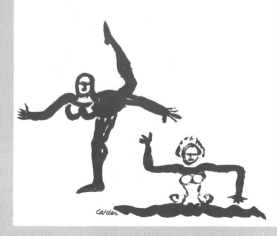

Cover for *Art in America*, No. 5, 1964.

Cover for *Derrière Le Miroir*, February 1971

DERRIERE
LE MIROIR

calder

152

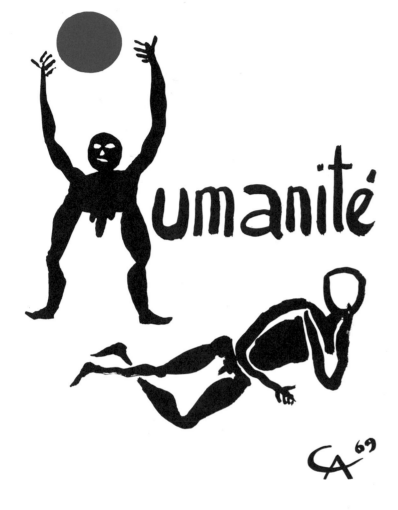

Humanité, 1969. Poster, 31 × 22½″. Collection of the author.

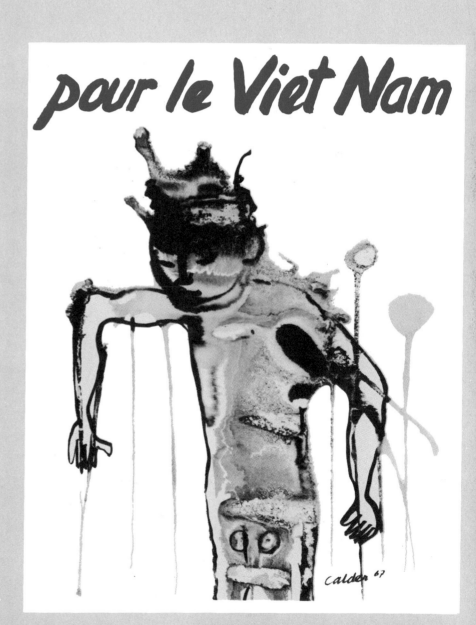

Pour le Viet Nam, 1967. Poster, 29⅜ × 17½″. Collection of the author.

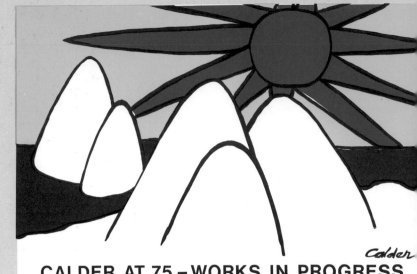

RIGHT: *Calder at 75—Works in Progress*, 1973. Poster, 29½ × 43″. Perls Galleries, New York.

CALDER AT 75 – WORKS IN PROGRESS
OCTOBER 2 - NOVEMBER 3, 1973   PERLS GALLERIES, NEW YORK

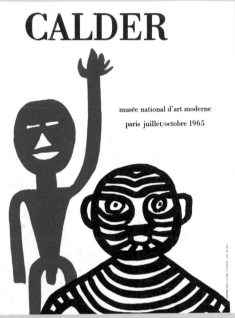

Calder, 1965. Poster, 23½ × 16″. Musée National d'Art Moderne, Paris.

BELOW: *Calder Flèches*, 1968. Poster, 28¾ × 20″. Galerie Maeght, Paris.

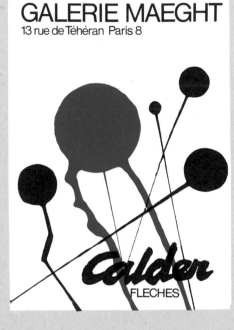

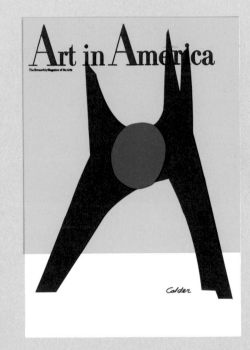

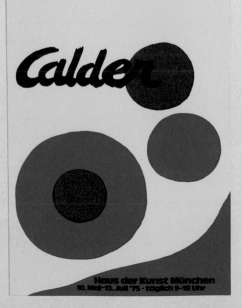

ABOVE: *Art in America*, 1962. Poster, 28½ × 19″. Collection of the author.

LEFT: *Calder*, 1975. Poster, 33 × 23¼″. Haus der Kunst, Munich.

Stabiles, 1963. Poster, 25½ × 19½″. Galerie Maeght, Paris.

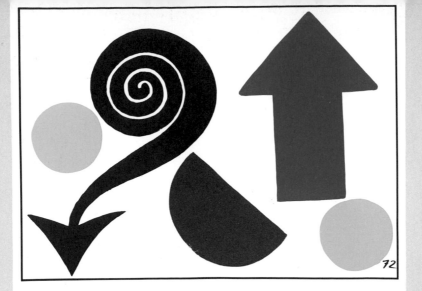

CALDER PAINTINGS/SCULPTURE/GRAPHICS oct. 15-nov. 16 HOKIN GALLERY, INC. 200 east ontario, chicago

Calder Paintings/Sculpture/Graphics, 1972. Poster, 24¼ × 29⅛″. Hokin Gallery, Chicago.

Calder, 1971. Poster, 18 × 21⅜″. Pace Gallery, Columbus, Ohio.

Terre des Hommes, 1974. Poster, 37⅜ × 23½″. Jean and Sandra Davidson, Saché, France.

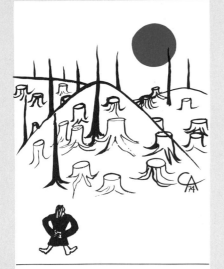

TERRE DES HOMMES

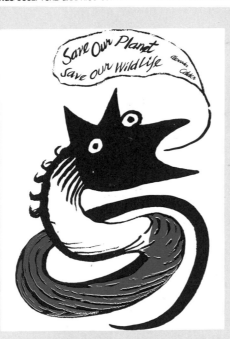

Save Our Planet, Save Our Wildlife, 1971. Poster, 29½ × 22″. Collection of author.

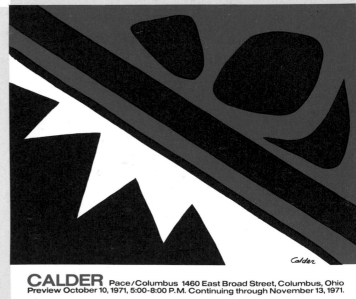

CALDER Pace/Columbus 1460 East Broad Street, Columbus, Ohio
Preview October 10, 1971, 5:00-8:00 P.M. Continuing through November 13, 1971.

Madison Square Boys Club, 1974. Poster, 30 × 24″. George Goodstadt Inc., New York.

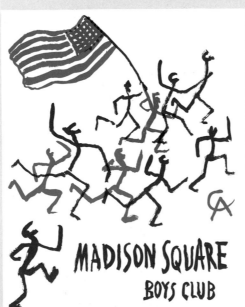

MADISON SQUARE BOYS CLUB

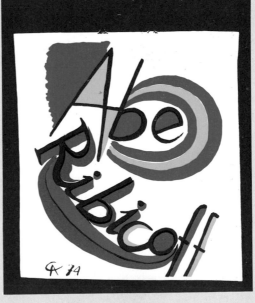

Abe Ribicoff, 1974. Plastic bag, 19 × 17″. People for Ribicoff, Hartford, Conn.

155

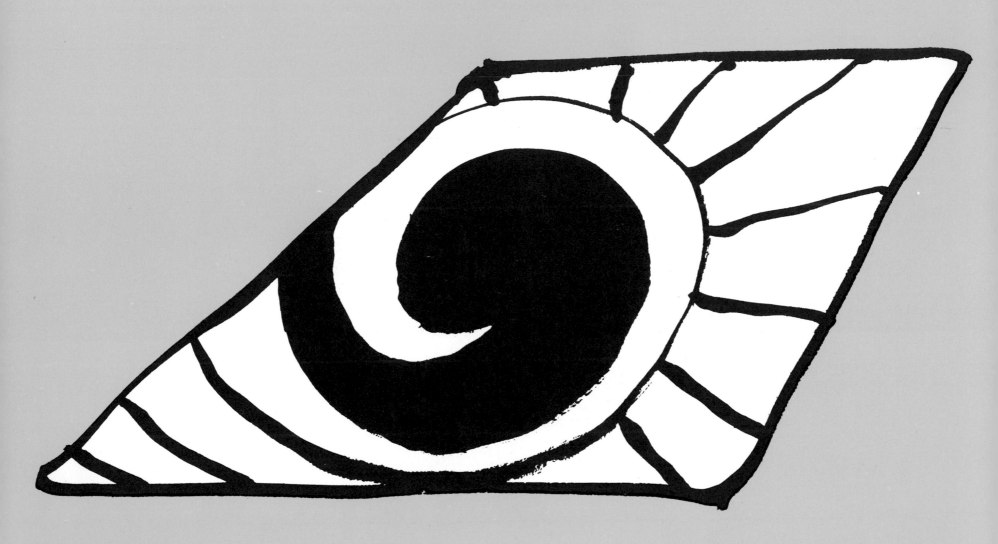

If you like what you give them, you have to like what you get back.

This is what Sandy said when I asked him how he felt about the way the Aubusson weavers interpret his exuberant tapestry designs. Since the early sixties he has made approximately fifty designs for execution by the skilled weavers of Aubusson and Felletin, two villages in the La Creuse area of France which have been famous for their tapestries since the Middle Ages.

In recent years many major artists, among them Calder's friend Miró, have created tapestry designs in the contemporary idiom, bringing fresh life to the ancient industry. Calder's interest began in 1960 when he designed a small Aubusson tapestry; this was followed in 1962 by a series of nine made under the direction of Pierre Baudoin. The following year Calder began working with the firm of Pinton Frères, one of the largest in the Aubusson region. His most monumental tapestry, measuring eight by twenty feet, was commissioned in 1973 by the IBM Corporation.

Calder prepares his tapestry designs in color on sheets of paper the size of his large gouaches. These function as maquettes, being mechanically enlarged to the size of the finished tapestry. The wools, imported from Australia, are dyed in Calder's brilliant, pure colors and spun, on a spinning wheel, onto large spools; the thread is transferred, as needed, from the spools to small bobbins, or flutes. Using these, the weaver follows the enlarged design which is placed beneath the loom so as to be visible through the warp threads. It takes about a month for a weaver to produce a square yard of tapestry. French law limits Aubusson tapestries to editions of six, plus two proofs for the artist. (Calder's IBM tapestry, however, was executed as a unique example; and the French government authorized special editions of two hundred for a set of six small tapestries which Calder designed in connection with the bicentennial celebration of the American Revolution.) Both Calder's signature and the weaver's trademark are woven into the fabric, with the number of the edition. Only one from an edition is executed at a time, on order, so there are variations in each example.

Calder's tapestries are closely related to his gouaches, but they are much larger and often more complex in design. As in all his work the compositions are deceptively casual and have the same playful element that enlivens even the most powerful of his abstractions. The tapestry medium—like lithography and large-scale sculpture—is an example of the successful collaboration with skilled craftsmen that has characterized Calder's later years. The weaver follows Calder's forms exactly but improvises to vary the weaves and textures in a free interpretation of the overall design. The tapestries are fresh works of art in their own right, blending the inventiveness of the artist with that of the weavers.

Tapestries and Rugs

157

Calder's rugs are cooperative ventures too. Like most of his jewelry, they have not been made for sale, only for the use of family and friends—with the exception of two editions of rugs, a project initiated by Marie Cuttoli, whom Calder has known since he exhibited his first mechanized sculpture at her Galerie Vignon in Paris in 1932. Sandy has been interested in rugmaking since the fifties, and Louisa has made a large number in cut wool, hooked and knotted, from her husband's designs. When Calder designs a rug, he outlines the elements on the canvas in black gouache, with a brush, and marks each color area at the same time—R for red, Y for yellow, and so forth. Some broad outlines are designed to be executed in black. Verbal instructions for the rugmaker, as well as design indications on the canvas, are simple and clear. He now also marks his formal initialed signature and date, to be hooked in black. Calder is freer in his use of color for the rug designs than for the gouaches; one executed by my husband has an unusual pale blue background for a yellow moon and a red man.

Louisa's rugs in the new Saché house.

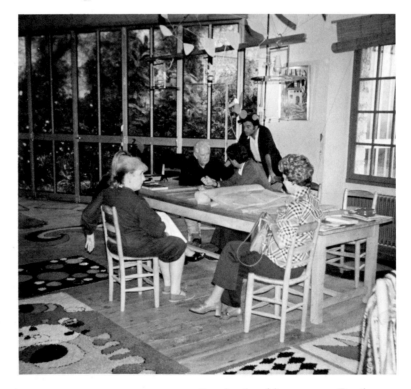

158

OPPOSITE: Louisa hooking a rug, Roxbury.

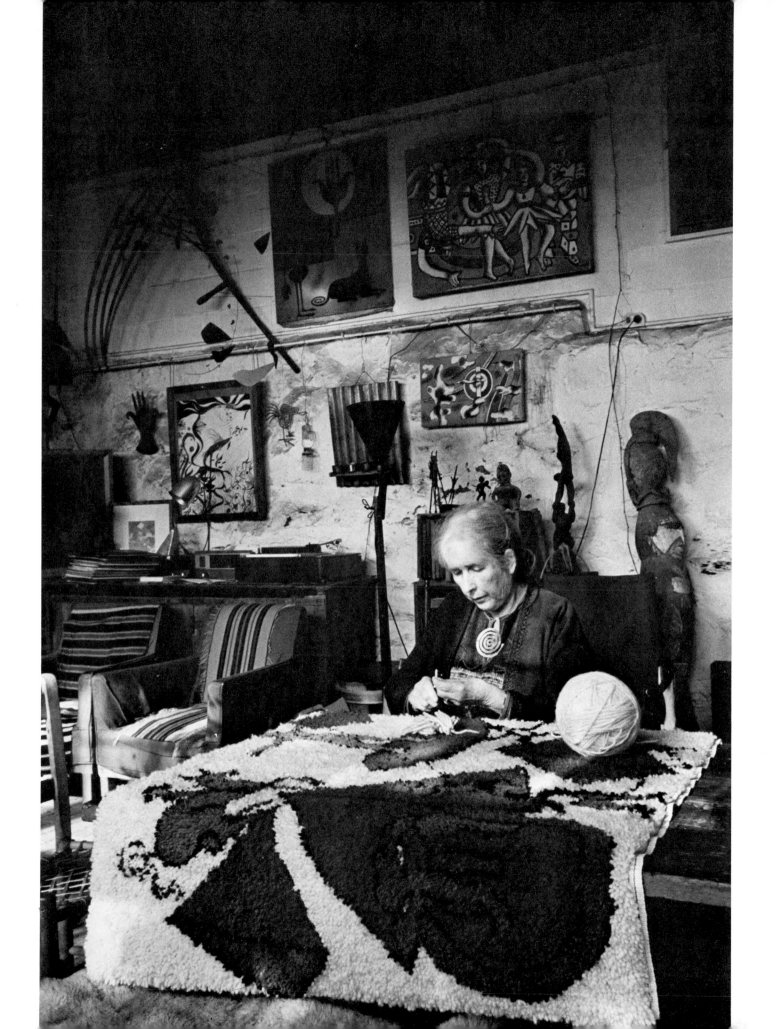

Spider, c. 1950. Wool rug, 5′ × 6′6″.
Jean and Sandra Davidson, Saché, France.

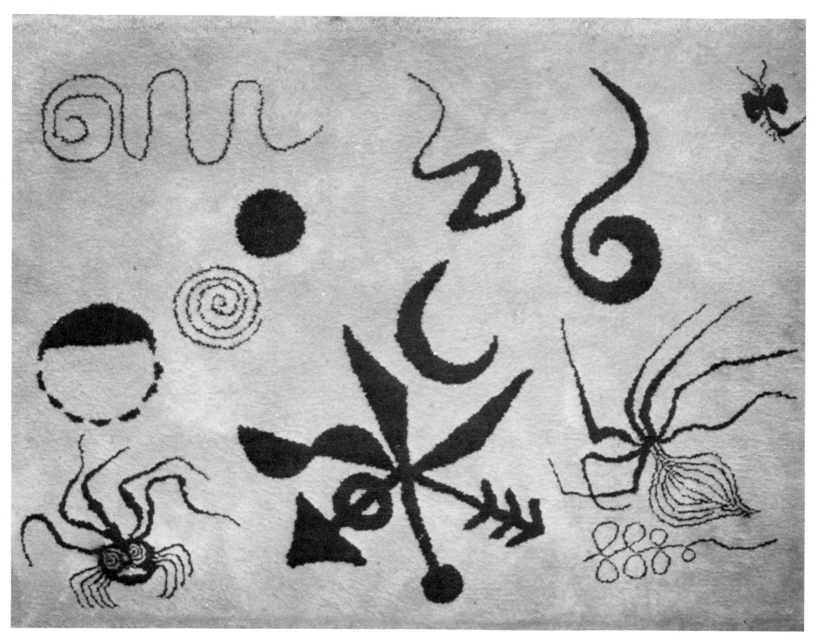

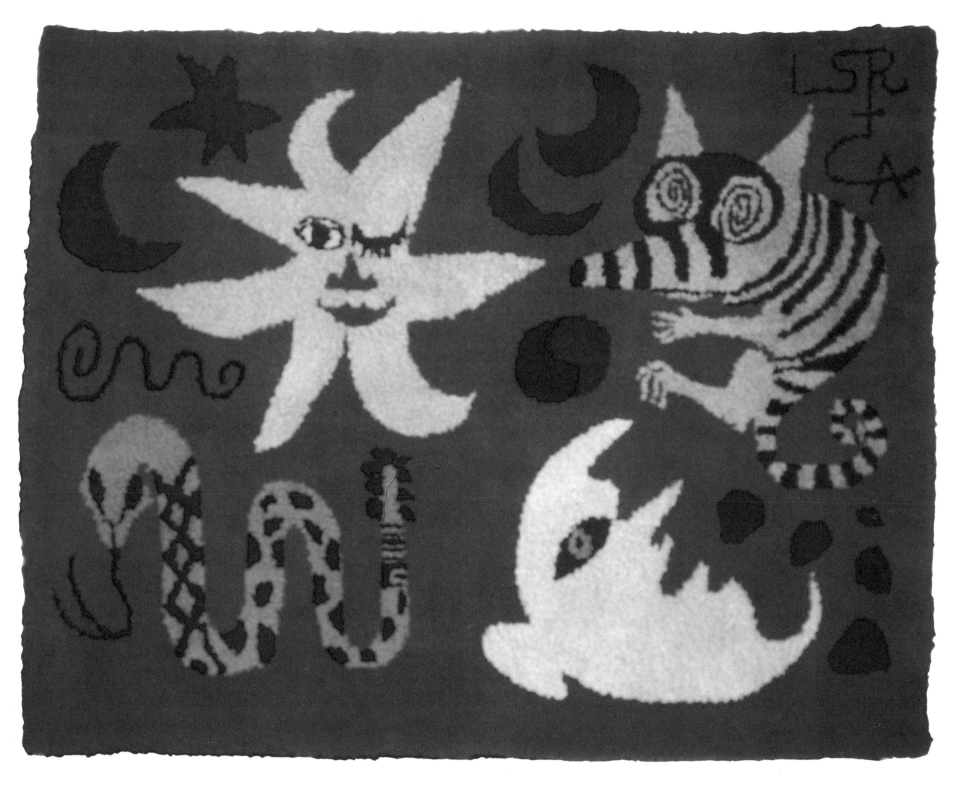

Untitled, 1965. Wool rug made by Leslie Stillman, 5′6″ x
6′10″. Mr. and Mrs. Rufus Stillman, Litchfield, Connecticut.

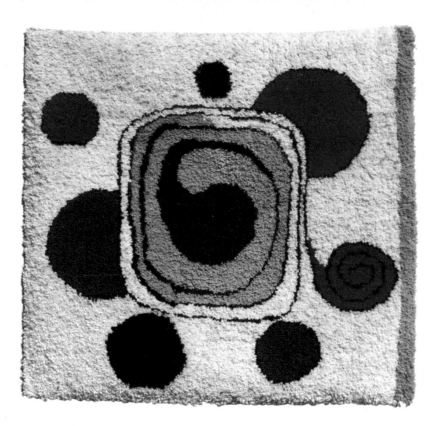

Square, 1974. Wool rug made by Louisa Calder, 36 × 36″. Collection of the artist.

Man and the Moon, 1974. Wool rug made by Howard Lipman, 32½ × 41½″. Collection of the author.

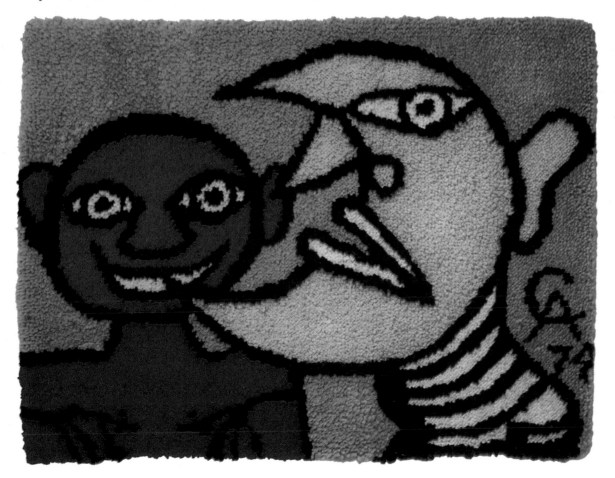

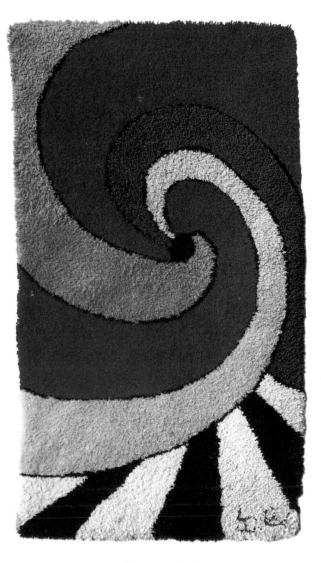

Spiral, 1972. Wool rug made by Louisa Calder, 3 × 6′. Collection of the artist.

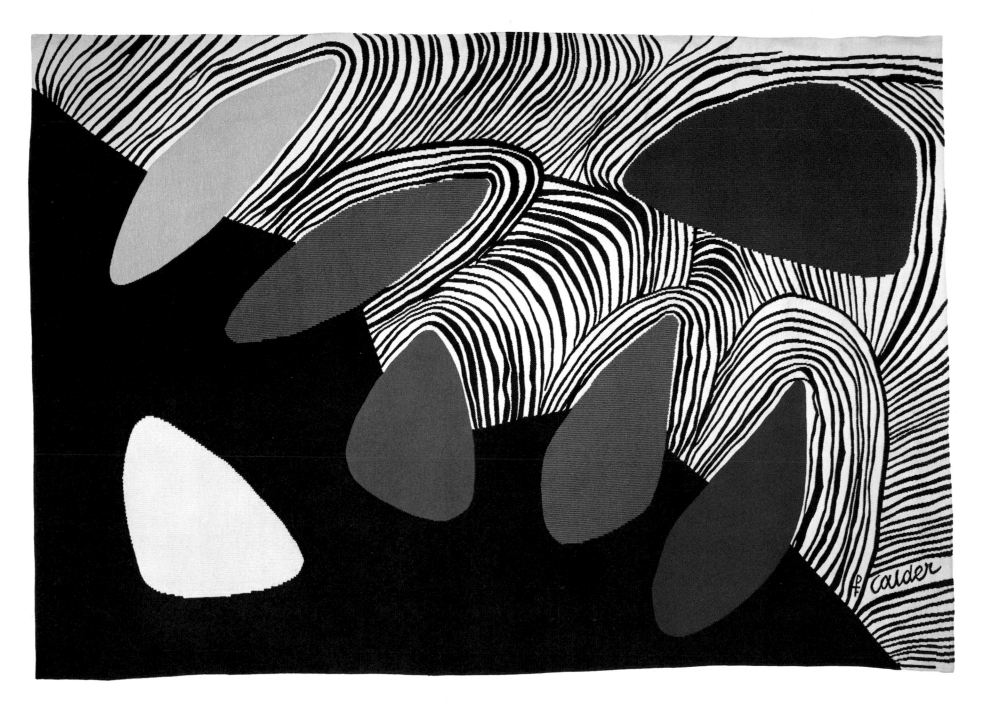

Glacier with Colored Petals, 1971. Aubusson tapestry, 5′6″
× 7′9½″. Whitney Museum of American Art, New York;
gift of the Howard and Jean Lipman Foundation.

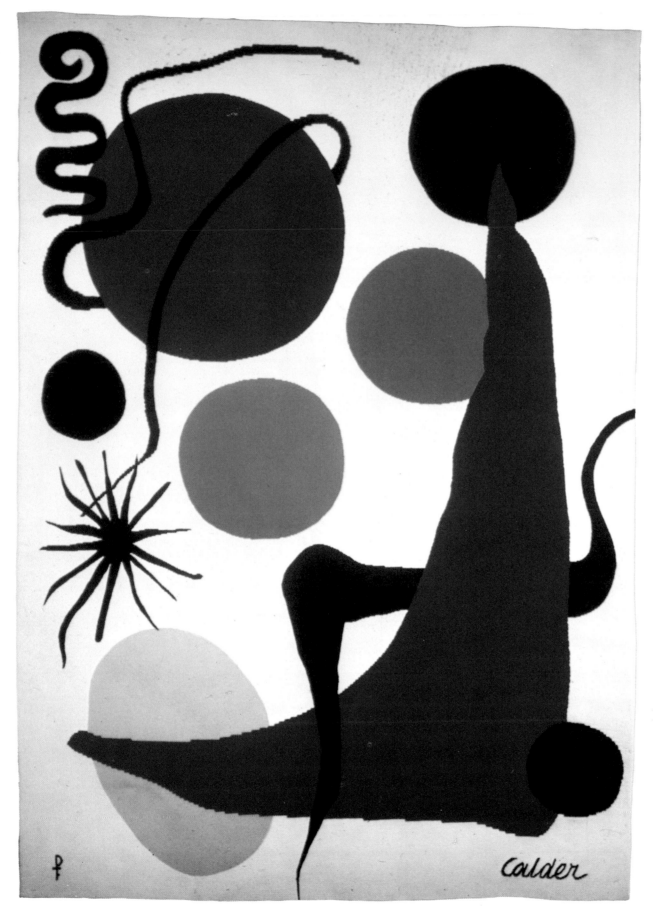

Green Ball, 1971. Aubusson tapestry, 6′7″ × 4′6½″. Shirley Polykoff, New York.

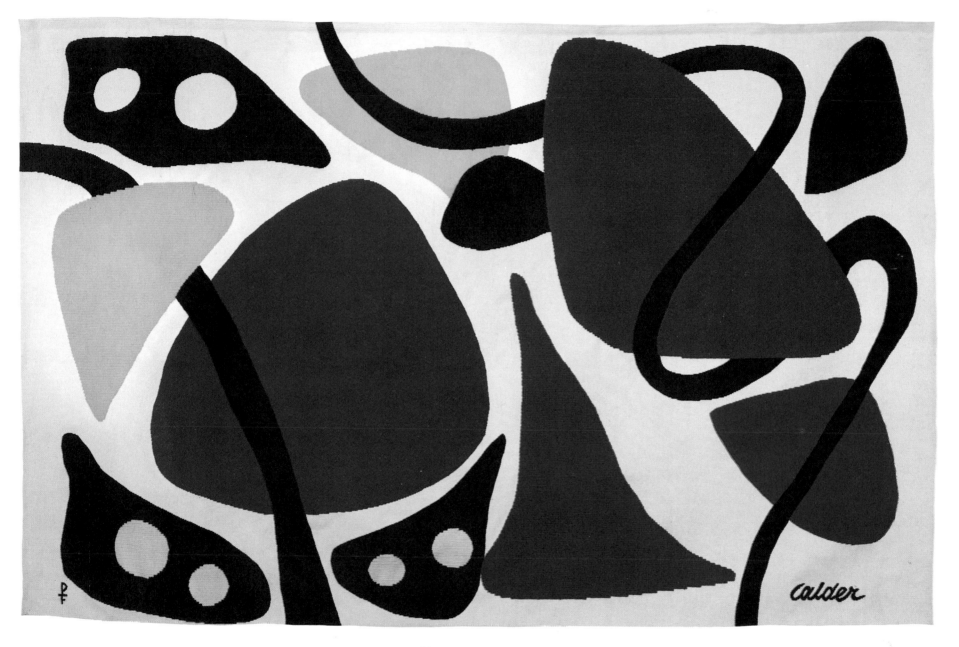

Les Masques, 1971. Aubusson tapestry, 5′4″ × 8′2″. Whitney Museum of American Art, New York; gift of the Howard and Jean Lipman Foundation.

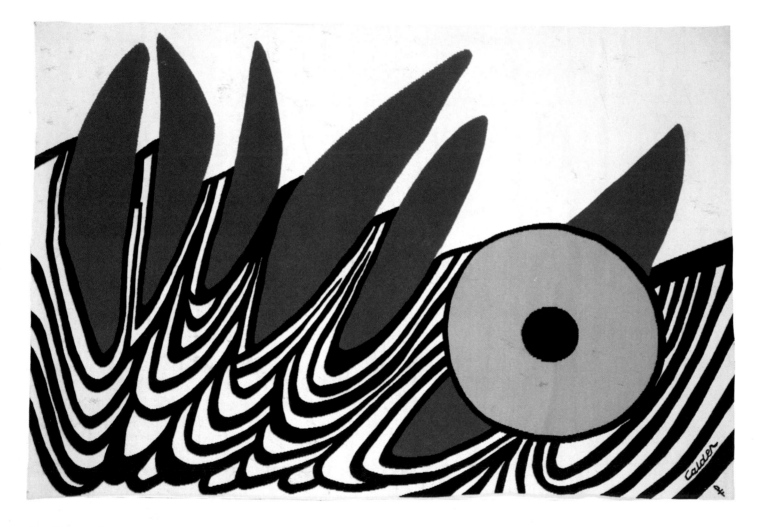

Six Dents Rouges, 1973. Aubusson tapestry, 5'2" ×
7'6". Art Vivant, Inc., New Rochelle, New York.

Une Floppée de Soleils, 1973. Aubusson tapestry, 8 × 20'. IBM Corporation, Armonk, New York.

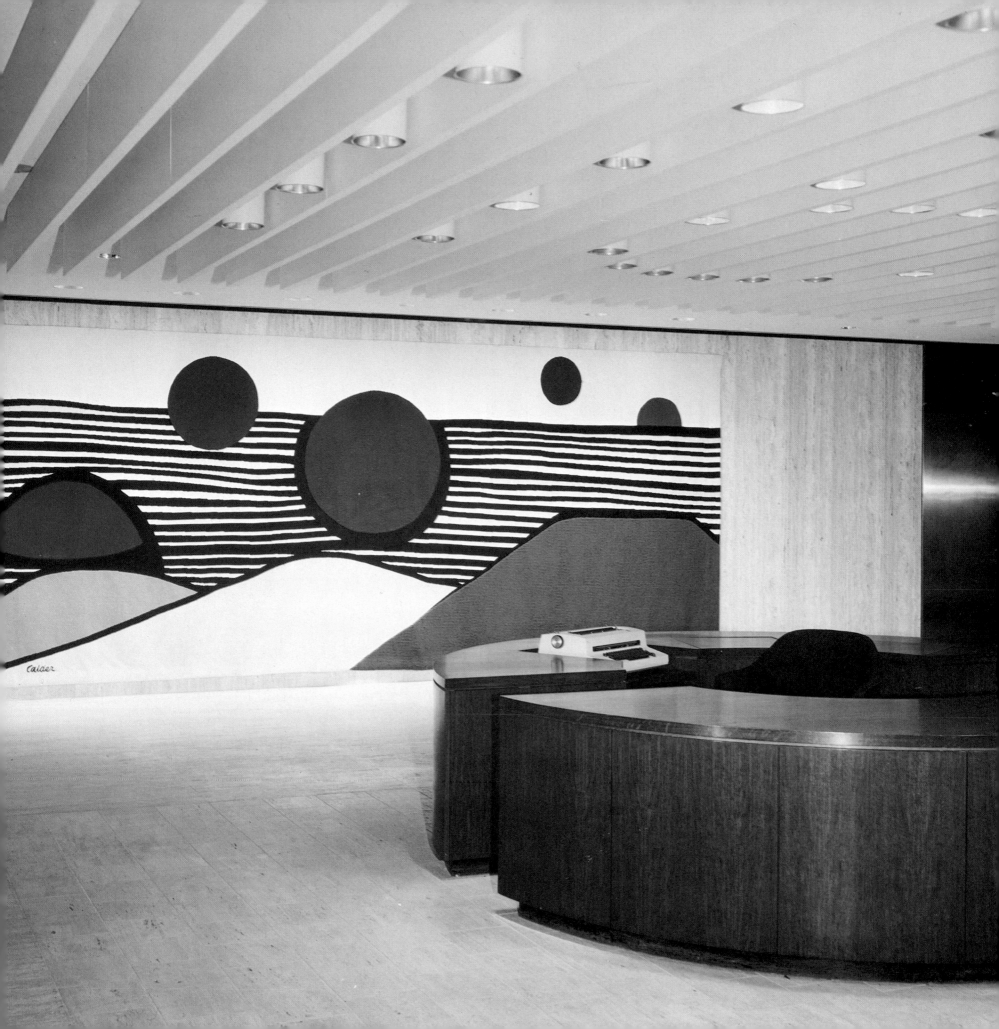

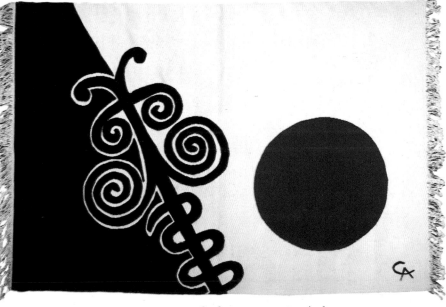

Signs, 1962. Aubusson tapestry, 15⅜ × 21¾". Galerie Maeght, Paris.

Mouth, 1962. Aubusson tapestry, 29⅛ × 41⅜". Galerie Maeght, Paris.

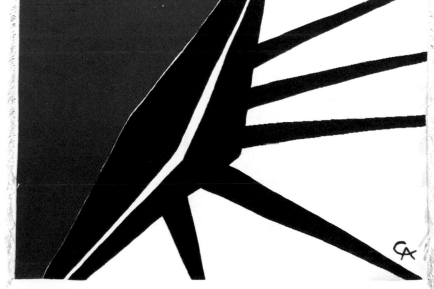

Caduceus, 1962. Aubusson tapestry, 28¾ × 41⅞". Galerie Maeght, Paris.

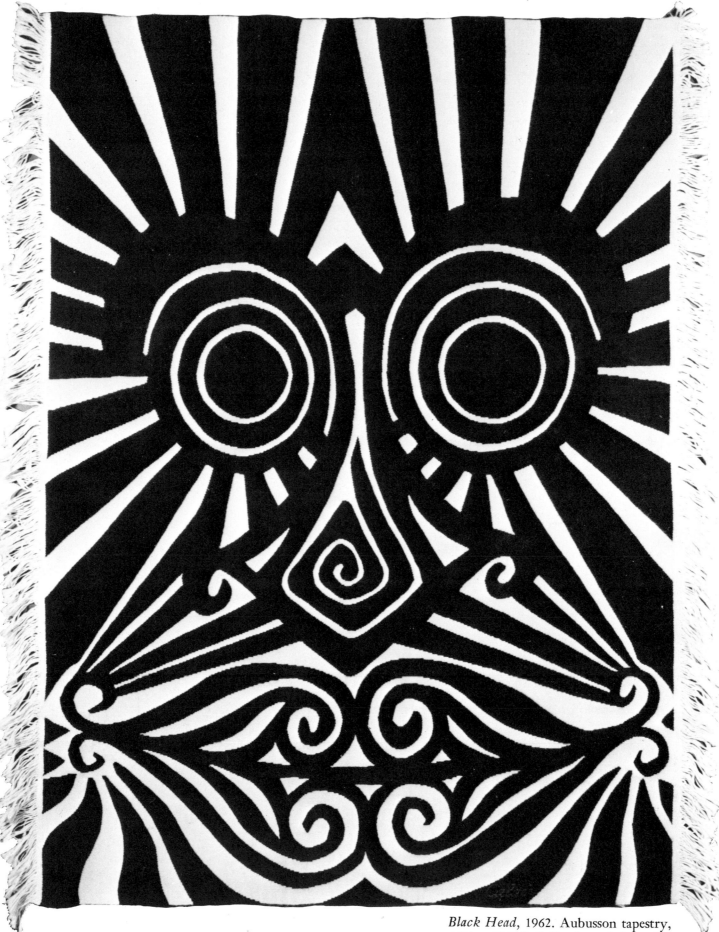

Black Head, 1962. Aubusson tapestry,
41½ × 29⅛". Collection of the artist.

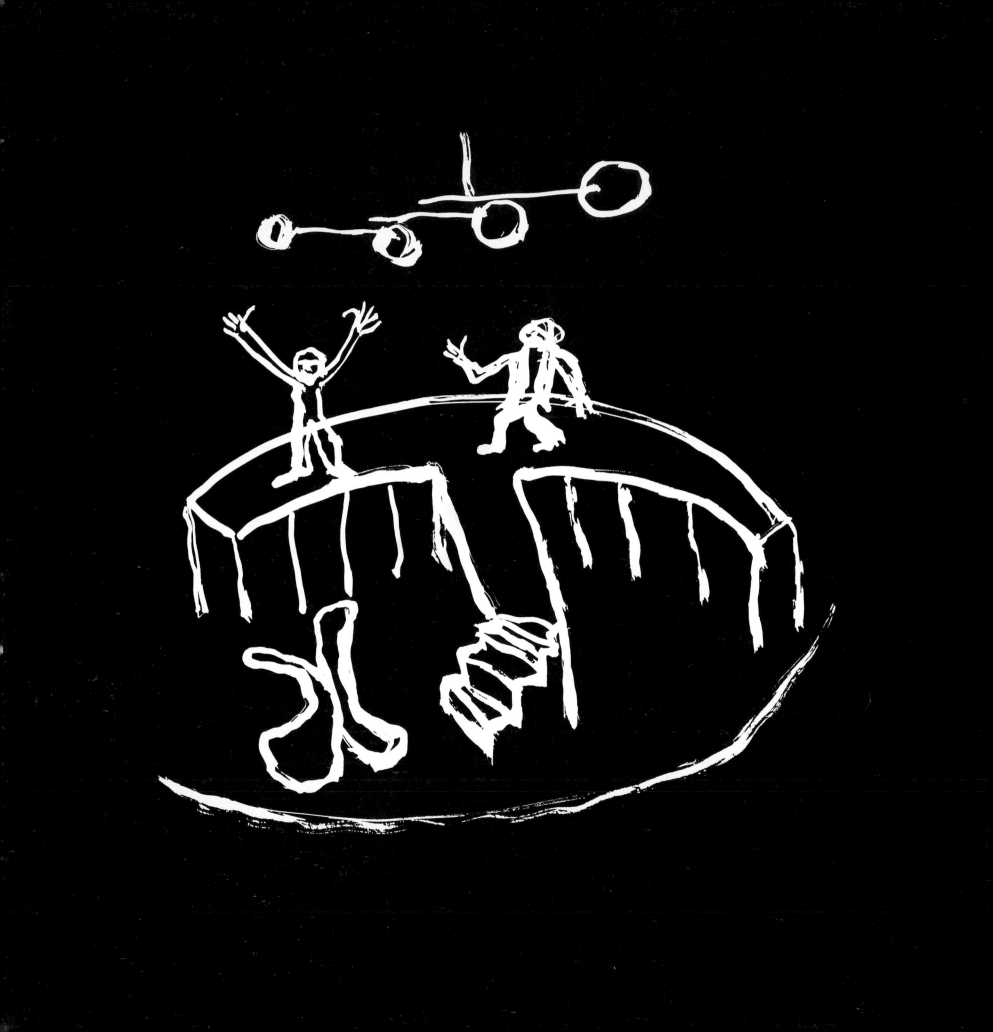

Maybe I should have called it [Work in Progress] *"My Life in Nineteen Minutes."*

Calder has created stage sets for more than a dozen various kinds of theatrical productions in the course of his career. Because these are the least known of his works—especially in the United States—it is worthwhile to list them all here, in chronological sequence:

Mobiles for Martha Graham's *Panorama* in Bennington, Vermont, in 1935 and for her *Horizons* in New York in 1936.

Mobile set for a production of Erik Satie's 1920 symphonic drama, *Socrate*, at the Wadsworth Atheneum, Hartford, Connecticut, in 1936. (Restaged in New York in conjunction with the exhibition *Calder's Universe*; a subsequent tour of the United States is planned.)

Mobiles for *Balloons*, a play by Padraic Colum, produced in Boston in 1946.

Mobiles for *Symphonic Variations*, a ballet by Tatiana Leskova with music by César Franck, performed in Rio de Janeiro in 1949.

Mobiles and other effects for the play *Happy as Larry* by Donagh MacDonagh, produced by Burgess Meredith in New York in 1950.

Sets for Henri Pichette's *Nucléa*, produced by the Théâtre National Populaire in Paris, 1952.

A stabile and a mobile for *The Glory Folk*, a ballet by John Butler performed in Spoleto, Italy, in 1962.

Sets for *La Provocation*, a ballet by Pierre Halet with music by Jean Ferrat, produced at the Comédie de Bourges, France, in 1963.

Sets for *Eppur Si Muove*, a ballet by Joseph Lazzini with music by Francis Miroglio, at the Marseilles Opera in 1965.

A mobile for *Calder Piece*, composed by Earle Brown and first performed by Diego Masson's orchestra at the Théâtre de l'Atelier, Paris, 1967. (The mobile, titled *Chef d'Orchestre*, functions both as a "conductor" determining the sequence and speed of the music, and as one of the instruments "played" by the four percussion musicians.)

Work in Progress, a "ballet" originated by Calder featuring hanging and standing mobiles, stabiles, and huge backdrops painted in gouache; the project was initiated by Giovanni Carandente and produced with electronic music by Niccolò Castiglione, Aldo Clementi and Bruno Maderna at the Rome Opera House, 1968.

Sets for *Métaboles*, a ballet by Joseph Lazzini, music by Henri Dutilleux, produced by the Théâtre Français de la Danse, at the Odéon, Paris, 1969.

Costumes and sets for *Amériques*, a ballet by Norbert Schmuki, music by Edgard Varèse, performed by the Ballet-Théâtre Contemporain in Amiens, France, in 1971.

A sense of drama is evident in much of Calder's work, and his predilection for strong color, movement and large scale led naturally to the theater. Some close observers of his work believe that he has not yet fully explored his capacities for theatrical inven-

Theatrical Productions

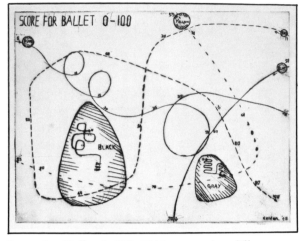

Score for Ballet 0–100, 1942, engraving. The Museum of Modern Art, New York.

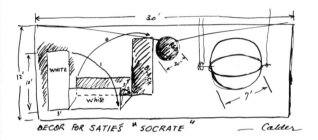

Calder's sketch of stage set for *Socrate*, published in *The Painter's Object*, 1937.

tion. When asked about his theatrical work, Calder singled out five productions as his favorites: *Nucléa*, his first theatrical work in Paris; the two Martha Graham productions; *Socrate*; and *Work in Progress*. The last four involved much more than designing stage props, costumes or accessories. No doubt they hold special meaning for Calder because they included performances in which he was the director and his sculptures the performers—just as he was the animator of his Circus troupe.

The art historian Albert Elsen recently observed that Calder's role "as a composer rather than initiator of movement in space . . . is not sufficiently recognized and appreciated." When Calder first became interested in developing an art based on actual motion—rather than an illusion of motion—he thought in terms directly related to musical composition or choreography, for music and the dance possessed the fourth dimension, time, that was missing from traditional sculpture. In an early essay (written before he became reluctant to commit his ideas to print), Calder commended the work of the Futurists, as well as Duchamp's *Nude Descending a Staircase* and Léger's 1924 abstract film *Ballet méchanique*, for their efforts to bring motion to art. Then he asks: ". . . why not plastic forms in motion? Not a simple translatory or rotary motion, but several motions of different types, speeds and amplitudes composing to make a resultant whole. Just as one can compose colors, or forms, so one can compose motions." In 1931 he began making motorized sculptures that follow a sequence of movements through a specific period of time, as dancers move through the steps of a ballet. Calder was making art that performed, and in this sense both the mechanized sculptures and his water ballet projects—illustrated and discussed in later chapters—could be considered theatrical works.

In discussing his moving sculpture, Calder sometimes used the analogy to dance: "I went to the use of motion for its contrapuntal value, as in good choreography." It is perhaps no coincidence that dancing plays an important role in Sandy's leisure activities. He has always enjoyed social dancing and, at times, performs solo to the accompaniment of Louisa's accordion. In his autobiography he reminisces happily about fraternity dances at Stevens Institute and about bringing samba records back from Rio and teaching his Roxbury neighbors the new Latin dance. On the *Flying Colors* inaugural flight in 1973, parties held during stopovers nearly always culminated in dancing, led by Sandy and Louisa.

As always, one learns most about Calder's art from his own comment. In his illuminating article "Mobiles," published in 1937, he describes the production of Satie's *Socrate* in exact detail:

There is no dancing in it. It is sung by two people—a man and a woman. The singing is the main thing in it. The proscenium opening was 12 feet by 30 feet. There were three elements in the setting. As seen from the audience, there was a red disc about 30 inches across, left center. Near the left edge there was a vertical rectangle, 3 feet by 10 feet, standing on the floor. Towards the right, there were two 7 foot steel hoops at right angles on a horizontal spindle, with a hook one end and a pulley the other, so that it could be rotated in either direction, and raised and lowered. The whole dialogue was divided into three parts: 9, 9, and 18 minutes long. During the first part the red disc moved continuously to the extreme right, then to the extreme left (on cords) and then returned to its original position, the whole operation taking 9 minutes. In the second section there was a minute at the beginning with no movement at all, then the steel hoops started to rotate toward the audience, and after about three more minutes they were lowered towards the floor. Then they stopped, and started to rotate again in the opposite direction. Then in the original direction. Then they moved upwards again. That completed the second section. In the third, the vertical white rectangle tilted gently over to the right until it rested on the ground, on its long edge. Then there was a pause. Then it fell over slowly away from the audience, face on the floor. Then it came up again with the other face towards the audience; and that face was black. Then it rose into a vertical position again, still black, and moved away towards the right.

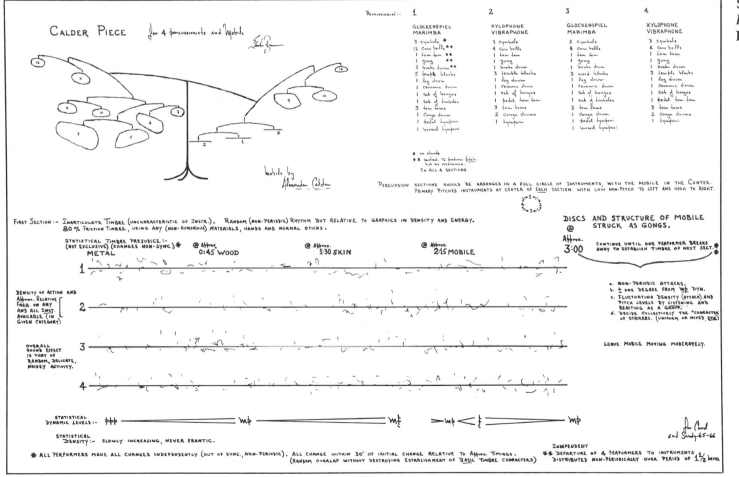

Score for *Calder Piece*, composed by Earle Brown, 1967.

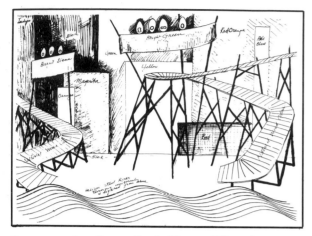

Stage set for Scene I of *00 to AH*, published in *Transition*, 1937 (never produced).

Then, just at the end, the red disc moved off to the left. The whole thing was very gentle, and subservient to the music and the words.

The Satie–Calder collaboration is an interesting one. The Dutch art historian A. M. Hammacher has pointed out that "Satie's place in music, anchored in the circus and the music hall, altogether removed from pompousness and self-importance, anti-Romantic and unconventional, is related to Calder's role in sculpture as representing free and unpretentious spatial play in life."

Calder's contribution to Martha Graham's *Panorama* was an arrangement of overhead discs which the dancers pulled by lines attached to their wrists. This was his solution to the problem of getting moving sculpture into a dance in an organic way. (*The New York Times* reviewer was kind in his comment on the production as a whole and most enthusiastic about Calder's dancer-pulled discs.) Graham's *Horizons*—the theme is the colonizing of new territory—was divided into four sections (it is sometimes referred to by the title *Four Movements*). To set the mood for each section, Calder designed "plastic interludes." These were large versions of his motorized Panels of the thirties (see "Mechanized Sculpture") in which circles and spirals spun around on the empty stage. He described the origin of these ideas in the article "Mobiles":

For a couple of years in Paris I had a small ballet-object, built on a table with pulleys at the top of a frame. It was possible to move colored discs across the rectangle, or fluttering pennants, or cones; to make them dance, or even have battles between them. Some of them had large, simple, majestic movements; others were small and agitated. I tried it also in the open air, swung between trees on ropes, and later Martha Graham and I projected a ballet on these lines. For me, increase in size—working full-scale in this way—is very interesting. I once saw a movie made in a marble quarry, and the delicacy of movement of the great masses of marble, imposed of necessity by their great weight, was very handsome. My idea with the mechanical ballet was to do it independently of dancers, or without them altogether, and I devised a graphic method of registering the ballet movements, with the trajectories marked with different colored chalks or crayons.

The idea of doing a ballet "independently of dancers, or without them altogether" never lost its fascination. In 1942 Calder made a sketchy engraving of a score for an imaginary ballet, with colored discs as the "dancers." It was not until the late sixties, when he was asked to do a production for the Rome Opera House, that Calder was able to mount a full-scale theatrical production of his own. A *Newsweek* report described *Work in Progress*, with Calder's comments, the week after it was produced:

The nineteen-minute work is a cosmic romp that begins with a galaxy of mobiles high above the stage like the universe before genesis. On the white screen of Part Two, the blue line of the sea is projected, across which swim black sea creatures and a giant red

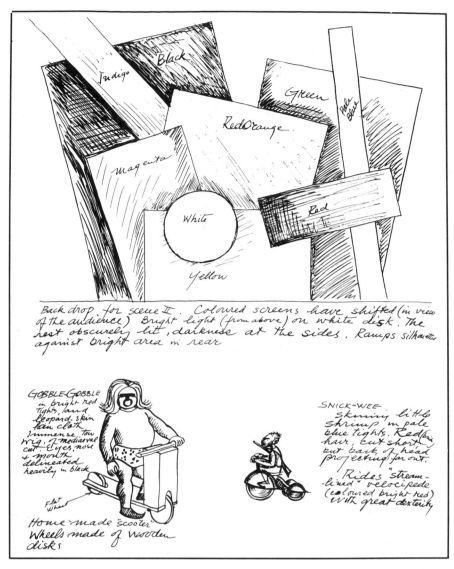

Sketches for Scene II of *00 to AH*.

starfish. The firmament has been divided. Then comes land, with birds of every hue, followed by man—fourteen bicyclists in brightly colored stretch suits.

FINALE: In the next to last part, dominated by a black pyramid and an enormous jolly sun beneath which a man waved a long red flag, Calder seemed to be noting the first stirrings of religion and politics. "Several people suggested I change the flag's color," says Calder. "I think red's the only color. There's no social significance." In his finale, a heaven and earth of mobiles and stabiles, of objects seeking and finding innocent and joyful communion, Calder once more affirmed his faith in the human spirit and his belief that art is the highest expression of man's imagination.

The Roman audience responded enthusiastically. Novelist Alberto Moravia said: "As a sculptor he revealed a great sense of theater. It was done with delicacy, with elegance, or maybe the word I mean is magic." Calder's new work is not only cosmogonical but personal, reflecting in the circusy bike riders and in the several replicas of past mobiles his creative life from its beginning. "Maybe I should have called it 'My Life in Nineteen Minutes,' " said the artist.

175

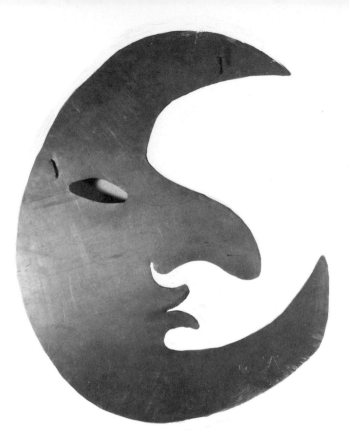

Stage set for *Nucléa*, play by Henri Pichette, presented in Paris, 1952.

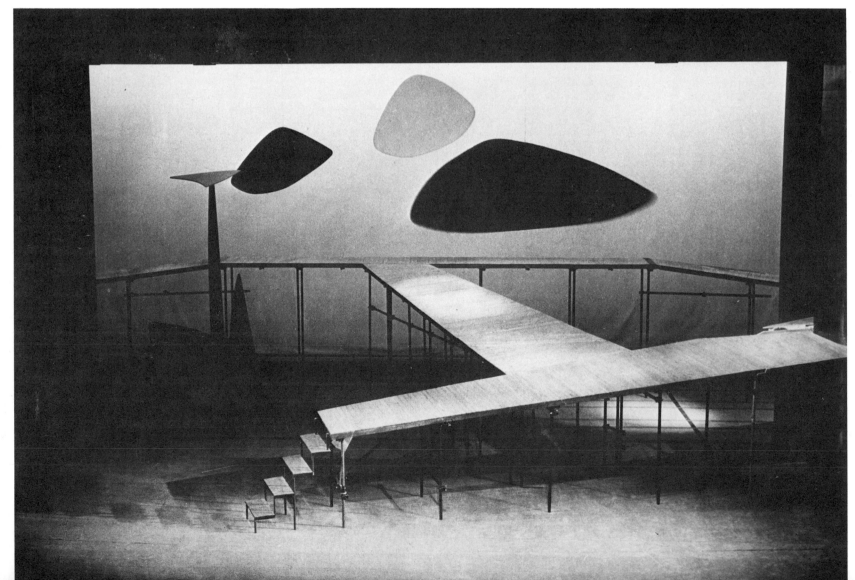

176

Stage props for *Happy as Larry*, play by Donagh MacDonagh, presented in New York, 1950. *Moon*, sheet metal, 33 × 26″, Perls Galleries, New York. *Sun*, painted sheet metal, 35 × 35″, Perls Galleries, New York. *Horse's Head*, sheet metal, 18 × 48″, William John Upjohn, Kalamazoo, Michigan.

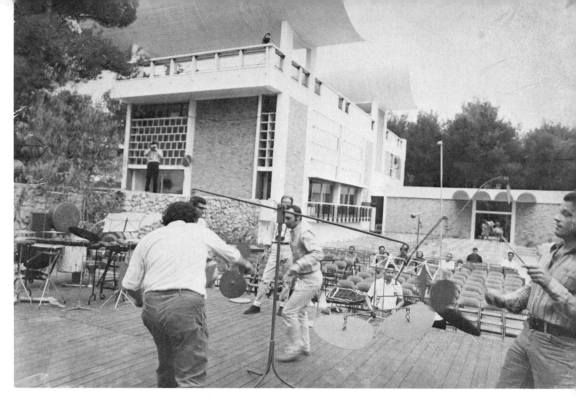

Rehearsal of *Calder Piece*, conducted by Diego Masson, with the mobile *Chef d'Orchestre*, Fondation Maeght, Saint-Paul-de-Vence, France, 1967.

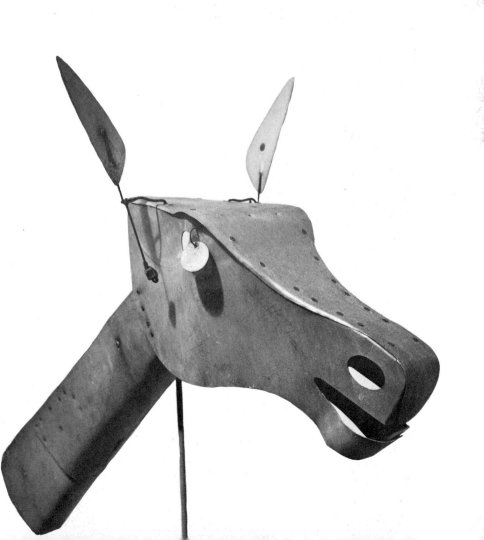

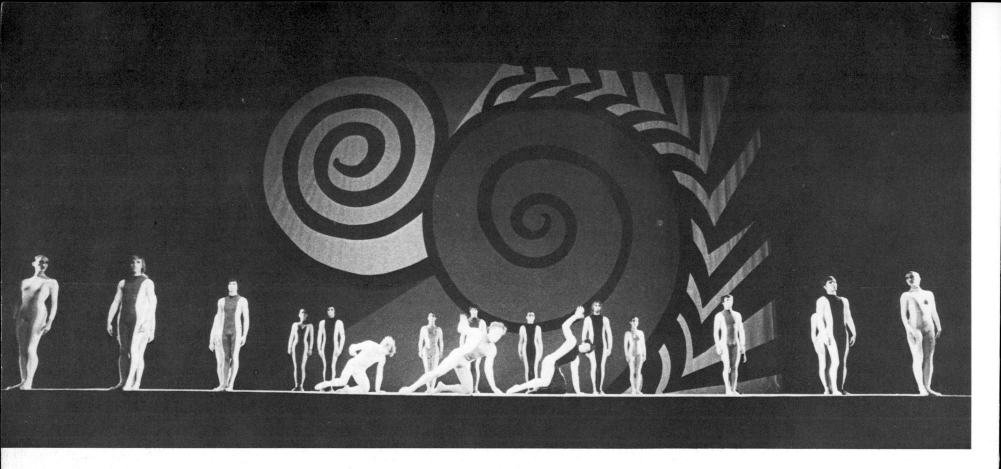

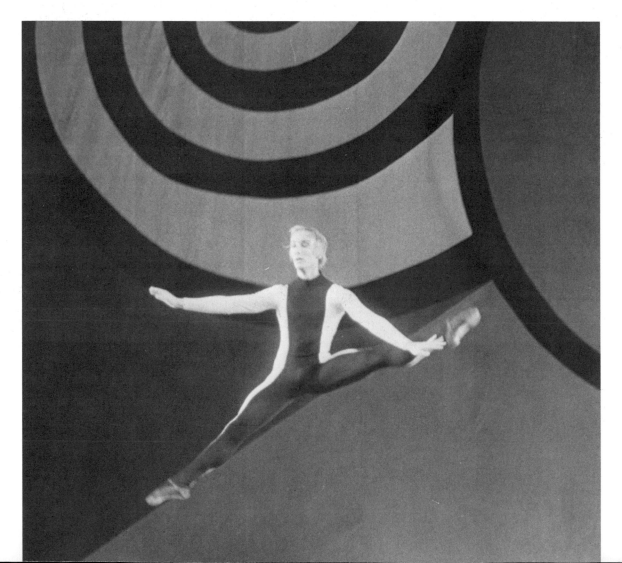

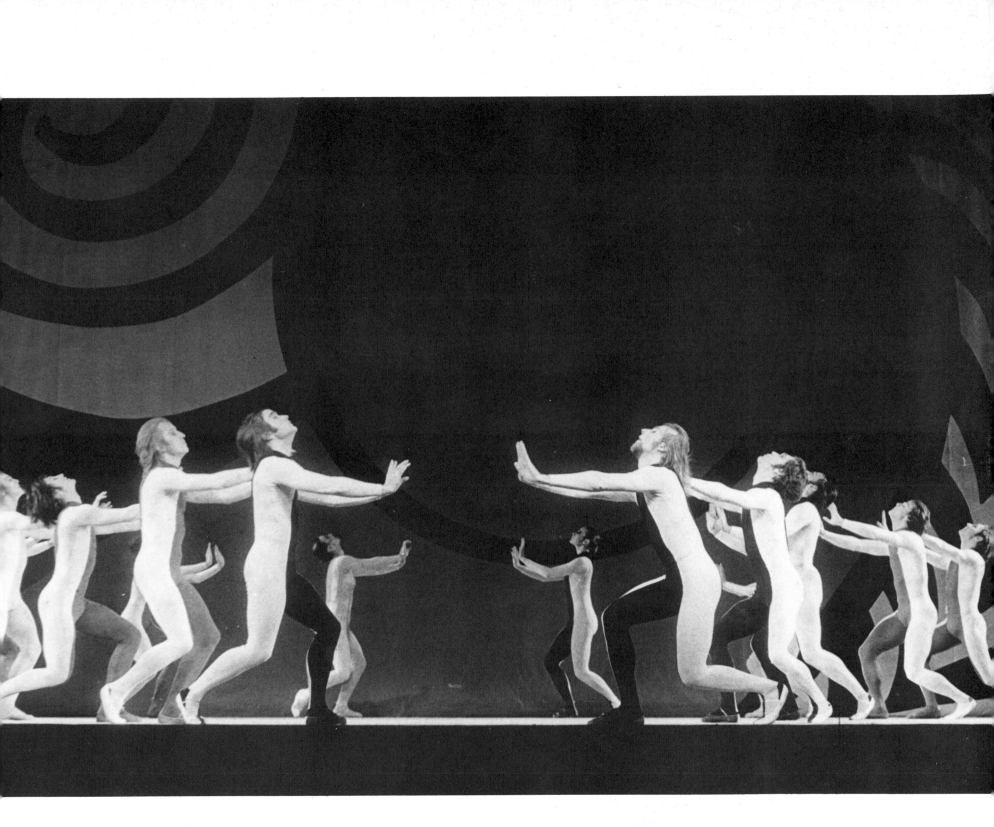

Stage set and costumes for *Amériques*, performed by the Ballet-Théâtre Contemporain, Amiens, France, 1971.

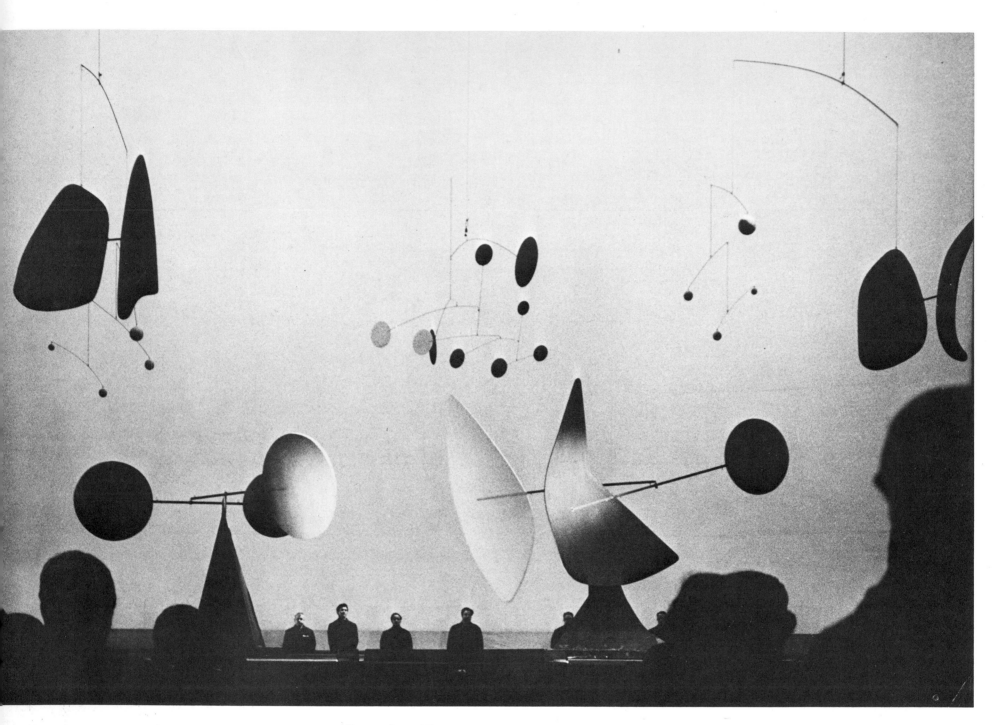

Scenes from *Work in Progress*, presented at the Rome Opera House, 1968.

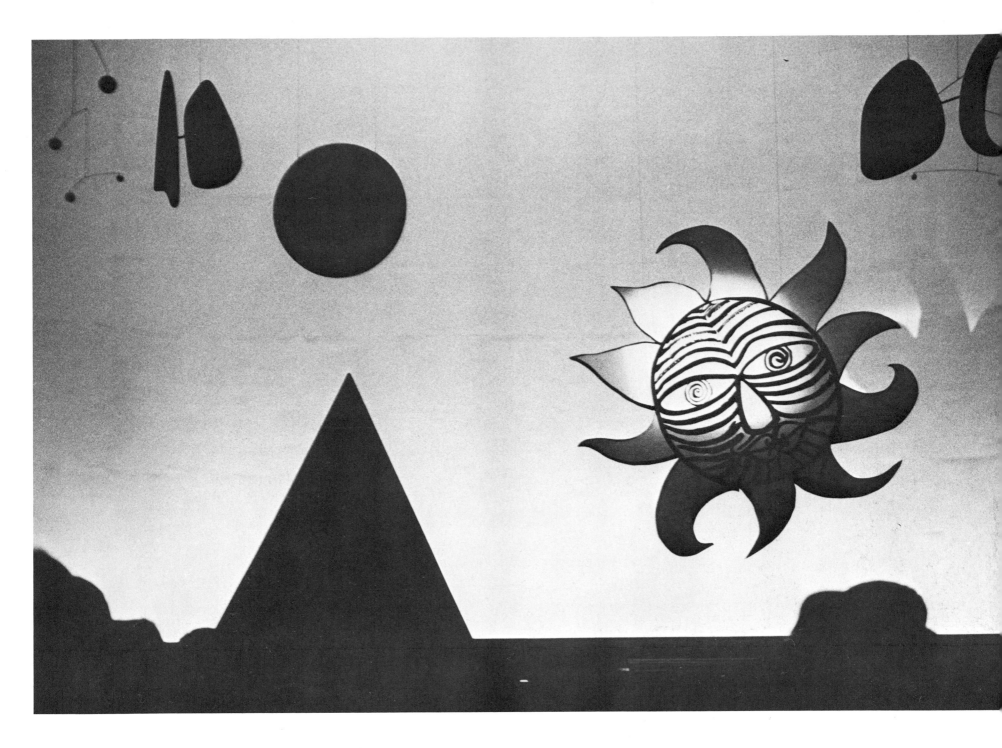

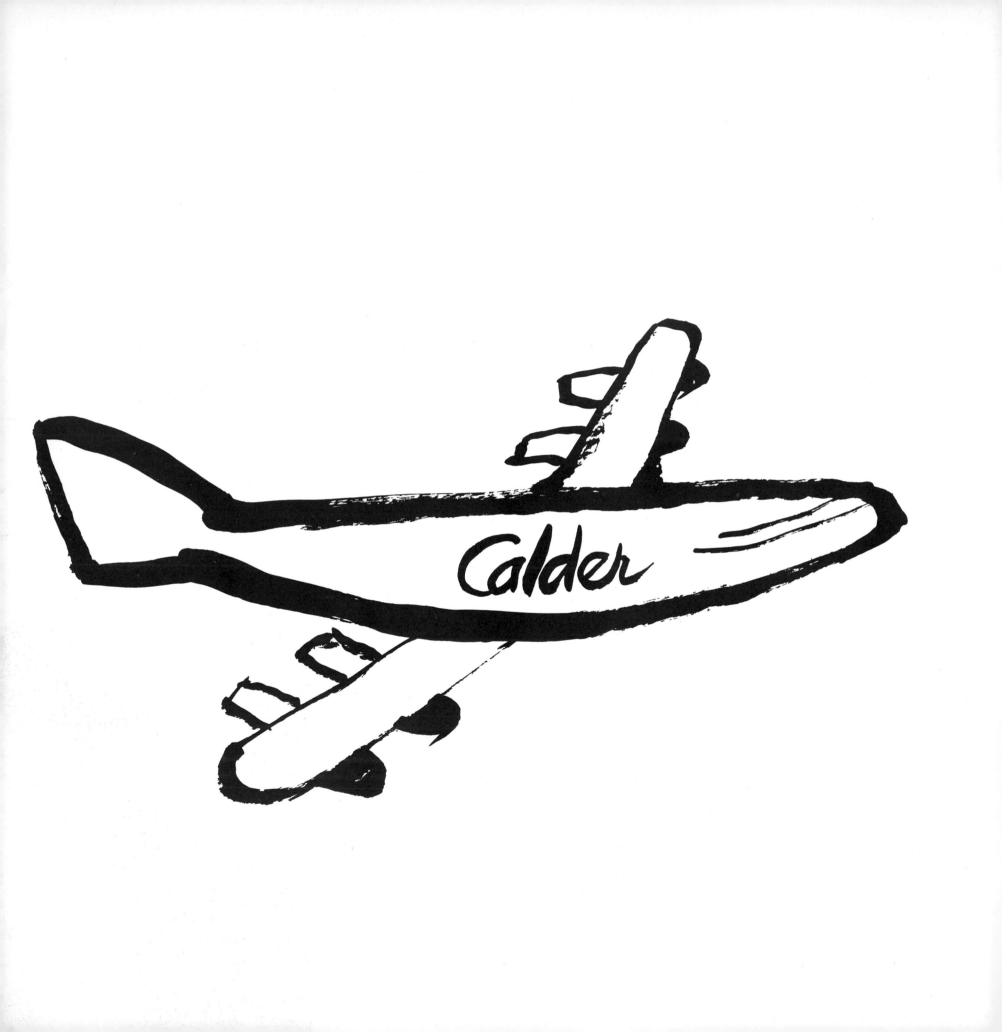

I like to work in any medium where I am free to do as I choose.

All one should need to say to introduce the various species of whatchama-Calders (a term recently coined by a newspaper reporter) is: Look at the illustrations and read the captions. But it is impossible to show all the original, unclassifiable objects Calder has made, many of which are long lost (and never intended for posterity). Here are Sandy's descriptions of a few:

One of the first animals I made was out of a loaf of bread. You know those long thin loaves called *ficelles*. I made a bird out of it. I showed it to José de Creeft. But the trouble was when I went to get it again the rats ate it—it was gone. [In 1929 *The New Yorker* reported another bread sculpture: "Conversation lagging one night at a dinner party in Paris some three years ago, Mr. Alexander Calder amused his table companion by making a chicken out of a piece of bread and a hairpin."]

[The stage designer Joseph] Urban had an assistant, Sheppard Vogelgesang. Sheppard wanted me to make a spider that would run up and down the tower wall. The main part of the spider was a float from a toilet tank; the rest of it was wire and shining glass objects borrowed from bicycles and automobiles.

Curt Valentin (then Calder's dealer) planned a birthday party for which Alfred Barr was to supply the cake and Sandy to design a candle:

I took two plumber's candles for the legs and one for the torso; the shoulders and arms were made by a fourth candle, and the head was the butt end of a burnt plumber's candle. The penis I made with the stump of an ordinary red candle.
All the wicks were carved clean so they could be lit, and when we proceeded to do this the revelation was disastrous. Apparently, red wax burns quickest.

One work that needs much more than a caption to describe it is the *Mercury Fountain* Calder made in 1937 for the Spanish Pavilion at the World's Fair in Paris (a journalist gave him the wonderful pseudonym Calderón de la Fuente). This work demonstrates Calder's innovative use of material and movement, his dual activity as engineer and artist, his spirit of play, all ingredients of a fascinating technical feat. Calder recently told Maurice Bruzeau that, with the Circus, he liked the *Mercury Fountain* as well as anything he had done.
Josep Lluis Sert, one of the architects of the Pavilion, has described how the commission came about, in a letter written for the introduction of this book. In his autobiography Calder tells exactly how the fountain worked:

Innovative Projects

Working on silkscreen mural, *A Piece of My Workshop*, 1948.

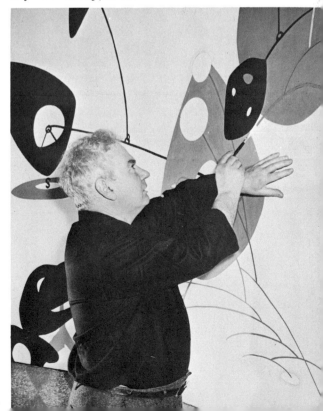

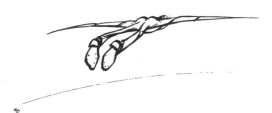

Robert Osborn drawings of Calder firing himself off to the stars.

To make the mercury circulate it was necessary to put a little water in with it so that it would wet the pipes and the pump; it would not work otherwise. The pump and a reservoir four feet across were located in a closet under a stairway. The reservoir was eighteen inches deep and full of mercury to maintain a steady pressure. The mercury was led to my fountain, underground, through a half-inch tube and then up thirty inches where it spewed onto an irregularly shaped dish of iron, lined with pitch. This dish was very nearly horizontal; otherwise the mercury would have rushed off. It trickled in turn onto another plate, differently shaped, and then from that onto a chute which delivered it rather rapidly against a sort of bat, attached to the lower end of a rod, which held at the upper end another rod—with a red disc at the bottom and in hammered brass wire the word A L M A D E N on top.

The impact of mercury against the bag made the combination of the two rods, the red disc, and the word "Almadén" weave in the air in a sort of figure eight.

A major architectural work, the acoustic ceiling for the Aula Magna of University City, Caracas, was done in 1952, and Calder told Katharine Kuh in a 1960 interview that he liked this assemblage of shaped plywood panels best of any of his work. He has mentioned it a number of other times as something that particularly pleased him, and he described it, with evident satisfaction, in his autobiography:

In the summer of 1955, Carlos Raúl Villanueva, of Caracas, arranged a show for me there. I had met him through Sert in 1951, and he came to Roxbury. I also saw him in 1952 in Paris. He had said then that he was doing an auditorium and wanted me to do something for the lobby, a mobile.

I said, "I'd rather be in the main hall."

And he said, "Oh! No! You can't do that because the ceiling is taken up with ribbons of acoustical reflectors."

I said, "Let us play with these acoustical reflectors." And I made him a sketch.

Carlos had engaged Bolt, Bereneck and Newman, of Cambridge, Massachusetts, as acoustical engineers. I had to collaborate with them, and had to redraw the whole layout all over, once or twice, for Carlos. Newman kept saying: "The more of your shapes, the merrier and the louder."

So we drew large round and oval shapes, some of them to be thirty feet or so long, painted different colors, and hung from the ceiling on cables from winches. There were also some of these shapes on the side walls. . . .

Apparently the acoustics are very successful.

Calder's work has pushed sculpture beyond its traditional definitions. He has literally taken sculpture off the age-old pedestal, abolishing the base altogether by hanging his works from ceilings and walls, or letting them sit quite casually on the floor or ground. When Calder had his first postwar exhibit in Paris in 1946, not even his dealer, Louis

Carré, seemed ready for it. Calder recalls that "Carré wanted to put them on some pedestals and I said, 'No, my wife insists these must be right on the floor.' And Carré said, 'Ce n'est pas noble' ['It is not dignified']." Both Calder's father and grandfather were "dignified" sculptors in the classical tradition. Calder's contemporary Henry Moore, often mentioned with Calder as one of the "old masters" of modern sculpture, represents the end of the line of this classical tradition, whereas Calder has always been in the forefront of the innovators. This is why his work is always fresh and interesting. It projects a sense of the future, as the poet Prévert has noted; Moore's work already seems to belong to the art of the past.

Calder's innovations and hybrids seem unlimited: painted jet planes and a racing car; a terrazzo sidewalk; murals in oil on concrete, silkscreen on canvas, ceramic tile; wallpapers and fabrics; shop-window displays; a huge rooftop painting; a water ballet; a mercury fountain. There are works made with just about every kind of material: wood, metal, bone, plastic, plywood, porcelain, cloth, paper, leather, wire, string, rubber tubing, corks, buttons, sequins, nuts and bolts, bottle caps, tin cans—and more. In every case the materials are used in new ways to produce original work.

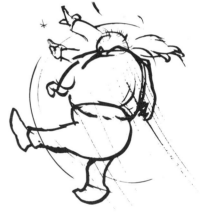

In 1939 he received first prize among 250 entries in a Museum of Modern Art competition for sculpture in Plexiglas—then a new medium. Calder's work is especially interesting not only for the fluid sense of motion and sweep in the whole composition but because light was also used as a medium. The entire piece was illuminated from a concealed source, and the design utilized a special property of Plexiglas: it can carry light around curves and from a source to an outlet without giving off light in transit. In Calder's red, purple and white sculpture, only the edges were lit and the extremities of the rods showed points of light—a dramatically innovative light sculpture. Calder also experimented with light in other ways long before the advent of "light art." In the thirties he made a series of simple, rather crude wood assemblages that he hung and illuminated in such a way that their shadows were as much a part of the total design as the actual elements. He describes an exhibition at the Freddy Mayor Gallery in London in 1938: "Some of the objects were very slender and filmy—little lines of fine wire—and I used to turn out the light and project them on the wall with a flashlight as they turned around." He admired the shadows of the cranes in a Frankfort workshop where the stabile *Hextoped* was being enlarged in 1955: "There were three traveling cranes, all on the same tracks. . . . When they were deployed by the men the artificial light threw fantastic shadows on the ceiling overhead. This made me feel I could do a wonderful ballet in that shop. . . ." Shadows are important to the overall effect of many of Calder's mobiles, wire sculptures and theatrical works.

Another experiment with immaterial, ephemeral sculpture occurred in 1939, when Calder designed an aquatic ballet with fourteen water jets, fifty feet high, for the New

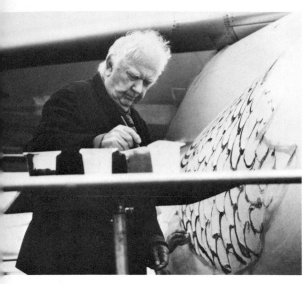

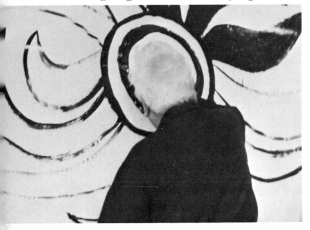

Painting engine covers of *Flying Colors*.

York World's Fair. This was not executed, but in 1954 the architect Eero Saarinen commissioned a similar work, *Ballet of the Seven Sisters*, for the General Motors Technical Center near Detroit. Here the idea of a programmed, moving sculpture, which Calder first developed in his mechanized works, is adapted to a complex interaction of water jets, producing a monumental water mobile.

The concept there was a large one, I'd say. Jets of water. Lines of water can be monumental too. I took one hundred feet and had one jet at each end rising and falling at different speeds, and then that comes to a halt. There were seven smaller jets that were almost vertical; I called them the seven sisters because they were slender jets, and some rotated one way and some the other way and they made a rotating pattern against the sky. Then there is a bathtubful of water shot into the air to make a big boom when it hits. Then a bar rotating makes a fishtail—that's rather fine.

Nancy Mulnix tells about the time Calder was invited to see his water ballet in action for the first time. Shortly before the big weekend it was discovered that the ballet was temporarily not working because the pond in which it was located had been drained for extensive remodeling and all the water was behind a coffer dam. Nancy's frantic messages reached a General Motors executive, who quickly ordered the coffer dam destroyed, and the water was returned to the pond in three minutes!

Some of Calder's most innovative work has been done on commission. He always welcomes the opportunity to work in new or unconventional media. In 1949 he made two designs for Laverne Originals, to be produced as both wallpaper and fabric. *Calder #1*, like many of Calder's works done at this time, relates to the paintings of Miró. *Splotchy*, dramatic in scale and concept, is very much like Jackson Pollock's black drip paintings, but (as Jack Baur pointed out when he saw the wallpaper sample in our research office) Calder's design *antedates* Pollock's great 1951 series. It is interesting to find that a Calder multiple—a ten-foot mural silkscreened on canvas, titled *A Piece of My Workshop* and produced in a limited edition of two hundred—was created in 1948, preceding by many years the "multiple originals" that became a popular new art form in the sixties.

Robert Osborn, a long-time friend, wrote in his foreword to Calder's autobiography that "Calder, a generation before our time, was in full orbit"; and Osborn illustrated his 1969 *Art in America* article "Calder's International Monuments" with drawings, shown here, of Sandy flying off into space. His concept was prophetic, for a few years later Braniff International commissioned Calder to paint a huge McDonnell–Douglas jet. *Flying Colors* could be considered a 157-foot Calder canvas, a skyborne mural, a giant mobile gouache. The plane was publicized to focus attention on South America as a colorful vacation continent, and it has attracted enormous attention—to

Calder fully as much as to Braniff. The Braniff name does not even appear on the plane; instead it carries the artist's signature, four feet high and thirteen long.

To arrive at the final design, Calder painted eight six-foot scale models that have since been exhibited in many museums. Before beginning to work on the models, he requested engineering drawings showing the ten per cent of the surface where paint could not be applied. With this sole limitation he painted the designs in eight work sessions in Saché. To duplicate the final model, Braniff engineers used special graph paper to trace the designs, then photographically enlarged the thirty-three abstract forms twenty-five times, and transferred them onto the fuselage, wings, engines, tail and nose of the plane, using high-pressure spray guns to apply the paint. The famous Calder colors were made to the artist's specifications in an aerospace paint that was color-computerized and formulated to withstand high speed, altitude and weather. The engine covers were hand-painted by Calder with the same paint colors, made in a special brushing consistency.

In 1975, Braniff came again to Calder with models of a 727-200 jet, asking him to design a flagship for their U.S. fleet in celebration of the Bicentennial. Although the original *Flying Colors* seemed a hard act to follow, Calder surpassed himself with *Flying Colors of the United States*, a ripple of red, white and blue that has been interpreted as an abstraction of the waving American flag.

In a letter to Klaus Perls and George Gordon, who originated the *Flying Colors* projects for Braniff, Calder commented, tongue-in-cheek, on the future implication of his latest innovative works: "George Gordon's inspiration to decorate airplanes opens up a whole new field to artists who are always crying out for areas to decorate (or desecrate)."

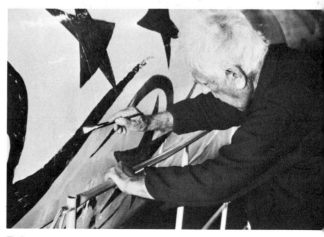

Painting engine cover of *Flying Colors of the United States*.

187

Sign, 1943–44. Sheet metal, 72″ w. Designed for hallway, Curt Valentin Gallery, New York. Present location unknown.

OPPOSITE: *Untitled*, 1939. Plexiglas, electric light, approx. 36″ h. Present location unknown.

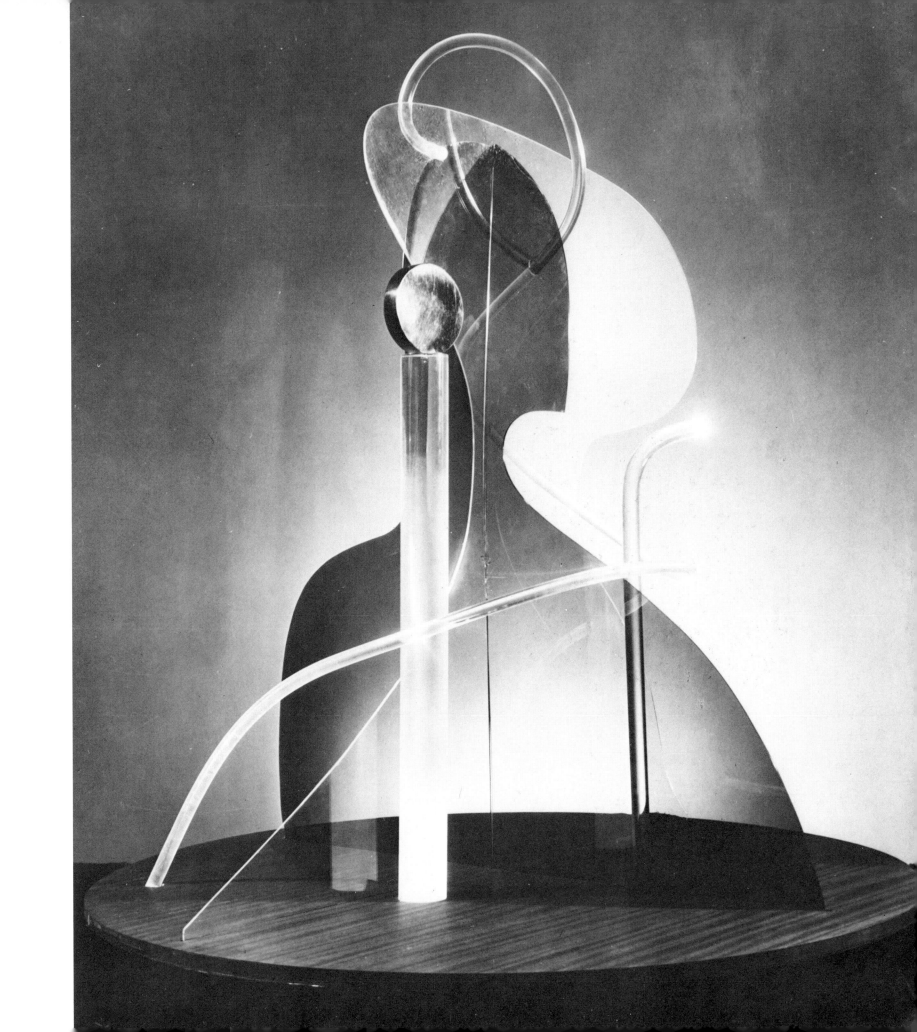

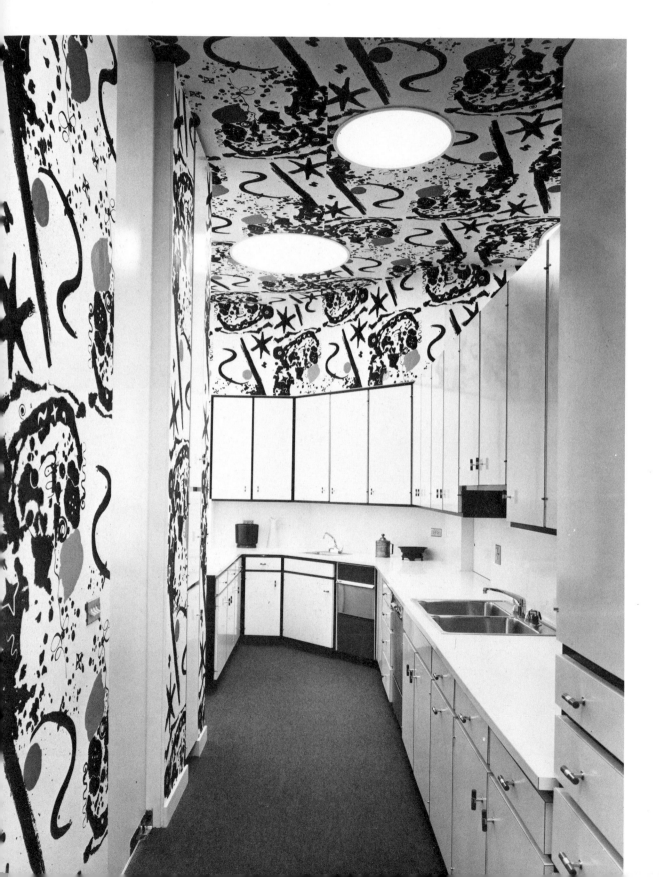

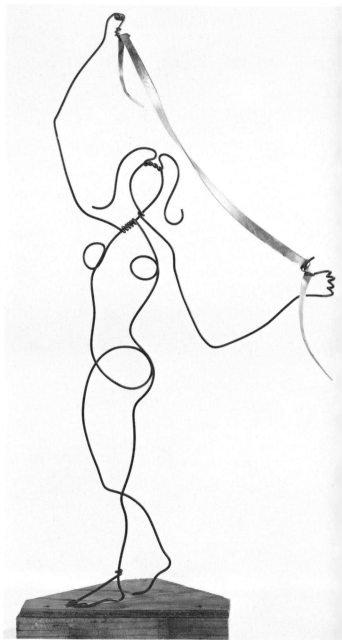

Maquette for fabric display, c. 1935-40. Sheet aluminum, wire, 21″ h. Private collection, New York.

Splotchy, 1949. Wallpaper designed for Laverne Originals, New York. Home of Mrs. Dorothy Rautford, Glencoe, Illinois.

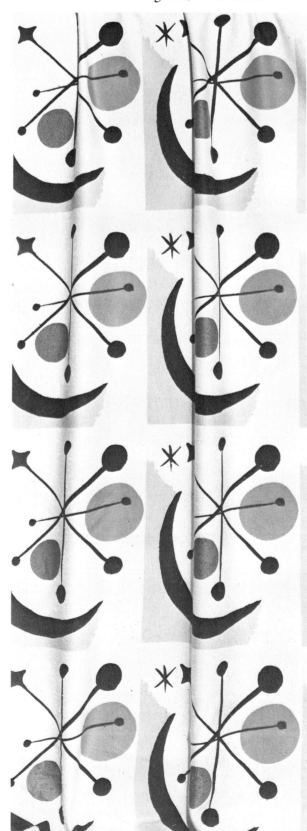

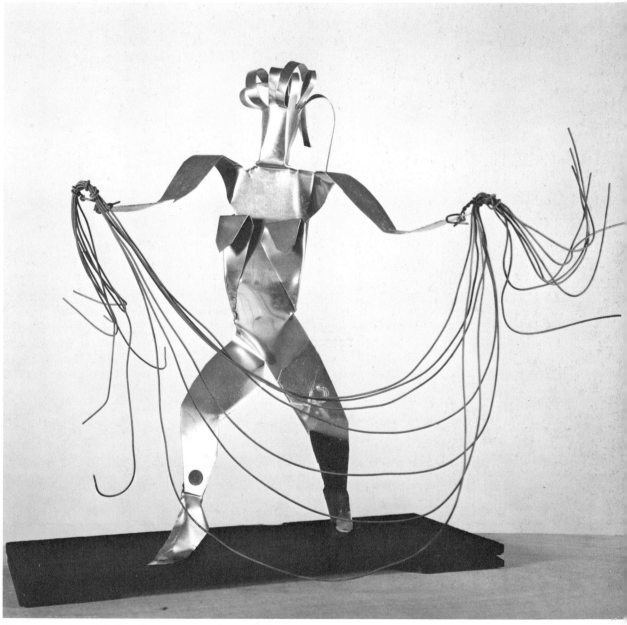

Maquette for fabric display, c. 1935–40. Sheet aluminum, wire, 14″ h. Perls Galleries, New York.

191

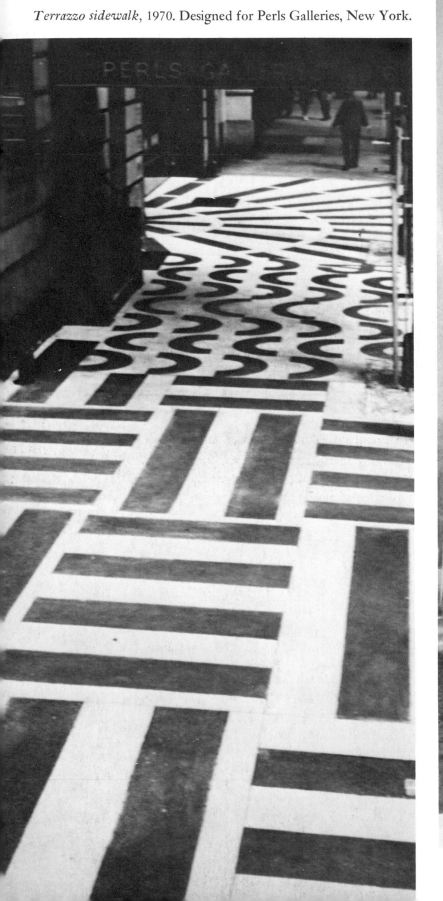

Terrazzo sidewalk, 1970. Designed for Perls Galleries, New York.

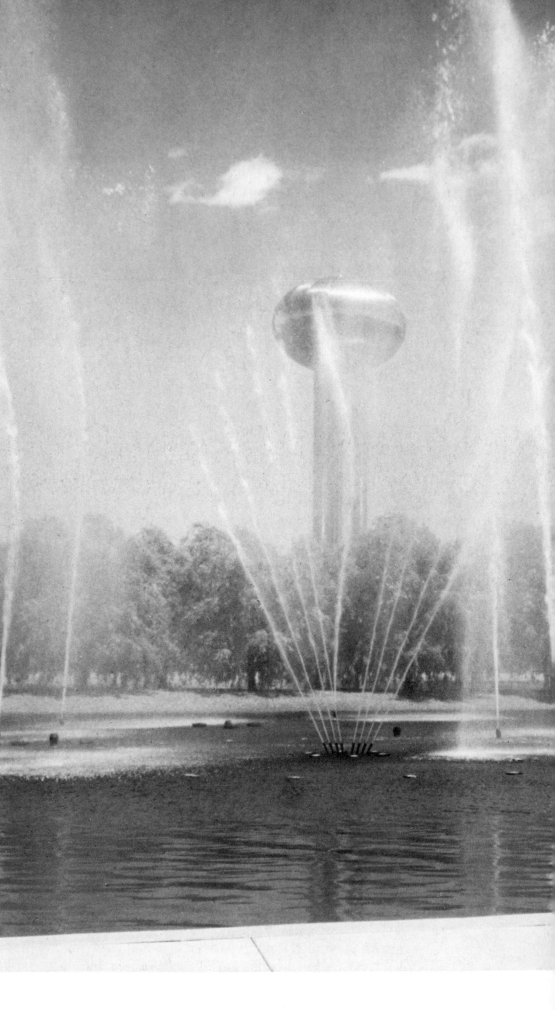

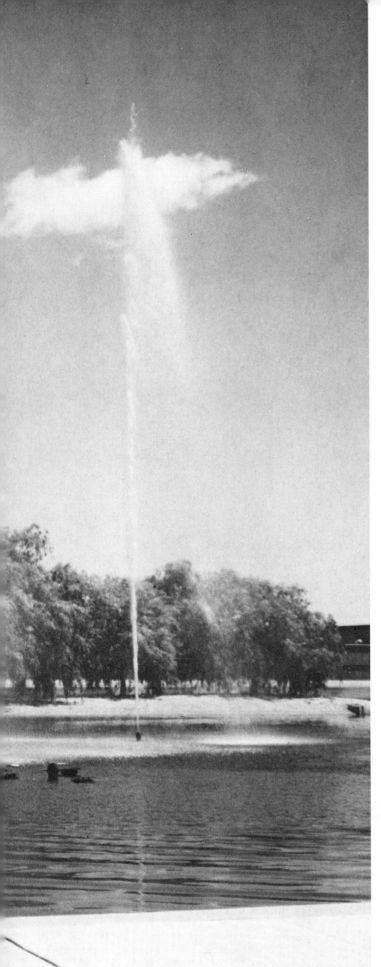

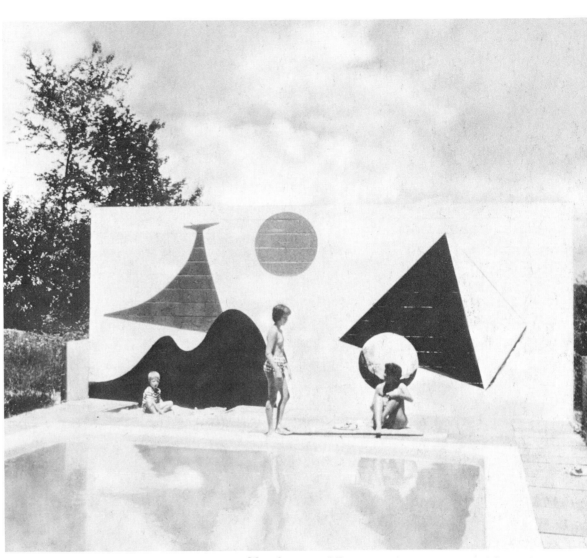

Mural, 1953. Oil on concrete, 10 × 30′. Mr. and Mrs. Rufus Stillman, Litchfield, Connecticut.

LEFT: *Ballet of Seven Sisters*, 1956. Programmed fountain designed for General Motors Technical Center, Warren, Michigan.

Mercury Fountain, 1937. Steel rod, sheet steel surfaced with pitch, mercury, 8′6″ h. Designed for Spanish Pavilion, Paris World's Fair.

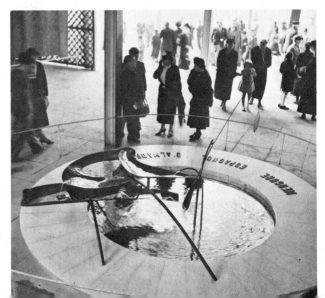

Flying Colors of the United States, 1975. Specially formulated
aerospace paint on 727–200 jet, 153' long. Braniff International.

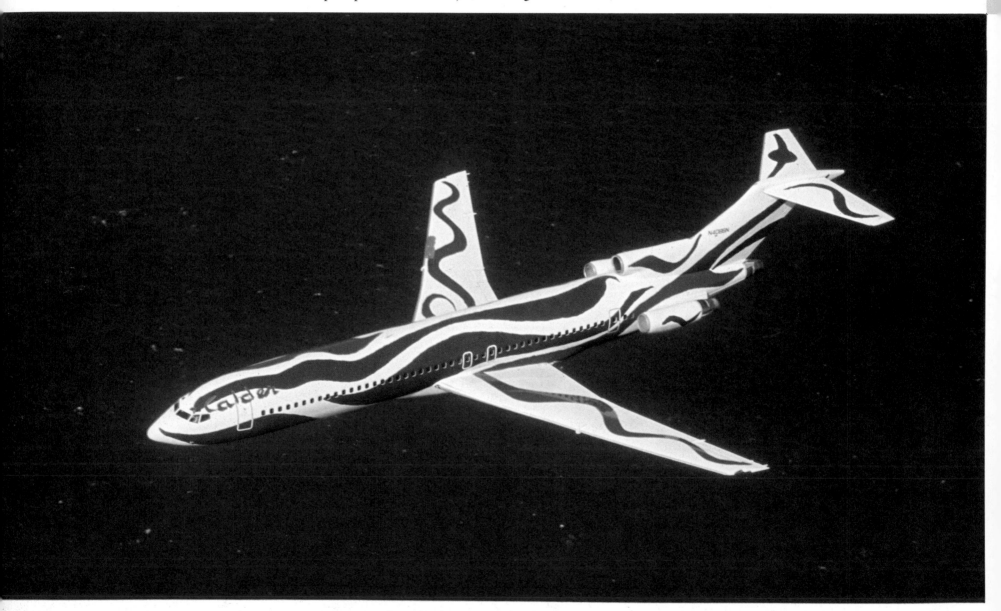

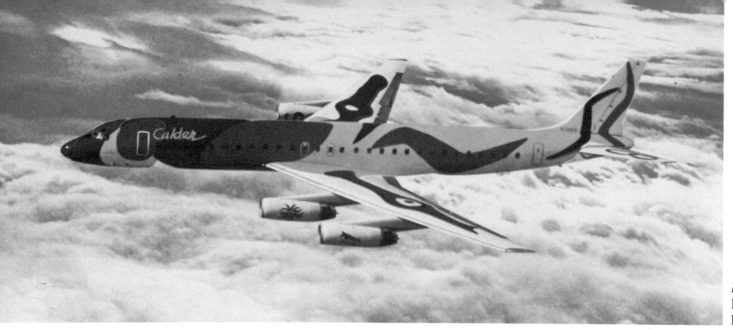

Flying Colors, 1973. Specially formulated aerospace paint on DC-8 jet, 157′ long. Braniff International.

BMW-Calder, 1975. Automotive paints on BMW 3.0 CSL. BMW Museum, Munich, Germany.

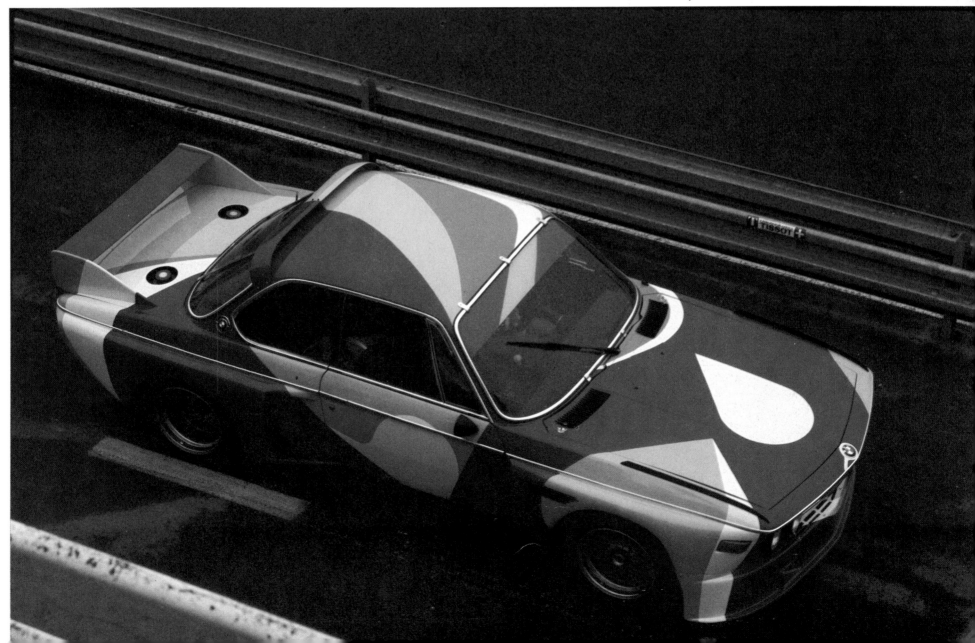

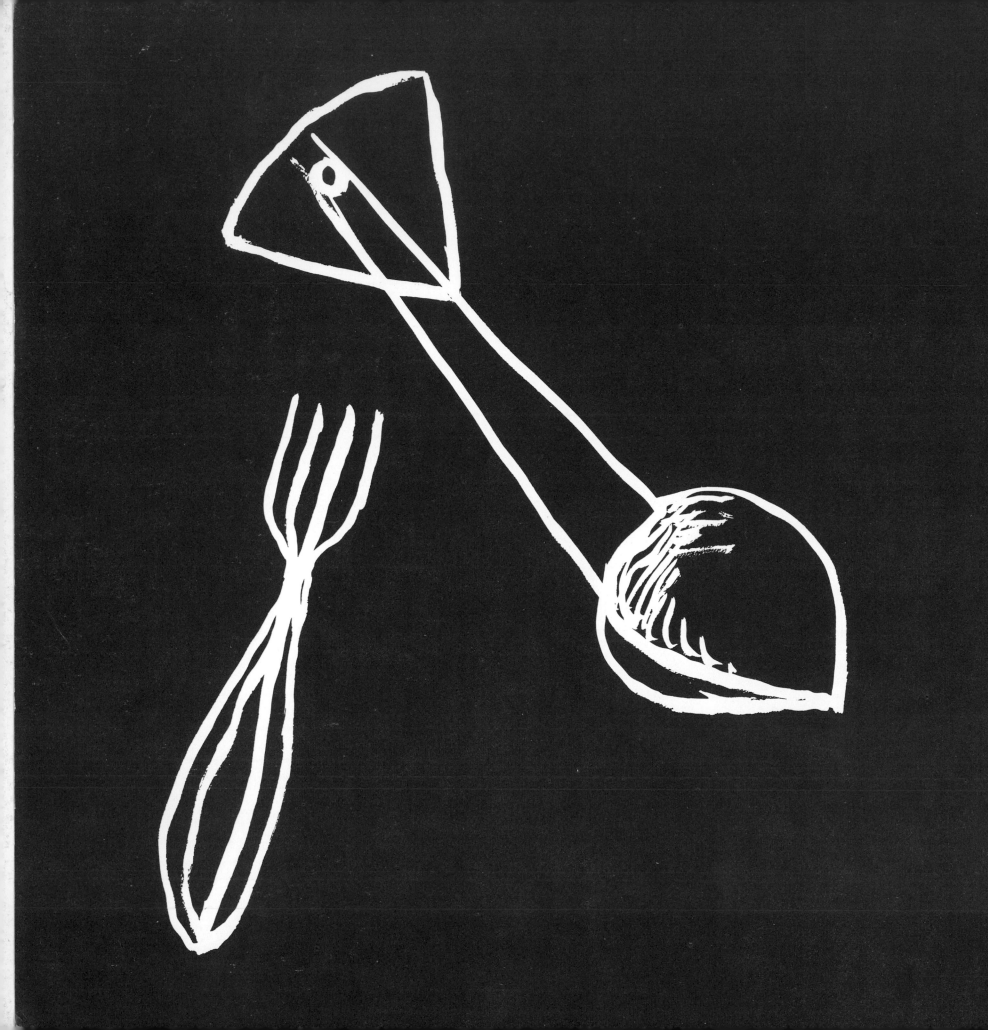

[Jean Davidson] had invited at least forty people to eat three-inch steaks and a dozen chickens in their skins. He had the meat and the fire, but no implements with which to cook them. So I . . . found an old garden chair made completely of iron. I wove some wire across where the back had been, and we cocked it up on the fire and it served very well as a grill. Steak à la chaise *came to be the* spécialité maison.

Sandy has been inventing ingenious gadgets all his life. Long before the chair-grill he rigged up a series of string pulleys at his bedside which he used to turn on the burner in the kitchen for morning coffee. Louisa said that when it didn't work, Sandy would get up, tinker with it until it did and then go back to bed, rather than simply turn on the burner.

Marcel Breuer remembers a gadget Calder surprised him with at one of the architect's goulash parties in Paris. Getting the sour cream out of its bottle and into the goulash at precisely the right moment was always a problem until Sandy devised a corkscrew-like object that cranked the cream out in a matter of seconds.

Just about anything that is needed, Sandy enjoys making. The present Calder homes are outfitted with all sorts of handmade things: kitchen utensils—serving forks and spoons, roasting pans, strainers—lighting fixtures, door hinges, fireplace equipment, ashtrays. Some are wittily conceived—camouflaged garbage cans, hand-shaped toilet-paper holders featuring an upright finger. Some, like a silver serving fork, its design derived from the Brazilian *figa* motif, are made in the style of Calder jewelry. Others, such as the unspillable tin-can ashtrays, are practical inventions. The wire holders for handleless coffee cups are modeled after soda-fountain glass holders; springy wire bases are an original addition to keep the cups from jarring and spilling coffee when they are set down on the table.

As with other varieties of his work, Sandy has been generous with gifts of homemade gadgets. He describes a bridge light he made for Louisa's great-aunt Mrs. Alice Cuyler: ". . . as she played bridge very often, I made her a light with a long slender cone hanging from a long sloping slender post . . . it seems it was successful." When his mother turned ninety, he made her a "birthday cake"—a mix of tin cans, a single candle and a mobile. And we have had one of his large ladles, made of folded sheet aluminum, in our Connecticut kitchen for many years.

During World War II Calder entertained hospitalized soldiers with his gadgetry. Once he spent the day at a military hospital on Staten Island "making tin ashtrays, little toys to encourage and inspire the wounded to make things of a similar nature." Another time he was invited to a rest home for merchant-marine sailors in Bernardsville, New Jersey: "I went out there, armed with tin cans, tinsnips, hammer, drawing ink, pen, paper, and so on. I spent the whole day doing little stunts. . . ."

Household Objects

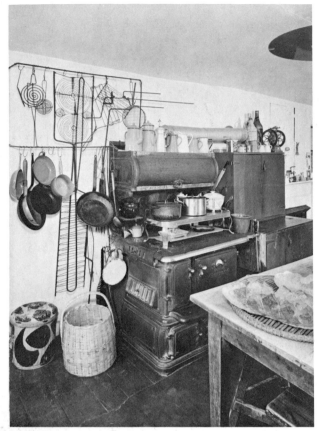

The Roxbury kitchen.

In recent years Calder designs have appeared on Sèvres china (one set of plates was made expressly for the late President Pompidou of France) and on hammocks and mats woven by Nicaraguan Indians. Calder made gouache designs available for the mats and hammocks, which were sold for Managua earthquake relief.

Calder's kitchen collection of serviceable gadgets has grown over the years because, so often, he found manufactured articles ugly and unfunctional. Cans that held olive oil, coffee and beer are favored materials because, as John Canaday observed, they "combine sprightly tints with remembrance of good things past in the Calder cuisine." In his article about a visit to Roxbury, Canaday describes some of his favorite Calder household objects. One is a silver serving fork that looks to him like a line drawing, held together by "a little scribble of silver wire at the proper spot." Another, devised after Miró had complained of the harsh light, is a perforated aluminum light guard which fastens onto an overhead bulb; the saw-toothed notches on the wing-like flange soften the shadow, and a curlicued wire attaches the contraption to the light cord. Canaday remarked that this object, exhibited out of context, could make a good percentage of contemporary abstract art look silly. He also described Calder at work, as he cuts, folds, punctures and brads with unhesitating skill, improvising his design as he works: "He is a deft craftsman, and when he is at work in his shop he smiles slightly as if bemused at watching another workman whose technique he finds fascinating but whose end product he cannot quite visualize."

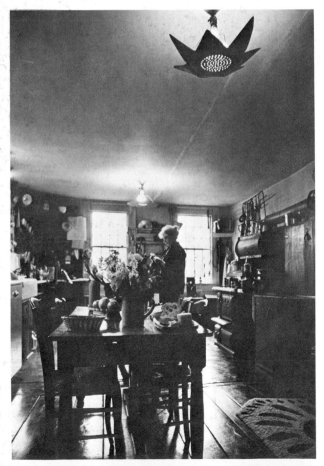

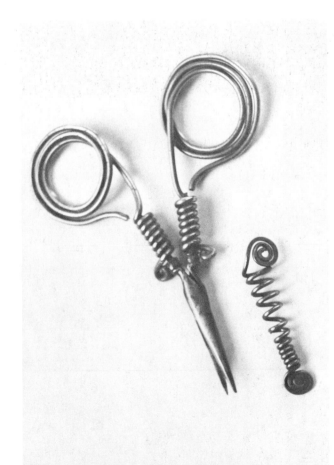

Scissors and Scabbard, c. 1920. Steel blades, brass handles and scabbard, 4½″ w. Margaret Calder Hayes, Berkeley, California.

OPPOSITE: *Andirons*, c. 1935. Brass, 22″ h. James Thrall Soby, New Canaan, Connecticut.

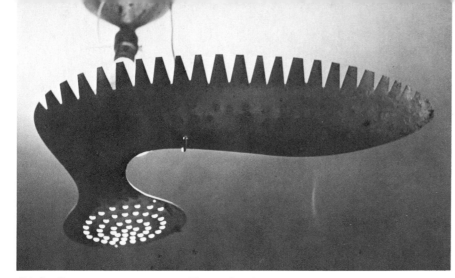

Light-fixture cover, c. 1940. Sheet aluminum, 20″ w. Collection of the artist.

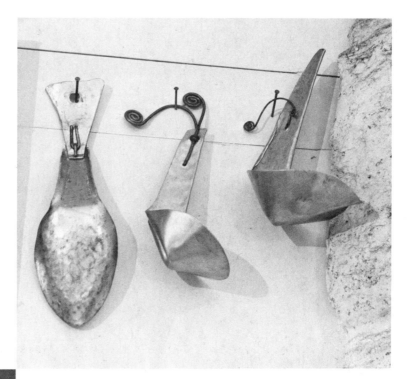

RIGHT: *Ladles*, c. 1940. Sheet aluminum, 12–14″ long. Collection of the artist.

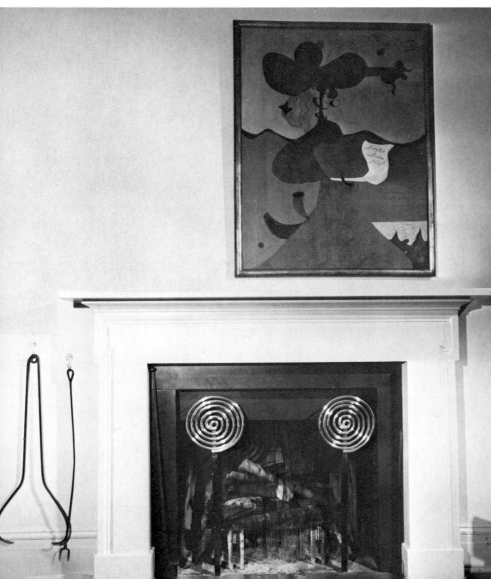

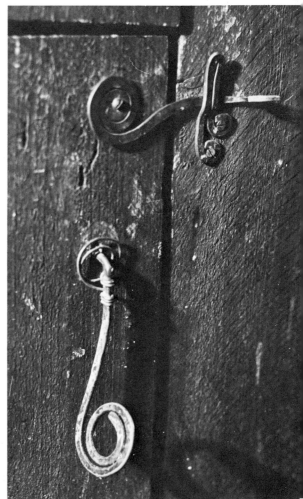

RIGHT: *Door latch*, c. 1940. Brass wire, 6″ w. Collection of the artist.

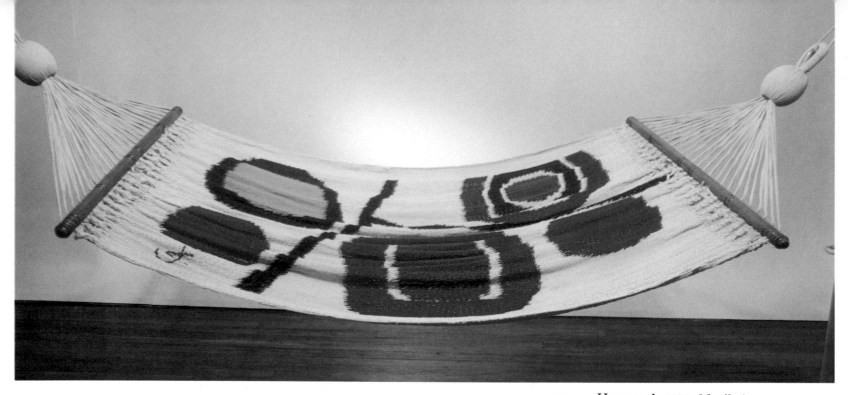

ABOVE: *Hammock*, 1974. Manila hemp,
7 × 4′. Private collection, New York.

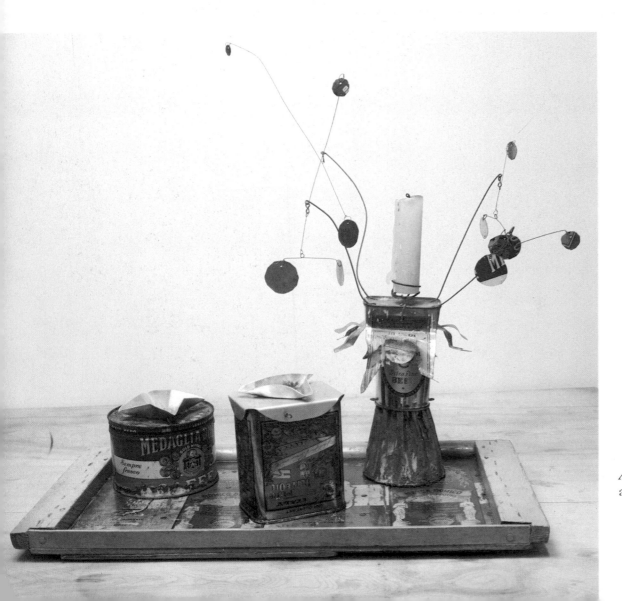

Ashtrays and *Birthday Cake*, c. 1955. Tin cans,
aluminum, wire, 5–17″ h. Collection of the artist.

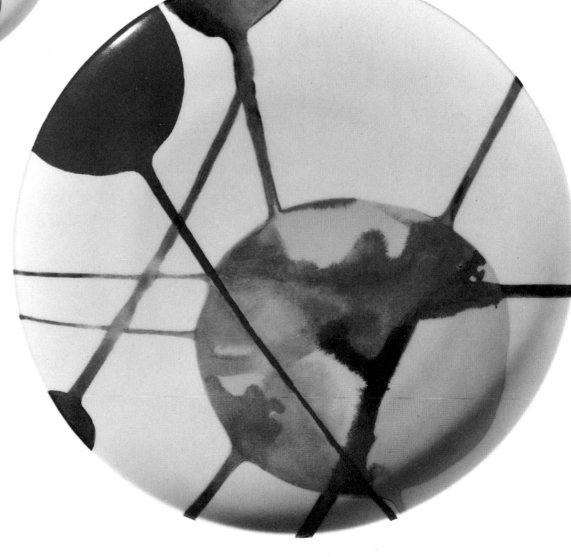

Sèvres plate, 1972. Glazed porcelain, 11½″ diameter. Private collection, New York.

Sèvres plate, 1969. Glazed porcelain, 10⅛″ diameter. Private collection, New York.

Sèvres plate, 1970. Glazed porcelain, 10⅛″ diameter. Private collection, New York.

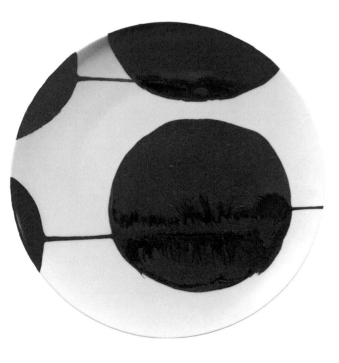

203

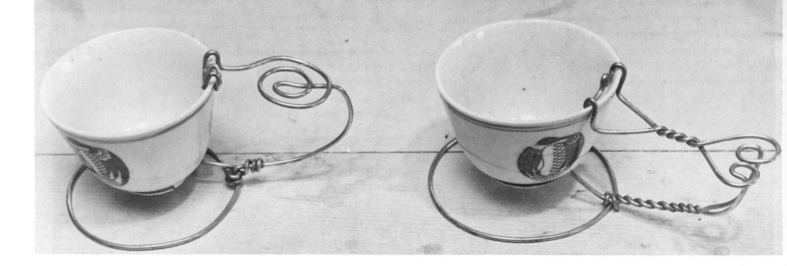

Serving forks, c. 1940. Silver wire, 8–13½″ long. Collection of the artist.

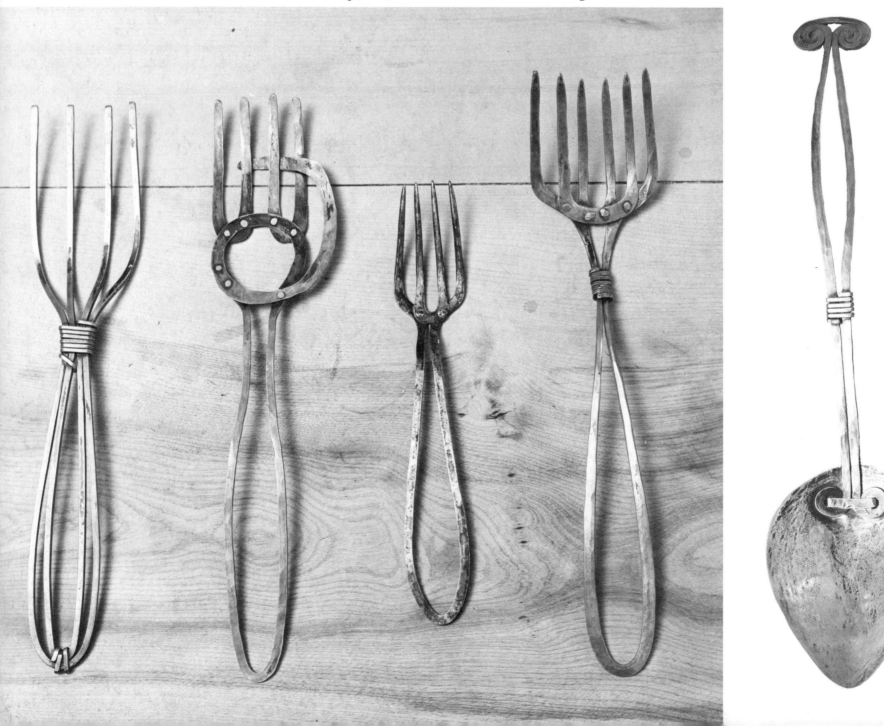

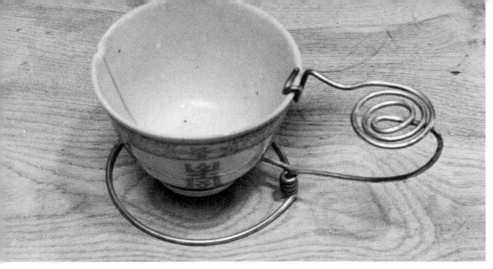

Coffee cups, c. 1940. Brass, porcelain cups, 3½″ h. Collection of the artist.

Kitchen spoons, c. 1940. Sheet aluminum, 15–17″ long. Collection of the artist.

OPPOSITE: *Serving spoon,* c. 1940. Silver wire, 13″ long. Collection of the artist.

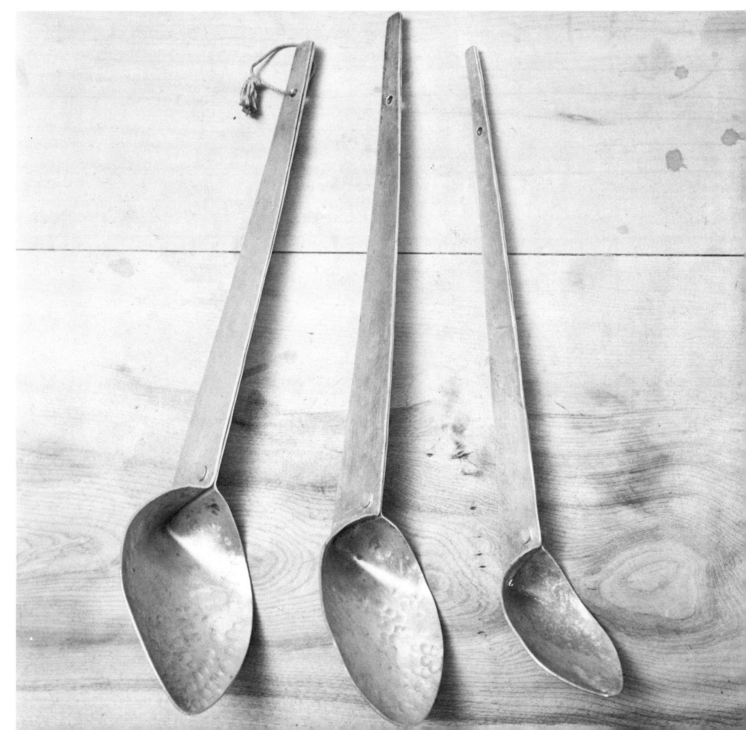

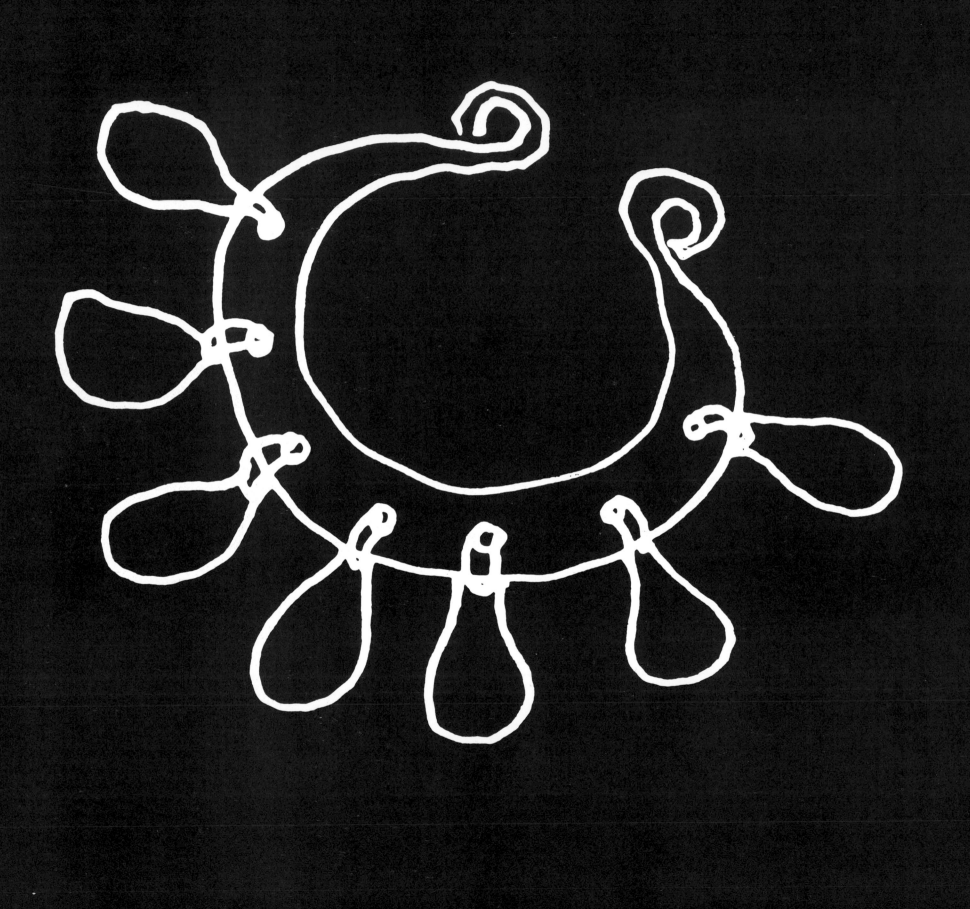

I picked up in the streets the bits of copper wire left from other people's spliced cables and made jewelry with little beads for Thomasine and other ladies.

Thomasine and the "other ladies" were Peggy Calder's dolls, for whom Sandy made his first wire jewelry. That was in Pasadena in 1906, when Sandy was eight years old. There are frequent references to jewelry making in his autobiography and elsewhere:

France, 1930:
Calder mentions a boat trip to Corsica, where he wandered around Calvi "picking up bits of what had been blue pottery, and with these and some wire I made a necklace which I sent to my mother for her birthday."

Jewelry

Concord, Massachusetts, 1931:
I had known a little jeweler in Paris, Bucci, and he had helped me make a gold ring—forerunner of an array of family jewelry—with a spiral on top and a helix for the finger. I thought this would do for a wedding ring. But Louisa merely called this one her "engagement ring" and we had to go to Waltham, near by, and purchase a wedding ring for two dollars.

Making jewelry, Roxbury, 1952.

Roxbury, 1940s:
Mrs. Blume's sister, Ann, had just married her dear old friend Heber Blankenhorn. During the evening, I discovered they had no wedding ring, so I found a piece of copper wire and made one for them.

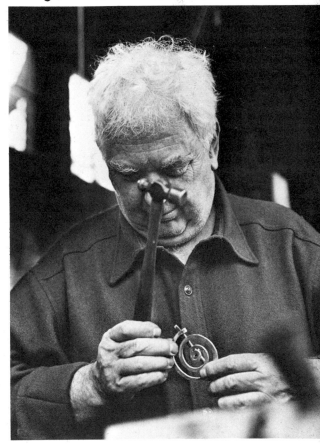

Rio de Janeiro, 1948:
Lota de Macedo Soares thought I ought to do some work while in Rio, so she took me to the district where one found hardware stores and I bought a hammer, an anvil, tinsnips, sheet aluminum, steel wire. I already had my favorite Bernard pliers (they have a parallel bite), which I take wherever I go.

At first, I worked on the second floor of a mechanic's shop. He was very nice, but there was a terrific current of air—even too much for me. I worked up a sweat and my fingers got so cramped that I could hardly open my hand.

I hastily took a piece of aluminum sheet and fashioned a *figa*—the Brazilian good-luck piece, which is also an emblem of fecundity and is composed of a hand in which the thumb passes under the forefinger. This seemed to do the trick, so I continued working, and finally I put a wire pin on the *figa* and gave it to Lota, who often wears it as a barrette." (Calder made several smaller silver *figa* pins after that, and one of them became my future daughter-in-law's engagement present; we didn't know its significance till Sandy told us much later, with a great guffaw. After her two sons were born in quick succession, Beverly asked if she could exchange the pin!)

Calder's jewelry was never intended to be mass-produced; except for exhibitions held in New York in 1940 and 1941 at the Marian Willard Gallery and in 1966 at the Perls Galleries, it has not been formally offered for sale. Some pieces were made especially for the Willard shows, and at the time a few others were commissioned. A number of the pieces sold by Perls came from Louisa's enormous gift stock accumulated over the years. Thus Calder jewelry has been acquired by a few collectors who bought examples as unique works of art.

However, there are many others who, as Tom Messer aptly phrased it, "merely stood in the path of the artist's generosity." Most of Calder's jewelry has been made for friends and given away on special occasions, like the magnificent (and witty) wedding-present brooch for Ingeborg ten Haeff. The printmaker Stanley William Hayter recalls that in the early days in Paris "everyone" was wearing Calder's silver and brass wire jewelry. More recently Calder openings at Perls Galleries have been annual fashion

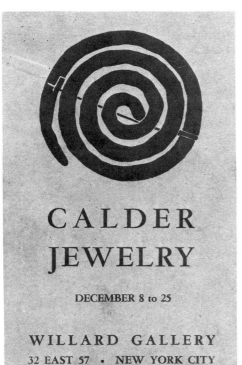

Exhibition catalogue, 1940.

Making jewelry, Saché, 1964.

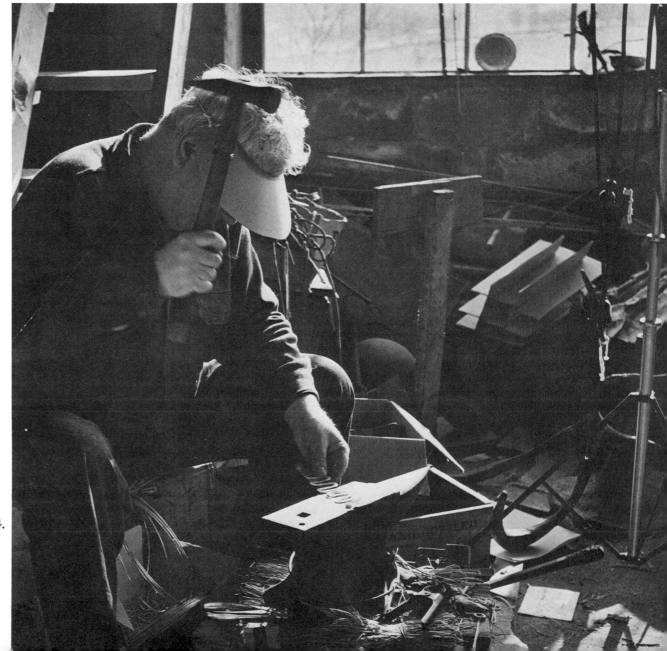

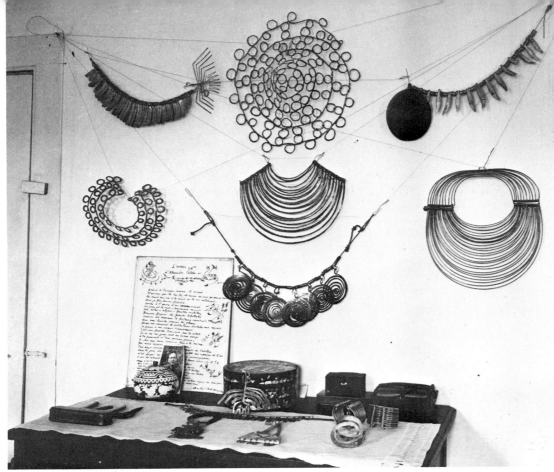

Louisa's dressing table with jewelry, Roxbury, 1940s.

shows of brooches, rings, necklaces, combs, earrings; Calder family and friends are easily identified. Owners' initials and visual puns (like a fish for Cordelia Pond or a hawk for Frances Hawkins) abound. The jewelry is made of silver, gold, brass and occasionally zinc, some set, cabochon fashion, with chunks of clear optical glass, colored glass, obsidian, pebbles, bits of pottery. I have a dramatic pin made of one such "found jewel" —a triangular gray-and-white striped stone which I collected at Lake Champlain. Sandy saw it at our house, asked if he could have it and surprised me by returning it, mounted with brass spirals and silver wire.

Calder's range of interests is always amazing: in painting from gouaches to murals, from black and white to brilliant color; in sculpture from monumental stabiles for city spaces to small, graceful table pieces—and minuscule jewelry. Within Calder's remarkably varied production, each genre is found to be linked to another in some significant way. The decorative linear design that is basic to his jewelry is directly related to his early wire portraits. When he began hammering the wire into flat strips and combining several metals—silver and brass, gold and zinc—and then adding stones, the jewelry took on the complexity, in miniature, of his sculptures. Calder's preoccupation with jewelry about 1940 seems in turn to have influenced his sculpture, for at that time his work became gayer, more slender, and the delicacy of some of the formal elements is reminiscent of the jewelry.

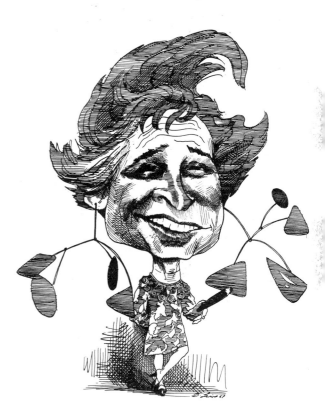

Dolly Perls with mobile earrings, drawn by David Levine, 1969.

209

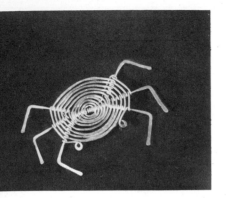

Spider pin, c. 1930–40. Silver, 5″ w. Present location unknown.

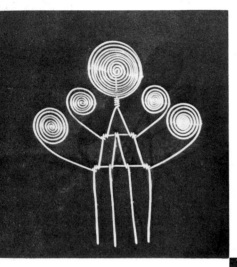

Comb, c. 1940. Brass, 8″ h. Private collection, Dallas, Texas.

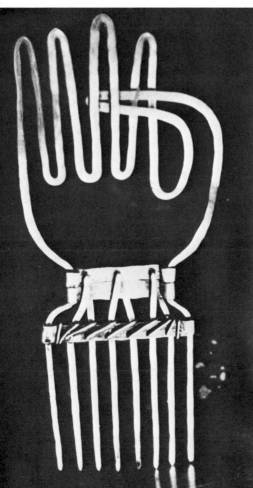

Figa comb, c. 1930–40. Brass, 6″ h. Louisa Calder, Saché, France.

Butterfly pin, c. 1930. Brass, 7″ w. Margaret Calder Hayes, Berkeley, California.

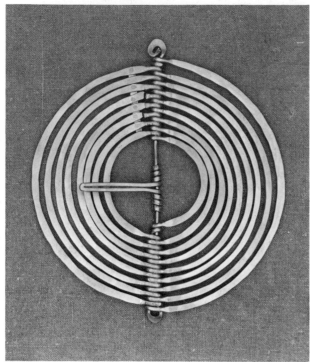

Buckle, c. 1943. Brass, 5⅜″ diameter. The Museum of Modern Art, New York; gift of the artist.

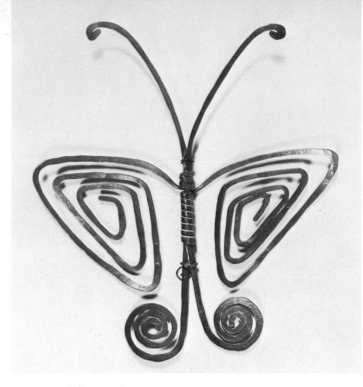

BELOW: *Obsidian pin*, c. 1960. Brass, obsidian, 3½″ diameter. Louisa Calder, Saché, France.

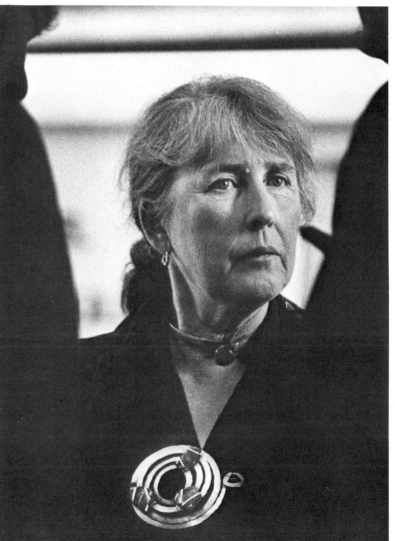

Reclining Bride, 1948. Silver, brass, glass, wire, 7¼″ w. Ingeborg ten Haeff, New York.

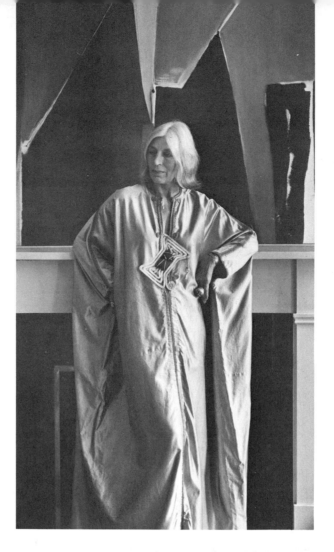

Bird pin, c. 1930–40. Brass, 6½″ w. Mary Carter Jones, New York.

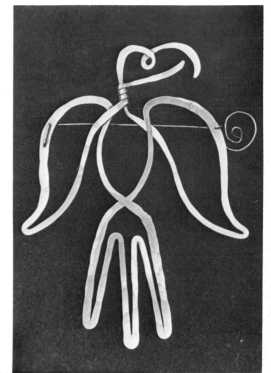

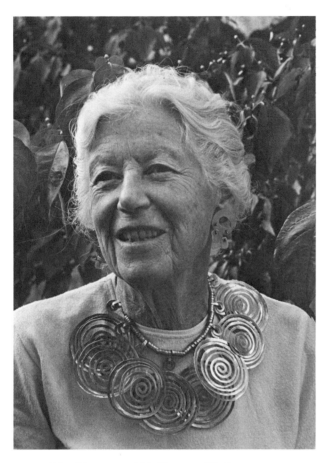

Necklace, c. 1933. Brass, 12″ diameter. Margaret Calder Hayes, Berkeley, California.

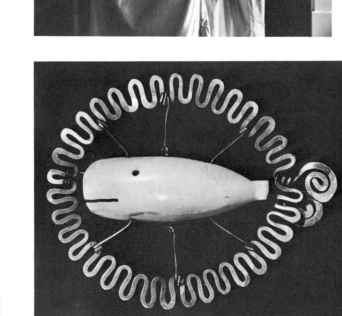

BELOW: *Brooch*, c. 1930–40. Silver, 12⅜″ w. The Museum of Modern Art, New York; gift of the artist

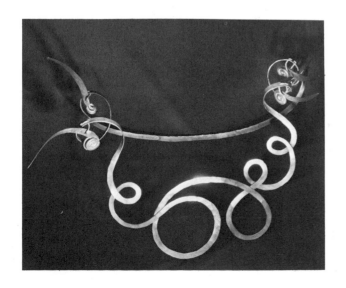

ABOVE: *Whale pin*, c. 1945. Gilded silver, whale ivory, 5″ w. Mrs. Albert Fink Milton, Washington, Connecticut.

LEFT: *The Jealous Husband*, c. 1940. Brass necklace, 15″ w. Muriel Kallis Newman, Chicago.

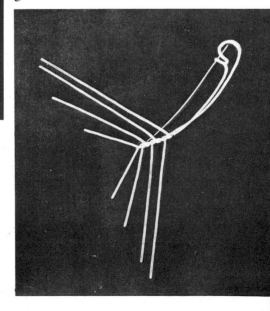

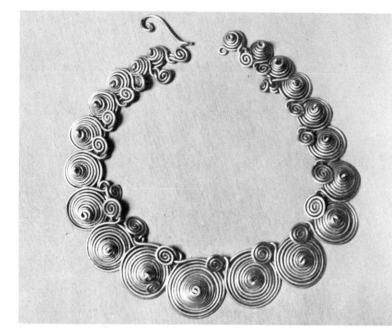

Necklace, c. 1940. Brass, 9″ diameter. Present location unknown.

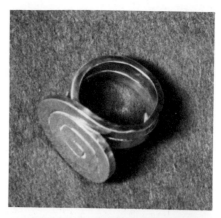

RIGHT: *Ring*, c. 1930–40. Silver, 1″ diameter. Howard Lipman, New York.

BELOW: *Earrings*, 1953. Gold, 1½″ h. Leslie Stillman, Litchfield, Connecticut.

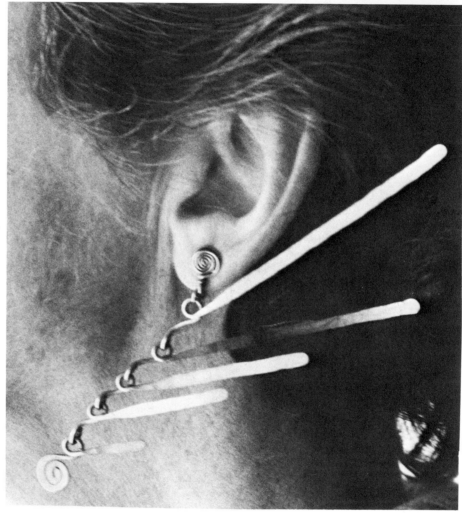

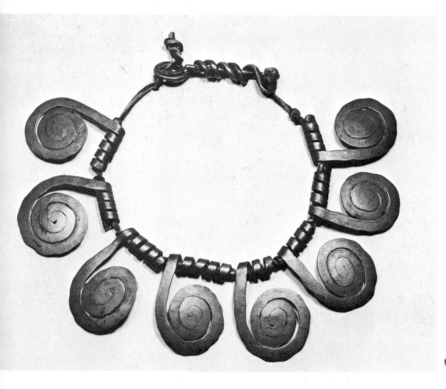

Necklace, c. 1926. Brass, leather thongs, 19¾″ long. Betty Parsons, New York.

212

Bones, c. 1940. Wood necklace, 21″ long. Mrs. Edwin A. Bergman, Chicago.

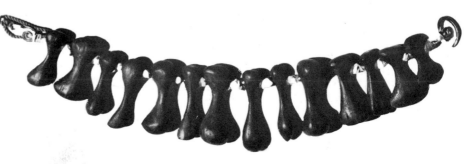

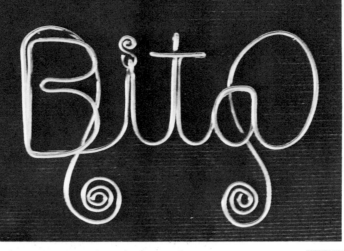

BELOW: *Figa pin*, c. 1948. Silver, 6¼″ w. Margaret Calder Hayes, Berkeley, California.

LEFT: *Pin*, 1940. Brass, 5½″ w. Bita Dobo, New York.

BELOW: *Belt buckle*, 1935. Brass 8″ h. Mrs. Marcel Duchamp, Villiers-sous-Grez, France.

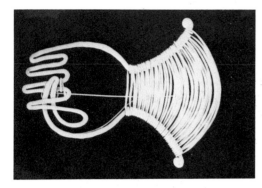

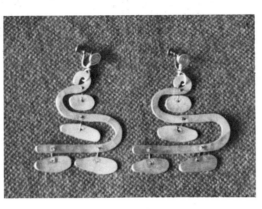

RIGHT: *Earrings*, c. 1935. Silver, 3½″ w. Anita Kahn, New York.

BELOW: *Tiara*, c. 1935. Brass, 4½″ h. Anita Kahn, New York.

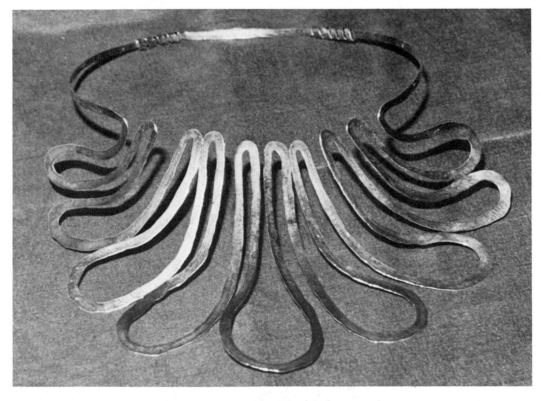

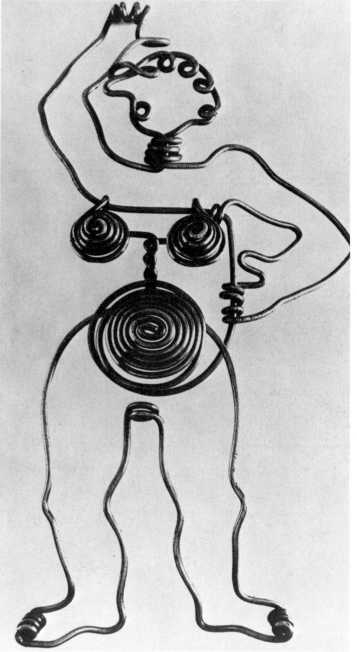

OVERLEAF: CLOCKWISE; *Glass pin*, c. 1930–40. Zinc, brass, optical glass, 4½″ w. *Pin*, c. 1960. Brass, silver, stone, 4½″ w. *Pig pin*, c. 1930–40. Brass 6½″ w. *Pin*, c. 1930–40. Brass, 6½″ w. *Bracelet*, c. 1930–40. Brass, silver, 2½″ diameter. *Alligator pin*, c. 1930–40. Silver, 7″ w. Collection of the author.

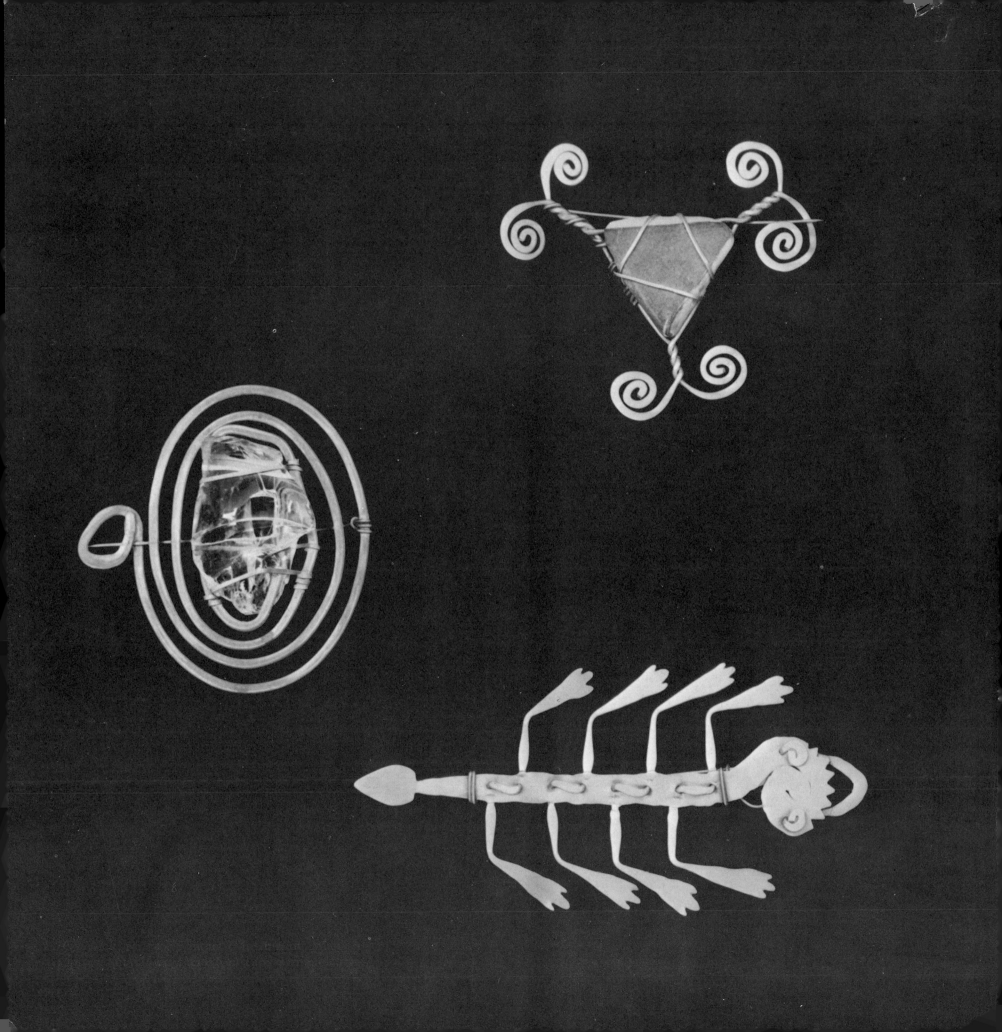

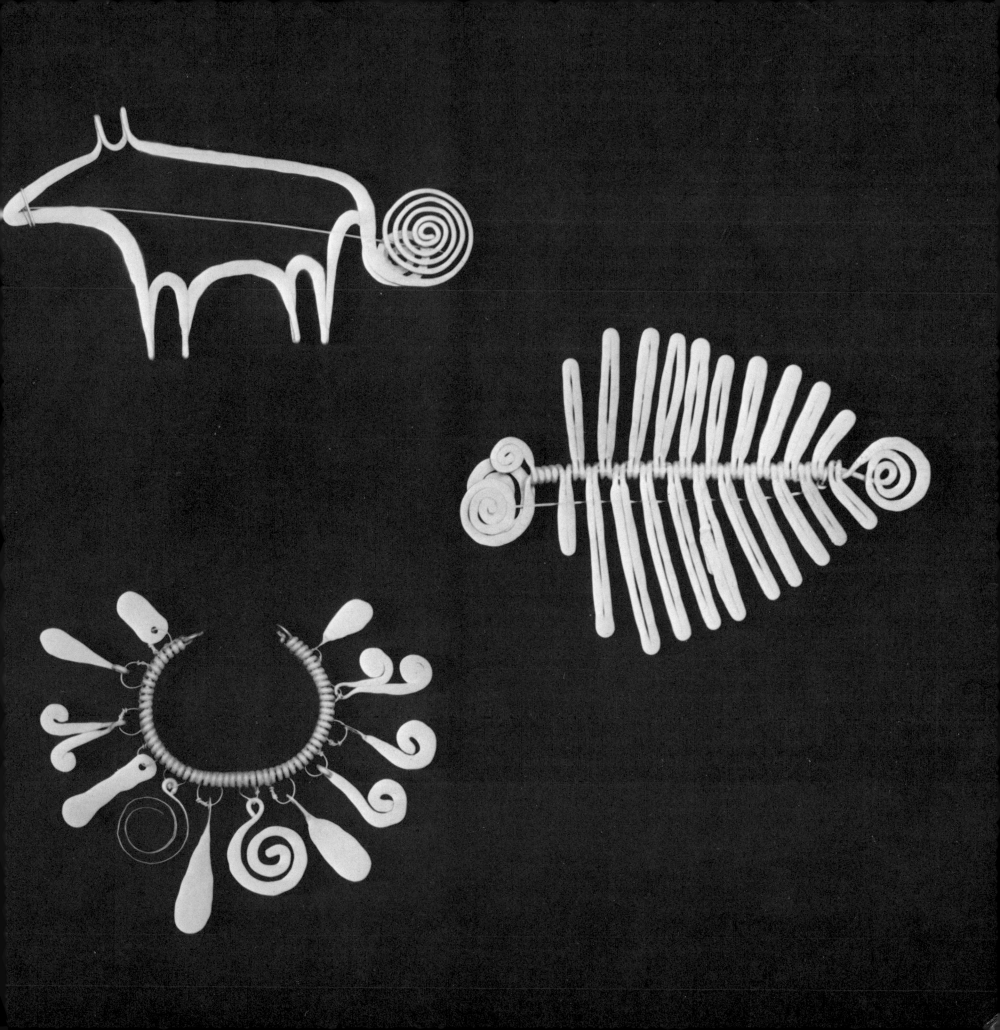

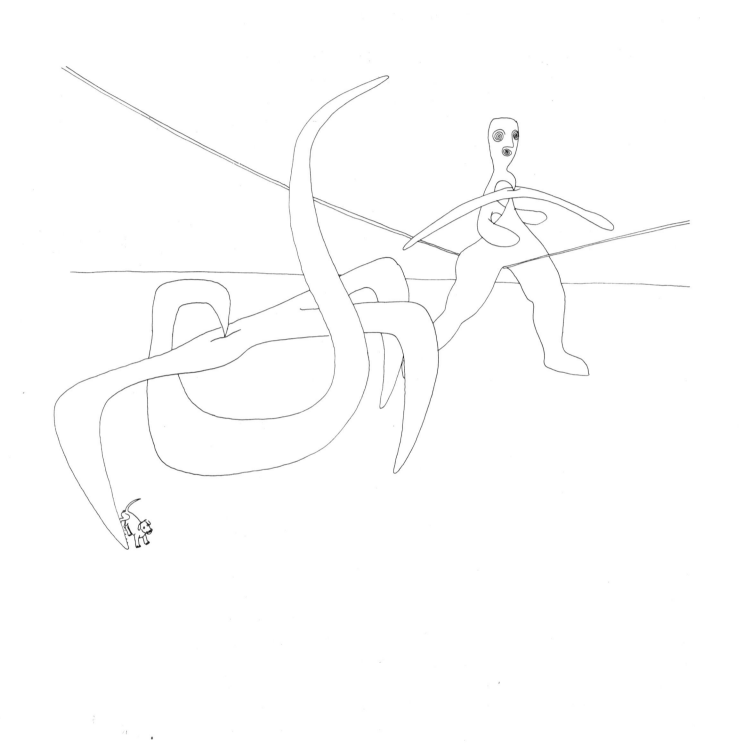

It was also disagreeable to have to check the manipulations
of some other person working on objects at the foundry.

Calder recalls that his first bronzes were done in Paris. "In 1930 I lived in Villa Brune, and Valsuani the bronze foundry was nearby. I did a cow, a horse, a lady recumbent, two or three little ladies who sat on a beach." His next venture in bronze came about in New York, in the spring of 1944, by a somewhat indirect route. Wallace K. Harrison suggested that Calder make some large outdoor objects to be done in cement. Calder wrote in his autobiography that Harrison "apparently forgot about his suggestion immediately, but I did not and I started to work in plaster. I finally made things which were mobile objects and had them cast in bronze [at the Roman Bronze foundry on Long Island]—acrobats, animals, snakes, dancers, a starfish, and tightrope performers." Calder showed his bronzes that fall at Curt Valentin's Buchholz Gallery in New York. He goes on to say, "This was rather an expensive venture and did not sell very well, so I abandoned it for my previous techniques. . . . However, I play with the idea, from time to time, of going back to this medium." He never did, although in 1968 he authorized bronze editions of eighteen of his 1944 sculptures, which had been stored in a basement in Roxbury. The new bronzes, limited to six numbered casts each and, like the earlier group, executed at Roman Bronze, were exhibited at the Perls Galleries a year later.

Bronzes

In our opinion the bronzes (and the Critters stabile series) are the least successful of Calder's many forms of expression. This is not a medium suited to his talents or temperament—he had clearly outgrown the "bronze age" of his grandfather, father and other exponents of traditional sculpture. The figures, which he modeled rapidly and roughly in white plaster, often look heavy and crude when translated into the somber formal-academic material of bronze. The casting, an intermediate mechanical process between the hand and the end product, seems generally to have destroyed Calder's spontaneity and, inevitably, the interest in and fidelity to materials that characterize the best of his work. Comparison with the sprightly Circus figures and the wire sculpture best makes the point. It is obvious that Calder has a strong liking—one might even say an affection—for certain materials, as for certain colors. He was never enthusiastic about bronze and did not preserve any of his experiments with stone sculpture.

We think the few bronzes selected for this chapter do qualify, despite the problems of the bronze medium, as outstanding examples of Calder sculpture. Interestingly, several date from 1930; not only do they represent his early efforts in bronze but they are also among his earliest sculpture in any medium, done at a time when Calder was exploring many materials, seeking those most appropriate to his sculptural ambitions.

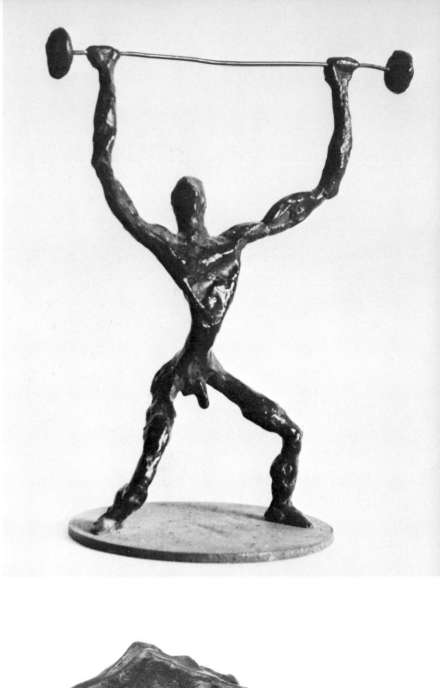

Weight Lifter, 1930. Bronze, 8⅝″ h. Jean and Sandra Davidson, Saché, France.

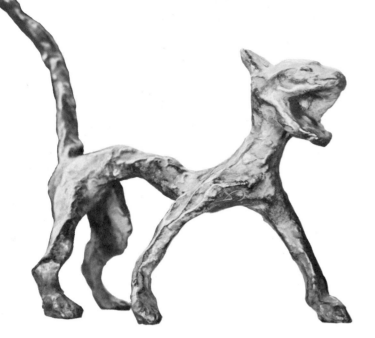

Le Chat, 1930. Bronze, 9″ w. Fondation Maeght, Saint-Paul-de-Vence, France.

Cow, 1930. Bronze, 8¼″ w. D. R. A. Wierdsma, Greenwich, Connecticut.

Lentil, 1944. Bronze, 20¼″ h. Mr. and Mrs. Andrew Gagarin, Litchfield, Connecticut.

Pierced Stone, 1944. Bronze, 36⅜″ h. Private collection, New York.

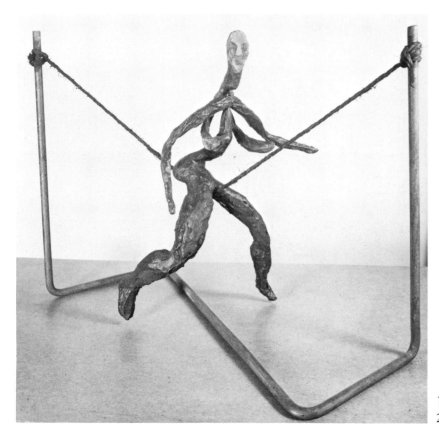

Woman on Cord, 1944 (cast 1968). Bronze, 21″ h. Perls Galleries, New York.

219

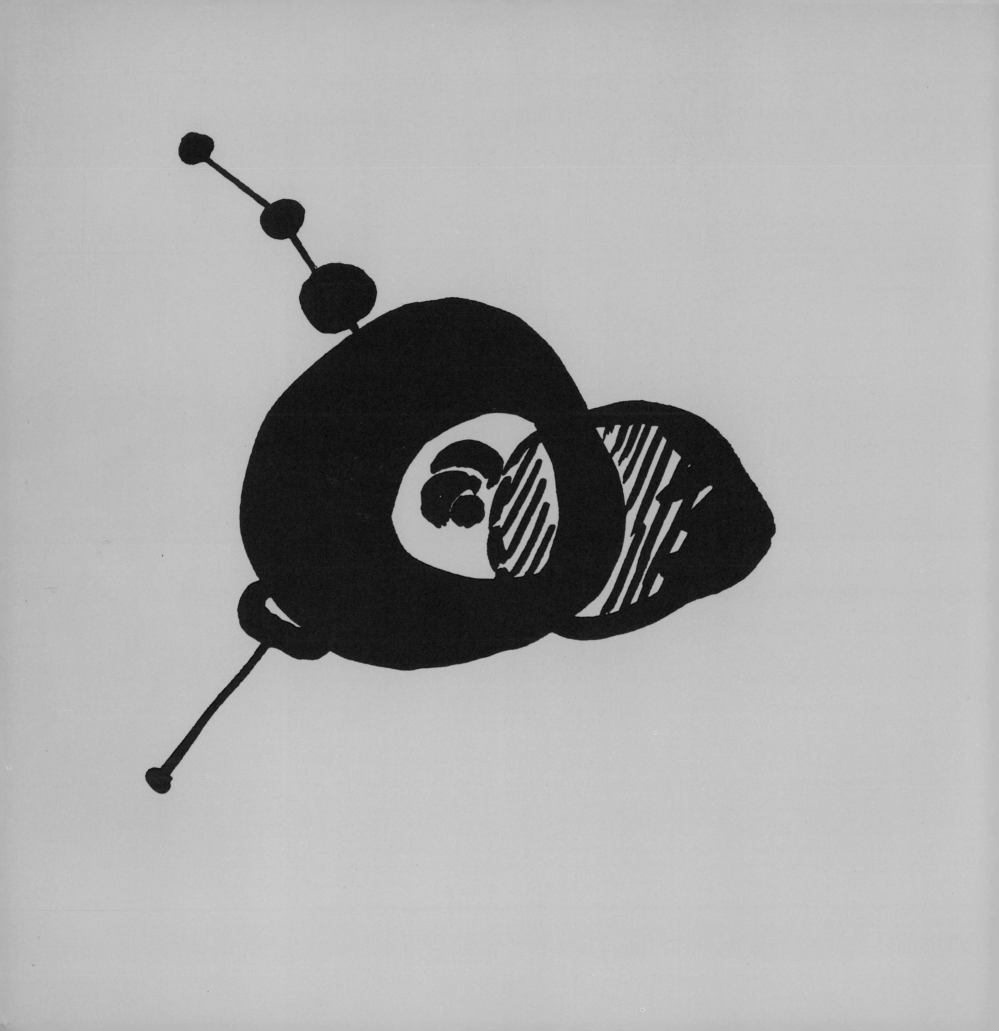

I made things in wood, taking a lump of wood and making very little alteration in its shape—just enough to turn it into something different.

Calder no longer does woodcarving, although wood was one of the first materials he used for sculpture. Right after he began making wire caricatures of people and animals in 1926, he started working with wood. The first pieces were only slightly altered from roots or a "lump of wood" that, as found objects, had already suggested to him some creature or other. Generally these works are not much more interesting than the bits of anthropomorphic driftwood that Sunday-sculptors pick up, alter slightly, and mount on free-form wooden bases. And Calder's early figurative wood sculptures—minimally carved from blocks of wood, surprisingly static and impersonal, bear a general resemblance to the "advanced" direct carving Calder saw in Paris and New York in the 1920–30 decade, such as that of his friend José de Creeft. They now look conventional and cannot be considered of more than minor interest in his oeuvre.

However, in 1929, when Calder first exhibited his woodcarvings at the Weyhe Gallery in New York, they were well received by the critics. Murdock Pemberton of *The New Yorker*, a Calder enthusiast since the young artist's first exhibit three years earlier, predicted that Calder's major work would be in wood. He was mistaken, but his general assessment of Calder's place in modern sculpture was astute: "Calder is nothing for your grandmother but we imagine he will be the choice of your sons. He makes a mockery of the old-fashioned frozen-stone school of sculpture and comes nearer to life in his creations than do nine-tenths of the serious stone-cutters."

There are a number of splendid sculptures to be found among Calder's early works in wood, such as the Museum of Modern Art's boxwood *Horse*, cleverly constructed from separate pieces of wood rather than carved from a single block. The reversibility of *Double Cat* makes it a delightful tour de force, and carvings such as *Cow* make interesting use of the natural grain and shape of the chosen piece of wood (". . . his cow is a cow with all of her pathos left in," said Pemberton). Seeing Calder's *Cow*, an entrepreneur suggested that it be mass-produced. The idea did not appeal to the artist, ever sensitive to his materials: "That piece of wood turned out to be a cow, but the next one might be a cat. How do I know?" The most important aspect of Calder's wood animal sculptures is that, as in the early animal drawings, he has captured a significant pose or movement with astonishing economy of means.

Calder talks about woodcarvings in his autobiography:

Peekskill, New York, 1928:
I worked outside on an upturned water trough and carved the wooden horse bought later by the Museum of Modern Art, a cow, a giraffe, a camel, an elephant, two elephants, another cat, several circus figures, a man with a hollow chest, and an ebony lady bending over dangerously, whom I daringly called *Liquorice*.

Wood Sculpture

Cambridge, Massachusetts, 1930:
I must have made a little money, somehow, in all this—I sold a few wood sculptures: for $100, $200 and $500. . . . So, I was in a position to go to Paris again, by March.

In the mid-thirties Calder turned again to wood sculpture, but now it was abstract, like the rest of his work. There were objects which might be classified as wood stabiles. One of these, *Gibraltar*, is a masterful sculpture in which contrasts of textures and shapes —rough wood, planed wood, wood spheres, thin steel rods—add up to a powerful and dramatic abstract composition; its title rightly emphasizes its monumentality. There were also more complex, abstract constructions which Calder named Constellations. Their origin, he explained in his autobiography, had to do with wartime shortages of metal:

In 1943, aluminum was being all used up in airplanes and becoming scarce. I cut up my aluminum boat, which I had made for the Roxbury pond, and I used it for several objects. I also devised a new form of art consisting of small bits of hardwood carved into shapes and sometimes painted, between which a definite relation was established and maintained by fixing them on the ends of steel wires. After some consultation with Sweeney and Duchamp, who were living in New York, I decided these objects were to be called "constellations."

Calder has said that both the shapes and title of his Constellations came from Miró's series of gouaches done a few years earlier, in 1940–41. They also bear a strong resemblance to objects in Yves Tanguy's canvases of the early forties; Tanguy was a friend and Connecticut neighbor at this time. However, it was more than a simple borrowing from his friends' themes: "[The Constellations] had for me a specific relationship to the *Universes* I had done in the early 1930s. They had a suggestion of some kind of cosmic nuclear gases—which I won't try to explain. I was interested in the extremely delicate, open composition."
Some Constellations are robust constructions of richly colored forms; others are small, simply painted black, as slender and graceful as spiders. Calder mounted some on flat bases, but more often—and these are more original in concept—he hung them from a wall without obvious means of support, a device used in some of his wall mobiles. The Constellations are undoubtedly among Calder's most beautiful sculptural inventions.

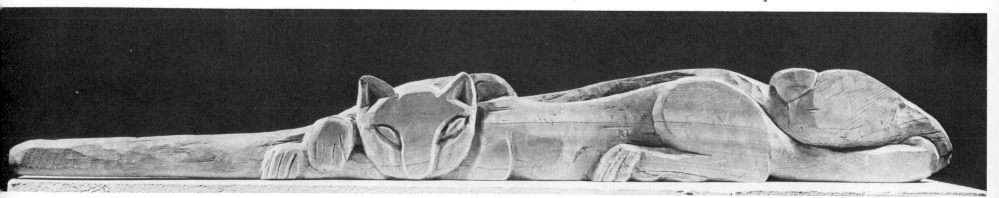

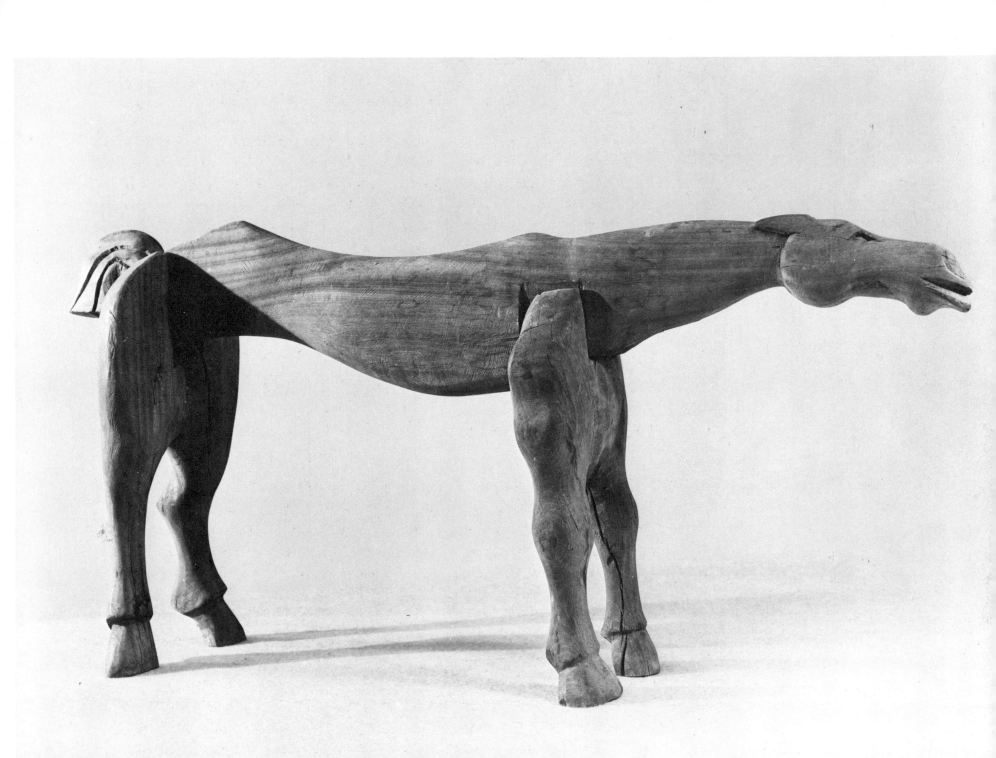

The Horse, 1928. Wood, 34¾″ w. The Museum of Modern Art, New York; acquired through the Lillie P. Bliss Bequest.

Double Cat, 1930. Wood, 51″ w. Whitney Museum of American Art, New York; gift of the Howard and Jean Lipman Foundation.

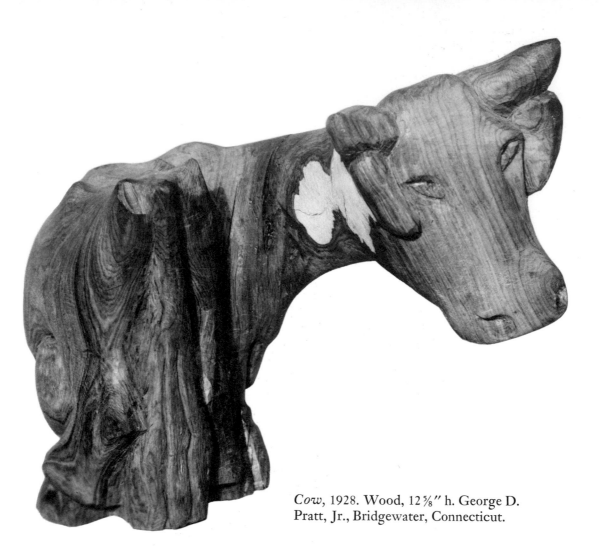

Cow, 1928. Wood, 12⅝″ h. George D. Pratt, Jr., Bridgewater, Connecticut.

Shark Sucker, 1930. Wood, 30⅞″ w. The Museum of Modern Art, New York; gift of the artist.

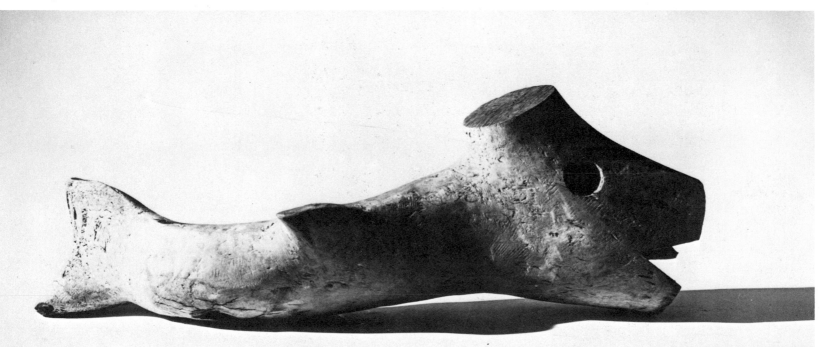

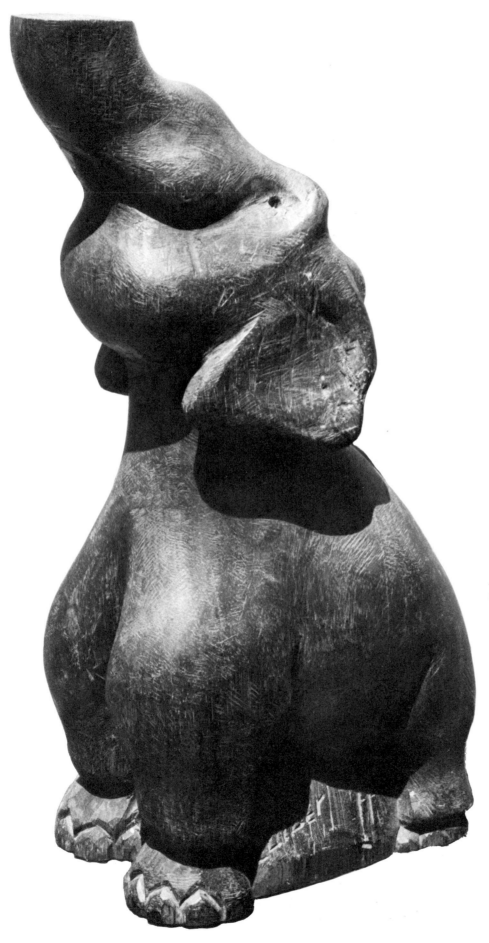

Elephant, 1928. Wood, 16″ h.
Collection of the artist.

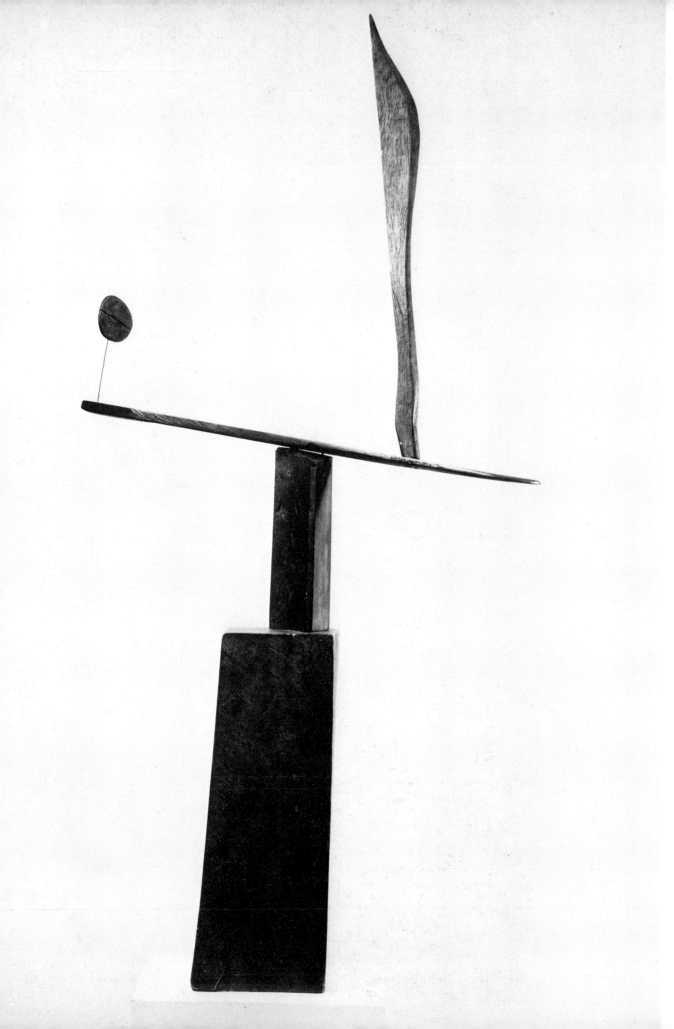

Wood Mobile, 1935. Wood, wire, 39⅜″ h. Ralph I. Goldenberg, Highland Park, Illinois.

OPPOSITE: *Gibraltar,* 1936. Wood, rods, 51⅞″ h. The Museum of Modern Art, New York; gift of the artist.

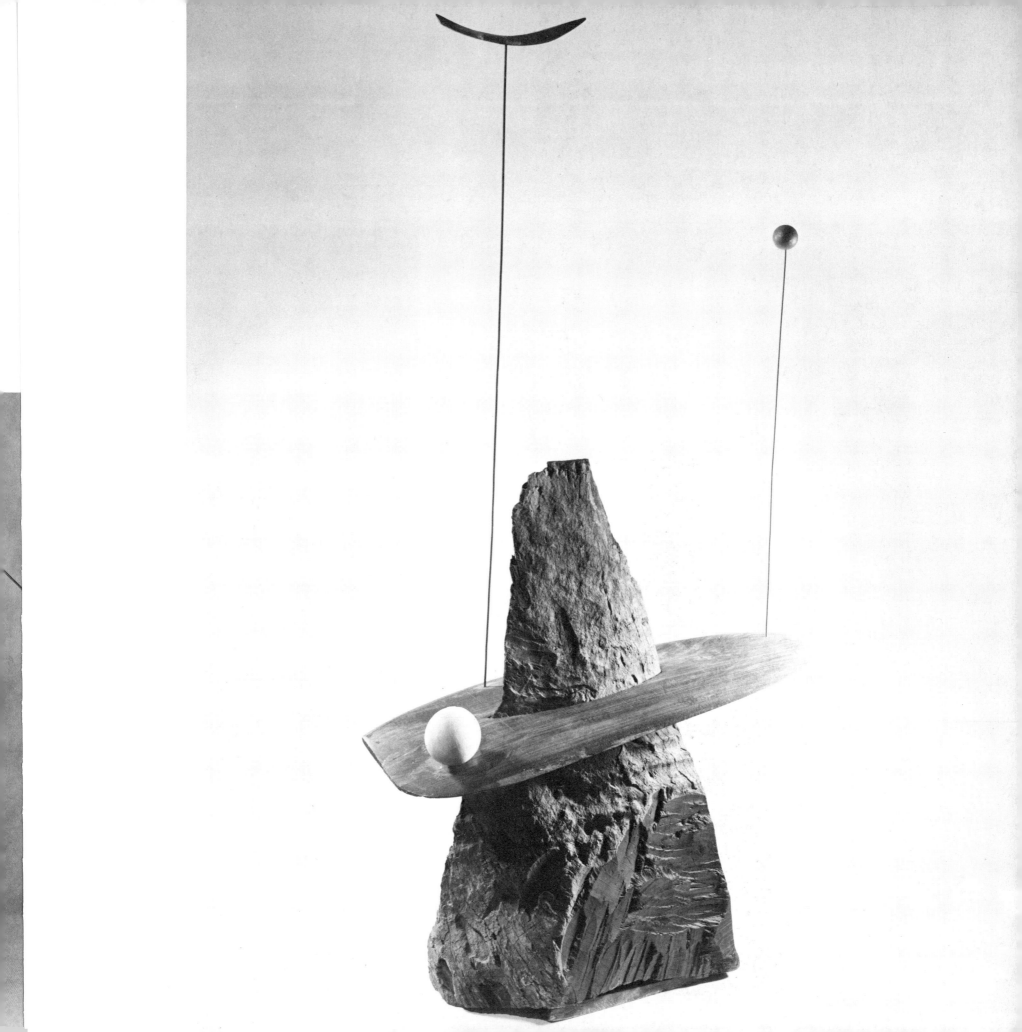

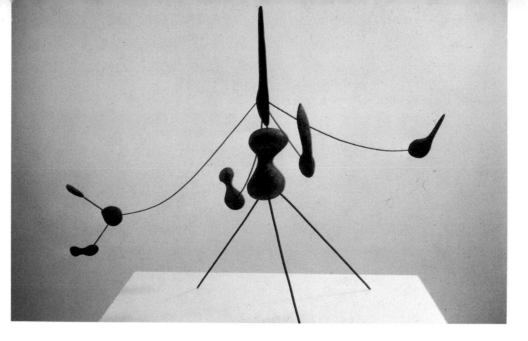

Constellation, c. 1943. Wood, wire, 32″ w. Private collection, New York.

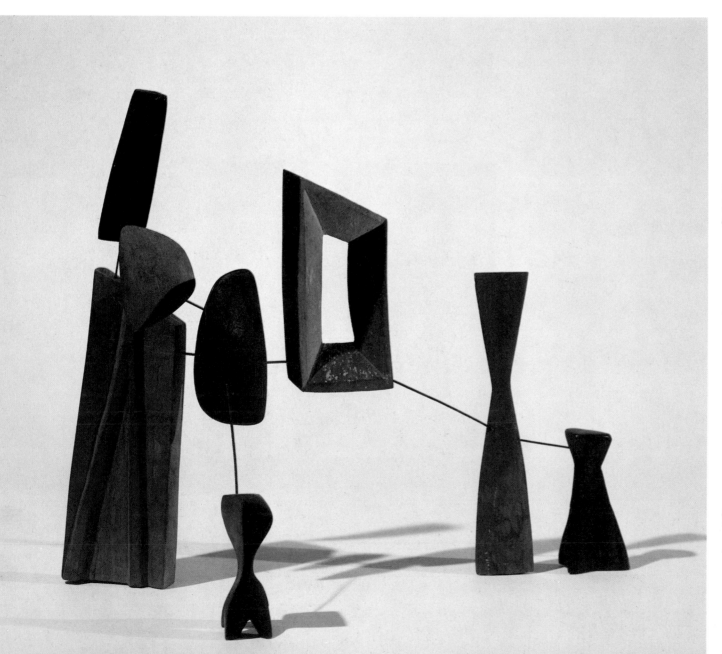

Constellation with Quadrilateral, 1943. Wood, wire, 18″ w. Private collection, Neuchâtel, Switzerland.

OPPOSITE: *Constellation*, c. 1943. Wood, wire, 51″ h. Mrs. Theodate Johnson Severns, New York.

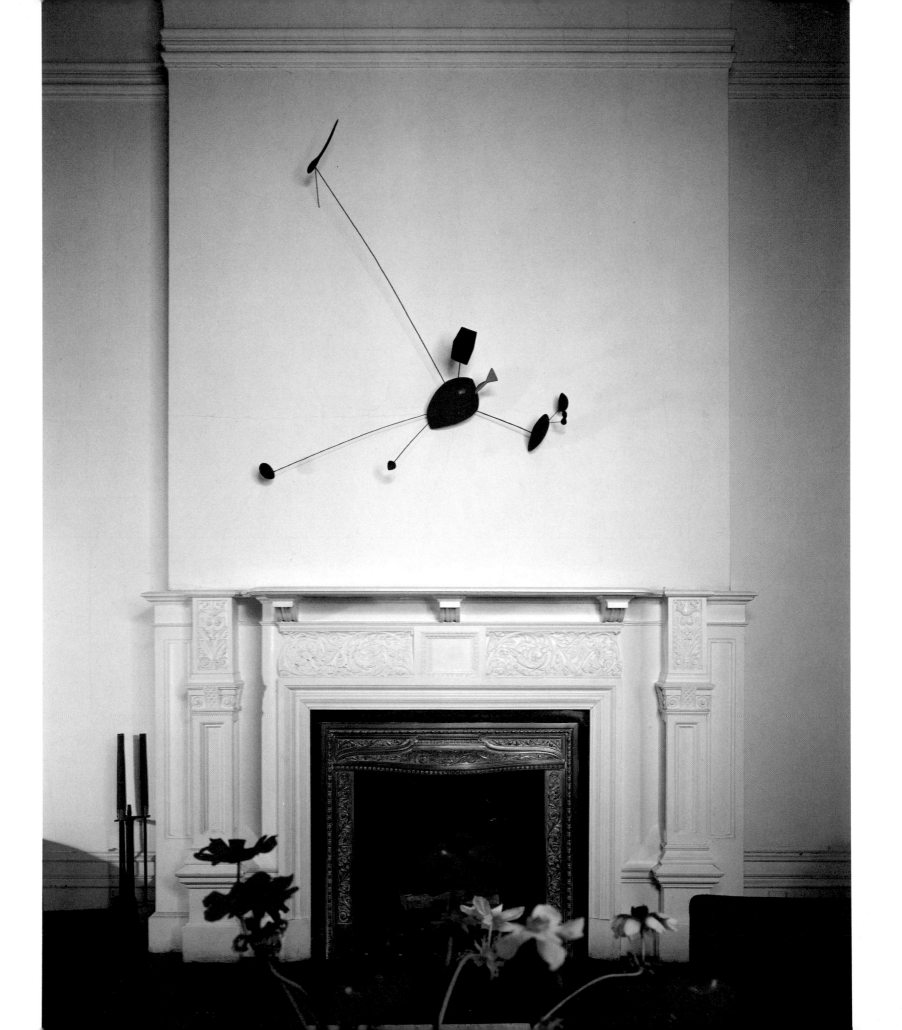

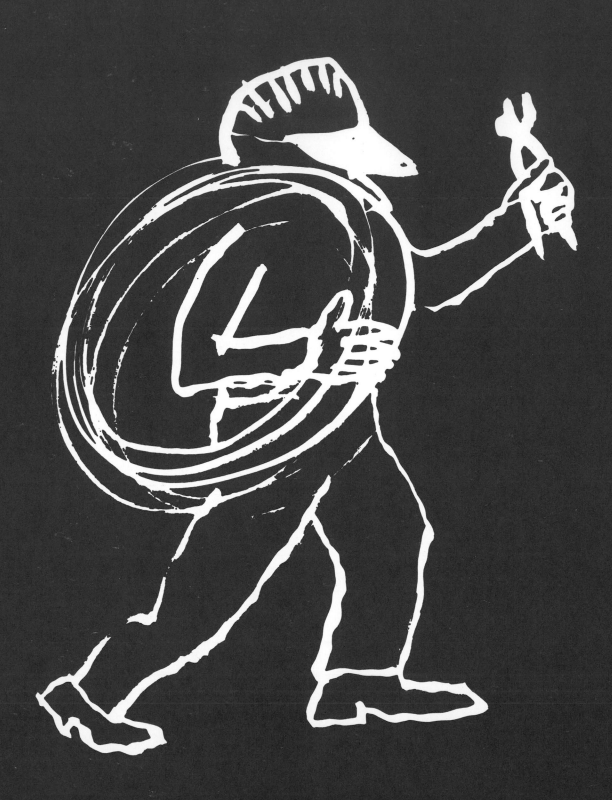

I even undid an old bale of wire I had had in storage since 1929, and took out Spring, *a seven-foot wire lady, and* Romulus and Remus *and an eleven-foot she-wolf in wire. I'd always thought these particularly humorous, but now they looked like good sculpture—after thirty-five years in the closet.*

Calder said this on the occasion of the 1964 retrospective at the Guggenheim Museum. Between the time of his first wire sculpture, made in New York in 1925, and the Guggenheim exhibition, public opinion about the importance of his work had changed as much as his had. The following comments by Calder, the critics and a few of his artist friends tell the story of the wire sculpture and of public reaction to it:

New York, 1925:
I'd made things out of wire before—jewelry, toys—but this was my first effort to represent an animal in wire. I don't know what became of it, so I have drawn it now, forty years later, as I remember it.

Paris, 1926:
I soon was making small animals in wood and wire and articulating them. I had made myself a little workbench and bought a few tools, some steel wire, and some soft wire in a hardware store on the avenue d'Orléans.

Clay Spohn . . . visited my studio and saw the objects I made out of wood and wire. . . . He said, "Why don't you make them completely out of wire?"
I accepted this suggestion, out of which was born the first Josephine Baker and a boxing Negro in a top hat.

1927
Stanley William Hayter recalls a time in Paris when he and Sandy were visiting José de Creeft. Sandy disappeared into the kitchen with his pliers and some wire. After some time he called them in. Attached to the water spigot was a dog outlined in wire; one hind leg, linked to the faucet, lifted as the water was turned on.

1928
In New York in February of 1928, I showed wire animals and people to Carl Zigrosser of the Weyhe Gallery and bookshop and he decided forthwith to give me a show. My first show. There were about fifteen objects and we priced these things at ten and twenty dollars. Two or three were sold. Among those sold was the first Josephine Baker which I had made in Paris. I think it is about then that some lady critic said:

"Convoluting spirals and concentric entrails; the kid is clever, but what does papa think?"

Wire Sculpture

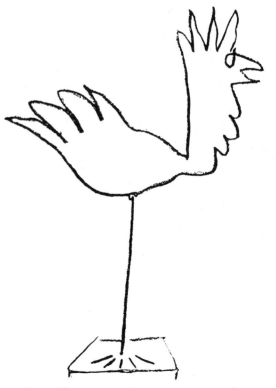

Drawing of lost 1925 wire rooster.

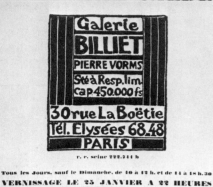

Galerie Billiet announcement, 1929.

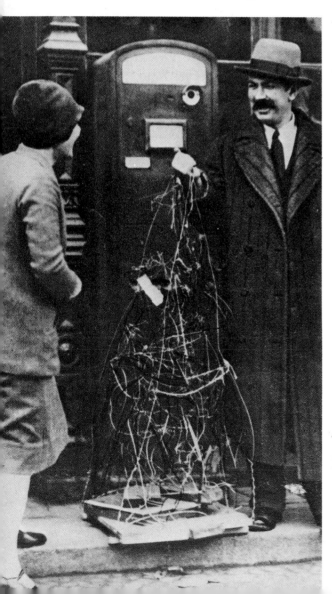

Calder with wire-sculpture bundle, Berlin, 1929.

The *Art News* review to which Calder referred began: "Of the wire sculpture of Alexander Calder, Jr., the best is silence."

A *Times* article begins with comment on *Romulus and Remus:* "Copper wire and bureau drawer knobs made their first appearance as mediums of artistic expression yesterday at the twelfth annual exhibition of the Society of Independent Artists. . . . The she-wolf was ten feet long and one wire thick."

Luckily, I had had a stroke of fortune. In the fall of 1928, somebody appreciated my wire portraits and ordered five objects in wire to illustrate the strength of the frames they manufactured for eyeglasses. Before leaving for Paris I completed this order. I did wire athletes tugging at the lenses for the firm of Batten, Barton, Durstine & Osborn, and I got my first check . . . with the thousand dollars—after having laid plans for my later New York show—I decided to go abroad again and to pay myself the luxury of taking the *De Grasse* of the French Line as a passenger.

I . . . had an orange bicycle with which I used to run around the *quatorzième arrondissement* to visit friends. I wore gray knickerbockers and red socks. At one point I had a cold and held a piece of camphor under my nose with a wire that looped and went behind my ears.

1929
A caption under a newspaper photo of the now-famous *Brass Family* presented it more as a curiosity than as a work of art: "It is only one of a number of fantastic groups he has created for his own amusement."

I had with me fifteen to twenty wire sculptures of different sizes. They made a great open bundle five to six feet long and two in diameter—awkward but light.
 I landed in Berlin. Sacha Stone had arranged a show for me at the Galerie Neumann und Nierendorf.
 The day following my arrival, we took a cab to the Berlin station, with Sacha and my wire-sculpture bundle. He intended to take the official picture of my arrival. The bundle was so large that we had to get the cab driver to open up the top. And he said:
 "What, for all that *Eisenschrott* [iron junk]?"
 Finally, the only object sold was a small wire dachshund. I believe he was taken to Mannheim. I am always hoping to find him in the museum there, some day, but I have visited Mannheim since and there was no trace of him.

Calder's first one-man show in Paris, at the Galerie Billiet, exhibited wood and wire sculptures. Jules Pascin's preface to the catalogue states: "I know that he will soon be accepted, in spite of his ugly mug, and he will exhibit with shattering success. . . ."

A *Paris Montparnasse* article is headlined, "Le fil de fer devient statue." ["Wire becomes statue."]

Paris, 1931:

The *Chicago Daily Tribune* (Paris edition) reviewed Calder's Galerie Percier show of wire portraits and abstract wire constructions: "Many of the works shown by Calder are extremely witty. His abstract compositions . . . are, according to Leo Stein, more complete and satisfying than the recent abstractions of Pablo Picasso. Mr. Stein, it is well known, was one of the 'discoverers' of Picasso. . . ."

Fernand Léger, in his preface to the Galerie Percier catalogue, wrote:

Before these new works—transparent, objective, exact, I think of Satie, Mondrian, Marcel Duchamp, Brancusi, Arp, those uncontested masters of inexpressible and silent beauty. Calder is of this line.
    He is American one hundred per cent.
    Satie and Duchamp are one hundred per cent French.
    How do they agree?

Calder was reluctant to include his wire portraits in the Galerie Percier show, feeling that they detracted from the new abstract work which he had begun shortly after his visit to Mondrian's studio in the fall of 1930. The gallery owner insisted (probably in the belief that the clever three-dimensional caricatures of leading artists and intellectuals would sell more readily), so Calder hung them near the ceiling, putting as much distance as possible between them and the abstract constructions. The Percier exhibition was clearly a landmark in Calder's career. Not only was it his first public showing of abstract sculpture, but it included the antecedents of both forms which are today considered his major contributions to twentieth-century sculpture, the mobiles and the stabiles. Most of the wire constructions were stationary—Arp later named them "stabiles"—but, as Calder has pointed out in his autobiography, there were also "two slightly articulated objects that swayed in the breeze." In the photograph of the Percier exhibition, one of these appears at far left and the other at center; these proto-mobiles were soon followed by more complex moving objects (see "Mechanized Sculpture").

In the early days in Montparnasse, Calder was called "the wire king." Today, a number of his wire sculptures must be considered—even when measured against his mobiles and stabiles—among the most original and remarkable sculptural achievements of our time. Often they were not appreciated, however, and numbers of them, like many of Calder's other early works, were casually discarded or lost by their owners. The Stillmans tell of a baby-sitter they shared with the Calders in Roxbury about 1940 who was indignant when, after an evening of child care at the Calders, she was offered "one of those big wire things" instead of her usual two dollars. When *The Brass Family* was exhibited in 1929, it was priced at $500—the highest figure in Calder's show at the Fifty-sixth Street Galleries in New York; the smaller wire sculptures ranged from $25

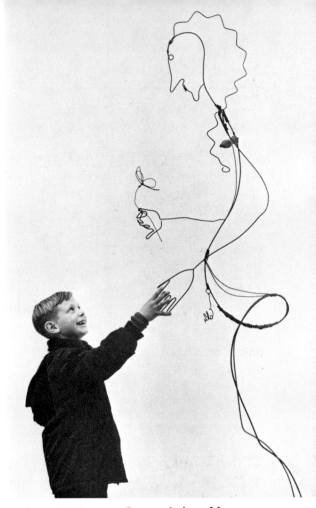

Spring, 1928, at Guggenheim Museum exhibition, 1964.

Studio, rue de la Colonie, Paris, 1931.

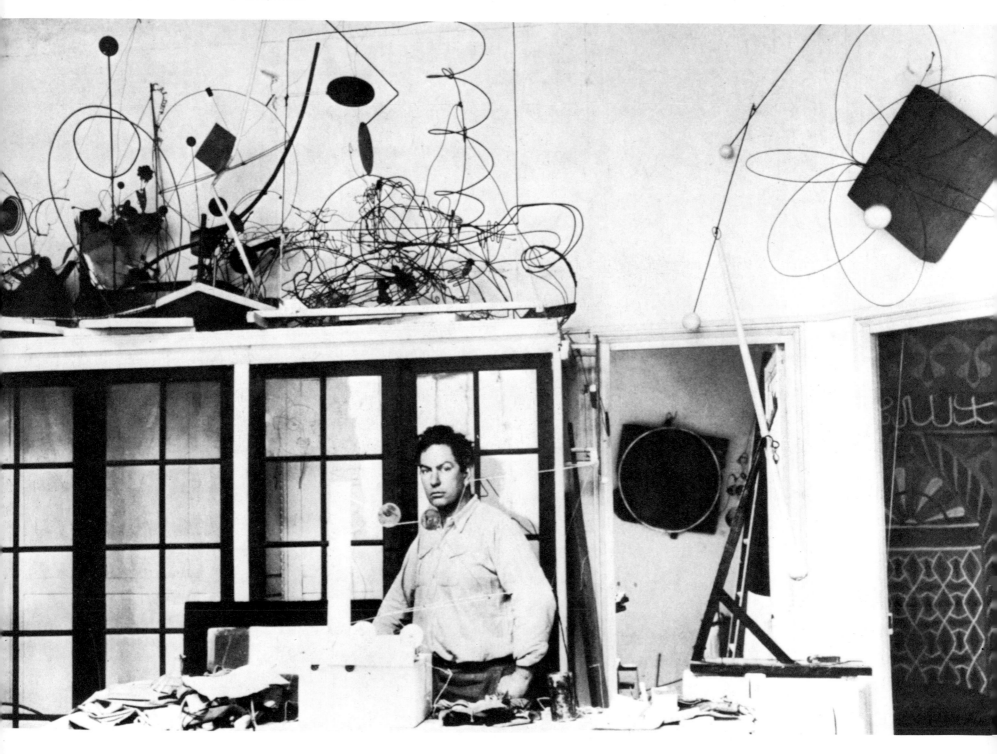

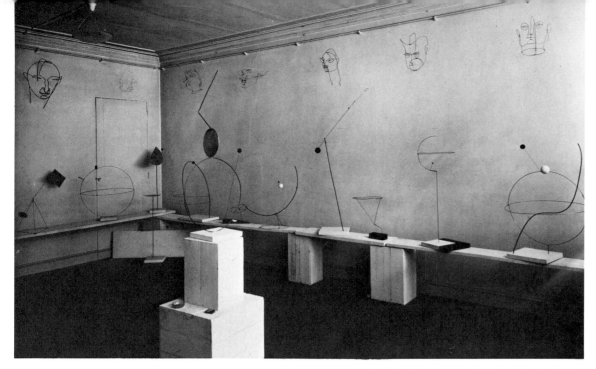

Galerie Percier exhibition, Paris, 1931.

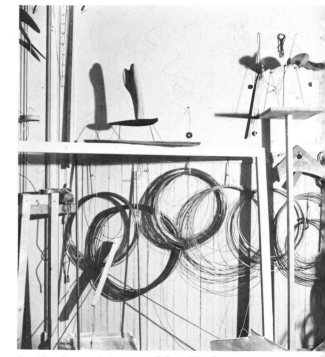

Studio, Second Avenue, New York, 1938.

to $50, with portrait heads $100 each. *The Brass Family* never sold, and Calder kept it in his personal collection until 1969, when he gave it to the Whitney Museum (its valuation was then $100,000).

The *Josephine Baker* made in Paris in 1926 was the first of a number of Calder's wire portraits of the American jazz singer who was then the rage of Paris. These calligraphic-sculptural caricatures are among Calder's most remarkable works in any medium. Some are prototypes of the mobile concept, designed to be suspended from a thread and quiver in the slightest breeze, the belly a shimmering spiral and the whole figure further animated and enlivened by the shadows on the wall. Jack Baur has remarked that it is "as if a tremor of life ran through them." Calder recently told Maurice Bruzeau that he had always worked with the idea of making things move, even his wire figures. "You think they were fastened down, as for an exhibition? At home, they were hung from the ceiling."

The bawdy humor of the huge *Romulus and Remus*, with its pendant wooden doorstops featured as equally appropriate for the she-wolf's dugs and the twins' penises, is hilariously funny but also, as Sandy has modestly remarked, "good sculpture."

The majestic *Brass Family* is surely the masterpiece of the wire sculptures. It is revealing to compare it with *Tumbling Family*, one of the large 1931 circus drawings; in photographs the wire and wire-like lines of the drawing look virtually interchangeable. The chief difference is that in the sculpture Calder used two different gauges of brass wire, the heavier making a strong, wavy triangle above the anchor man's legs—a functional and compositional support for his pyramidal acrobat family. *The Brass*

237

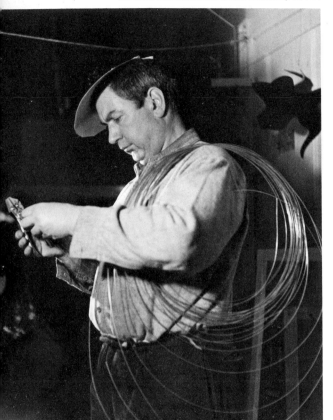

In the Second Avenue studio, 1938.

Family is a sculptural tour de force, and the wire acrobats evoke the same tense excitement that one would experience while watching actual performers. The composition is stable and symmetrical, but there are enough variations to avoid rigid frontality or any possibility of monotony; notice, for instance, the faces, some blank, some with features. Everything is presented in lively and entertaining shorthand, from a lady acrobat's flying hair and hefty hips to the gigantic strong man's powerful chest muscles and his impressively displayed sex. It's all playful, and monumental.

Wire, more than any other material, is Calder's special medium. In his childhood he had twisted discarded bits of copper wire into jewelry for his sister's dolls; he used wire for his little Circus performers and for his caricature-like sculptures. His first abstract sculptures were made of wire, and as the mobiles developed, wire continued to be one of his principal materials, used to connect the other elements. In the early days Calder sometimes appeared at his gallery openings carrying shears and pliers, with a roll of wire hung over his shoulder (as in the 1938 photograph shown here), and produced an entire show of wire sculptures on the spot. Calder works as quickly in this medium as some other artists make pencil sketches. He once told his sister, Peggy, "I think best in wire."

Romulus and Remus, 1928. Wire, wood, 9′4″ w.
The Solomon R. Guggenheim Museum, New York.

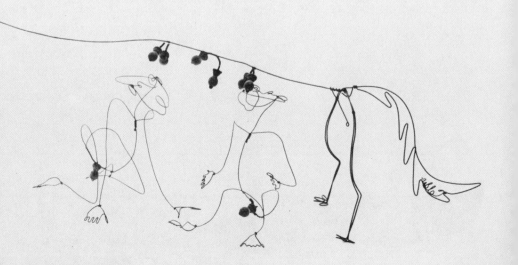

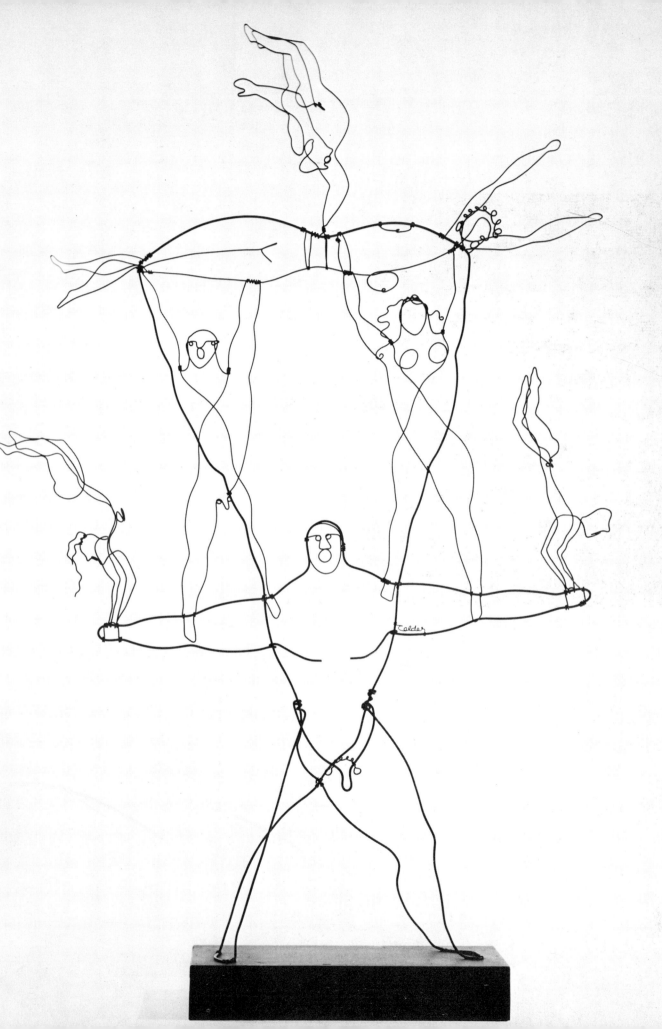

BELOW: *Wire Sculpture by Calder*, 1928. Wire, 46½″ h. Sign for Weyhe Gallery exhibition. Whitney Museum of American Art, New York; gift of Howard and Jean Lipman.

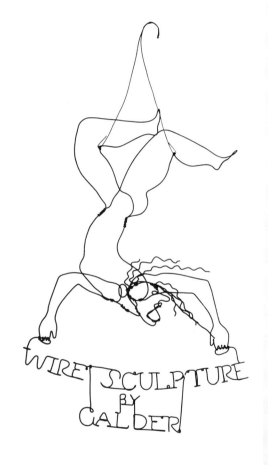

The Brass Family, 1929. Wire, 64″ h. Whitney Museum of American Art, New York; gift of artist.

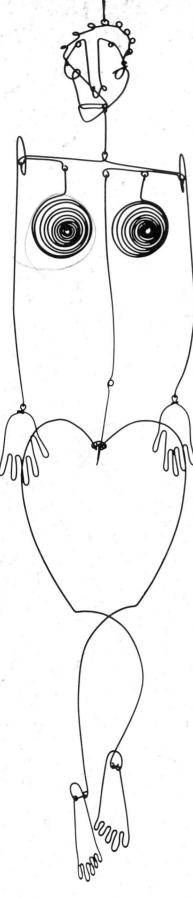

Aztec Josephine Baker, 1930. Wire, approx. 39″ h. Present location unknown.

Josephine Baker, 1927–29. Wire, 39″ h. The Museum of Modern Art, New York; gift of the artist.

OPPOSITE: *Josephine Baker*, 1926. Wire, 39¾″h. Musée National d'Art Moderne, Paris; gift of ·the artist.

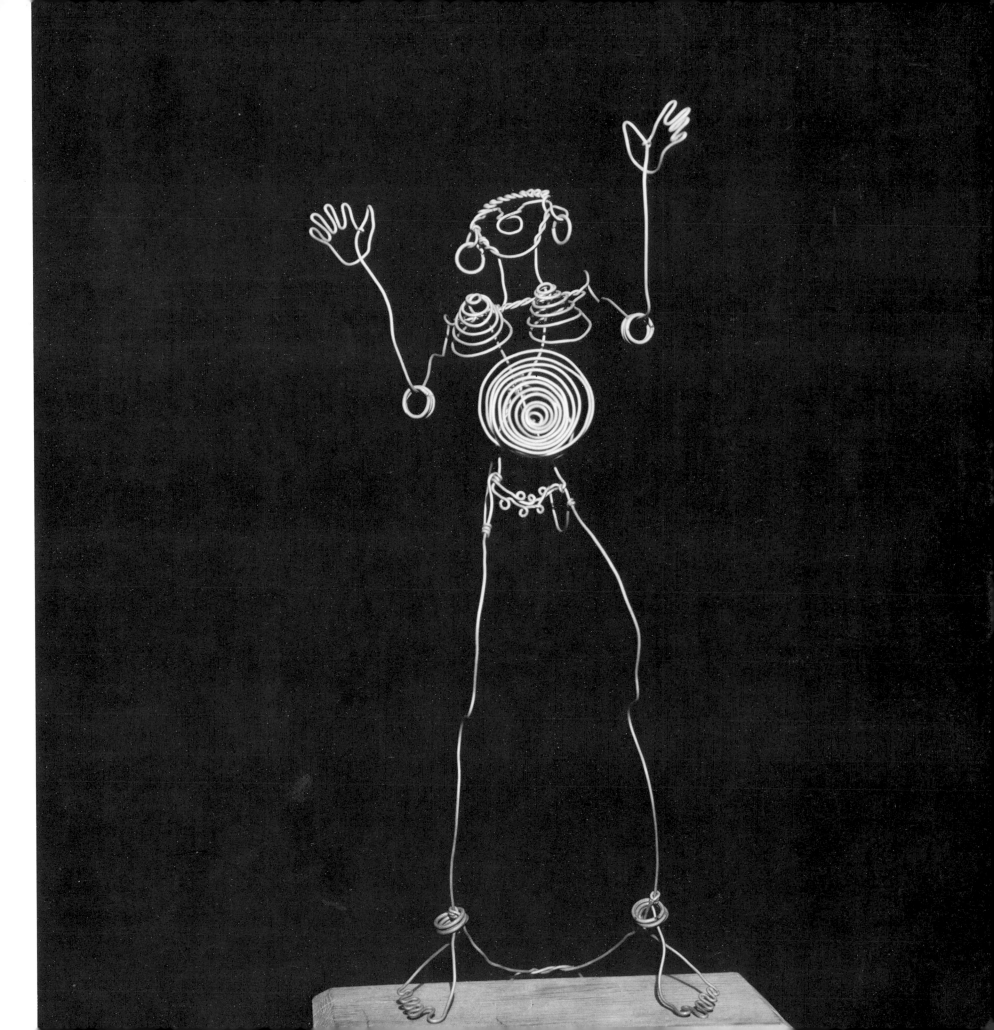

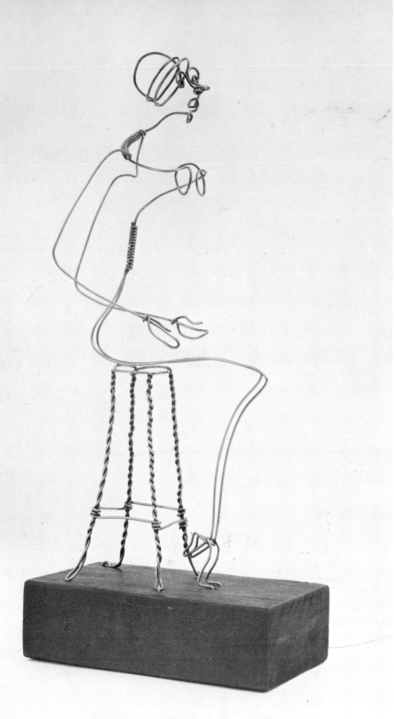

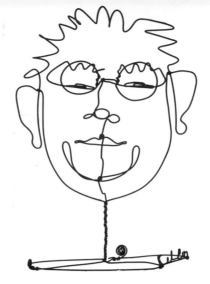

ABOVE: *Dr. Hans Cürlis*, 1929. Wire, 12½″ h. Dr. Hans Cürlis, Berlin.

LEFT: *Soda Fountain*, 1928. Wire, 10¾″ h. The Museum of Modern Art, New York; gift of the artist.

RIGHT: *Erhard Weyhe*, 1928. Wire, 21″ h. Weyhe Family Collection, New York.

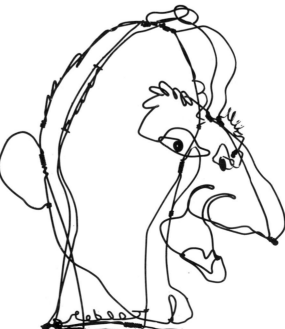

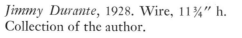
Jimmy Durante, 1928. Wire, 11¾″ h. Collection of the author.

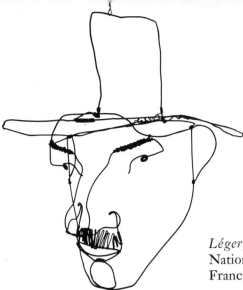

Léger, 1930. Wire, 16″ h. Musée National Fernand Léger, Biot, France.

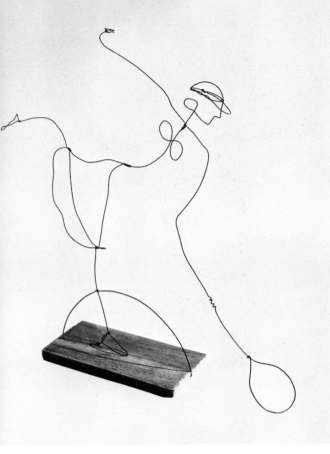

Helen Wills, 1928. Wire, 11″ h. Private collection, New York.

LEFT: *Varèse*, 1931. Wire, 14″ h. Louise Varèse, New York.

RIGHT: *The Hostess*, 1928. Wire, 11½″ h. The Museum of Modern Art, New York; gift of Edward M. M. Warburg.

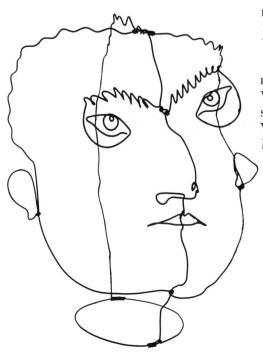

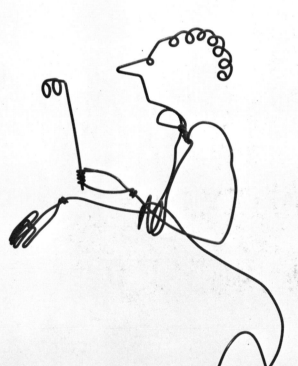

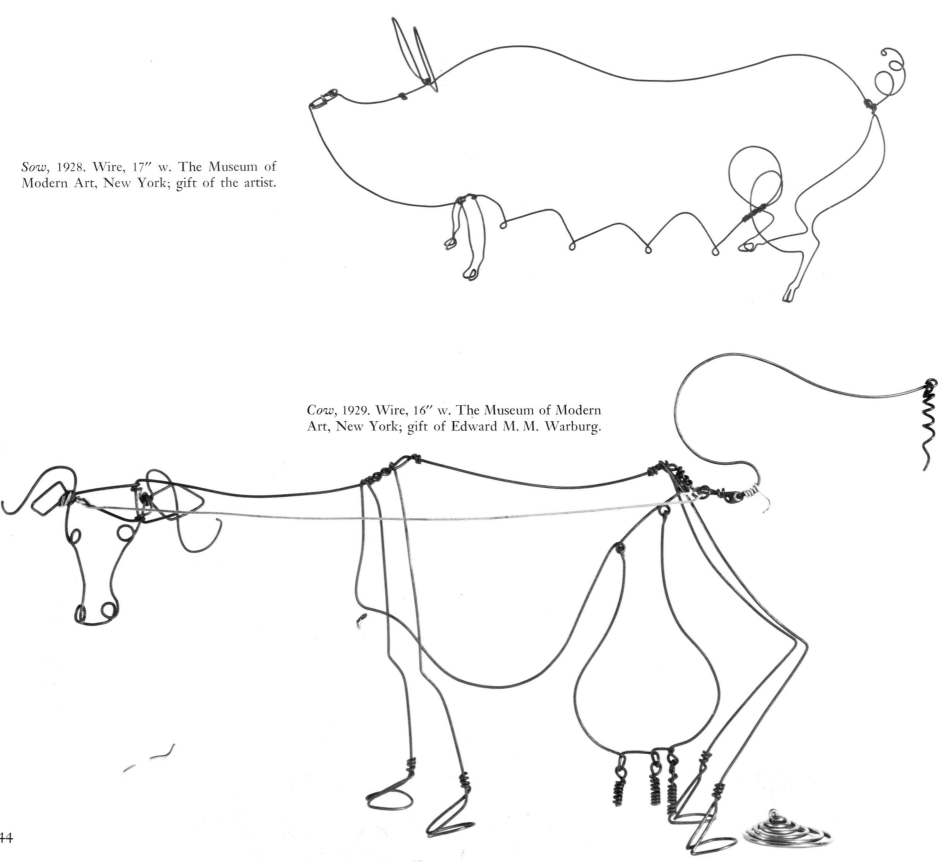

Sow, 1928. Wire, 17″ w. The Museum of Modern Art, New York; gift of the artist.

Cow, 1929. Wire, 16″ w. The Museum of Modern Art, New York; gift of Edward M. M. Warburg.

244

OPPOSITE: *Rearing Stallion*, c. 1928. Wire, 22¾″ h. Mr. and Mrs. Klaus G. Perls, New York.

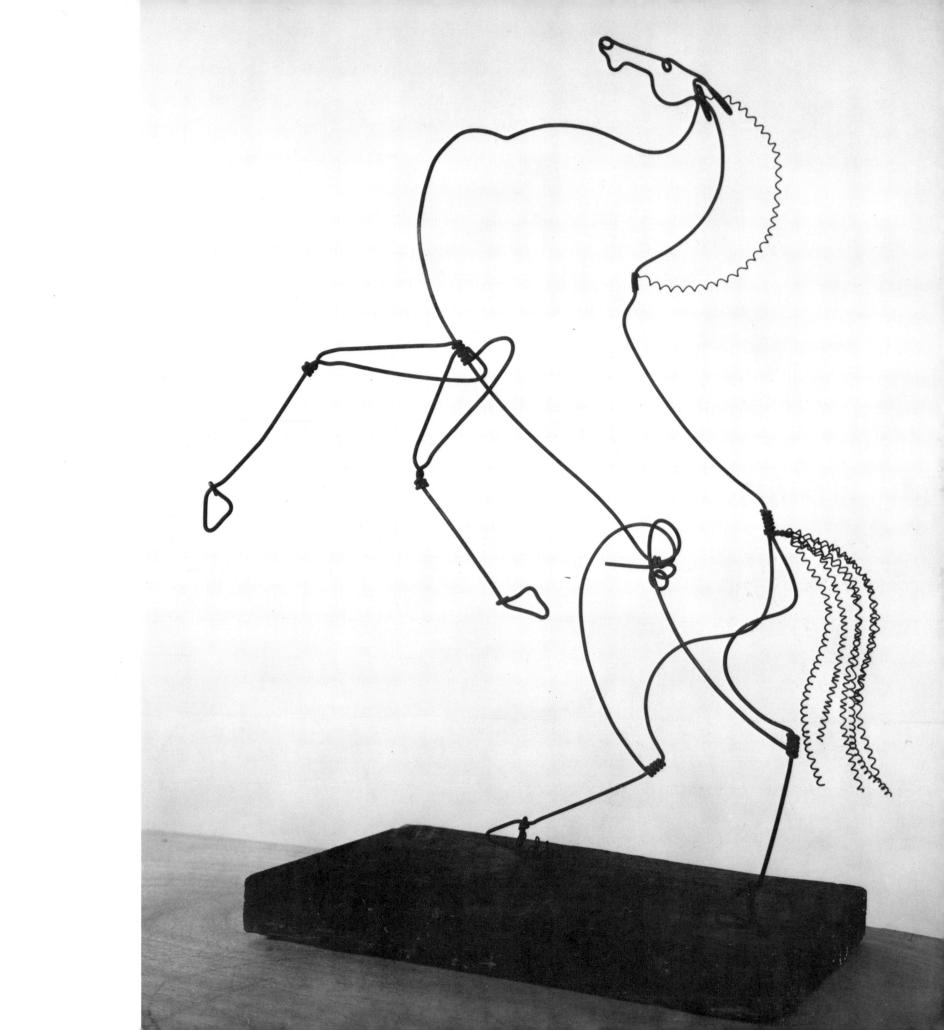

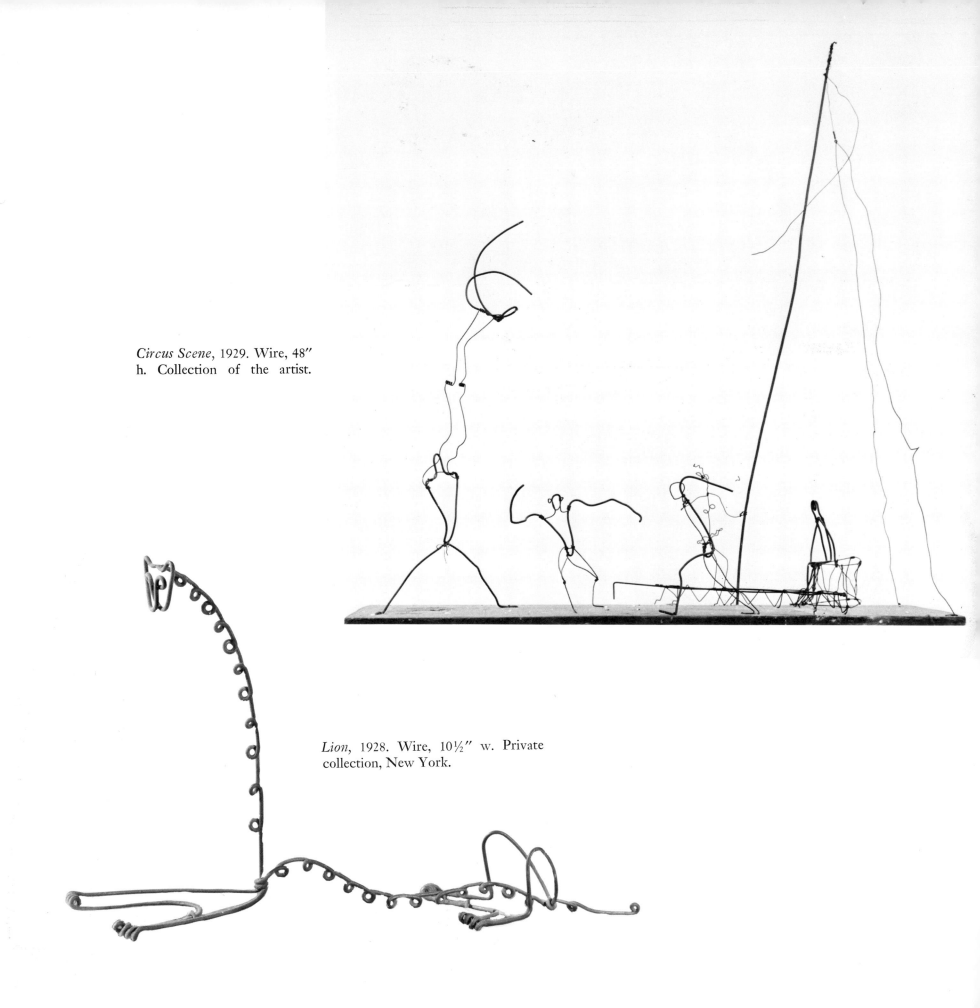

Circus Scene, 1929. Wire, 48″ h. Collection of the artist.

Lion, 1928. Wire, 10½″ w. Private collection, New York.

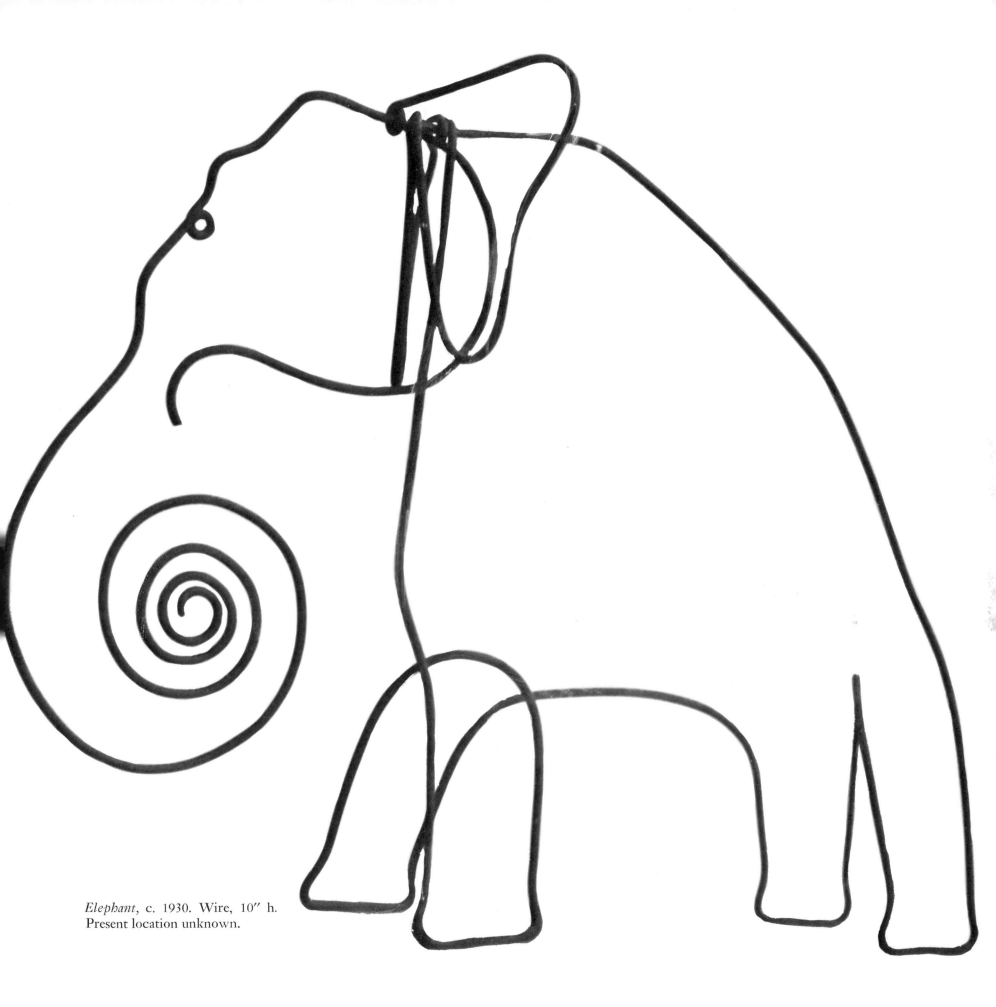

Elephant, c. 1930. Wire, 10″ h.
Present location unknown.

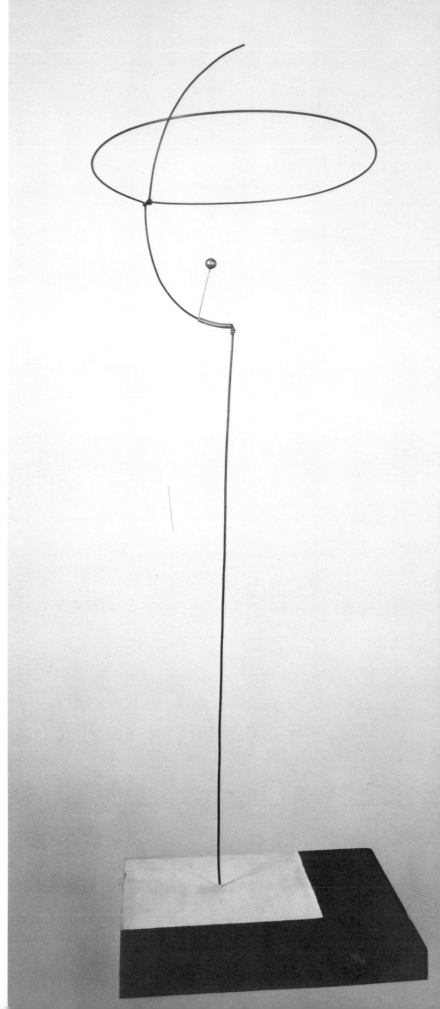

The Pistil, 1931. Wire, brass, 38″ h. Whitney Museum of American Art, New York; gift of the Howard and Jean Lipman Foundation (and purchase).

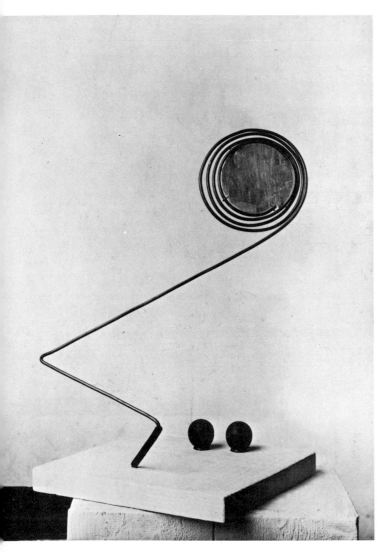

Kiki's Nose, 1931. Wire, tin, 18″ h. Formerly collection of Siri Rathsman, Paris.

248

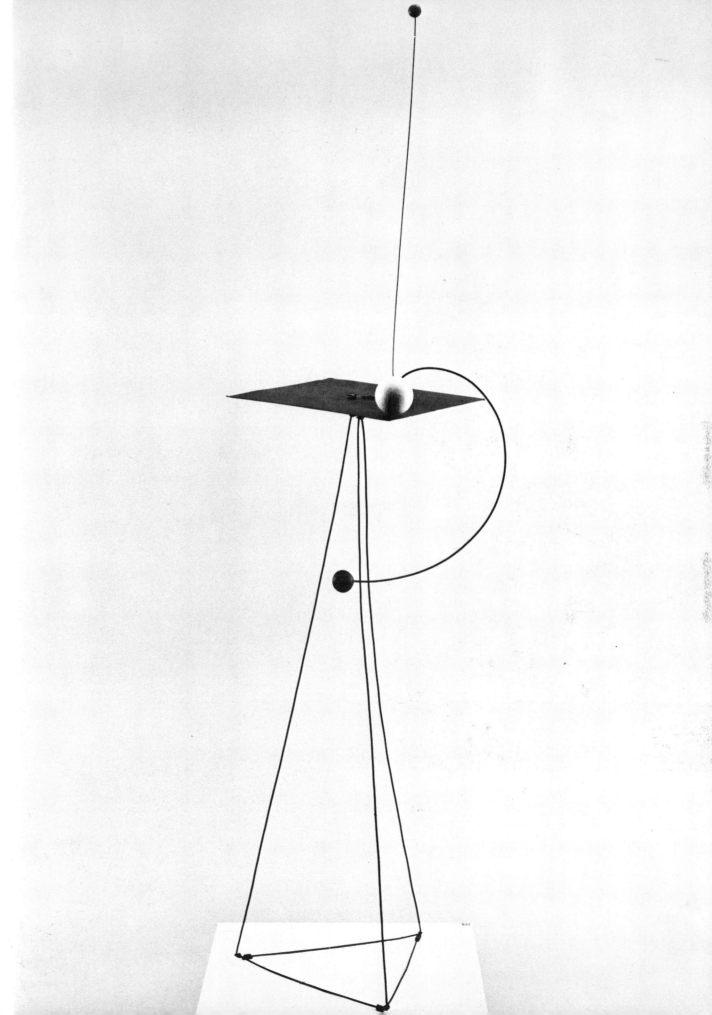

Little Ball with Counter-weight, c. 1930. Sheet metal, wire, wood, 63¾″ h. Mr. and Mrs. Leonard J. Horwich, Chicago.

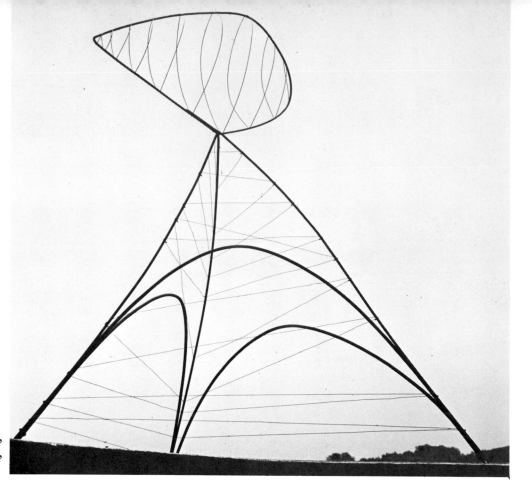

Untitled, c. 1940. Wire, rods, 54″ h. Mrs. Albert Fink Milton, Washington, Connecticut.

Tightrope, 1937. Wood, rods, wire, weights, 9′3½″ w. Collection of the artist.

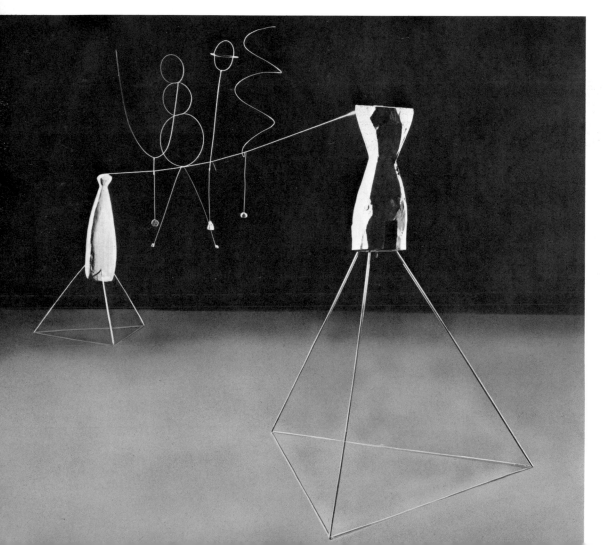

OPPOSITE: *Universe*, 1931. Wire, wood, 36″ h. Collection of the artist.

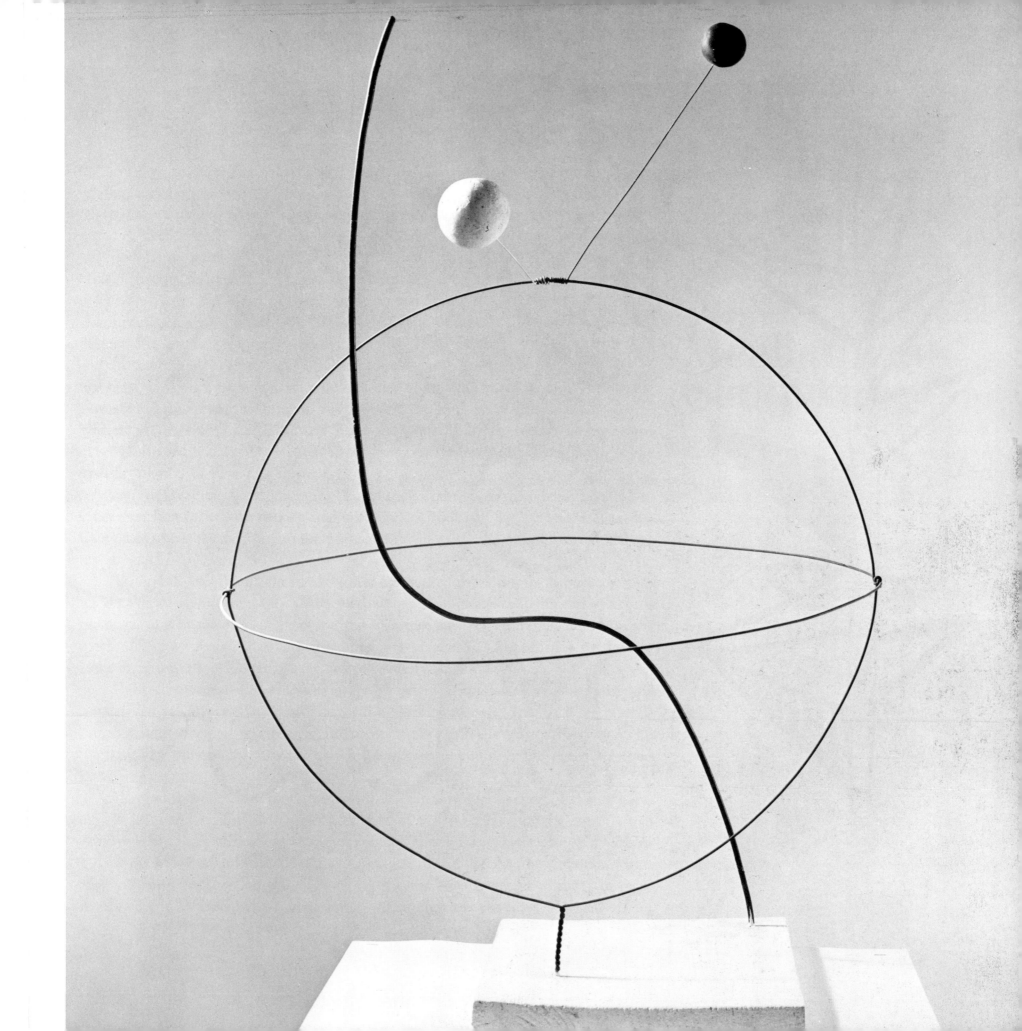

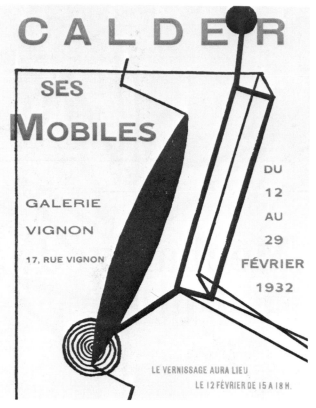

adapted and used ideas found in the abstract paintings of Mondrian and Miró and especially in the painted reliefs of Arp, themselves hybrids of painting and sculpture.

Experiments with motorized moving sculpture continued until the forties, but the predictable mathematical relationships, exactly repeating themselves, lost their appeal for Calder, who has always valued the elements of chance and spontaneity. He concentrated his attention on the free-swinging, infinitely variable mobiles and did not work with motorization in any significant way until 1974. He then revitalized some of the basic ideas of his early motorized sculptures and stage sets for a monumentally scaled and magnificently composed moving wall sculpture commissioned for the lobby of the Sears Tower in Chicago. It weighs 16,174 pounds, is 55 feet wide and 33 feet high; the total cost is discreetly placed at "under a million dollars." (It is interesting to note that when the Museum of Modern Art purchased its first Calder, a small motorized mobile titled *A Universe*, the artist asked $100 but settled for $60.) Initially Calder called the new Sears work *Pendulum*, for one of its main elements, but he eventually chose the title *Universe*, which refers back to his wire constructions of the early thirties. In a 1958 questionnaire Calder stated that one of these earlier Universes was "based on what the worlds must look like." His monumental new *Universe* is based on the same cosmic concept.

When Katharine Kuh asked him, in 1960, how he felt about his mechanized sculpture, Calder answered, "The motorized ones are too painful—too many bugaboos. Even the best are apt to be mechanically repetitious." Albert Einstein would have disagreed: he once spent forty minutes watching the ninety cycles of the Museum of Modern Art's *A Universe*, and is reported to have said he wished he had thought of it himself. He would surely have been mesmerized by the new Sears *Universe*, with its brilliantly colored elements, activated at varying speeds by seven separate motors to perform a monumental abstract ballet.

254

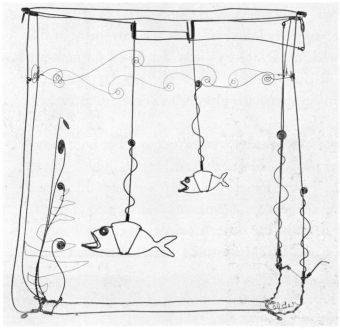

Fishbowl with Crank, 1929. Wire, 15⅞″ h. Private collection, New York.

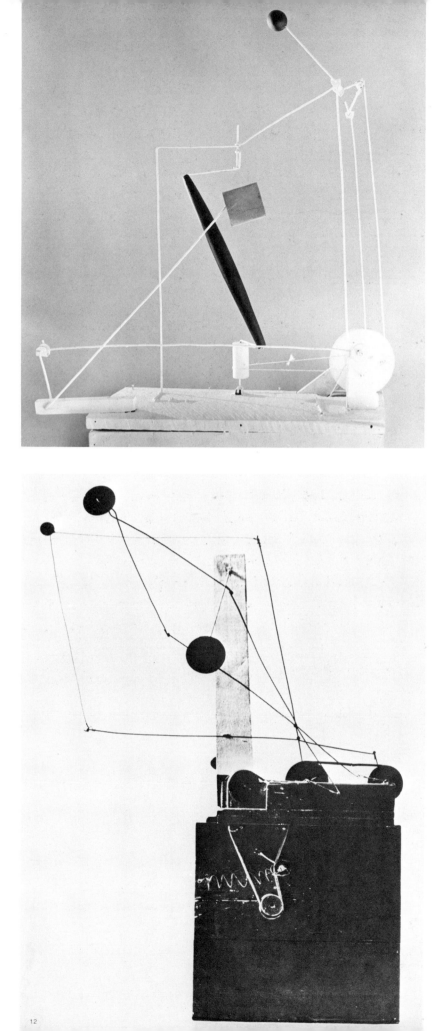

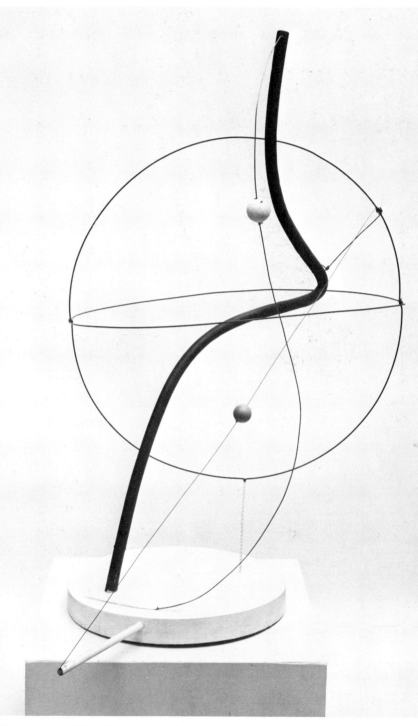

LEFT: *Dancing Torpedo Shape*, 1932. Painted wood, wire, sheet metal, motor, 28″ h. The Berkshire Museum, Pittsfield, Massachusetts.

A Universe, 1934. Painted steel pipe, wood, wire, string, motor, 40½″ h. The Museum of Modern Art, New York; gift of Abby Aldrich Rockefeller.

LEFT: *Pantograph*, 1933. Painted wood, wire, sheet metal, motor, 52″ h. Moderna Museet, Stockholm.

255

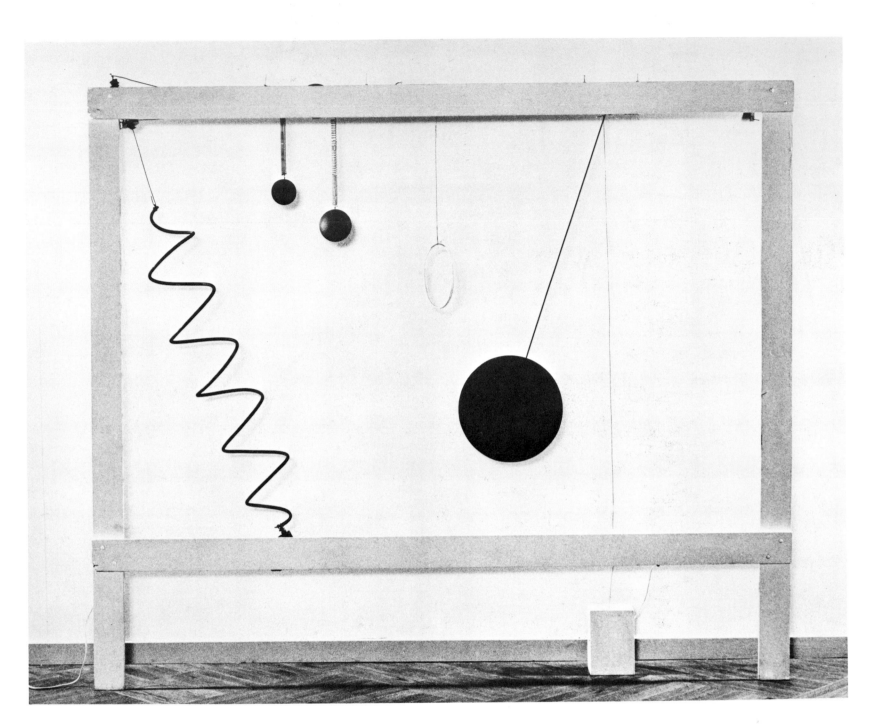

The White Frame, 1934. Painted wood, sheet metal, wire, motor, 7'6" × 9'. Moderna Museet, Stockholm.

OPPOSITE: *Half-circle, Quarter-circle and Sphere*, 1932. Painted wire, sheet metal, motor, 6'6¼" h. Whitney Museum of American Art, New York; gift of the Howard and Jean Lipman Foundation.

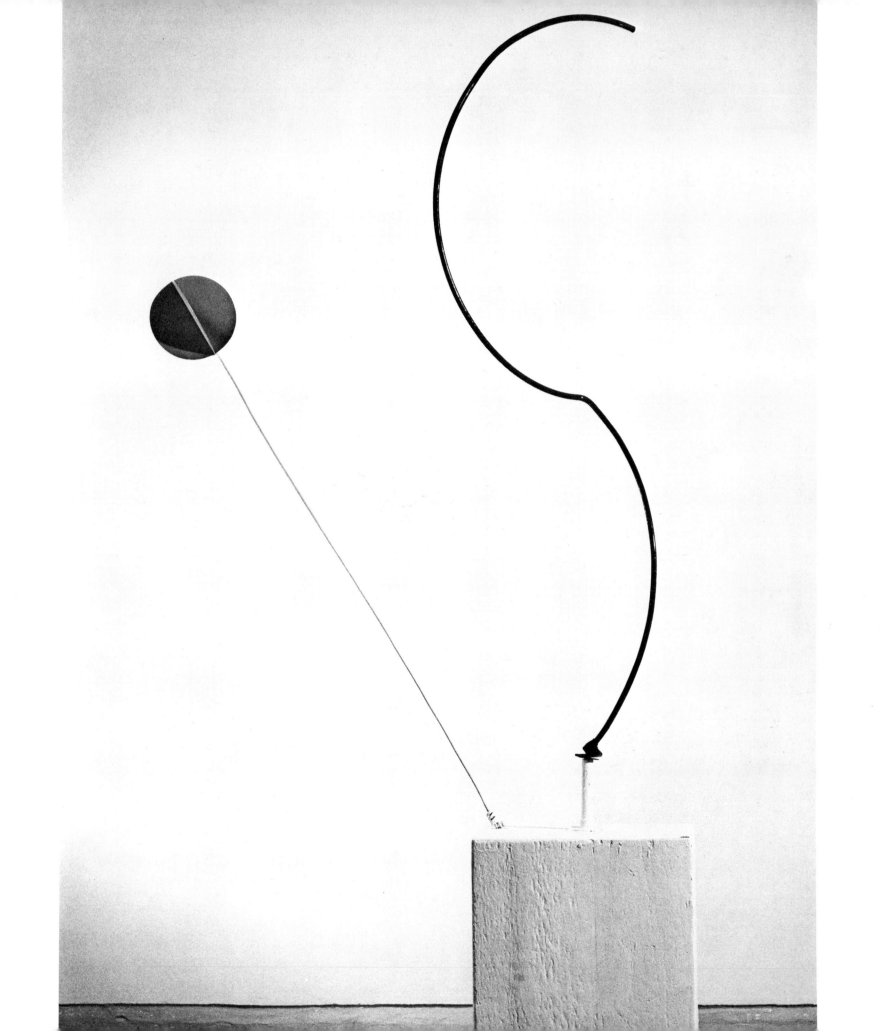

257

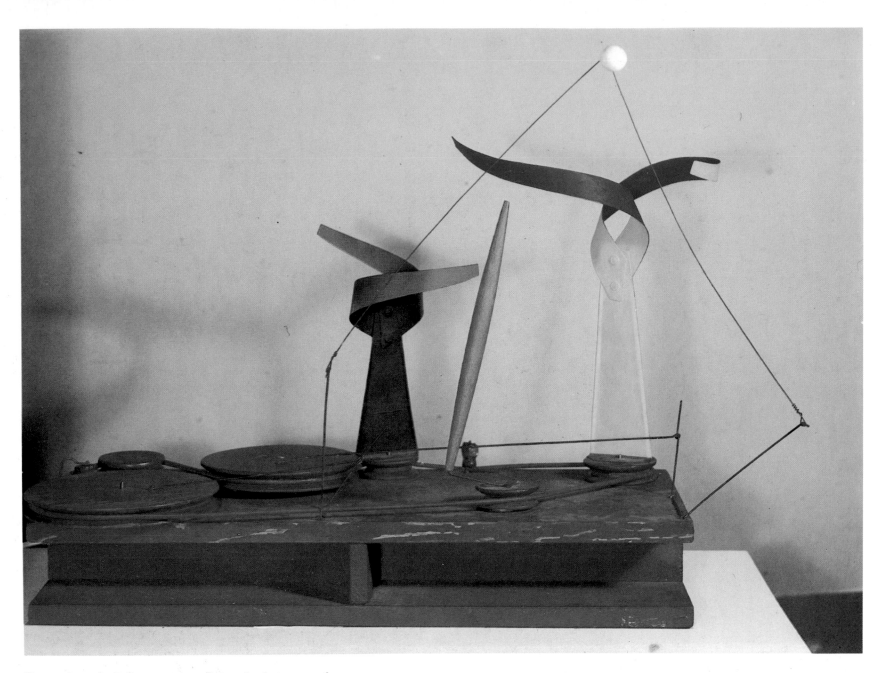

Dancers and Sphere, 1936. Painted sheet metal, wood, wire, motor, 17¾″ h. Galerie Maeght, Zurich.

258

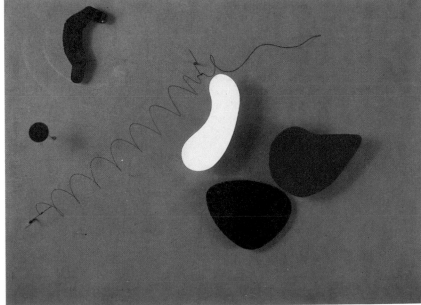

The Orange Panel, 1943. Painted wood, sheet metal, wire, motor, 36 × 48″. Mrs. H. Gates Lloyd, Haverford, Pennsylvania.

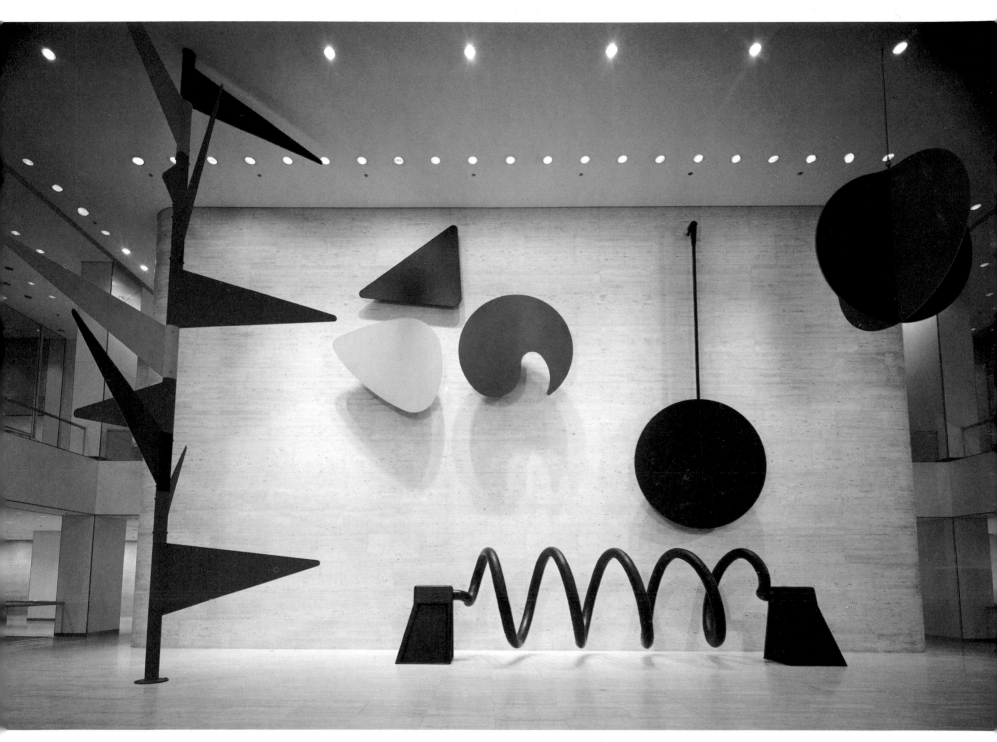

Universe, 1974. Painted stainless steel plate, aluminum plate, motors, 33 × 55'. Sears Tower, Chicago.

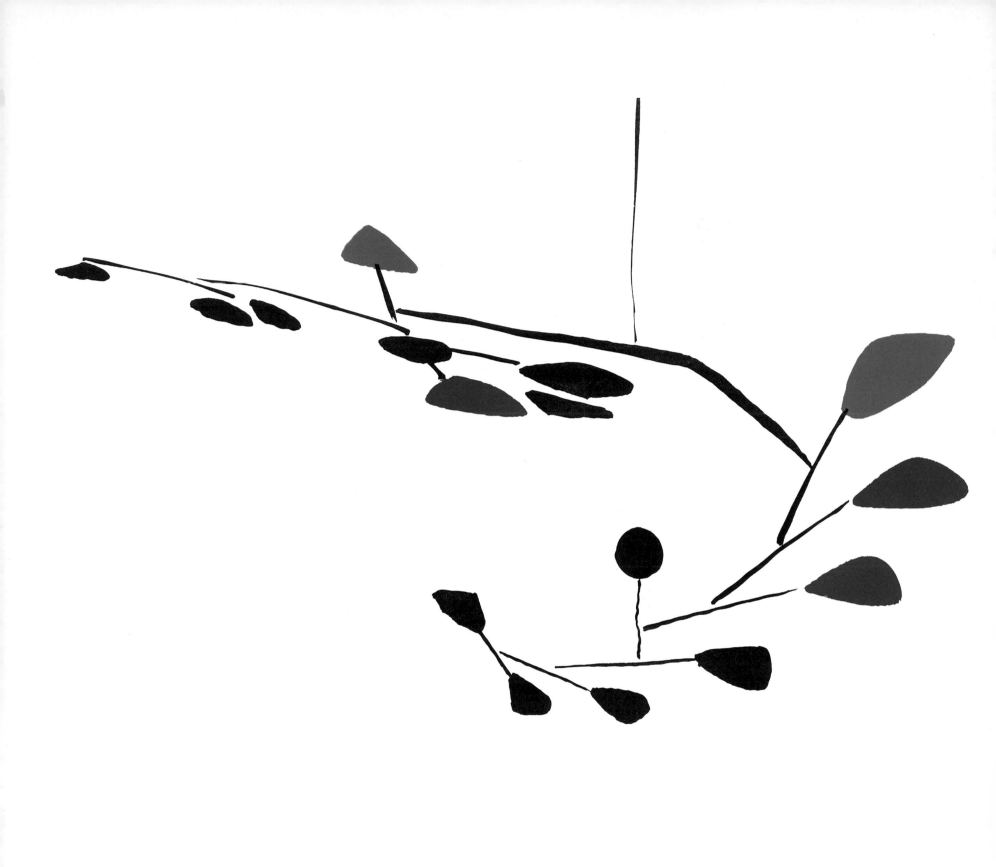

A classic interpretation of Calder's mobiles was written by the philosopher Jean-Paul Sartre to preface the Galerie Louis Carré catalogue for an exhibition in Paris in 1946. Excerpts from Sartre's poetic essay splendidly amplify Calder's mini-definition, quoted above:

A mobile, one might say, is a little private celebration, an object defined by its movement and having no other existence. It is a flower that fades when it ceases to move, a pure play of movement in the sense that we speak of a pure play of light. . . .

. . . A mobile does not suggest anything: it captures genuine living movements and shapes them. Mobiles have no meaning, make you think of nothing but themselves. They are, that is all; they are absolutes. There is more of the unpredictable about them than in any other human creation. No human brain, not even their creator's, could possibly foresee all the complex combinations of which they are capable. A general destiny of movement is sketched for them, and then they are left to work it out for themselves. . . . It is a little jazz tune, evanescent as the sky or the morning: if you miss it, you have lost it forever. Valéry said of the sea that it is a perpetual recommencement. A mobile is in this way like the sea, and is equally enchanting: forever rebeginning, forever new. No use throwing it a passing glance, you must live with it and be fascinated by it. Then and only then will you feel the beauty of its pure and changing forms, at once so free and so disciplined. . . .

I was talking with Calder one day in his studio when suddenly a mobile beside me, which until then had been quiet, became violently agitated. I stepped quickly back, thinking to be out of its reach. But then, when the agitation had ceased and it appeared to have relapsed into quiescence, its long, majestic tail, which until then had not budged, began mournfully to wave and, sweeping through the air, brushed across my face. These hesitations, resumptions, gropings, clumsinesses, the sudden decisions and above all that swan-like grace make of certain mobiles very strange creatures indeed, something midway between matter and life.

. . . In short, although mobiles do not seek to imitate anything . . . they are nevertheless at once lyrical inventions, technical combinations of an almost mathematical quality and sensitive symbols of Nature.

Michel Seuphor devotes a chapter to Calder in his book *The Sculpture of this Century,* and his quotation of Ben Nicholson's description of one mobile makes them all come alive:

The first time I encountered a Calder was in Paris some years ago when I borrowed one and hung it from the center of the ceiling of a white room overlooking the Seine, and at night, with the river glistening outside, this mobile object turned slowly in the

Mobiles

breeze in the light of an electric bulb hung near its center—a large black, six white, and one small scarlet, balls on their wires turned slowly in and out, around, above and below one another, with their shadows chasing, round the white walls in an exciting interchanging movement, suddenly hastening as they turned the corners and disappearing, as they crossed the window, into the night—it was alive like the hum of the city, like the passing river and the smell of Paris in early spring, but it was not a work of art as many people think of a work of art—imprisoned in a gold frame or stone-dead on a pedestal in one of our marble-pillared mausoleums. But it was "alive" and that, after all, is not a bad qualification for a work of art.

The origin of the mobiles has been variously explained by art critics: Selden Rodman mentions Calder's interest in eighteenth-century toys that demonstrated the planetary system; his exposure to antique mechanical twittering birds has also been noted; Sweeney points out that the Chinese wind-bells Calder saw in his youth in San Francisco are recalled in the mobiles. But in a statement published in 1932, when he was a member of the Abstraction-Création group, Calder said that his mobiles were "abstractions which resemble nothing in life except their manner of reacting."

Pinpointing the date of the first mobile is difficult. One of the earliest is *Une Boule Noire, une Boule Blanche*, in which a white wood ball and a black iron ball are suspended above red metal saucers of varying sizes; when the heavy iron ball is given a push, the lighter wooden one skips from one saucer to another, producing a series of sounds. This innovative sculpture, which incorporates the dimensions of both sound and motion, was made in 1930, the year of Calder's earliest abstract work. His moving sculpture did not follow a neat evolutionary process, one form developing from another; rather, he worked simultaneously on wire constructions, mechanized sculpture and mobiles during the years 1930 to 1933 in Paris. These were decisive and enormously creative years for Calder, a period during which he developed an entirely new form of abstract sculpture based on motion and at the same time continued figurative work of great originality, making his great series of circus drawings, illustrating *Fables of Aesop* and experimenting with sculpture in bronze and stone.

Calder estimates that he has made a couple of thousand mobiles in his life, and he has made them in great variety, using many materials, as can be seen from the illustrations. Our selection was necessarily tight; there were dozens more we could well have included in this most important section of the book. Here, they are divided into three categories: standing, wall and hanging, which do not form a strict chronological sequence. There are many subdivisions, for example: Animobiles, Louisa Calder's contraction of *animaux-mobiles;* Totems, which Calder has described as "tall black pyra-

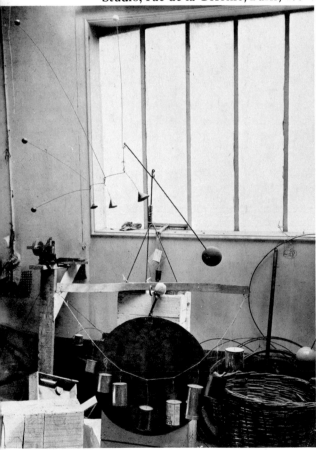

Studio, rue de la Colonie, Paris, 1932.

midal shapes with mobile festoons on their heads"; Crags, a recent series of large standing mobiles; Towers, which could be considered wire wall mobiles. Calder has said he was thinking of oil derricks when he made the Towers, but they also suggest a lighthearted remodeling of the Eiffel Tower, as well as the ubiquitous construction cranes that dominate our cityscapes. Calder had previously experimented with the element of sound, and in the early fifties he made a number of mobiles called Gongs. These have polished brass elements which, when struck by other mobile parts, produce a resonant ring. Calder explained to Katharine Kuh how he came to use sound as a medium: "It was accidental at first. Then I made a sculpture called *Dogwood* with three heavy plates that gave off quite a clangor. Here was just another variation. You see, you have weight, form, size, color, motion, and then you have noise." *Chef d'Orchestre*, a mobile made for a musical performance in the sixties (see "Theatrical Productions"), is a further logical development—noise to music.

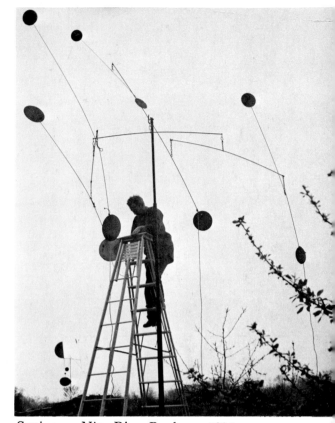

Setting up *Nine Discs*, Roxbury, 1936.

The common denominator of all the mobiles is, obviously, mobility. Calder has said that even before he visited Mondrian's studio he "felt that art was too static to reflect our world of movement." Another time he said: "I don't know whether it was the moving toys in the circus which got me interested in the idea of motion as an art form or whether it was my training in engineering at Stevens." Motion is indeed at the core of all Calder's work—toys, Circus figures, wire and bronze sculpture (some of the latter have balancing and rotating elements). Even the stabiles have implied movement: their design is always active, and they are in another sense mobile—like mobile homes—in that they are constructed so as to be easily taken apart and moved. Pierre Descargues has said that just about everything Calder makes can be taken to pieces: "Even his largest stabiles are made for the nomads whom Le Corbusier recognized in modern societies." The mobiles have almost all been designed to be unhooked in sections and flattened out for packing. Asked by Katharine Kuh how he happened to make collapsible mobiles, Calder replied in detail:

When I had the show in Paris during 1946 at Louis Carré's gallery, the plans called for small sculptures that could be sent by mail. The size limit for things sent that way was 18 × 10 × 2 inches, so I made mobiles that would fold up. Rods, plates, everything was made in two or three pieces and could be taken apart and folded in a little package. I sent drawings along showing how to reassemble the pieces.

Mentioning how he made a small mobile for a Brazilian friend so that it could easily be taken apart for his flight to Rio, Calder adds: "I often regret not having made him a cloth vest with pockets, each the color of the part contained."

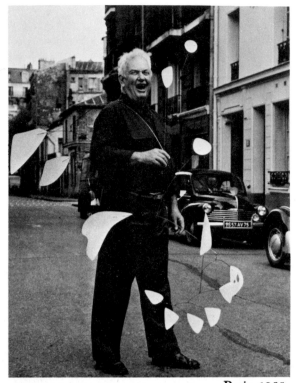

Paris, 1955.

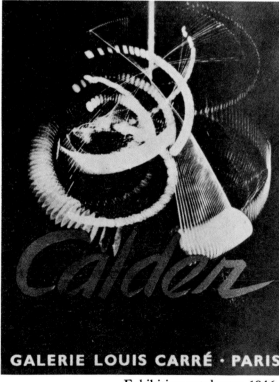

GALERIE LOUIS CARRÉ · PARIS

Exhibition catalogue, 1946.

264

The evolution of the mobiles can best be observed by studying the caption dates. The earliest ones often incorporate found objects such as bits of colored glass and pottery and free-form pieces of carved wood, naturally weathered or painted in earth colors like many of the Constellations. Later, the mobiles were made entirely of metal and the colors usually limited to red, yellow and blue with black and white. In his first metal mobiles Calder sheared the individual elements out of aluminum, sometimes making cutouts in one or more of them and thus adding to the complexity of the overall composition. In recent years Calder has had his largest mobiles fabricated from steel, the same material used for his great stabiles. The potentials of movement became increasingly complex—the parts moving up and down as well as around to form infinitely varied patterns in space. The size of the mobiles changed dramatically. It has been suggested that when Calder moved to the United States in 1938, the open countryside of Connecticut—after the confined studio quarters of Montparnasse—had something to do with the increased scale of the mobiles, and with the origin of the outdoor standing mobiles that could skylark freely in the air. In 1953 the Calders rented a house in Aix-en-Provence: "I looked for and found a blacksmith, near Aix, on our road and made four large outdoor mobiles in his shop." After the Calders moved to Saché the outdoor pieces multiplied and grew steadily larger. In 1962 a huge new studio was built, principally to accommodate the large mobiles and stabiles.

Everyone asks Calder how he makes the mobiles, and though he avoids pronouncements on esthetics, this kind of technical inquiry is one he never minds answering.

Katharine Kuh interviewed him for *The Artist's Voice:*

Question: How do you get that subtle balance in your work?
Calder: You put a disc here and then you put another disc that is a triangle at the other end and then you balance them on your finger and keep on adding. I don't use rectangles—they stop. You can use them; I have at times but only when I want to block, to constipate movement.

To Selden Rodman he explained:

About my method of work: first it's the state of mind. Elation. I only feel elation if I've got ahold of something good. I used to begin with fairly complete drawings, but now I start by cutting out a lot of shapes. Next, I file them and smooth them off. Some I keep because they're pleasing or dynamic. Some are bits I just happen to find. Then I arrange them, like *papier collé*, on a table, and "paint" them—that is, arrange them, with wires between the pieces if it's to be a mobile, for the overall pattern. Finally I cut some more on them with my shears, calculating for balance this time.

When Curtis Cate asked him how he calculated the size of the counterweight needed to hold up the other elements, Calder explained it very simply (Cate's article is titled "Calder Made Easy"):

I begin with the smallest and work up. Once I know the balance point for this first pair of discs, I anchor it by a hook to another arm, where it acts as one end of another pair of scales, and so on up. It's a kind of ascending scale of weights and counterweights.

A *Look* article described in detail how Calder works to make a mobile, and some of his basic ideas about techniques, tools and art:

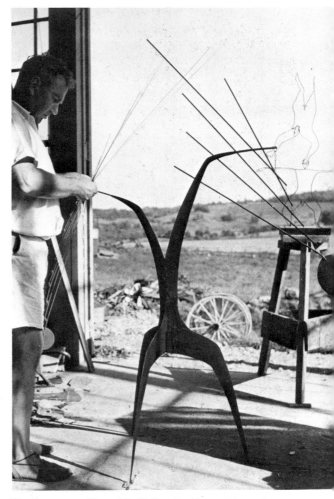

A Calder mobile begins as a scale model. Working amidst the skeletons of a hundred half-finished or discarded mobiles in the cluttered barn that is his studio, he first takes large sheets of very light aluminum, "that you can cut like paper." He chops them into rough shapes, which, in turn, suggest more shapes. ("I like a hard shape, something like a fresh fruit, rather than an old, rotten shape.") When he has 20 or 30 forms he likes, Calder lays them out on a board. His stubby fingers move over them with great deliberation, selecting, discarding, rearranging until they form a relationship that pleases him. In four or five hours, he has these wired together in a completed model. It takes scarcely longer to complete the finished mobile out of stronger wire and metal and paint it in circus-bright, primary colors. Calder is never certain how the mobiles will behave when the wind strikes them and they begin their dancing movements. "Oh, I know pretty well what will happen," he says, "but it's all 'cut and try,' and sometimes they surprise me."

As he resists complicated theory, Calder also resists complicated tools and techniques. Relaxing before a fire, sipping a glass of wine in his living room, with a jumble of paintings and mobiles, he says, "having a lot of equipment dedicates you to its use. You go off in the direction your equipment carries you. You should set limits. The trouble with a lot of artists is that they have too much technique. They don't know what to do with it all. If you cut down on it, you can work more strongly within narrower limits."

Roxbury studio with *Effet du Japonais* and *Acrobats,* c. 1945.

Not only does Calder preach simplicity of equipment, he has practiced it consistently throughout his career. In his travels he usually carries a few small tools and can set up a workshop almost anywhere. When he was invited to Beirut in the fifties to make a mobile for Middle East Airlines, he had a bad case of flu, and the doctor who treated him asked for a small mobile. "A few days after our arrival in Beirut, I had been allotted a small room by the Middle East Airlines, in their new building. And with two planks across two wooden horses and a few borrowed tools, I set to work on the mobile. I had my pliers with me." Calder uses no power tools: he prefers rivets and bolts

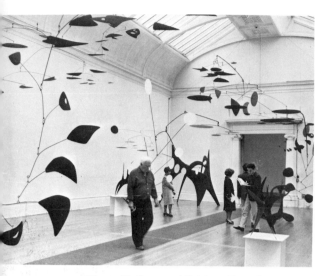

Tate Gallery exhibition, London, 1962.

Studio, Saché, 1965.

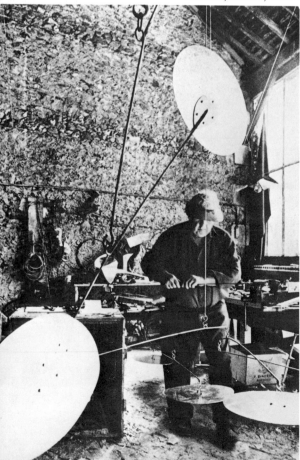

to welding and still uses a brush to paint with, not a spray gun. He has invented many of his hand tools, including a gadget for locating the center of gravity on a piece of material. Although the larger mobiles and stabiles are built in foundries from his models, under his supervision, he shuns the factory-finish look. Speaking of the welding of ribs and gussets, Jacques Bazillon, the director of Etablissements Biémont, Calder's foundry in Tours, said: "Mr. Calder does not want us to use automatic apparatus, but on the contrary he wants the weldings to be done manually so that the Public may see the 'scars of workmanship.' "

George Staempfli, a dealer in contemporary art, wrote an article featuring conversation with Sandy and Louisa about the construction of *Spirale*, commissioned by Marcel Breuer for the UNESCO Building he designed in Paris. It was made in Connecticut, at Carmen Segre's Iron Works. Sandy boasts that Segre was "the best welder in the U.S. Army once." The following is a compressed account of some of the talk:

Sandy: We worked together, in the evenings, in his backyard. We started with the top pieces and worked our way down. . . . We got a big crane and worked from the roof of the shop one night, to test the upper section. Segre wouldn't believe until the last moment that it would really rise up like that. But it did, there it was.
Louisa: They jumped up and down like children. They drank two bottles of champagne to celebrate.
Sandy: We put it up in two days. First day the base, second day the top. We beat the Bible, got everything created in *two* days.
Staempfli: Is there any symbolic meaning in it?
Sandy: Well, it goes up, it's something like a flame. But there's no history attached. Sorry. . . .
Louisa: Sandy is about as unsymbolic a person as I know.

For a recent *New York Times Magazine* story by Ted Morgan, Calder described some of the engineering as well as design problems of the largest mobiles. When they are more than forty feet wide, the angle of movement has to be limited. The top bar can weigh as much as a ton, but if it drops too far, the mobile elements snarl in the stem. In a strong wind, a big mobile can start whirling like a gyroscope, and elements could spin off—very dangerous. Calder tries out the models in the wind tunnel of a Poitiers aeronautics firm to study potential problems. Morgan gave the following account of a conference in Jacques Bazillon's office at Etablissements Biémont:

At one end of the room hung a model of a mobile for the Federal Reserve Bank in Philadelphia that will weigh between seven and eight tons and hang 100 feet down between two walls. Engineers brought out blueprints showing each part of the mobile in profile, full-face and cross-section.

Armed with slide rules and thick notebooks full of mathematical calculations, the engineers began subjecting Calder to the tyranny of their laws. "Remember the one we made for Dallas?" Bazillon said. "This is the same problem: the width of the bars in relation to the weight of the elements. In any case, we'll have to use aeronautical high-resistance tubing." The engineers talked thrust bearings, steel swivels, off-center axis, rotation surface and other arcana. In English, Bazillon asked: "O.K.? Get it?"

The necessity for complex mechanical calculations is in no way a negative factor, because the machine esthetic—structural integrity, energy and rhythm—is an important part of the artistic personality of the mobiles.

However carefully engineered, Calder's mobiles always seem to retain their freedom to move at the will of the wind, and they move with gaiety. The idea of playfulness in abstract sculpture—like the humor Klee, Kandinsky and Miró brought to modern painting—has been one of Calder's most significant contributions. The never-failing Calder humor is inherent even in his totally abstract work, and many of his pun-titles reflect this. Some years ago he was commissioned by industrialist Otto Spaeth to make a mobile, and Mrs. Spaeth recalls that Sandy couldn't decide whether to call it the *Otto-mobile* or the *Spaethmobile;* this was long before the "space age," and he settled for the former.

Calder has been called, because of the mobile, the only artist who has invented and then practiced an art of his own. In 1972 a *Daily News* article stated categorically: "Calder is a school of one." Indeed, he has never been interested in teaching or working with artist-assistants. Nevertheless, distinguished sculptors such as George Rickey derived their mobile art directly from Calder's, as did most of the recent kinetic sculptors. The mobiles have been copied by interior decorators and amateur artists everywhere, as well as by manufacturers of toys and decorative objects. Sandy is not flattered by the imitators and says he tries to ignore them but finds it a bit difficult. "A woman wrote me she made a mobile and got seventy-five dollars for it; she wanted me to brush her up so she could get a hundred and fifty. They have books for children now on how to make mobiles out of Ping-Pong balls and marbles, and they teach them in school. People write me and say, 'I've read your book.' "

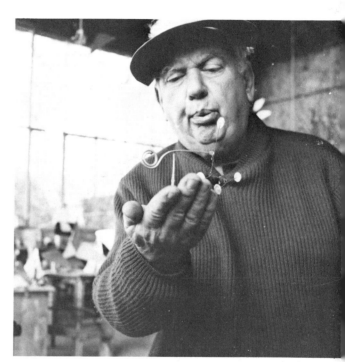

Saché, 1965.

It was hard to choose a single comment of Calder's about his mobiles to begin this chapter; he has said so many interesting things about them. So I saved some of the others for the end, to give him the last word:

A mobile is a very modest thing.

I asked him [Marcel Duchamp] what sort of a name I could give these things and he at once produced "mobile." In addition to something that moves, in French it also means motive.

They're meant to be touched delicately. I like the "whang" they make—noise is another whole dimension.

I do a lot of things that look like snowflakes. The round white disc is pretty much a standard thing in life—snowflakes, money, bubbles, cooking devices.

Then there is the idea of an object floating—not supported. The use of a very long thread . . . seems to best approximate this freedom from the earth.

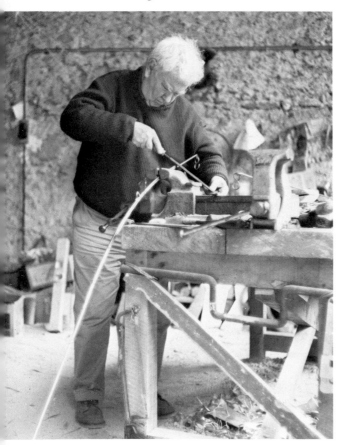

Filing rods for a mobile, Saché, 1965.

I have made a number of things for the open air: all of them react to the wind, and are like a sailing vessel in that they react best to one kind of breeze. It is impossible to make a thing work with every kind of wind.

To most people who look at a mobile, it's no more than a series of flat objects that move. To a few, though, it may be poetry.

People think monuments should come out of the ground, never out of the ceiling, but mobiles can be monumental too.

OPPOSITE: *Calderberry Bush*, 1932. Painted sheet metal, wood, wire, rod, 7′ h. Mr. and Mrs. James Johnson Sweeney, New York.

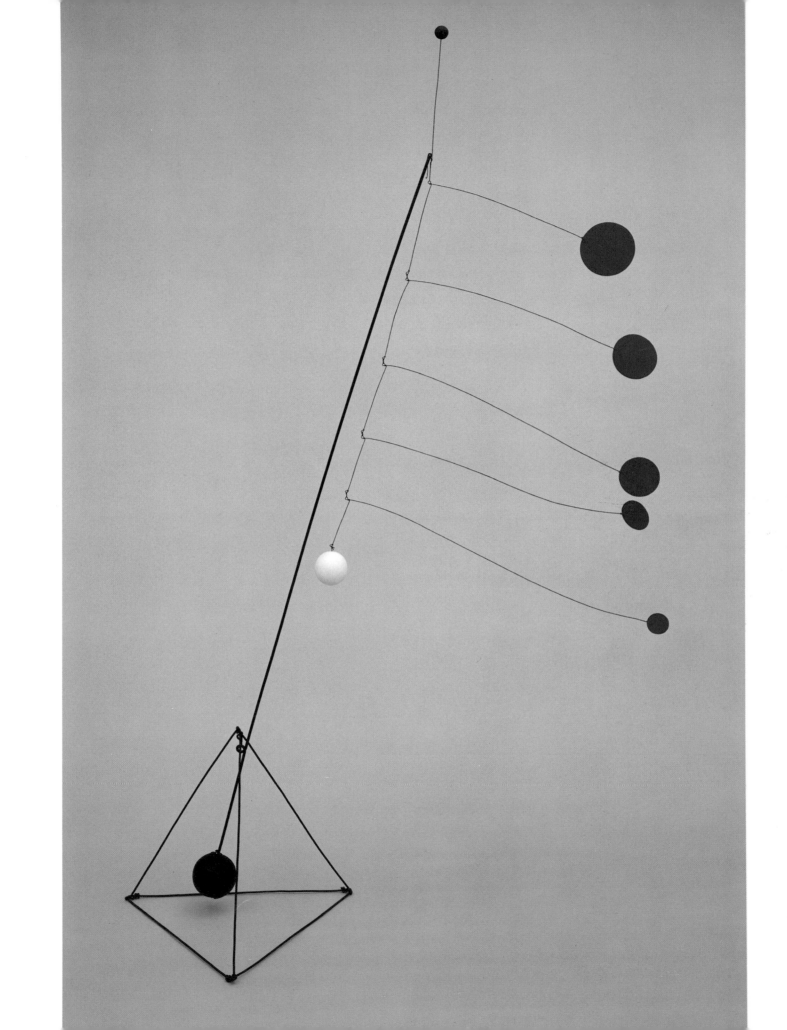

The Praying Mantis, 1936. Painted wood, rod, wire, 6′6″ h. Wadsworth Atheneum, Hartford, Connecticut.

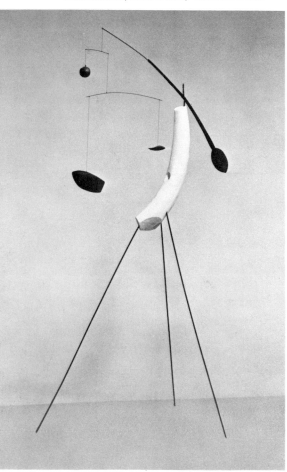

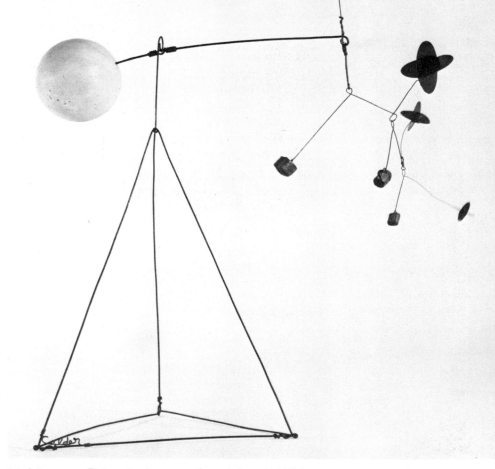

Mobile, 1933. Painted wire, wood, weights, 33½″ h. Musée National Fernand Léger, Biot, France.

OPPOSITE: *The Circle*, 1935. Painted sheet metal, wood, ceramic, string, wire, 35⅞″ h. Vassar College Art Gallery, Poughkeepsie, New York; gift of Agnes Rindge Claflin.

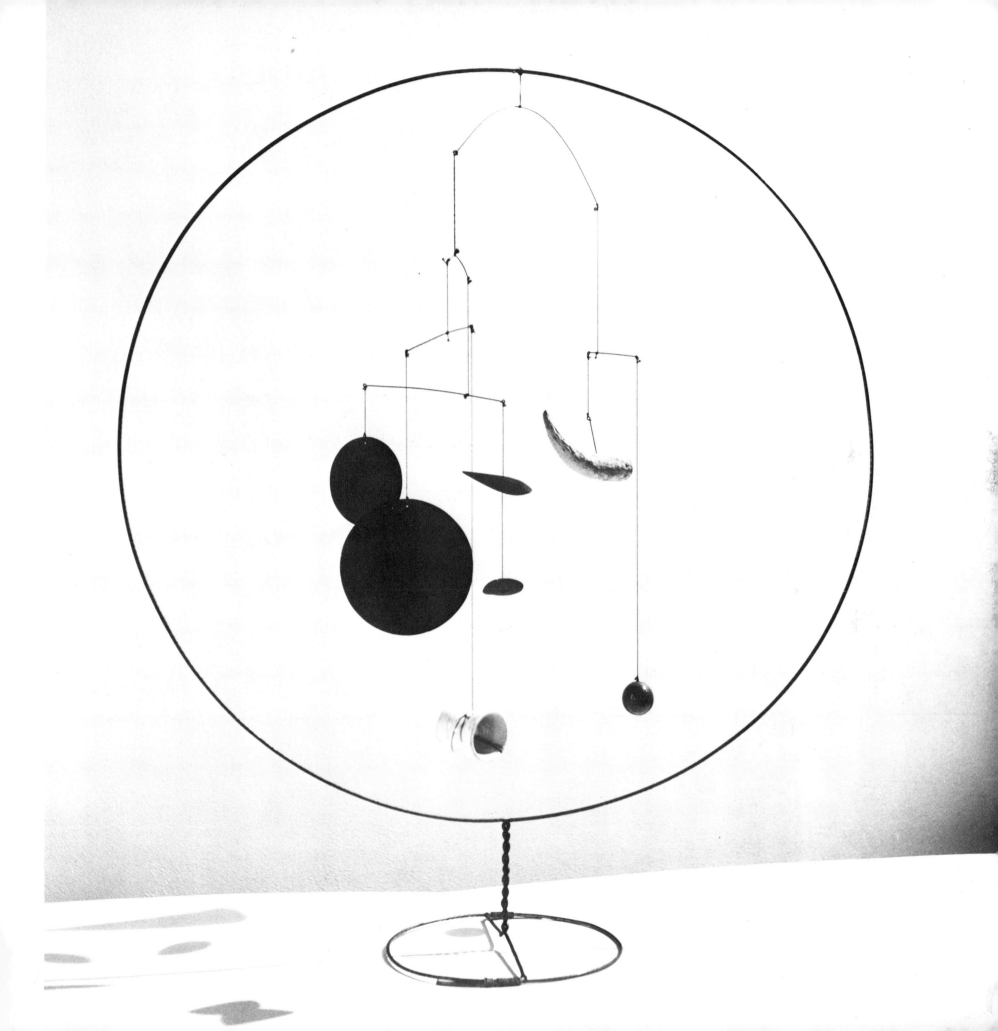

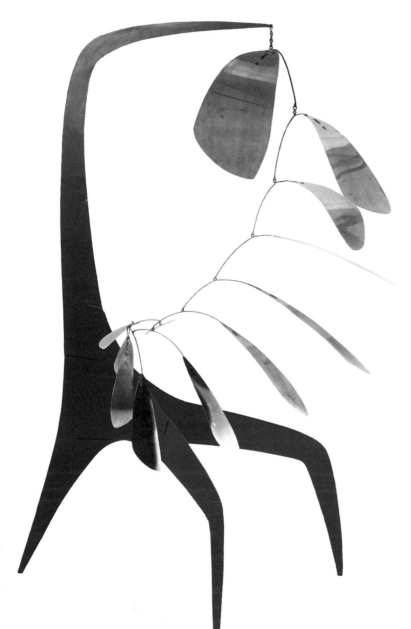

Aluminum Leaves, 1940. Painted sheet metal, sheet aluminum, wire, 61″ h. Collection of the author.

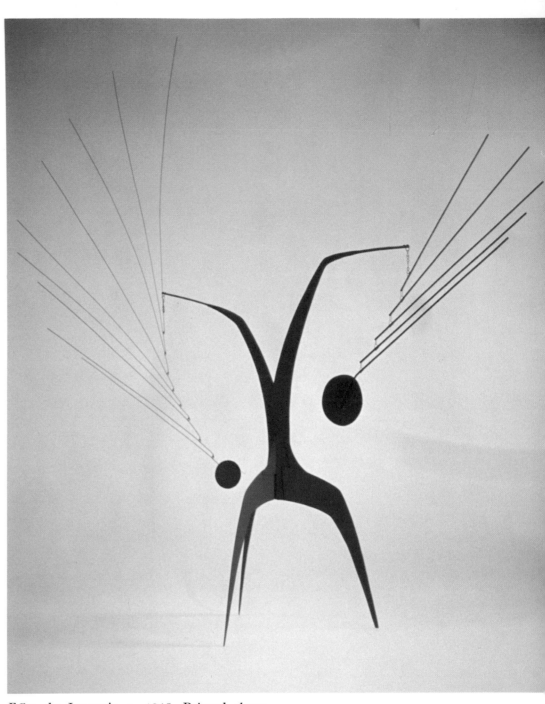

Effet du Japonais, c. 1945. Painted sheet metal, rod, wire, 54″ h. Private collection, New York.

OPPOSITE: *Little Spider*, c. 1940. Painted sheet metal, rod, wire, 55″ h. Mr. and Mrs. Klaus G. Perls, New York.

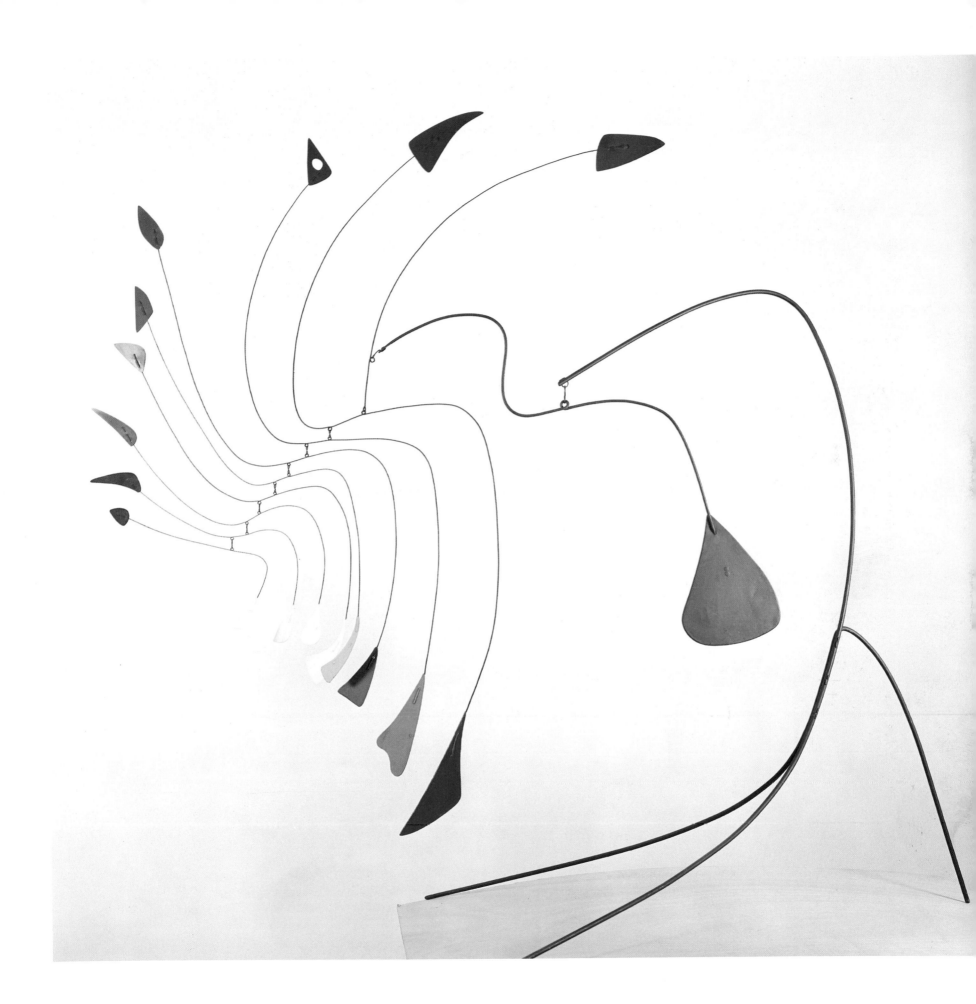

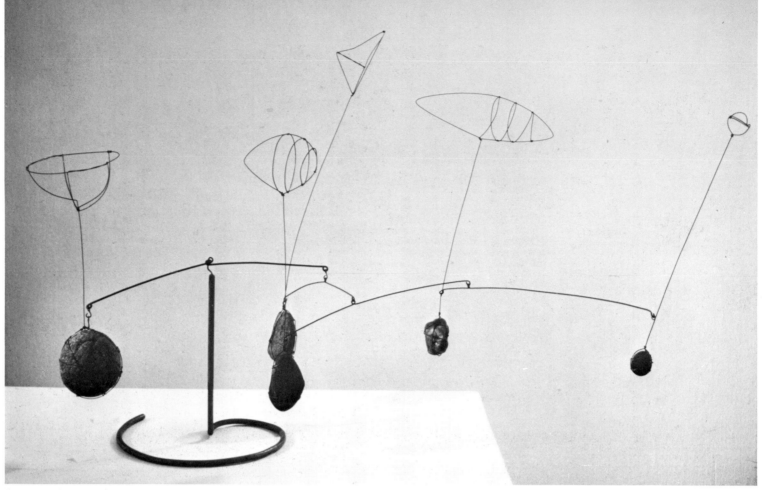

Stonymobile, 1948. Wire, rod, stones, 36″ w. Mrs. H. Gates Lloyd, Haverford, Pennsylvania.

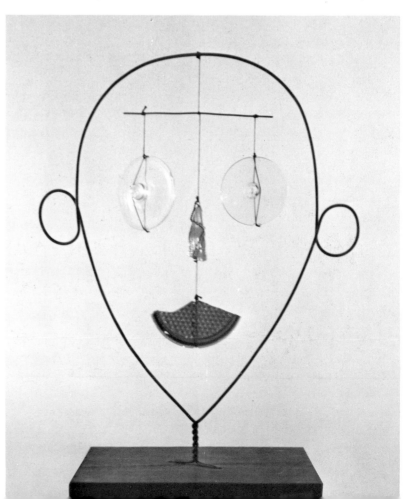

RIGHT: *Little Face*, c. 1945. Glass, wire, 13½″ h. Mr. and Mrs. Leonard J. Horwich, Chicago.

OPPOSITE: *Cage within a Cage*, 1939. Painted rod, wire, wood, 58″ w. Whitney Museum of American Art, New York; gift of the Howard and Jean Lipman Foundation.

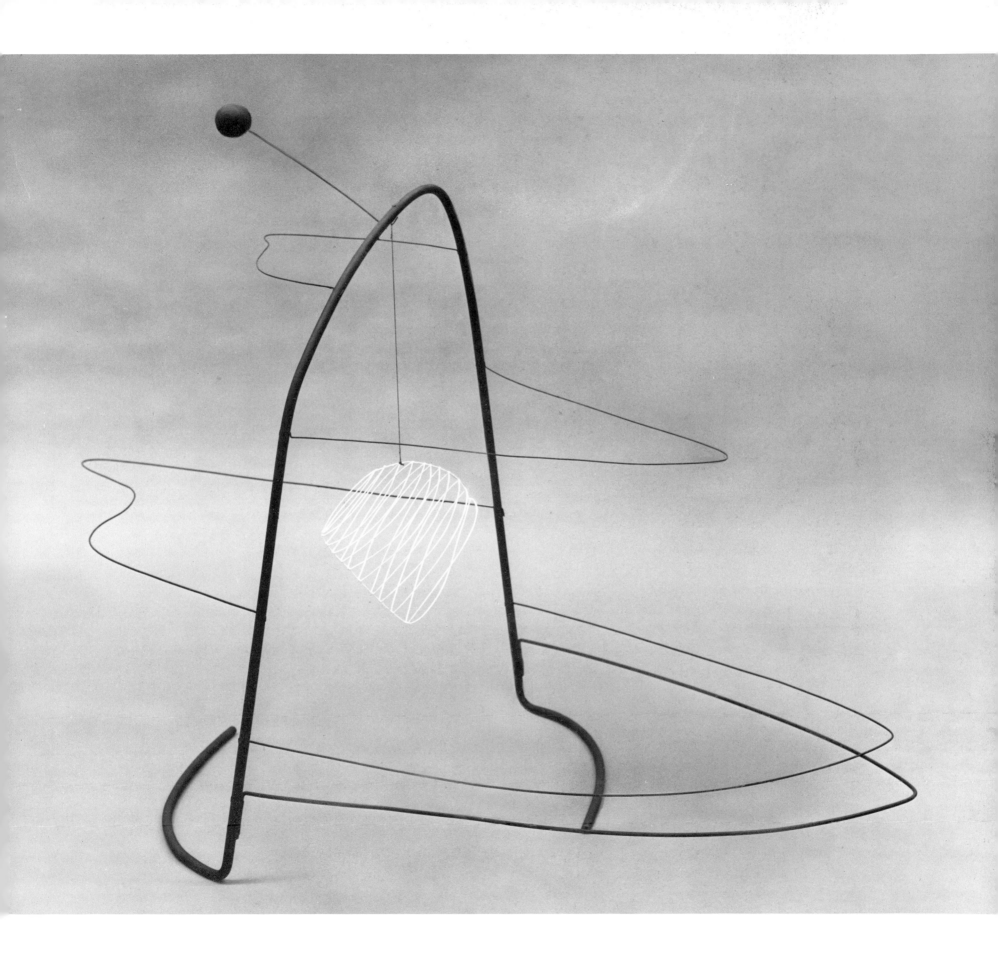

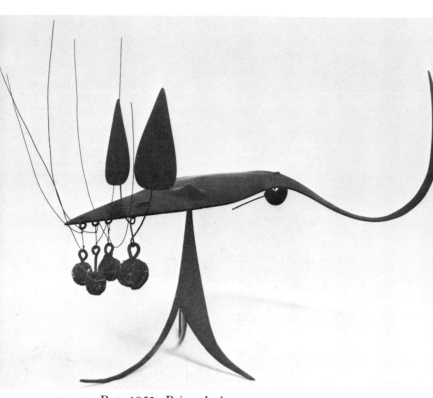

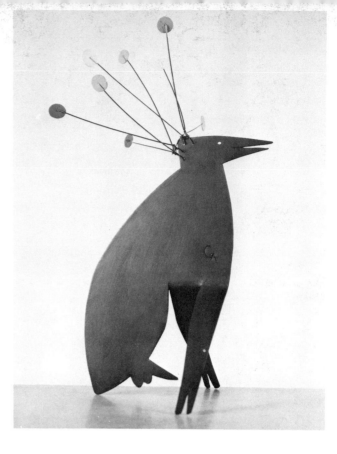

ABOVE: *Rat*, 1952. Painted sheet metal, wire, 10½″ h. Private collection, New York.

ABOVE, RIGHT: *The Crested Crow*, 1972. Painted sheet metal, wire, 16½″ h. Mr. and Mrs. Klaus G. Perls, New York.

BELOW: *Louisa's Valentine*, c. 1955. Painted sheet metal, wire, 13½″ h. Collection of the artist.

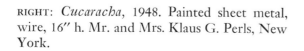

RIGHT: *Cucaracha*, 1948. Painted sheet metal, wire, 16″ h. Mr. and Mrs. Klaus G. Perls, New York.

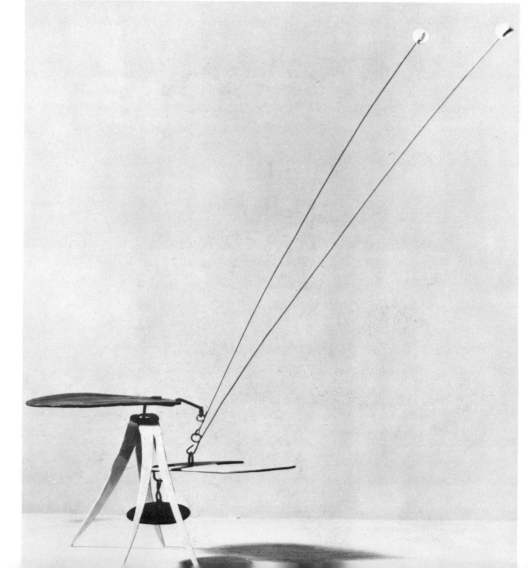

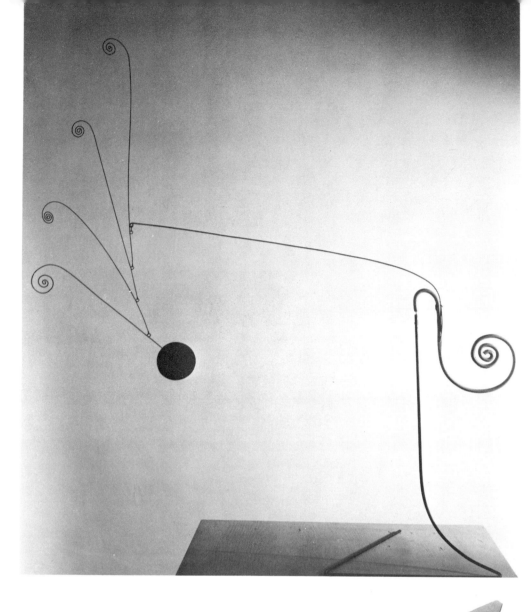

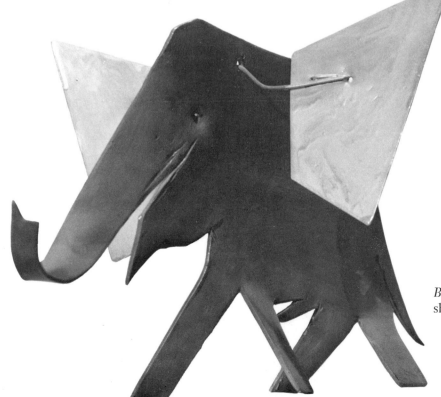

ABOVE, LEFT: *Five Curlicues*, 1952. Painted sheet metal, rod, wire, 32″ h. John C. Stoller, Minneapolis, Minnesota.

ABOVE: *Kitty*, 1967. Painted sheet metal, wire, 24″ h. Milada S. Neumann, Caracas.

Blue Elephant with Red Ears, 1971. Painted sheet metal, 14″ w. Galerie Maeght, Paris.

279

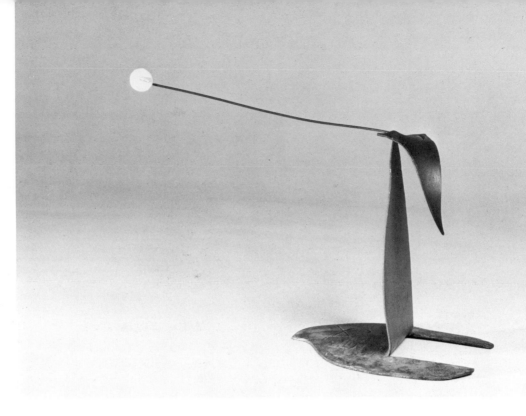

Point Blanc, 1970. Painted sheet metal, wire, 12″ w. Daniel Lelong, Paris.

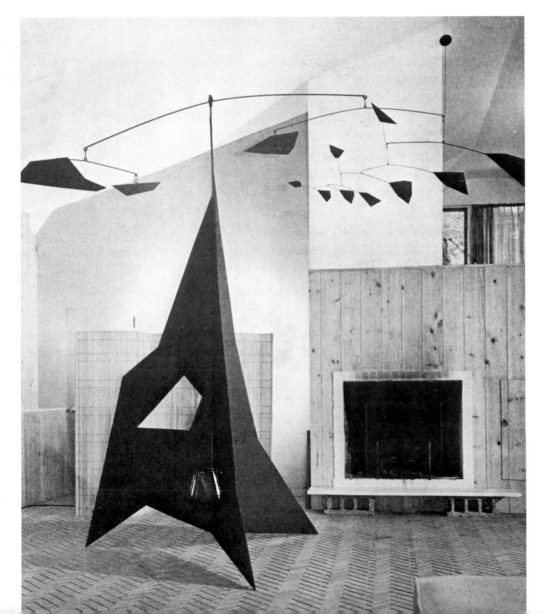

LEFT: *El Corcovado*, 1951. Painted steel plate, sheet metal, rod, wire, 11′ h. Mr. and Mrs. Josep Lluis Sert, Cambridge, Massachusetts.

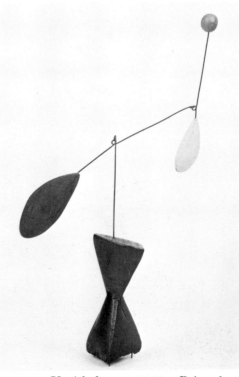

ABOVE: *Untitled*, c. 1945. Painted wood, wire, 10½″ h. Solomon & Co. Fine Art, New York.

OPPOSITE: *Performing Seal*, c. 1950. Painted sheet metal, wire, 33″ h. Mr. and Mrs. Leonard J. Horwich, Chicago.

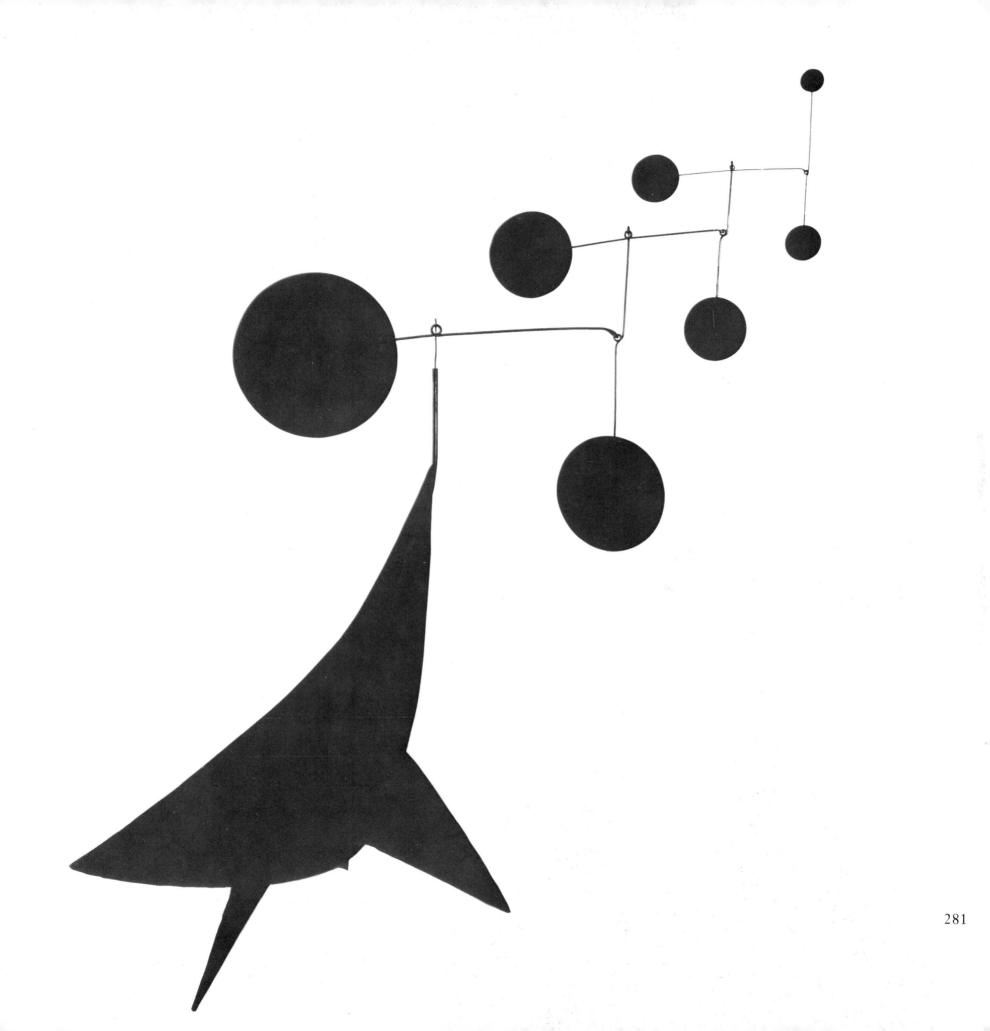

281

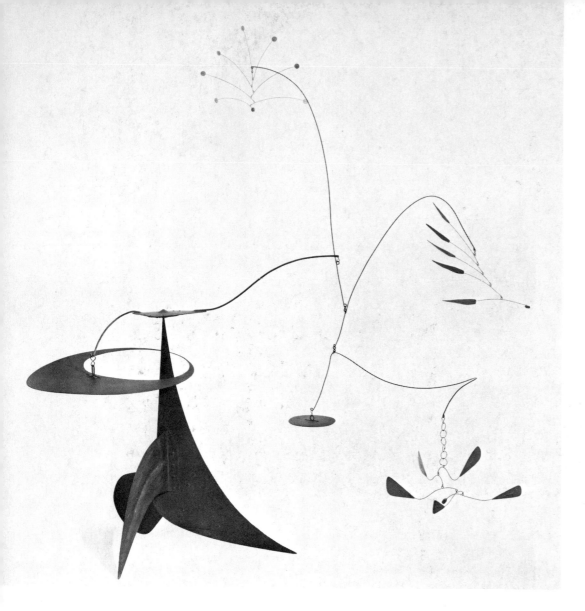

Bougainvillea, 1947. Painted sheet metal, wire, weights, 6'5" h. Mr. and Mrs. Burton Tremaine, Meriden, Connecticut.

OPPOSITE: *Spirale*, 1958. Painted steel plate, rod. 16'5" h. UNESCO, Paris.

BELOW: *Totem-Saché*, 1974. Painted steel plate, aluminum plate, 13' w. Saché, France; gift of the artist.

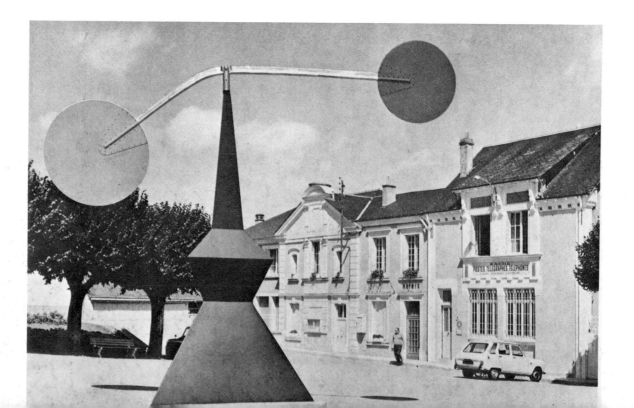

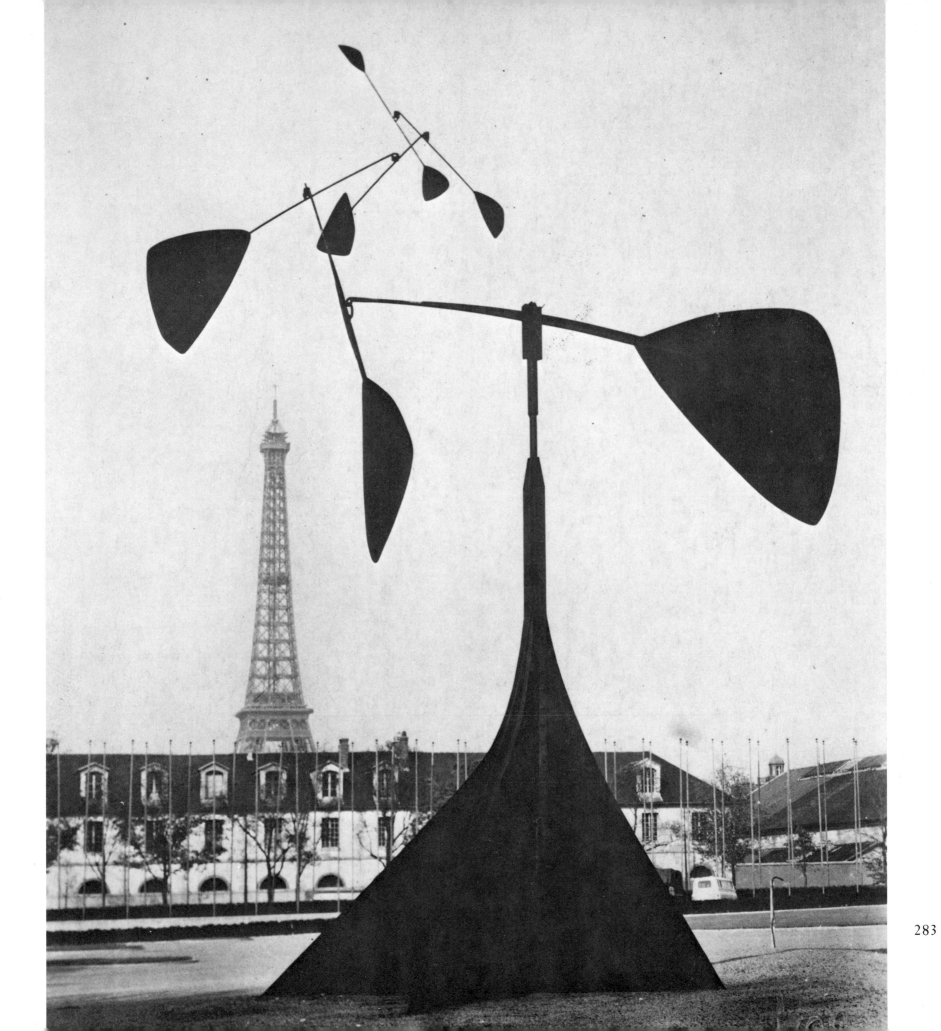

283

The Spider, 1940. Painted sheet metal, rod, 10′ w. Mr. and Mrs. Herbert Matter, New York.

OPPOSITE: *Indian Feathers*, 1969. Painted sheet metal, rod, 11′4¾″ h. Whitney Museum of American Art, New York; gift of the Howard and Jean Lipman Foundation.

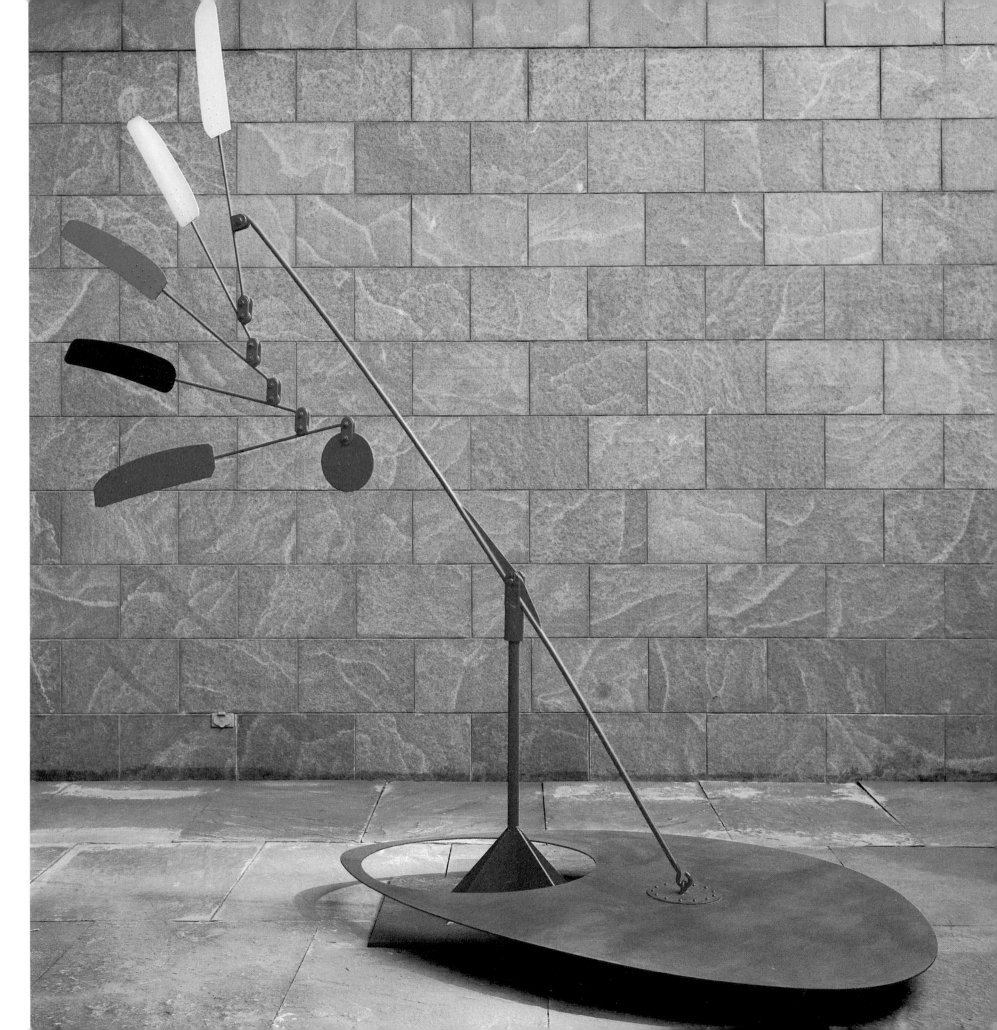

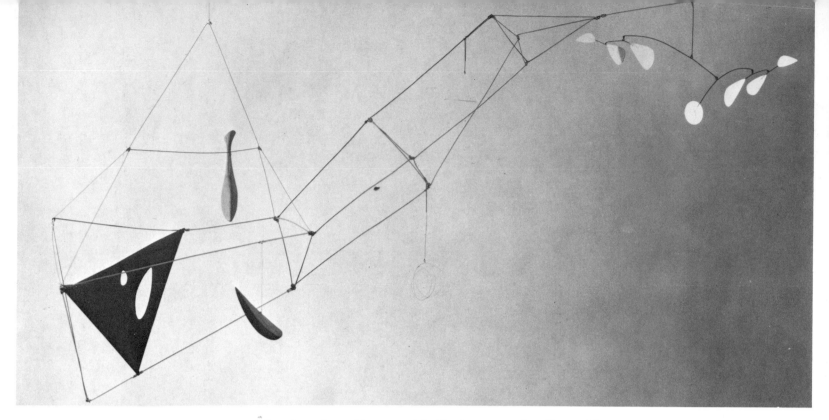

The Aeroplane—Tower with Six Leaves and a Dot, 1951. Painted rod, sheet metal, wood, wire, 53″ h. Dr. and Mrs. Arthur E. Kahn, New York.

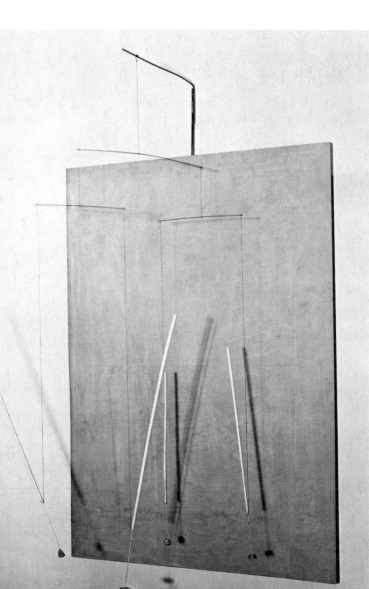

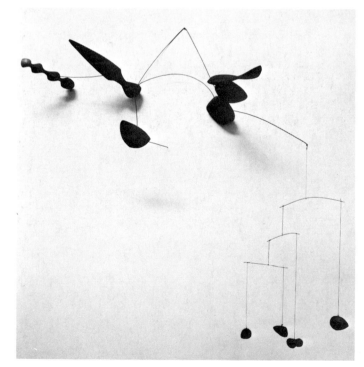

Constellation with Mobile, 1946. Wood, wire, string, 37″ w. Leo Lionni, Lavagna, Italy.

Swizzle Sticks, 1936. Painted wood, wire, weights, 48 × 33″. James Thrall Soby, New Canaan, Connecticut.

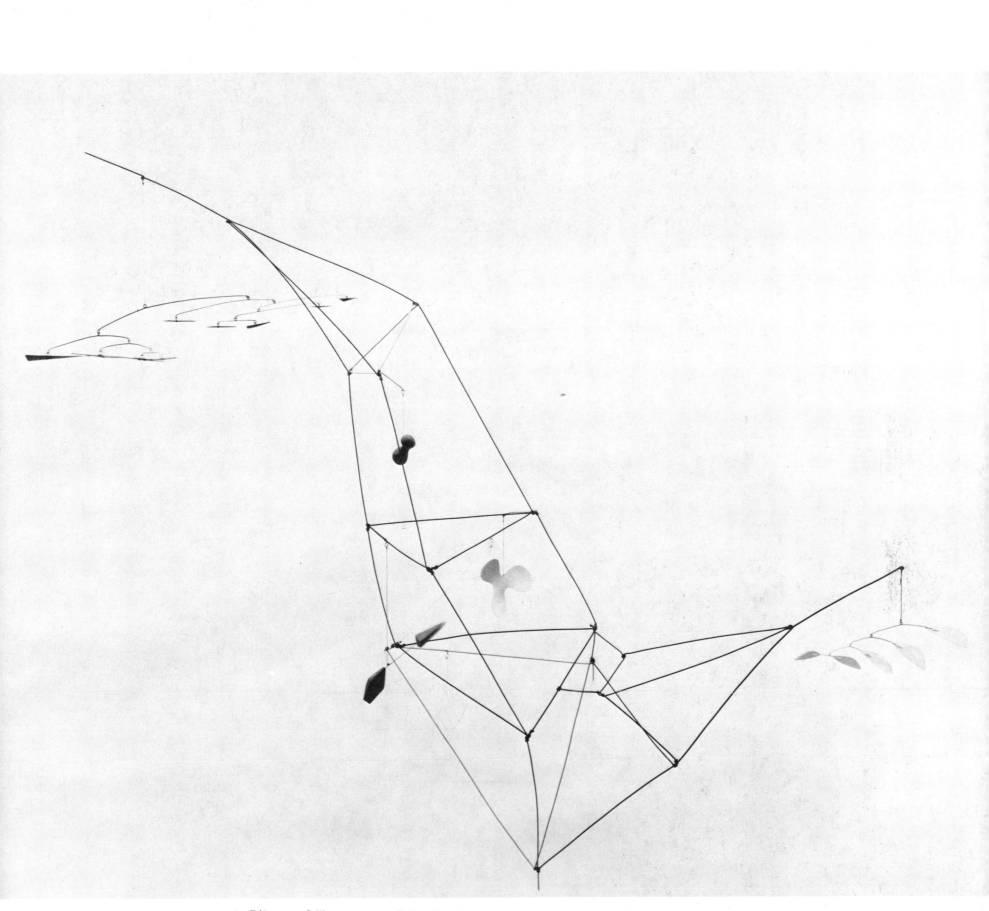

Bifurcated Tower, 1950. Painted rod, sheet metal, wood, wire, 6′ w. Whitney Museum of American Art, New York; gift of the Howard and Jean Lipman Foundation.

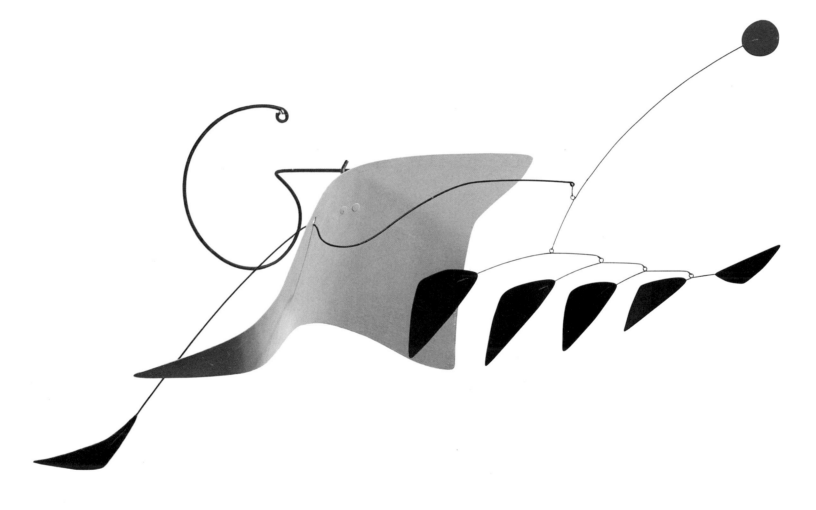

Yellow Whale, 1958. Painted sheet metal, wire, 45″ w. Collection of the author.

OPPOSITE: *Lobster Trap and Fish Tail*, 1939. Painted sheet metal, wire, 9′6″ w. The Museum of Modern Art, New York; gift of the Advisory Committee.

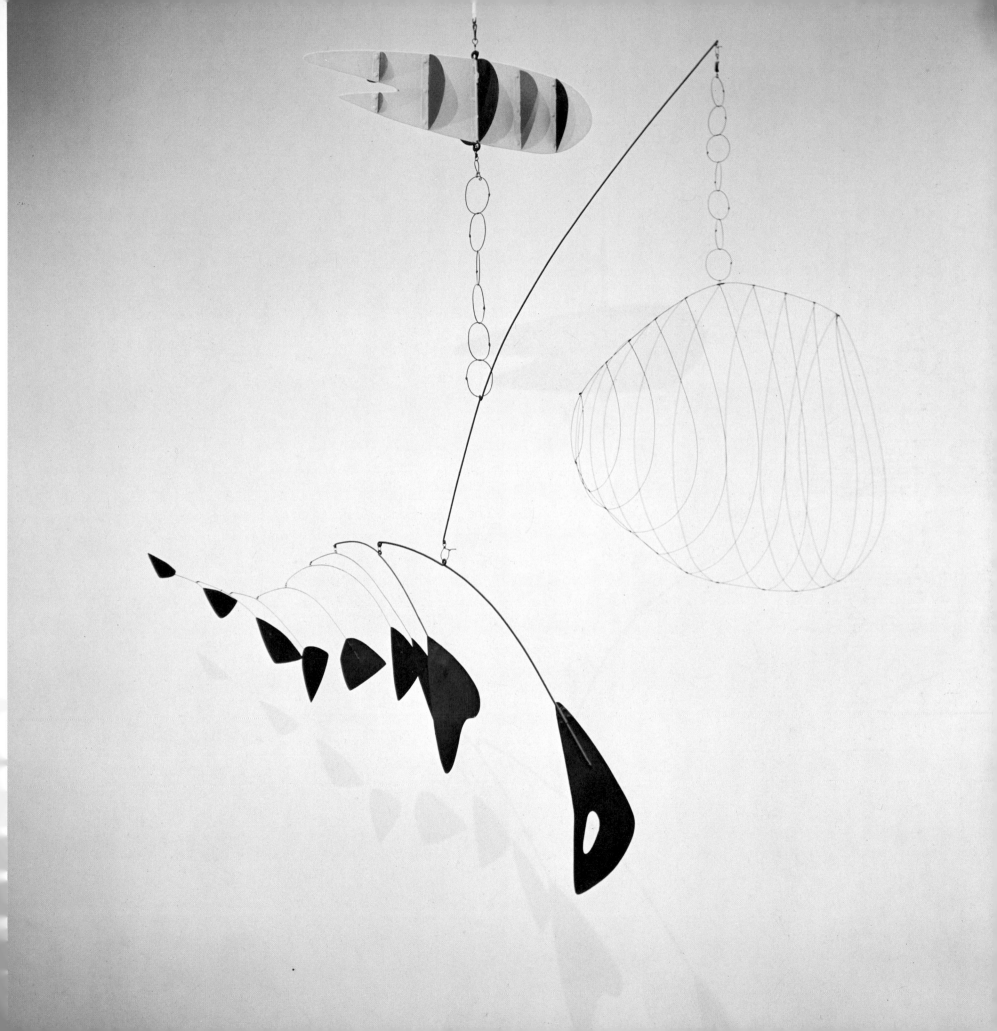

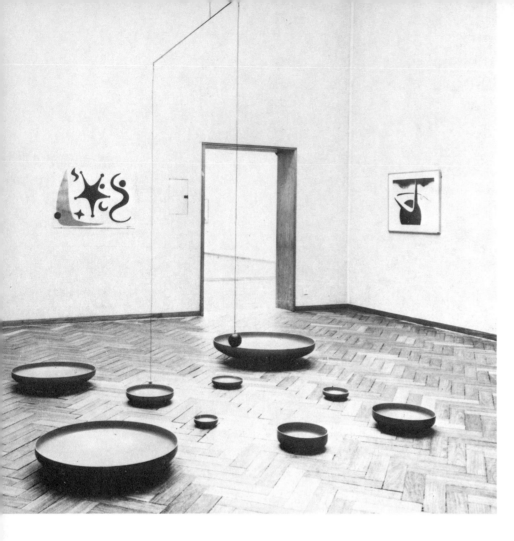

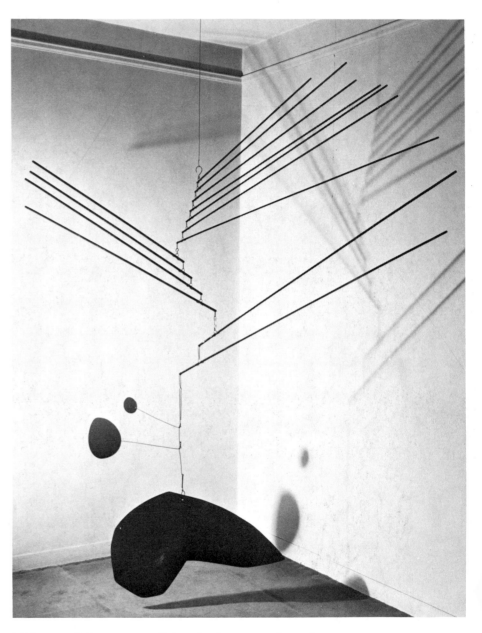

Une Boule Noire, une Boule Blanche, 1930 (reconstructed 1969). Painted metal, wood, wire, rod, 8′ h. Fondation Maeght, Saint-Paul-de-Vence, France.

Mobile with Hats, 1951. Painted wire, 40″ w. Mrs. Joan Prats, Barcelona, Spain.

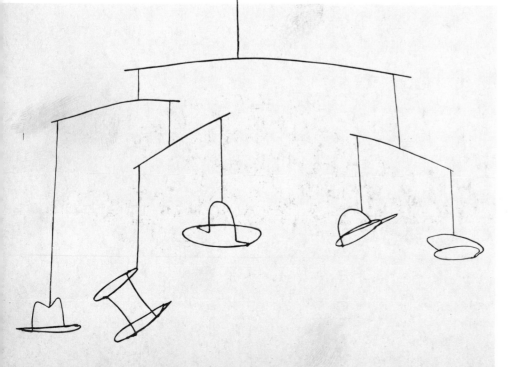

Thirteen Spines, 1940. Painted sheet metal, rod, wire, 7′ h. Wallraf-Richartz-Museum, Cologne, Germany.

OPPOSITE: *MoMA Whale*, 1936. Painted sheet metal, rod, wire, 7′3″ w. Collection of the author.

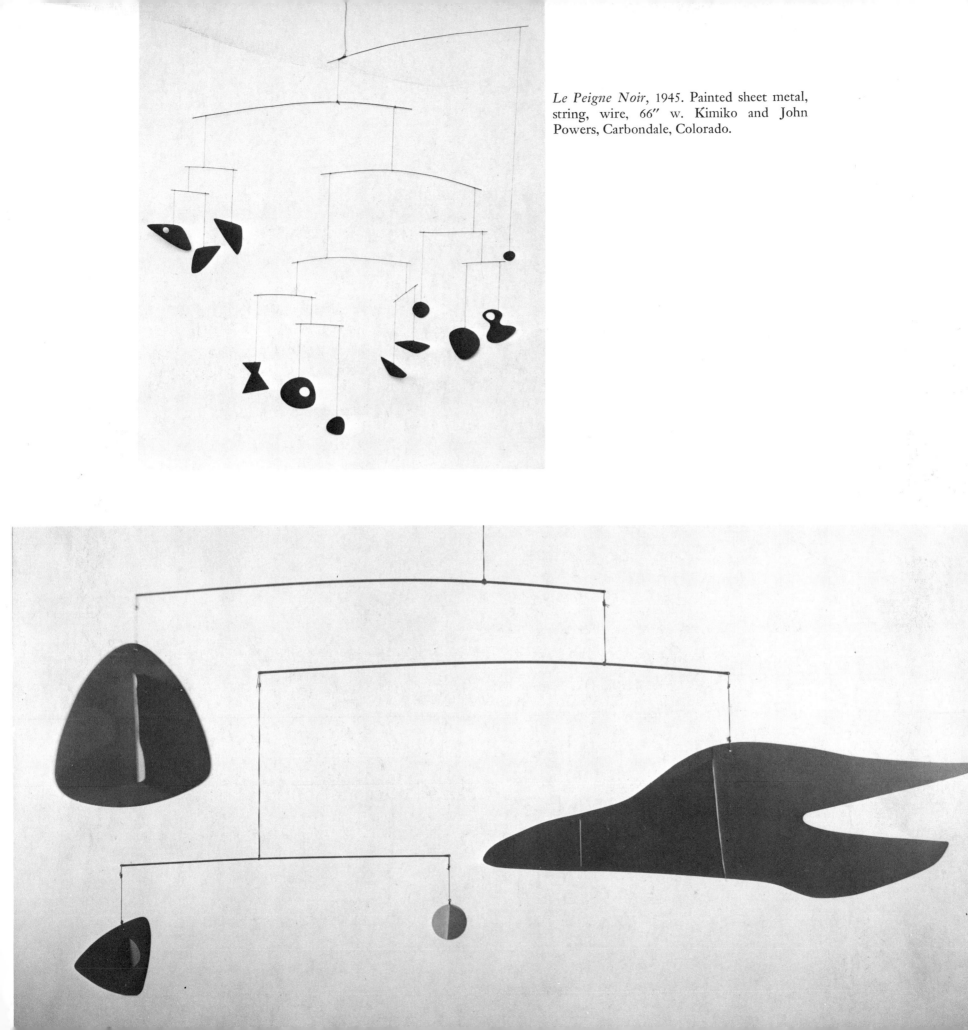

Le Peigne Noir, 1945. Painted sheet metal, string, wire, 66″ w. Kimiko and John Powers, Carbondale, Colorado.

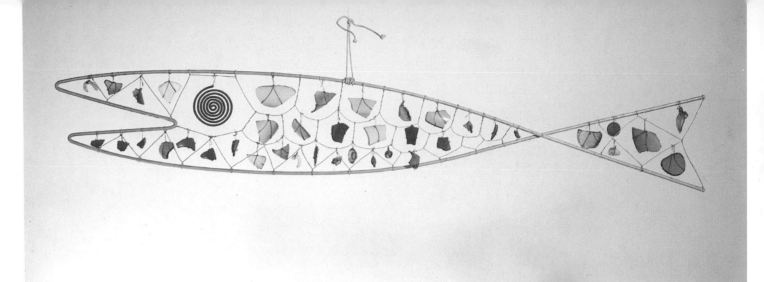

Fish, 1948–50. Glass, wire, 60″ w. Collection of the artist.

Sea Scape, 1947. Painted wood, sheet metal, string, wire, 60″ w. Whitney Museum of American Art, New York; gift of the Howard and Jean Lipman Foundation (and purchase).

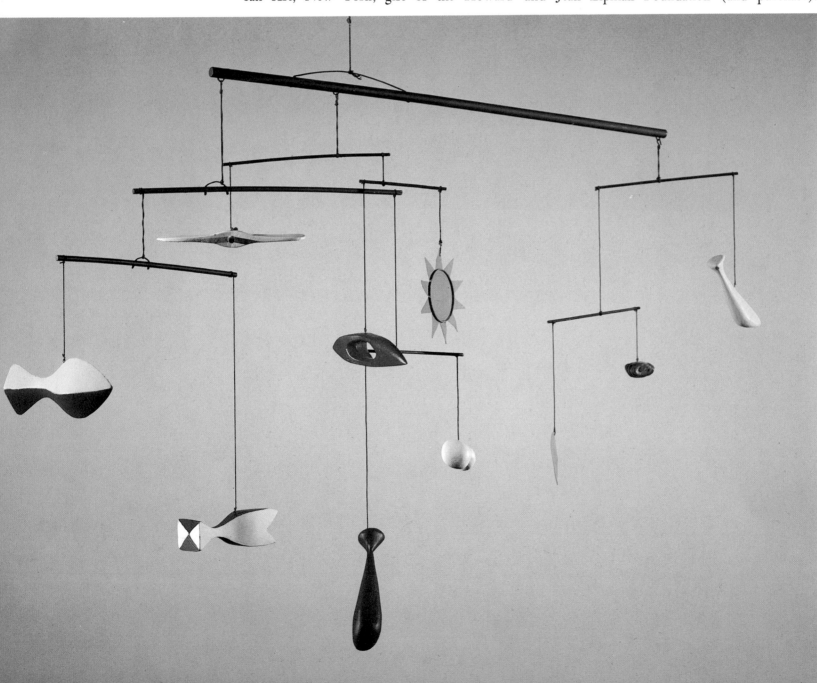

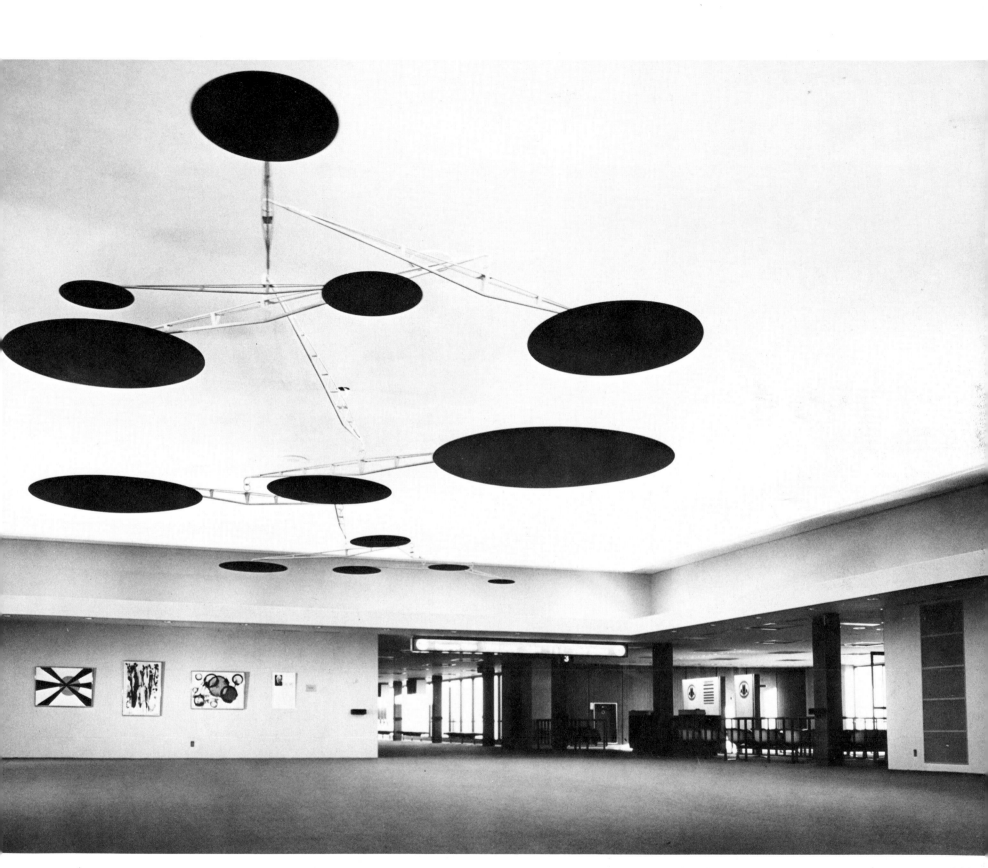

Red, Black and Blue, 1968. Painted aluminum plate, stainless steel struts, motor, 35′ w. American Airlines, Dallas–Fort Worth Airport (photographed at Love Field, Dallas).

293

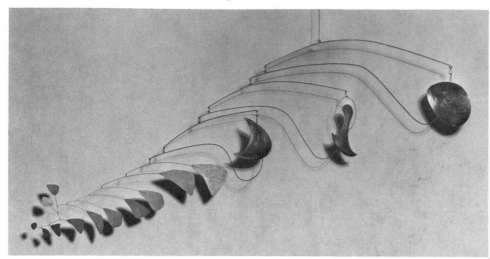

Red Gongs, c. 1950. Painted sheet metal, sheet brass, rod, wire, 12′ w. The Metropolitan Museum of Art, New York; Fletcher Fund.

Floating Wood Objects and Wire Spines, c. 1940. Painted sheet metal, wood, wire, 6′ w. Ingeborg ten Haeff, New York.

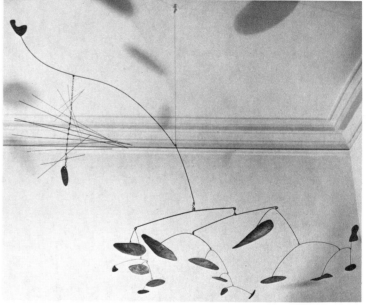

Chagall Mobile, 1944. Painted sheet metal, wire, string, 45¼″ h. Ida Chagall, Paris.

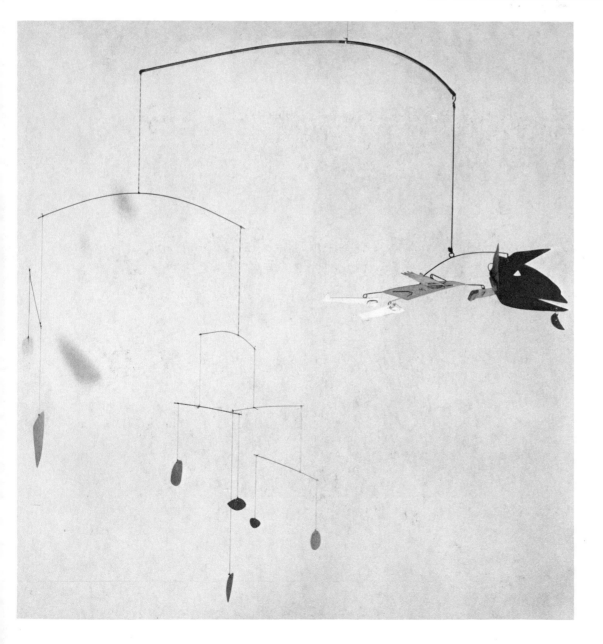

OPPOSITE: *Hanging Spider*, c. 1940. Painted sheet metal, wire, 51″ h. Mrs. John B. Putnam, Cleveland, Ohio.

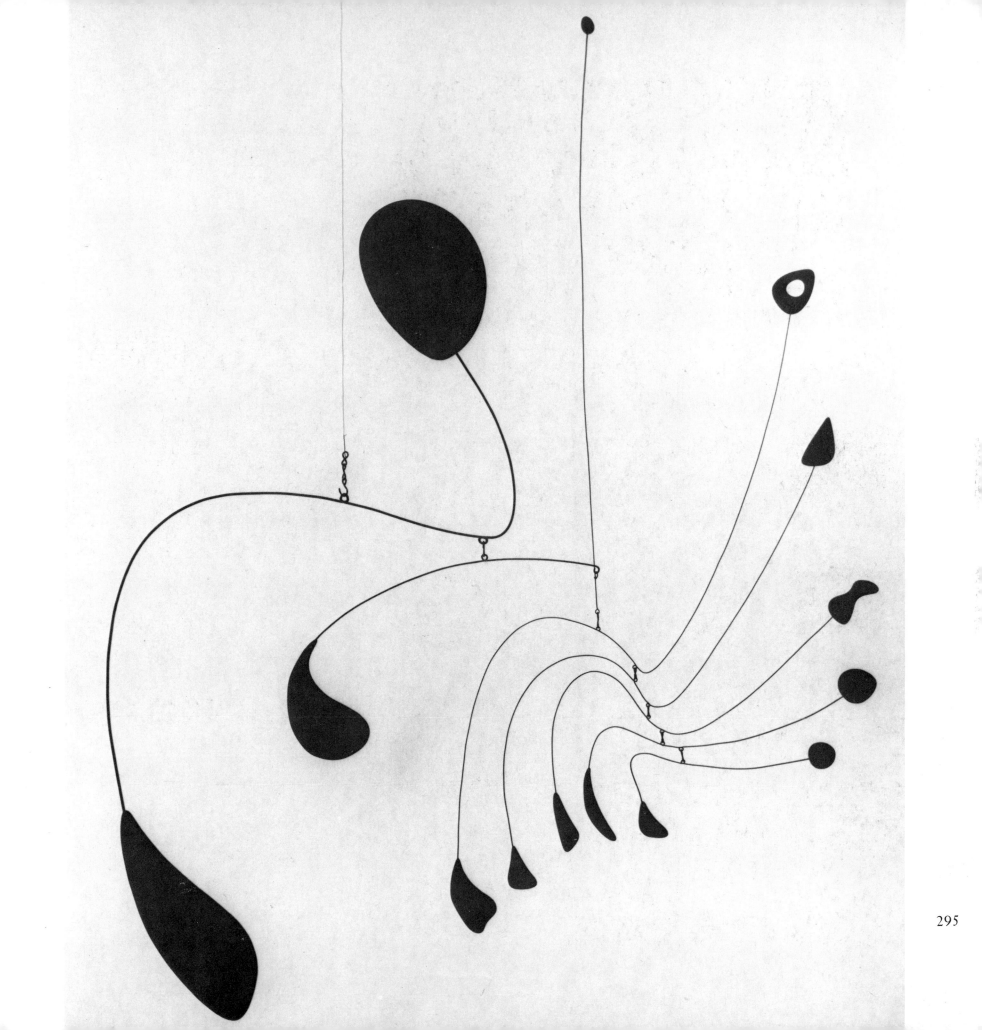

295

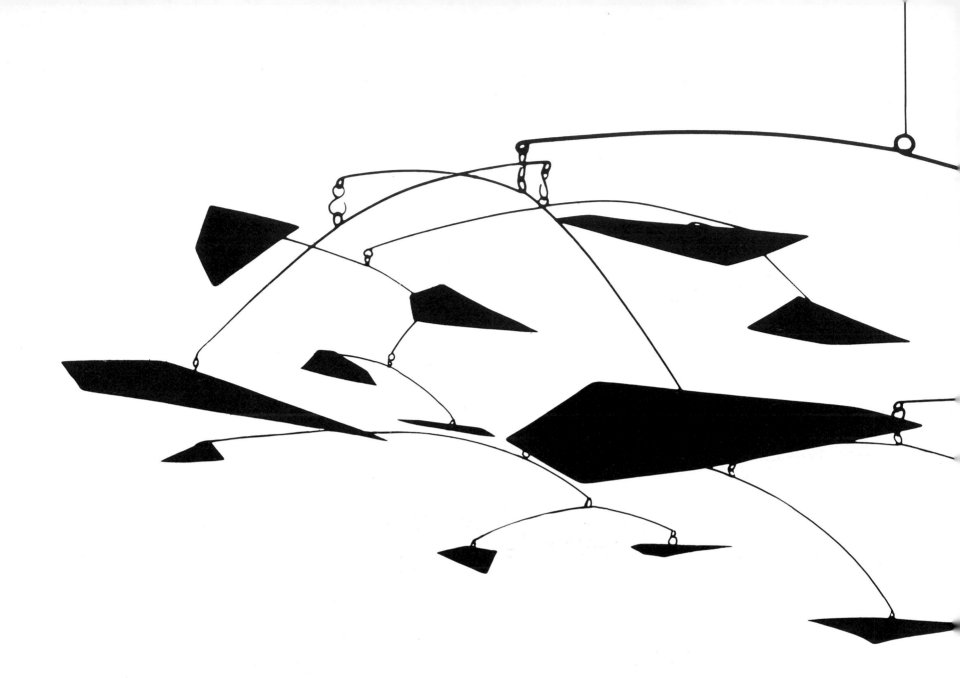

Polygones Noirs, 1947. Painted sheet metal, wire,
7′2″ w. Mr. and Mrs. Joan Miró, Mallorca, Spain.

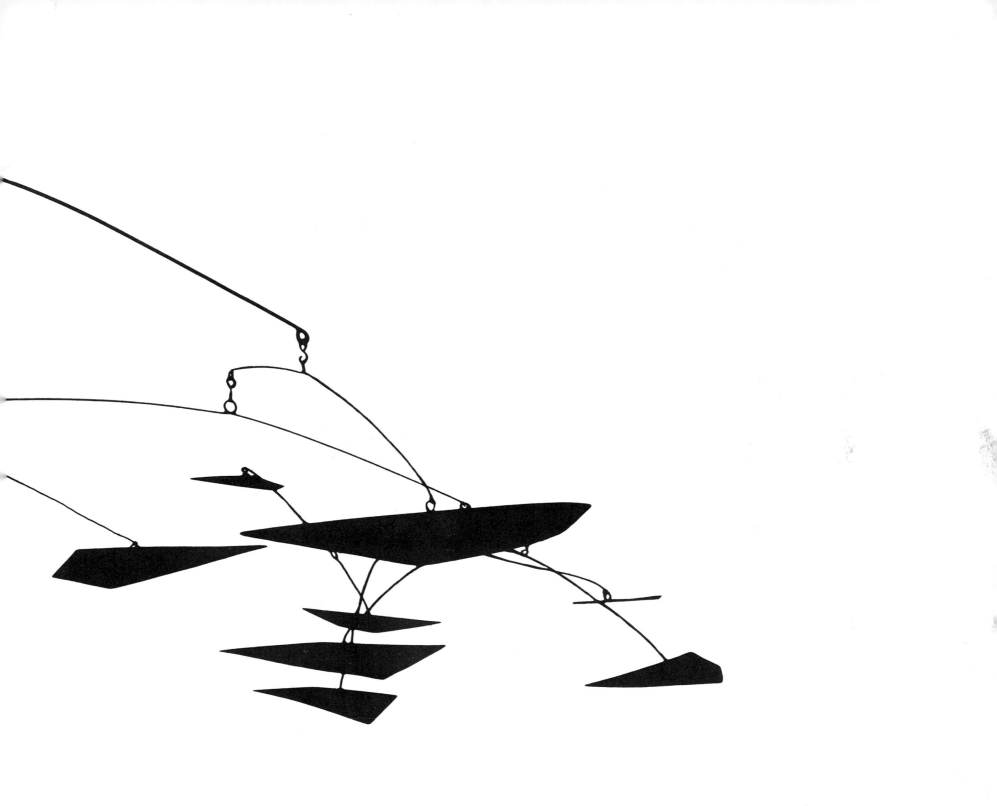

31 Janvier, 1950. Painted sheet metal, wire, 18′ w. Musée National d'Art Moderne, Paris.

Untitled, 1959. Painted sheet metal, rod, wire, 20′ w. Chase Manhattan Bank Art Collection, New York.

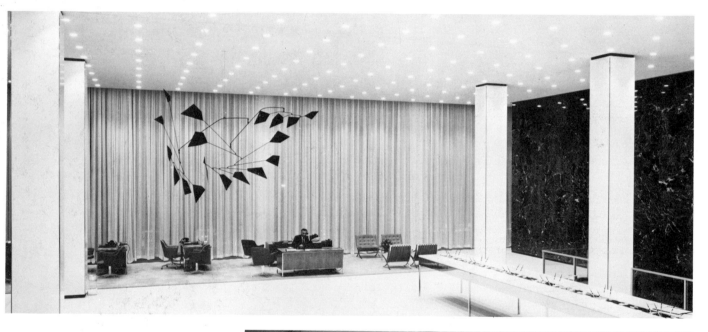

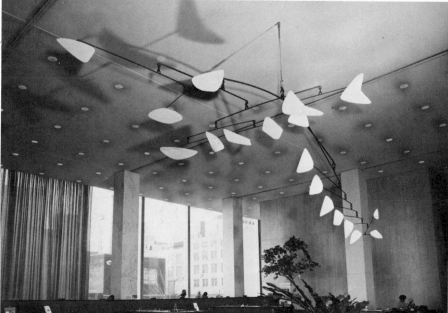

Mobile, 1963. Painted sheet metal, rod, 27′ w. The Connecticut Bank and Trust Company, Hartford.

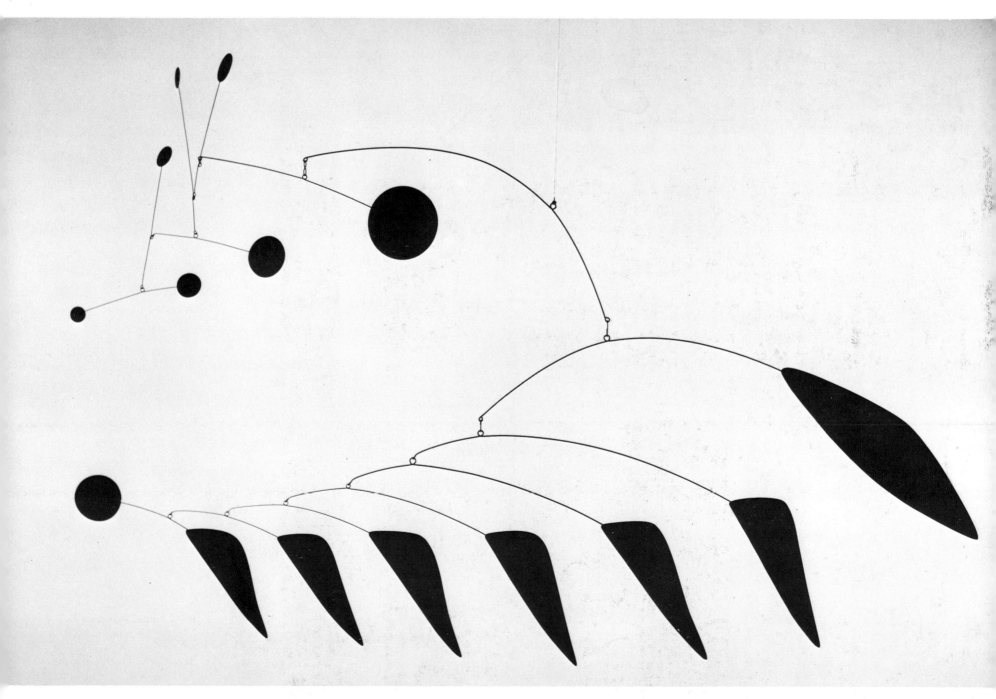

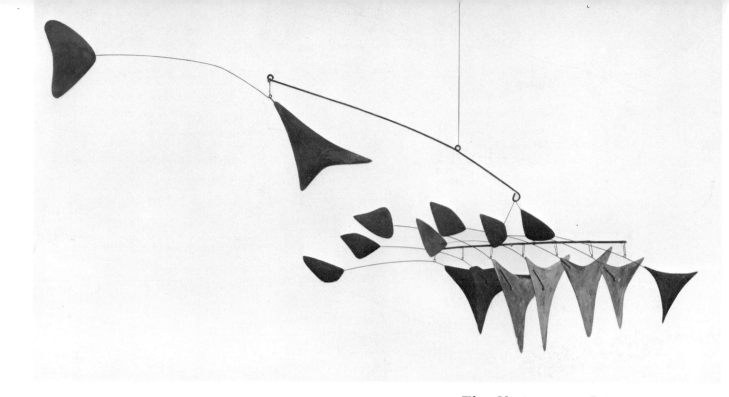

The Chariot, 1961. Painted sheet metal, wire, 63″ w. Collection of the author.

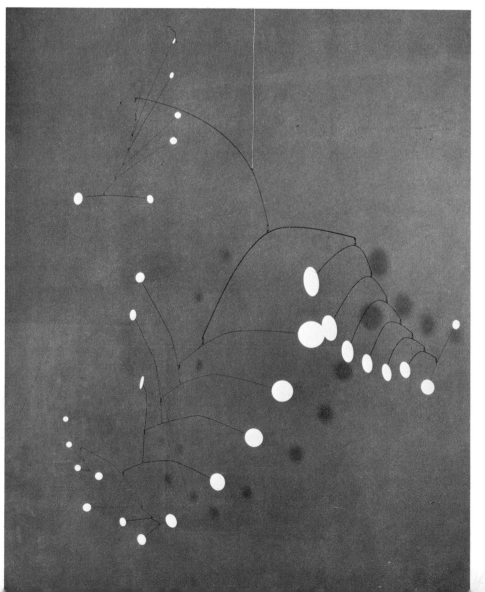

Snow Flurry I, 1948. Painted sheet metal, wire, 7′10″ h. The Museum of Modern Art, New York; gift of the artist.

OPPOSITE: *Five Red Arcs*, 1948. Painted sheet metal, rod, wire, 56″ w. The Solomon R. Guggenheim Museum, New York.

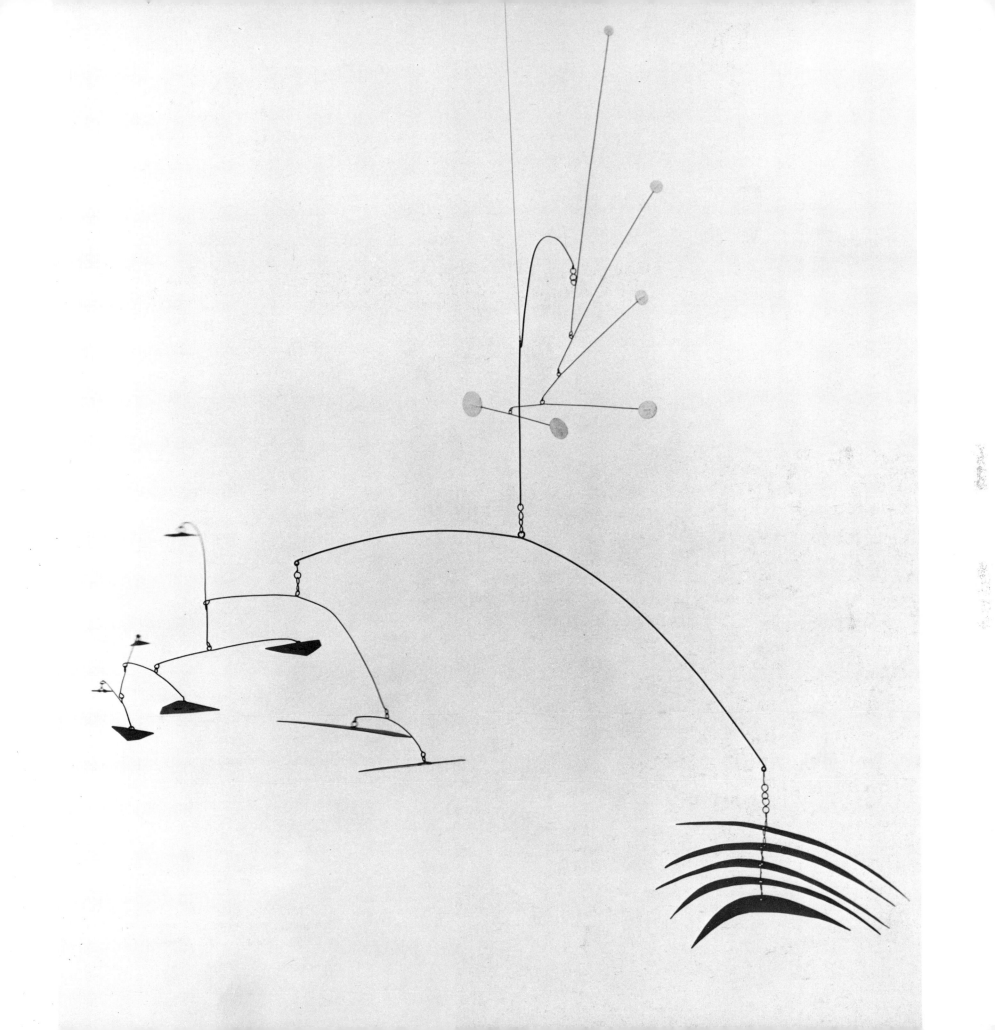

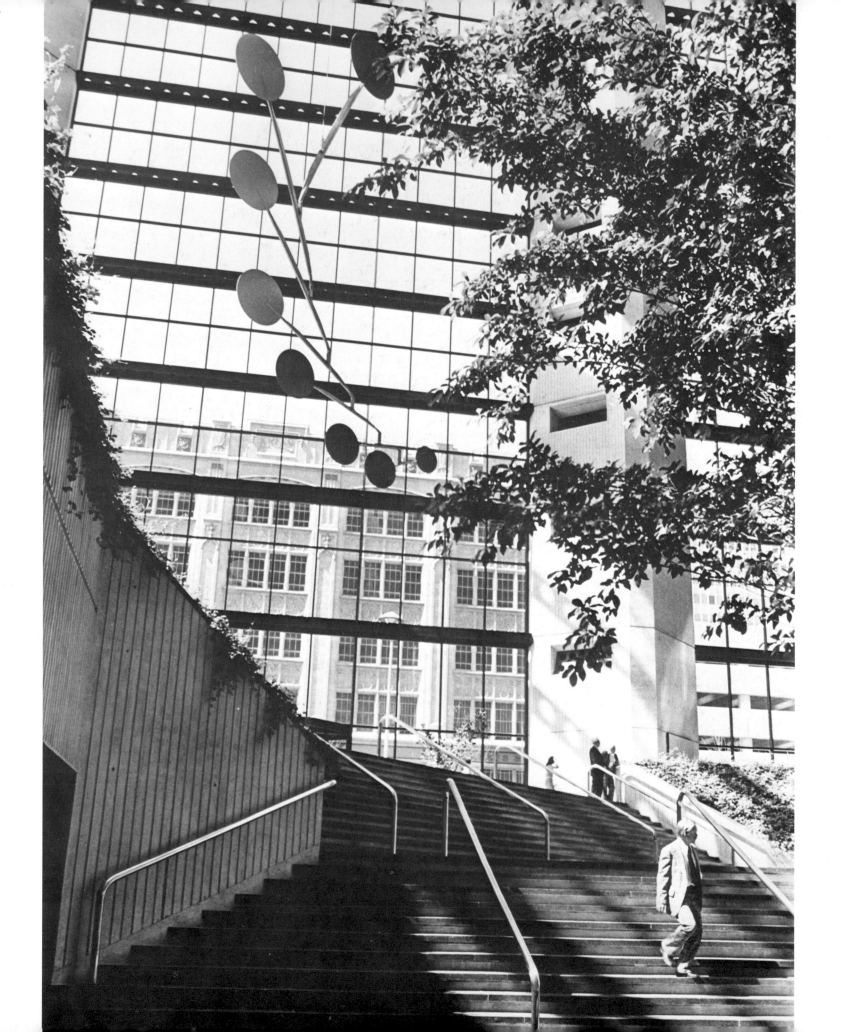

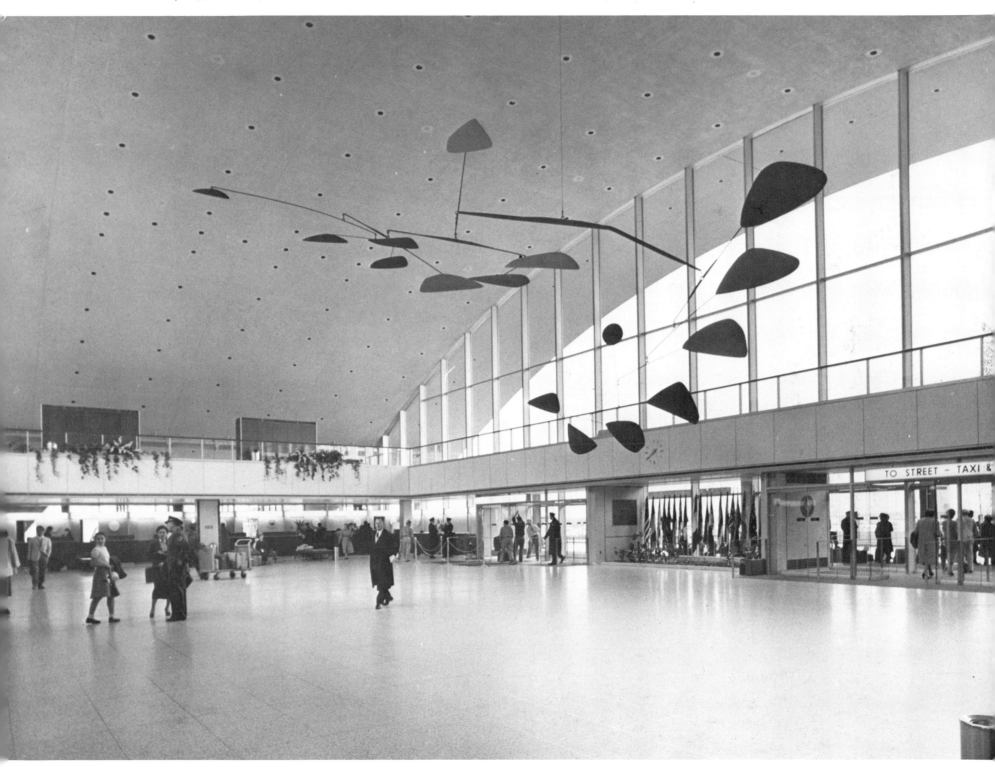

.125, 1957. Painted steel plate, rod, 45′ w. John F. Kennedy International Airport, The Port Authority of New York and New Jersey.

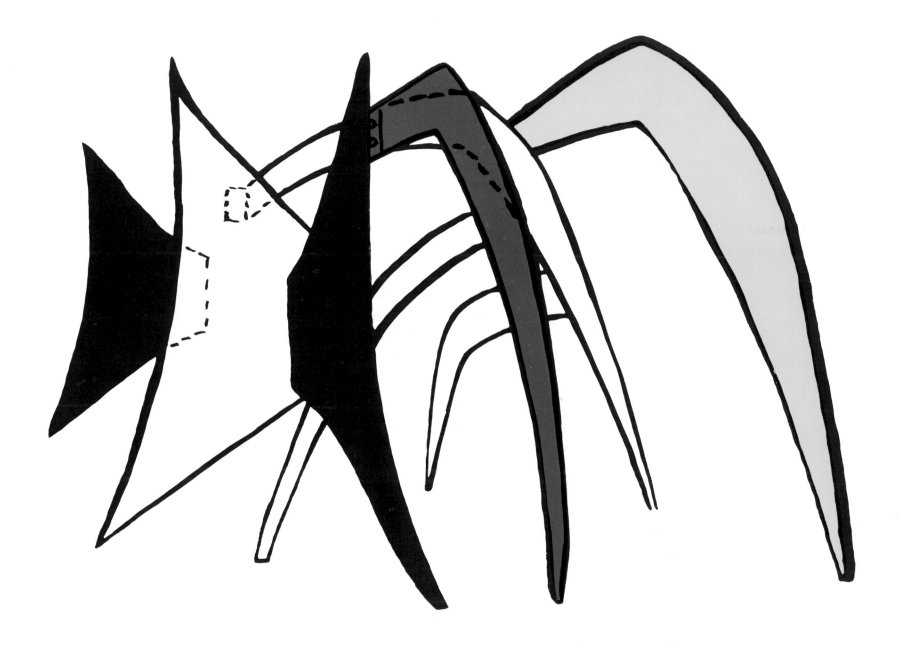

Calder continues: "Whereupon I seized the term and applied it first of all to the things previously shown at Percier [abstract wire sculpture, 1931] and later to the large stabile objects I am now involved in. . . ." The quality of the "large stabile objects"—and the more modestly scaled ones as well—can be judged to some extent from the reproductions here, but fortunately a great many people who read this book will have seen at least one of them. Today Calder mobiles and stabiles are hard to miss. There seems to be great interest in the way the stabiles are made, and Calder has described this clearly.

For the small stabiles—and the models for the large ones—he cuts strips of sheet aluminum with shears, punches holes for the bolts, shapes the pieces in a vise between blocks of wood, files the edges smooth, then bolts them together. (In some of the small early stabiles Calder used rivets instead of bolts, as he does for his small maquettes.) He makes all this look easy, working rapidly and without hesitation.

In the late fifties, as large commissions began coming his way, Calder's works outgrew his studios—and his own ability to execute them by hand. He tried out several metal shops in the vicinity of Roxbury and soon settled down with Carmen Segre in Waterbury, Connecticut. Today all Calder's large works are executed either at Segre's Iron Works or at the Etablissements Biémont in Tours, near his home in France.

In 1966 Calder began making, besides the original maquette for a large stabile, a one-fifth scale model to study the overlapping of plates and piercing of the holes. For the final piece the technique is that of industrial metal work. Plates of heavy steel are machine-cut, curved between rollers, lifted by cranes to be set into one another at various angles, and put together with bolts. Metal ribs and gussets are welded on wherever needed to give stability, but it should be noted that welding is a minor rather than a major aspect of Calder's work as a sculptor. Even the largest stabiles are made so that they can be easily unbolted and taken apart for shipping, then reassembled at their destination. The Biémont factory has railroad tracks running right up to the main hangar, and the only size limitation for the stabiles is that they must fit in freight cars. "All I had to do was have enough nerve to tell them how big I wanted them," said Sandy, in a colossal understatement of what goes into the execution of a giant stabile.

On the occasion of the major retrospective organized by the Fondation Maeght in 1969, Sandy wrote a simple "*Comment Faire*"—"how-to-do-it"—for his stabiles:

I make a little maquette of sheet aluminum, about 50 cm. high. With that I'm free to add a piece, or to make a cutout. As soon as I'm satisfied with the result I take the maquette

Stabiles

to my Biémont friends . . . and they enlarge the maquette as much as I want. When the enlargement is finished, provisionally, I go to add the ribs and the gussets, or other things which I hadn't thought of. After that they work out my ideas on the bracing. And that does it.

When Calder experimented with the bronze medium, one of the things he says he disliked was having his work executed by others. Recently he has had happier experiences with lithographers and weavers—who interpret his gouaches as prints and tapestries—and especially with the skilled metal workers who execute his monumental mobiles and stabiles. With Carmen Segre and a number of Biémont foremen, Calder has a relationship of shared work and easy camaraderie. Introducing Segre to an interviewer, Calder explained, "I've become *his* helper, he's doing the work." To which Segre readily replied, "Sandy does all the figuring. He works right in here with us. He gets a sledge hammer . . . he keeps right up with us. It's tough to work with a sledge." One of the French foremen had never been in an art museum and seldom traveled outside his own village until he went to Dallas to help install Calder's huge motorized airport mobile. He, and other equally unsophisticated workmen, have become Calder's devoted collaborators, willing to follow and give shape to the artist's flights of fancy. For his part, Sandy draws inspiration from the technical problems they confront and solve together. The technicians have become working partners who enlarge and extend Calder's artistic intentions in much the same way that construction engineers bring into being an architect's concept of a building.

Indeed, Calder's largest stabiles are monuments that approach architecture in both scale and physical presence. It is not surprising that he understands and works well with architects; as Klaus Perls says, Calder respects the professional always. Scattered through his autobiography are the names of the leading architects of his time: Le Corbusier, George Nelson, Gordon Bunshaft, Wallace K. Harrison, Eliot Noyes, Marcel Breuer, Alvar Aalto, Eero Saarinen, Philip Johnson, I. M. Pei. Many of them have been Calder's personal and professional friends, commissioning great stabiles for public places.

One article that should be considered required reading for any study of the stabiles is Robert Osborn's interview with Calder, published in 1969 as an eighteen-page feature in *Art in America*. Titled "Calder's International Monuments," it presents Calder's comments on the development of the large metal sculptures, the foundries where they are made, and how twenty-two monumental works—all illustrated—were commissioned and executed. Osborn begins his introduction by saying:

At heart, Calder has always been an engineer. He has clothed the forces of his engineering with his joyful imagination and his lithe sense of beauty. But the wellspring of his

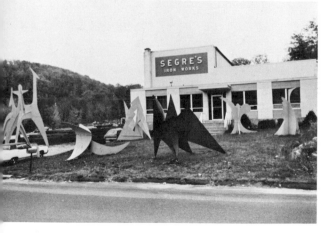

Segre's Iron Works, Waterbury, Connecticut. FROM LEFT: *Hats Off*, 1969; *Brontosaurus*, 1970; *Lightning*, 1970; *The Kite that Never Flew*, 1967; *The Clove*, 1970; *The Snuck*, 1969.

art remains the thrusts, the tensions, the stress loads, the balances, the forces of gravity which he, the engineer, proceeds to adjust and join. . . .

Normally, an artist has learned laboriously from his heritage and his immediate predecessors and then *slightly* altered these gifts. But not Calder. He fought off his father's *solid* teaching, admonishments and deprecatory remarks and brought forth his entirely new concept of sculpture.

. . . Now in full command of his materials and armed at last with honor (which is never a detriment for any man), he can achieve the nobility he desires through a variety of new avenues, steadily explored and extended.

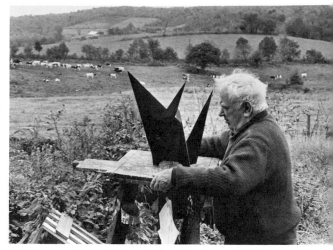

With maquette of *Gwenfritz*, Roxbury, 1965.

In connection with the last comment it is interesting that in 1938, when Calder had a large exhibition at the George Walter Vincent Smith Art Gallery in Springfield, Massachusetts, many distinguished guests attended the opening—among them Alvar Aalto, Fernand Léger and Siegfried Giedion—but nothing was sold. In 1955 an important show was held at the Curt Valentin Gallery, but, as Calder puts it, "nothing came of it." Asked in the 1940s about stabile prices, Calder said, "The big ones are seven hundred dollars, but we'll take any reasonable offer." Now the big ones (bigger than those Calder mentioned) are priced in the hundreds of thousands, some of them partially subsidized by government funds.

The Onion at Segre's Iron Works, 1965.

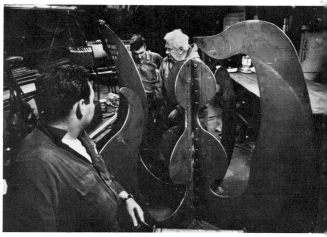

A few excerpts from Osborn's interview should give a good idea of the origin and growth of the great stabiles, and of the artist's attitude toward the work that now most interests him:

When did the large metal constructions begin?
It was when Eliot Noyes asked me to remake an object I'd made earlier to show at Pierre Matisse—*The Black Beast*—only make it of thicker metal. . . . I'd already done the one in 1958 for UNESCO in Paris [*Spirale*] and that was a pretty good size, but now I had the impulse and the means (two thousand dollars) to make things at a larger scale of one-quarter-inch iron plate. So I decided to have a show of fairly large stabiles at Perls in the winter of 1958.

Tell me about the Biémont ironworks. How many men are employed there?
Between sixty and eighty work in the plant, but only three or four work on one piece.
Have certain men become specialists and therefore improved in doing your things?
Yes, but now they are all becoming "art critics."
But I should think it would be handy to be able now to just produce the model and then know that they can enlarge it without loss of power.
Yes, it's almost ideal now. But I always like to have a finger in the pie.
While we're on it, talk about the enlarging process.
I used to make a small model, then cut out full-sized parts in paper. Then the iron-workers in Waterbury would translate these paper templates into metal plates. Now

307

Studio terrace, Saché. FROM LEFT: *Sabot*, 1963; *Dent de Sagesse*, 1964.

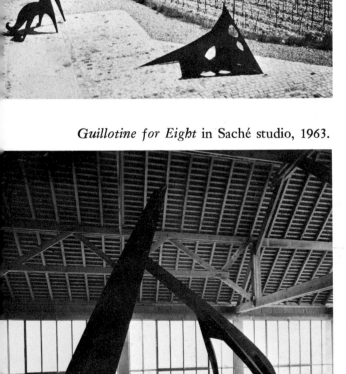

Guillotine for Eight in Saché studio, 1963.

the Biémont people are so trained that they make the templates themselves. Even Waterbury can do this now.

Which was the first really monumental stabile—Spoleto [Teodelapio]?
Yes, Giovanni Carandente, assistant director of the Museum of Modern Art in Rome, organized the outdoor sculpture for Spoleto in 1962. . . . Because it was to arch the crossroads at the entrance, I made the model higher in the crotch—thirty inches long, thirty inches high. Italsider, a shipbuilder in Genoa, built the thing. . . .
Was it fun to do something that large?
Yes. People keep giving it a phallic meaning. I wasn't aware of any such influence, but that may give it its nice force.

Sandy then tells an amusing incident about an unforeseen technical problem with a model for *El Sol Rojo,* made for the 1968 Olympics in Mexico City:

When I got to Mexico—I'd sent a three-foot model of what I wanted ahead and suggested that they make one nine or ten feet high—they'd made this intermediate model and *welded* it all together. When I arrived they asked: "Now, where do we put the holes?"
They were going to bore them and bolt them after the fact.

Osborn asked how important Calder felt color was to his large stabiles:

Against certain backgrounds, yes—it can help. For instance, a new one at Grand Rapids [*La Grande Vitesse*] will be red because the piece is set against a black glass building. . . . But otherwise, plain black will do it if I've made it right.

Calder also mentioned that *Man,* made for Expo 67 in Montreal, was unpainted:

They wanted it bare, which was natural because the Nickel Company put up the money, so they wanted it to look like nickel.

The last question has to do with the carefully conceived ribbing, the bracing, which, as Osborn points out, has acquired an esthetic of its own, to be enjoyed as an integral part of the design:

I try something new each time. With the model at three meters you can wobble it and see where it gives, where the vibrations occur, and then put your reinforcement there. If a plate seems flimsy, I put a rib on it, and if the relation between the two plates is not rigid, I put a gusset between them—that's the triangular piece—and butt it to both surfaces. How to construct them changes with each piece; you invent the bracing as you go, depending on the form of each object. . . .

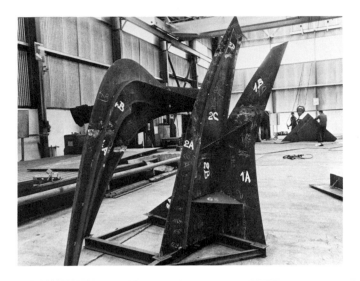

Intermediate-sized model for *Crossed Blades* at Etablissements Biémont, Tours, 1966.

With *Five Wings* at Etablissements Biémont, 1967.

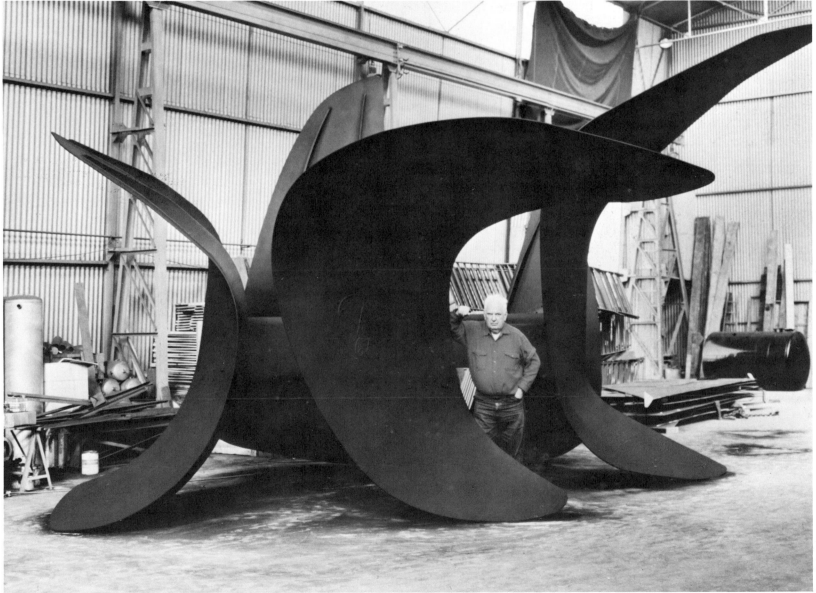

I crossed the Atlantic once on the *Bremen*. The partitions were all going, "Baaroop, baaroo, baaroop, baaroo." That's what you have to avoid.

From these last comments it is clear that even in his recent huge stabiles Calder continues to follow the intuitive method he described in 1951:

. . . when I use two or more sheets of metal cut into shapes and mounted at angles to each other, I feel that there is a solid form, perhaps concave, perhaps convex, filling in the dihedral angles between them. I do not have a definite idea of what this would be like, I merely sense it and occupy myself with the shapes one actually sees.

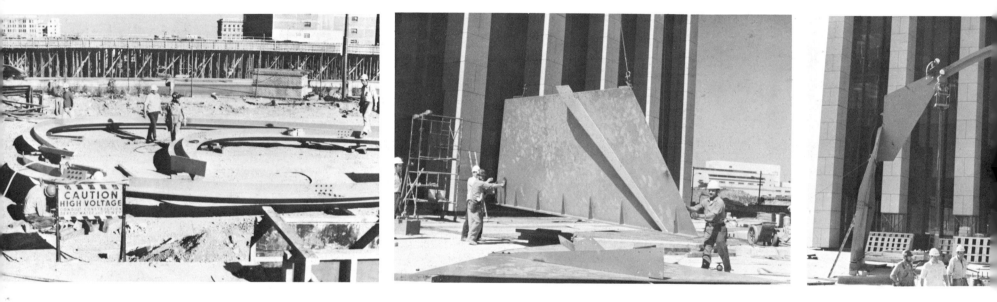

In one city after another across the globe, Calder stabiles are being installed in public places. Beginning with Spoleto, Italy, where a stabile serves as a monumental gateway spanning one of the town's main thoroughfares, a partial list of stabile sites would include New York, Philadelphia, Princeton, Grand Rapids, Kansas City, Cambridge, Albany, Des Moines, Washington, D.C., Houston, Fort Worth, Detroit, Hartford, Los Angeles and Chicago in the United States; Montreal and Toronto in Canada; Mexico City; Caracas, Venezuela; Sydney, Australia; Brussels, Belgium; Rotterdam and Amsterdam in the Netherlands; Stockholm and Göteborg in Sweden; Hanover and Berlin in Germany. In France there are outdoor stabiles in Amboise, Bourges, Grenoble and Saché, and in 1975 Paris acquired the monumental stabile *La Défense*, named for and located in the section where a new complex of skyscraper office buildings has been developed.

In many cities Calder's monuments have become the objects of enormous civic pride and celebration. Chicago staged a full-scale "Calder Festival," including a real circus parade, on the occasion of the dedication of *Flamingo* in 1974. Even more striking is the case of Grand Rapids, Michigan, where in the late sixties a stabile was commissioned as part of the city's downtown urban renewal program, financed by public subscription as well as government funds. *La Grande Vitesse* (the poetic title is Calder's pun on "Grand Rapids") was dedicated in 1969; at that time Gerald Ford, the city's Congressman, said that when the grant request was first made he didn't know what a Calder was, but he later realized it had "really helped to regenerate Grand Rapids." Since then it has multiplied its influence; its site is now named Calder Plaza; it is repro-

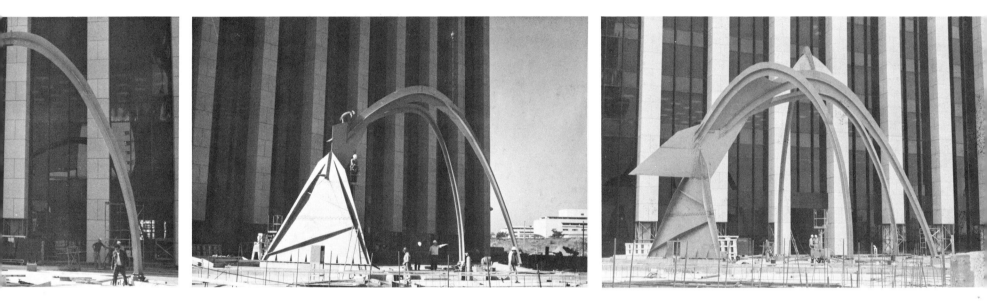

duced on the official city stationery and on the sides of the garbage disposal trucks; all the fire engines have been repainted to match the Calder red of the stabile: Calder has executed a roof-painting for a building on the Plaza; the music specially composed for the dedication is now well known in Grand Rapids; and the stabile's success is credited with having changed Ford's vote on funding the National Endowment for the Arts.

The monumental stabiles are—with the mobiles and the latest *Universe*—the most impressive achievements of Calder's lifetime of work, but we must not overlook marvelous early pieces such as *Morning Star*, which might be considered a Constellation evolved into a stabile. Some of the early stabiles, such as *The Monocle*, are small *only* in size; they have the same potential of scale as the maquettes for the recent monumental ones. Today, as Calder nears eighty, the stabiles continue to be the focus of his attention, growing steadily in scale and grandeur.

Installation of *Four Arches* at Security Pacific National Bank, Los Angeles, 1974.

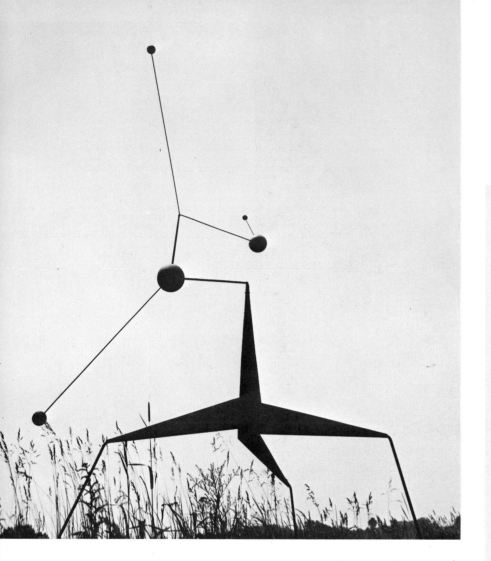

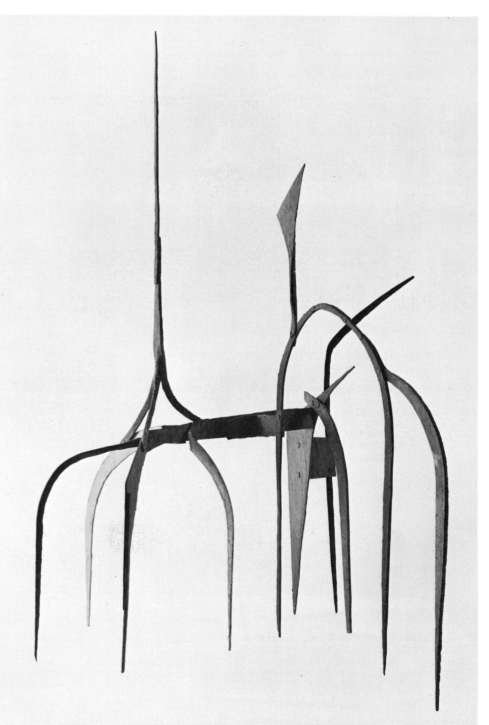

Morning Star, 1943. Painted sheet metal, rod, wood, 6′4¾″ h. The Museum of Modern Art, New York; gift of the artist.

Gothic Construction from Scraps, 1939. Painted sheet metal, 31⅝″ h. Collection of the artist.

312

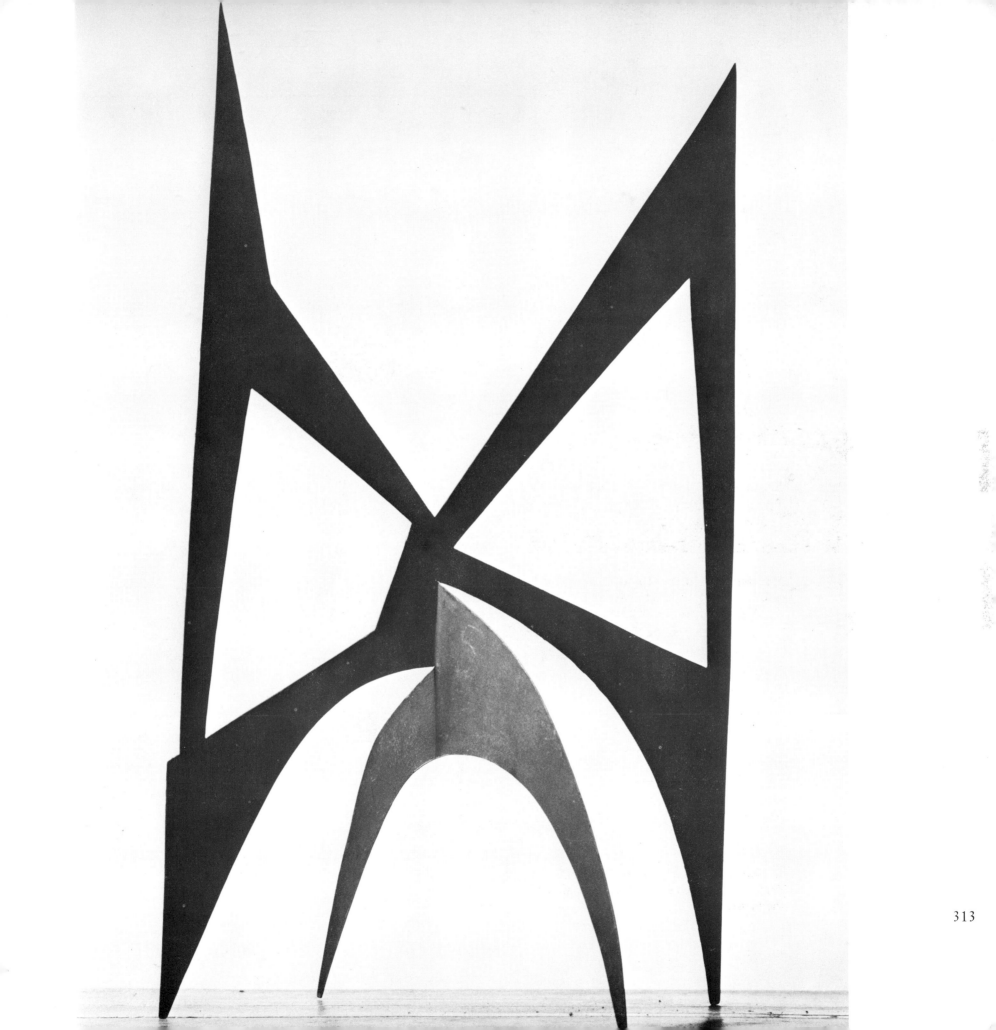

313

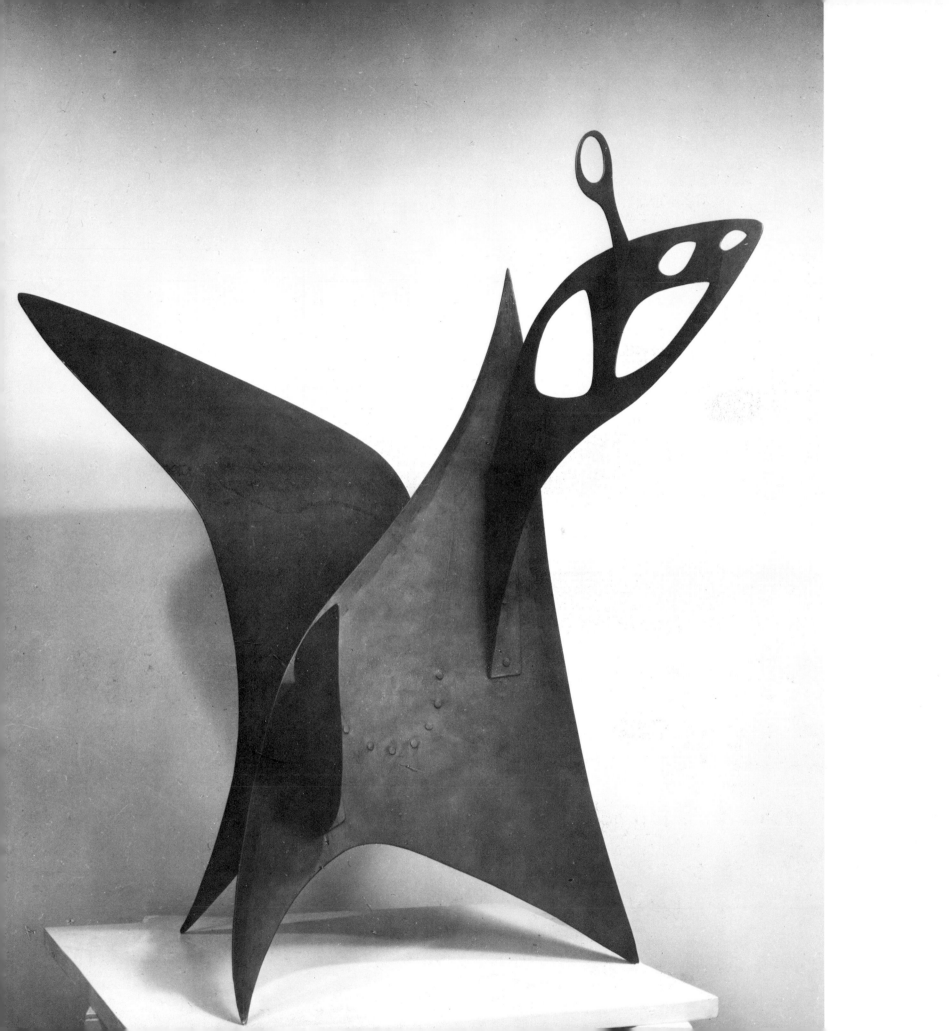

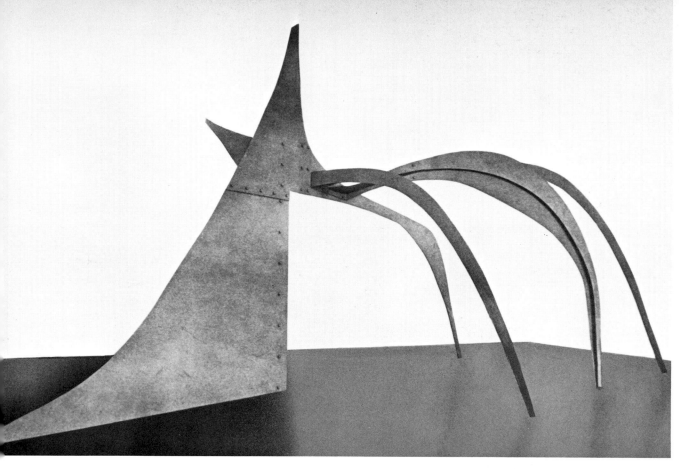

The Crab, 1962. Painted steel plate, 20′ w. The Museum of Fine Arts, Houston, Texas.

OPPOSITE: *The Monocle*, c. 1950. Painted sheet metal, 36″ h. Collection of the author.

Bucephalus, 1963. Painted steel plate, 10′6″ w. Fresno, California.

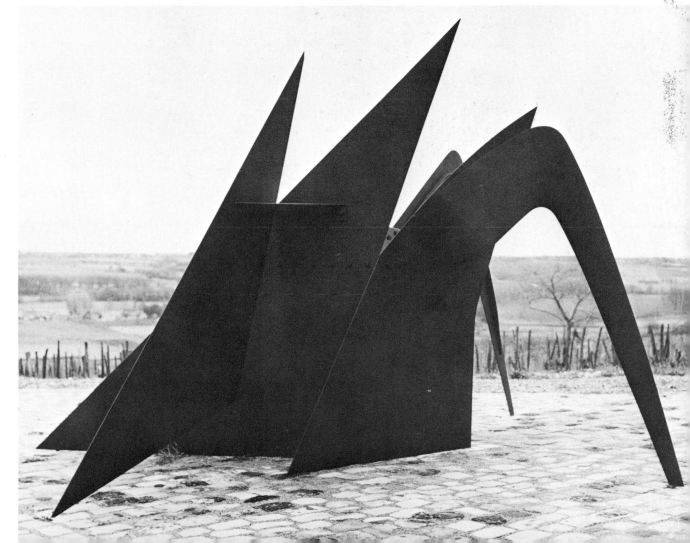

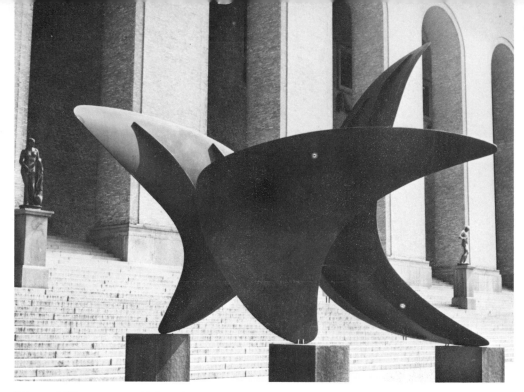

Three Wings, 1963. Painted steel plate, 13′ h.
Göteborg, Sweden; The Charles Felix Lindberg
Donation Fund.

The City, 1960. Painted steel plate, rod, 16′10⅜″
w. Museo de Bellas Artes, Caracas.

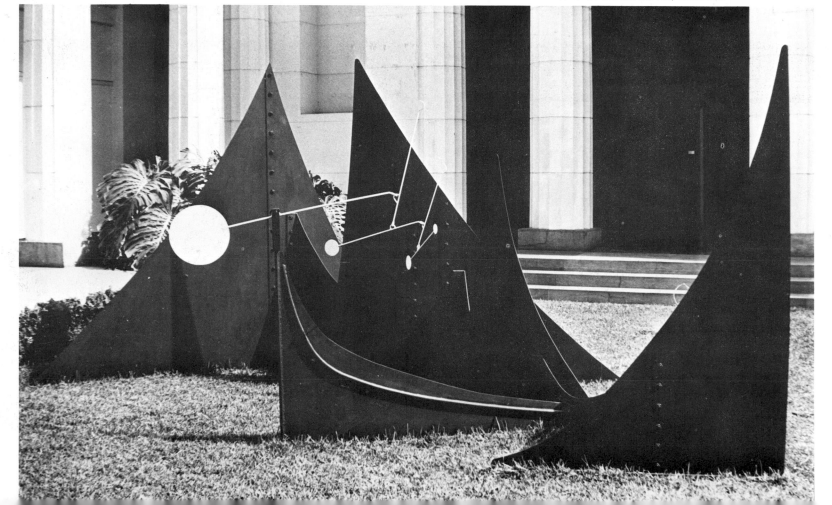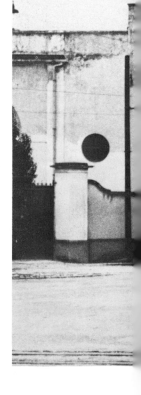

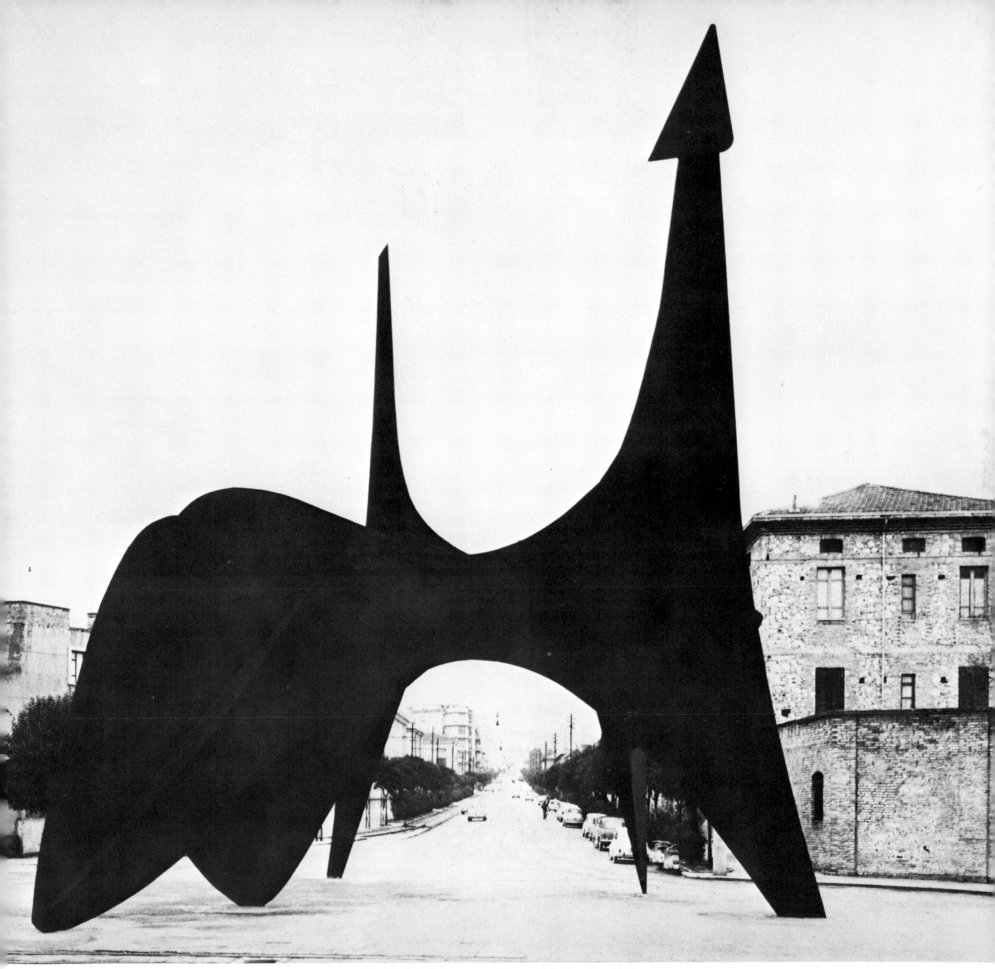

Teodelapio, 1962. Painted steel plate, 59′ h. Spoleto, Italy.

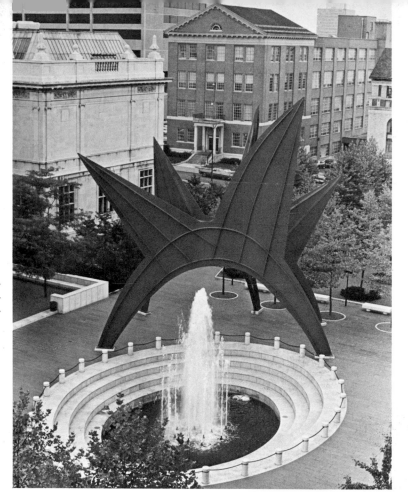

Stegosaurus, 1973. Painted steel plate, 50′ h. Alfred E. Burr Mall, Hartford, Connecticut; gift of the Trustees of the Ella Burr McManus Fund.

Man, 1967. Stainless steel plate, 70′ h. Montreal, Canada.

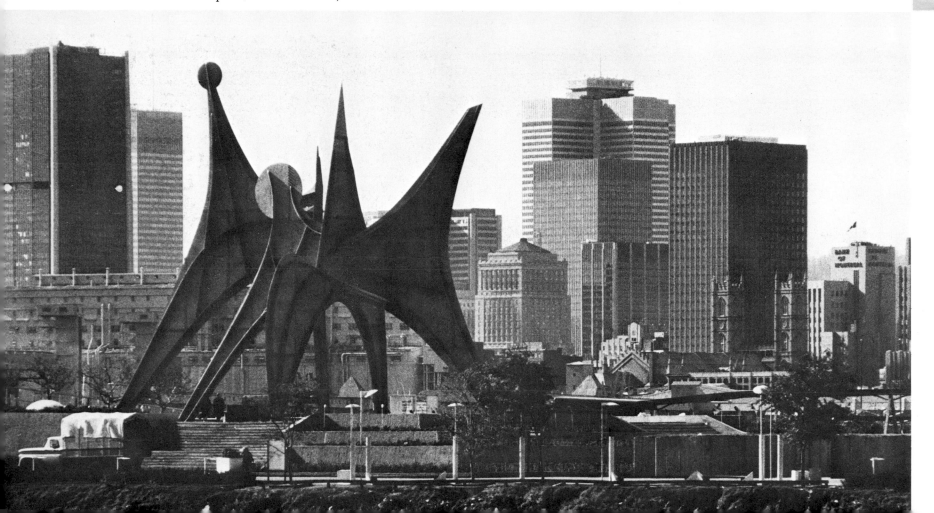

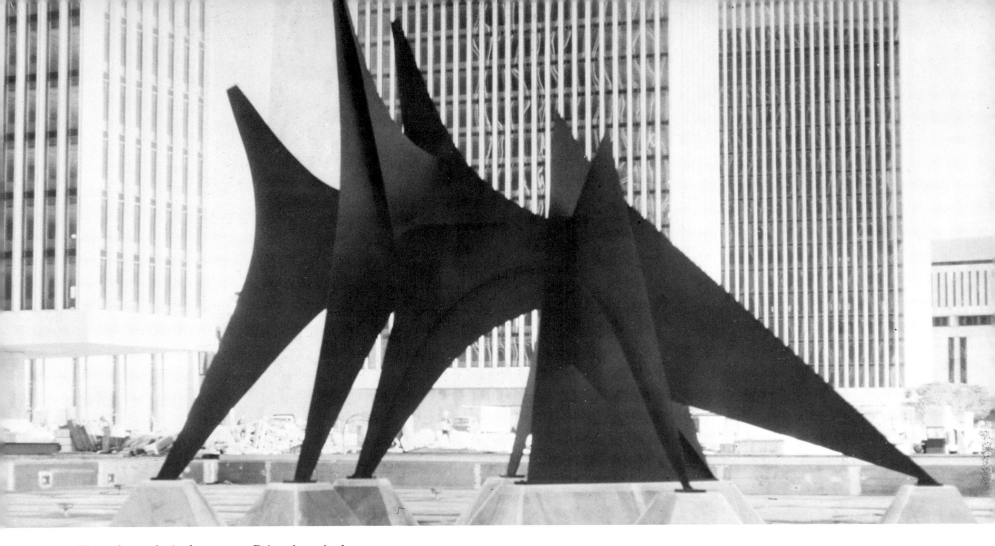

Triangles and Arches, 1965. Painted steel plate,
30′ w. Empire State Plaza, Albany, New York.

La Grande Voile, 1966. Painted steel plate, 40′ h.
Massachusetts Institute of Technology, Cambridge, Massachusetts.

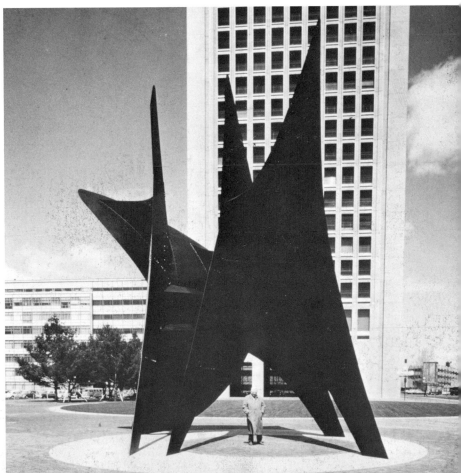

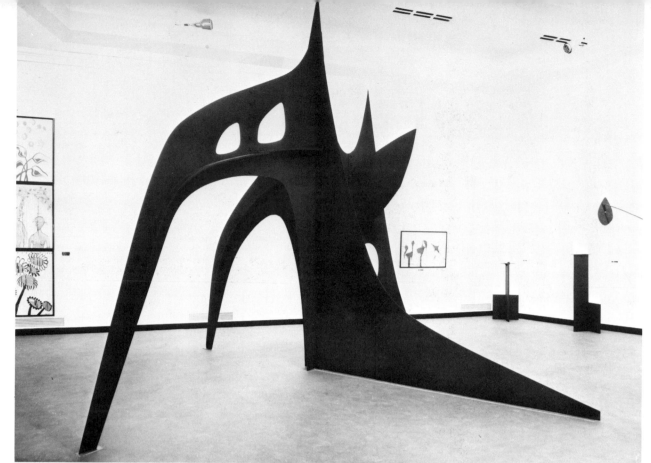

Nageoire, 1964. Painted steel plate, 18'6" w. Musée National d'Art Moderne, Paris; gift of the artist.

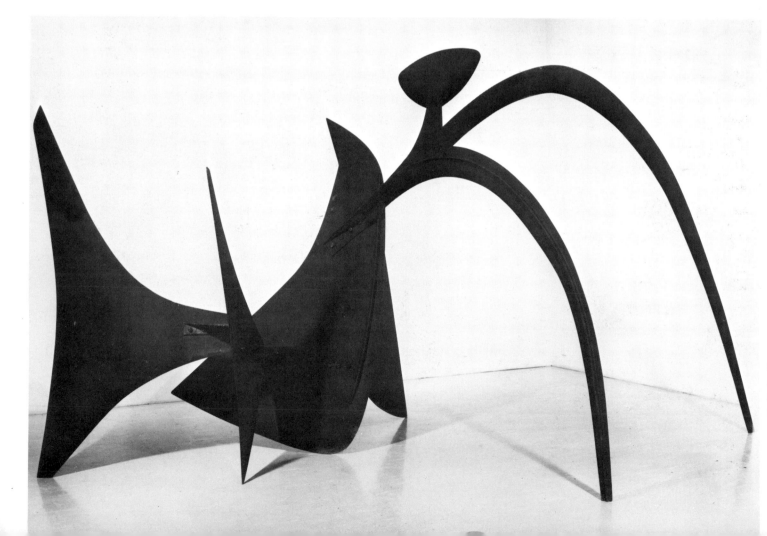

Black Widow, 1959. Painted steel plate, 14'3" w. The Museum of Modern Art, New York; Mrs. Simon Guggenheim Fund.

OPPOSITE: *Portrait of a Young Man*, c. 1945. Painted sheet metal, 35¼" h. Collection of the author.

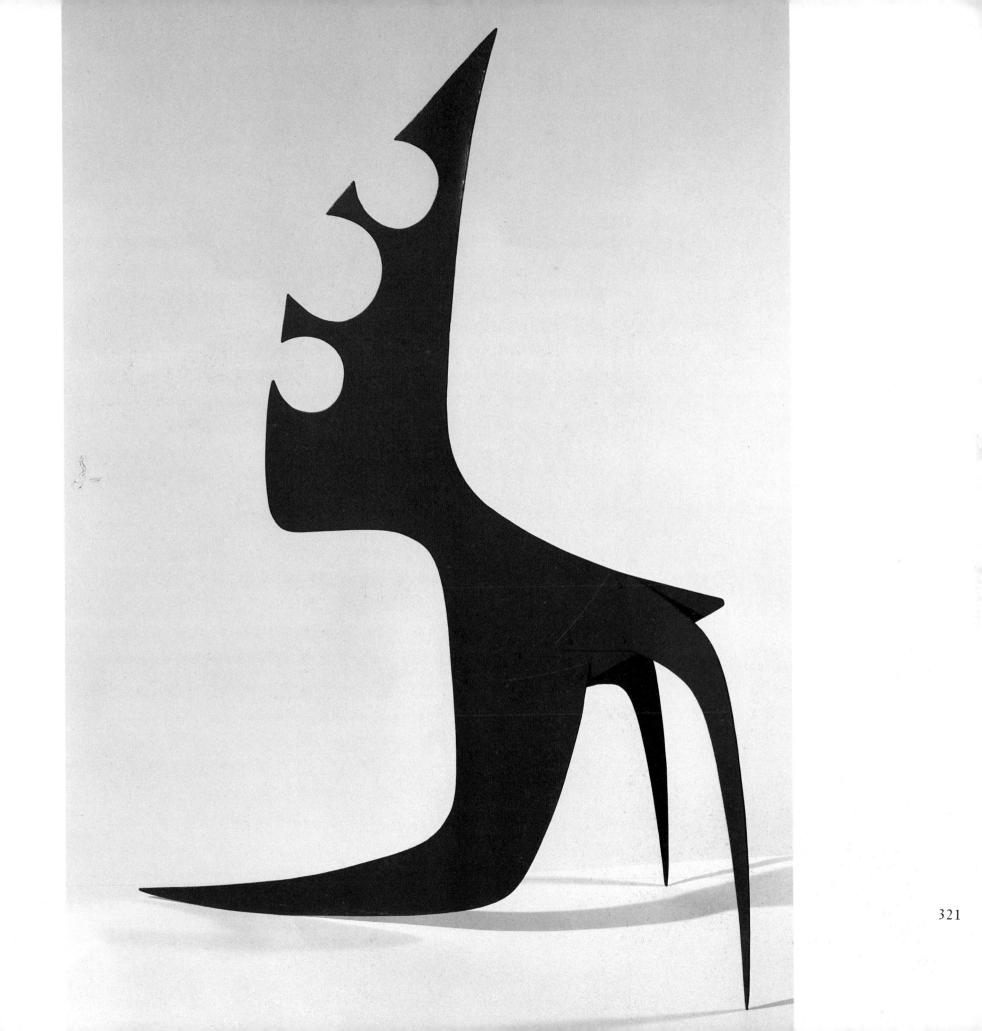

321

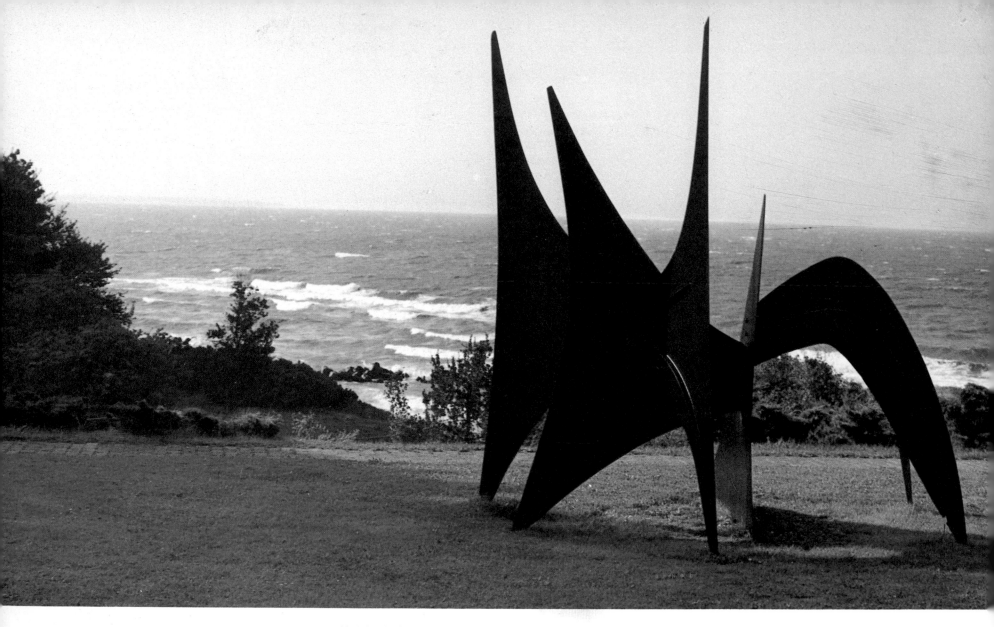

Slender Ribs, 1963. Painted steel plate, 11'9" h. Louisiana Museum, Humlebaek, Denmark; gift of the New Carlsberg Foundation.

Tom's (for Thomas M. Messer), 1974. Painted steel plate, 28'2" h. Collection of the artist.

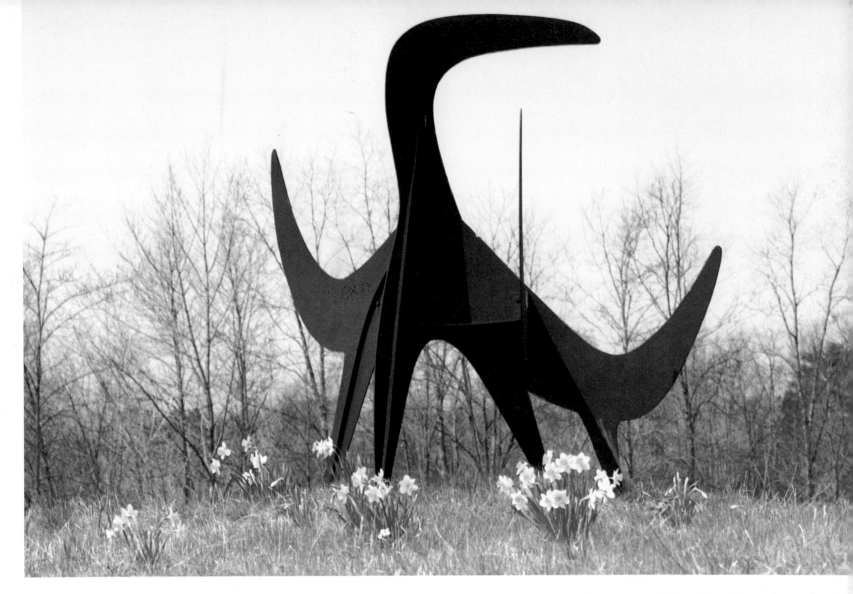

Longnose, 1957. Painted steel plate, 8'2" h. Collection of the author.

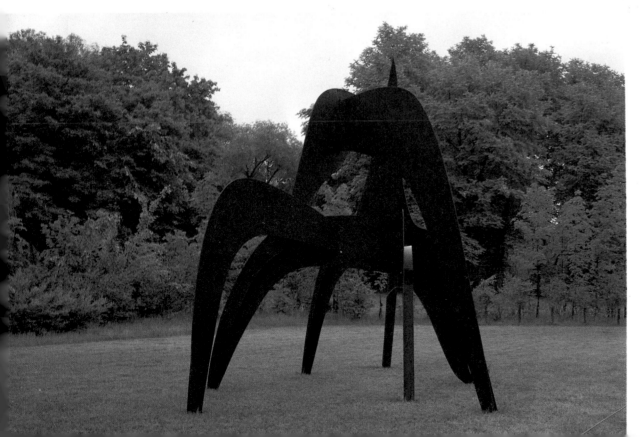

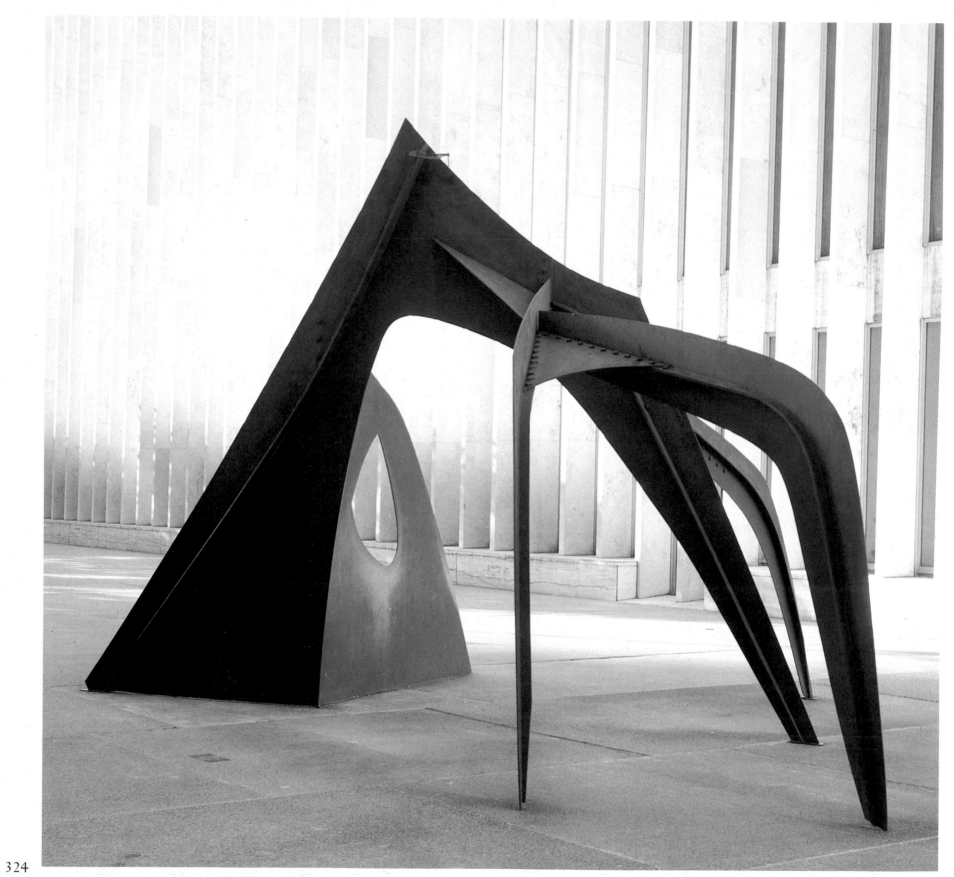

324

Le Guichet, 1963. Painted steel plate, 22′ w. Lincoln Center for the Performing Arts, New York; gift of Howard and Jean Lipman.

OPPOSITE: *La Grande Vitesse,* 1969. Painted steel plate, 55′ w. Calder Plaza, Vandenberg Center, Grand Rapids, Michigan.

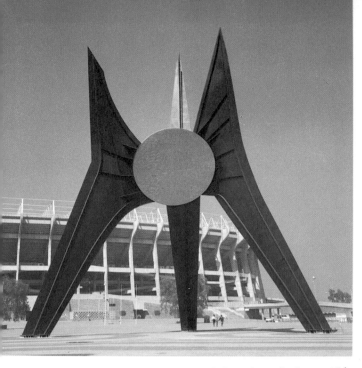

El Sol Rojo, 1968. Painted steel plate, 80' h.
Aztec Stadium, Mexico City.

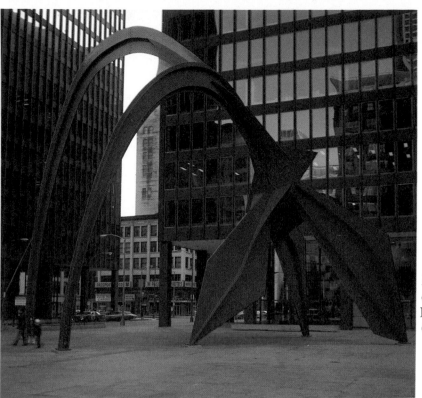

Flamingo, 1974. Painted steel plate, 53' h.
Federal Center Plaza, Chicago.

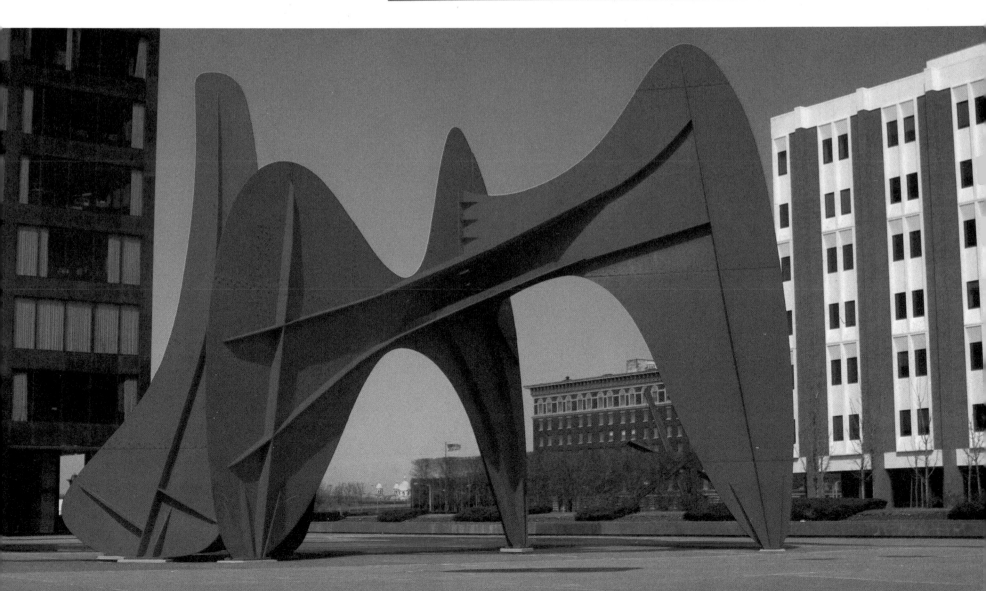

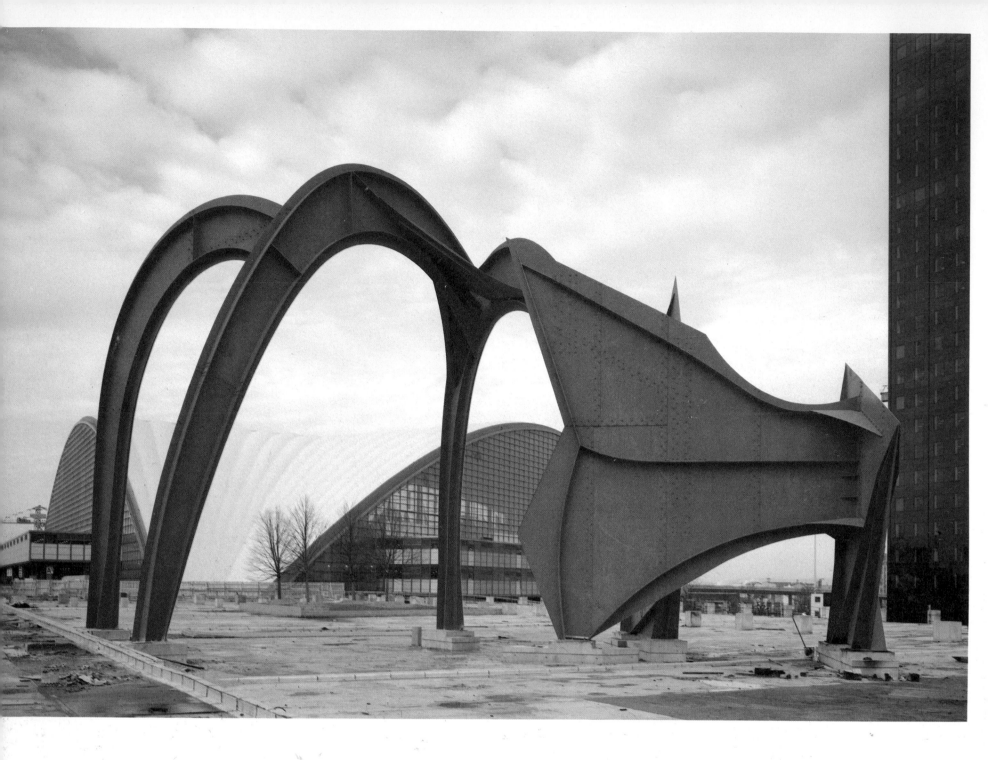

L'Araignée Rouge, 1975. Painted steel plate, 98′ w. Rond Point de La Défense, Paris.

Flying Dragon (under construction, 1975). Primer paint on steel plate, 56′ w. Collection of the artist.

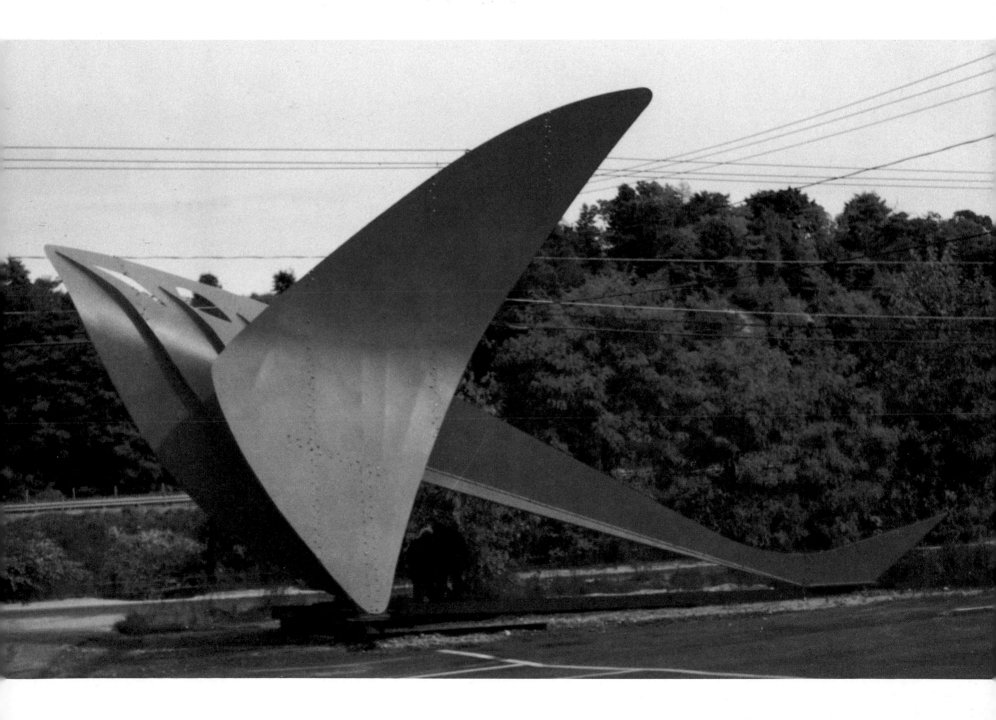

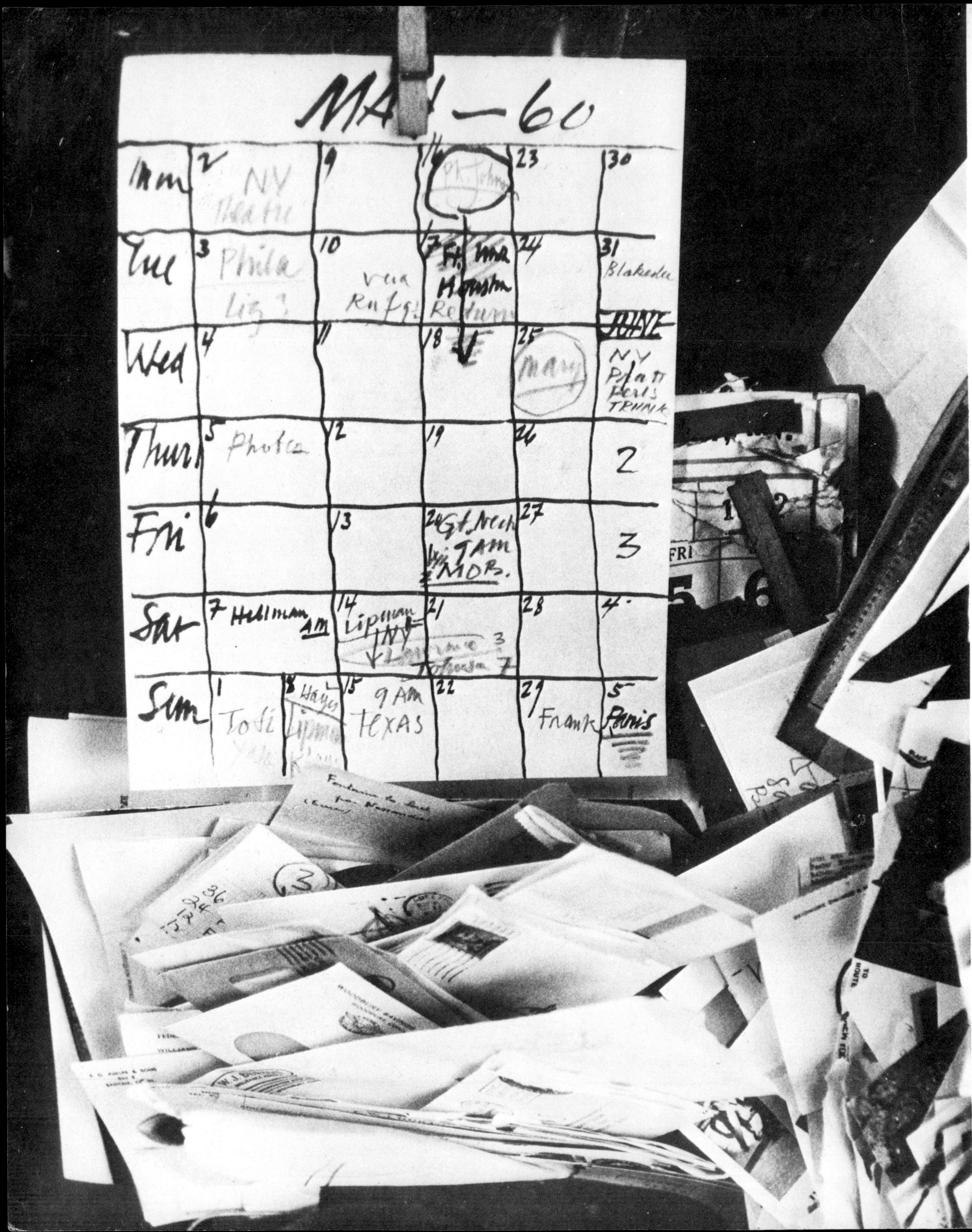
60
Mon
Tue
Wed
Thur
Fri
Sat
Sun
NY
Theatre
Phila
Photo
Hellman AM
Lipman
NY
9 AM
TEXAS
Frank
Paris
Blakeslee
JUNE
NY
TRUNK

Calder's Calendar

Calder's autobiography, especially the French edition, was the primary source for this chronology; information on the years since 1972 was compiled with the assistance of the artist, Jean Davidson, Daniel Lelong and Dolly and Klaus Perls.

1898

Alexander Calder is born in Lawnton, Pennsylvania (now a part of Philadelphia), on July 22, into a family of artists: his mother, Nanette Lederer Calder, was a painter, and both his grandfather Alexander Milne Calder, and his father, Alexander Stirling Calder, were well-known sculptors.

For years there was some confusion about the exact date of his birth: "I always thought I was born—at least my mother always told me so —on August 22, 1898. But my grandfather Milne's birthday was on August 23, so there might have been a little confusion. In 1942, when I wrote the Philadelphia City Hall for a birth certificate, I sent them a dollar and they told me I was born on the twenty-second of July, 1898. So I sent them another dollar and told them, 'Look again.' They corroborated the first statement."

1906–15

Calder and his older sister, Peggy, join their parents in Oracle, Arizona, where the elder Calder is recuperating from a heart ailment. The family then settles in Pasadena, California. In 1910 they return east to New York, living in Croton-on-Hudson and Spuyten Duyvil. In 1913 his father is appointed Acting Chief of Sculpture for the World's Fair to be held in San Francisco in 1915; the family moves to California, where they live in San Francisco and then Berkeley. In each new home young Sandy sets up a workshop and busies himself making jewelry for his sister's dolls, and toys and gadgets for his own use.

". . . on Euclid Avenue in Pasadena, I got my first tools and was given the cellar with its window as a workshop. Mother and father were all for my efforts to build things myself—they approved of the homemade."

1915–19

Graduating from Lowell High School in Berkeley, Calder decides to become an engineer and enters Stevens Institute of Technology in Hoboken, New Jersey. His marks for descriptive geometry are the highest ever given. He graduates in June 1919 with a degree in Mechanical Engineering (M.E.); senior thesis topic—"Stationary Steam Turbines." During the last months of World War I, he serves in the Students' Army Training Corps, Naval Section, at Stevens.

"I took every course as it came. I had some facility in mathematics— won a hundred once or twice in exams."

OPPOSITE: Calder's appointment calendar, Roxbury, 1960.

1919–21

A succession of jobs—automotive engineer, draftsman, trade-journal staff member, efficiency engineer, insurance company investigator, machinery salesman, mapmaker, letterer for machine designers—take Calder around the country, to New Jersey, New York, Connecticut, Missouri, Ohio and West Virginia.

"None of these experiences meant too much to me or discouraged me greatly, because I had never been too enthusiastic over the jobs in the first place."

1922

Returning to New York, he attends drawing classes taught by Clinton Balmer at a public night school on East 42nd Street. In June he joins the crew of the passenger ship *H. F. Alexander* on its New York–San Francisco run via the Panama Canal; he works in the boiler room. On the West Coast he visits his sister, now married to Kenneth Hayes, in Washington State. He works as a timekeeper, then as a draftsman, in logging camps; in between, he finds other odd jobs.

"I made one or two inventions during this trip [on the H. F. Alexander]. I rigged up a baffle where the breeze came down in the boiler room and directed it toward me. . . . The other invention was to spew a mouthful of drinking water up into the air—it would come down with a shower effect."

1923

In the fall he enters the Art Students League in New York and takes classes briefly with Kenneth Hayes Miller and Thomas Hart Benton; with Guy Pène du Bois and Boardman Robinson, for about one month each; with George Luks for two to three months; and with John Sloan every evening. He continues to study at the League until his departure for Paris in 1926. His grandfather Alexander Milne Calder dies.

". . . Father had known a certain Canadian engineer . . . we had quite a talk about what career I should follow. He advised me to do what I really wanted to do. . . . So, I decided to become a painter."

1924

Calder gets his first job as an artist, free-lancing for the *National Police Gazette* and working at a variety of commercial art assignments.

"I seemed to have a knack for doing it with a single line. And once, in one of my job-hunting moments, I tried the Police Gazette. *The editor, Robinson, was interested in this single-line drawing and gave me a modest job, doing half-pages of boxers training, which developed into covering other sports as well."*

1925

With his *Gazette* pass, Calder spends two weeks in the spring sketching Ringling Bros. and Barnum & Bailey Circus, the beginning of his fascination with this subject; he sells a circus drawing to the *Gazette* for its May 23 issue. He decorates A. G. Spalding, a sporting equipment store on Fifth Avenue, with drawings of athletes. During his Art Students League years, he lives alternately with his parents and in rented quarters. While in a small room at Fourteenth Street and Seventh Avenue, he creates his first wire sculpture, a rooster-sundial.

"I had no clock and faced south, so I made a sundial with a piece of

wire—a wire rooster on a vertical rod with radiating lines at the foot indicating the hours. I'd made things out of wire before—jewelry, toys —but this was my first effort to represent an animal in wire. I don't know what became of it. . . ."

1926

Animal Sketching, based on drawings made at the Bronx and Central Park zoos, is published in the spring. He makes his first woodcarving, Flattest Cat, from a fence rail found in the country. His first exhibition of oil paintings is held at The Artists' Gallery, East Sixty-first Street. In June he sails for Europe on a British freighter, Galileo, working as a day laborer; he debarks at Hull, England, and after a few days in London, continues on to Paris. He begins attending sketching classes at the Académie de la Grande Chaumière. That fall he earns round-trip passage, France–New York–France, on the Holland-American line, sketching life aboard ship for an advertising brochure. Returning to Paris, he takes a studio-room at 22 rue Daguerre. There he makes movable wood and wire animals and the first figures for his miniature Circus. He meets the English engraver Stanley William Hayter, who introduces him to the sculptor José de Creeft, his first acquaintance in the Paris art world. At the Salon des Indépendants he exhibits a bird made of bread and wire and a toy hippopotamus made of wood. He makes his first wire portrait, Josephine Baker.
"I finally took a room and studio at 22 rue Daguerre. I was walking along the street when I saw advertised at a hotel, 'room for hire.' It was a four-meter by five-meter room, one flight up in the rear, with a skylight. This place was heated by a little gas stove on top of which was balanced a receptacle of water. It would evaporate, condense on the skylight, and dribble down on my neck. There was also a radiator, heated by water, barely warm enough to dry a handkerchief, if you waited all day. I still considered myself a painter and was happy to be in my own workroom, in Paris."

1927

Calder begins giving performances of his miniature Circus for his friends and receives enthusiastic reviews from leading Paris circus critics. He exhibits animated toys at the Salon des Humoristes. In the fall he returns to New York, where he stays with his parents. He travels to Oshkosh, Wisconsin, to supervise production of the "action toys" which he had begun designing for the Gould Manufacturing Company.
". . . I met the man who introduced me eventually to the Gould Manufacturing Company of Oshkosh, Wisconsin. We all had lunch together. He was a banker; I said I made toys. Being from Oshkosh, he looked up the companies there. Later, in the fall of 1927, when I went back to America, I went to see Gould."

1928

In New York he takes a room on Charles Street at Seventh Avenue and gives Circus performances. His first exhibition of wire animals and caricature portraits is held at the Weyhe Gallery (February–March). His wire sculptures Romulus and Remus and Spring are included in the New York Society of Independent Artists exhibition at the Waldorf-Astoria Hotel (March). Summer is spent on a farm near Peekskill, New York, where he experiments with wood sculpture. He

earns his first big fee making wire sculptures for an advertising agency. Returning to Paris in the fall, he takes a studio at 7 rue Cels. There he resumes his Circus performances, which increasingly become a celebrated attraction in Parisian intellectual and artistic circles. He meets Pascin and visits Miró's studio; the latter becomes a lifelong friend. His wire sculptures are exhibited in a group show at the Salon de l'Araignée.
"I did wire athletes tugging at the lenses for the firm of Batten, Barton, Durstine, & Osborn, and I got my first check for a thousand dollars. I was about thirty and Hoover already had a million dollars by that time. Mine came much slower."

1929

Calder has his first one-man show in Paris at the Galerie Billiet (January–February), exhibiting wood and wire sculpture. Pascin writes a short catalogue introduction for the show. The Weyhe Gallery, New York, exhibits his wood sculpture (February). In the spring Calder exhibits Romulus and Remus and Spring, which he had brought from New York, at the Paris Salon des Indépendants. He travels to Berlin, where an exhibition of wire sculpture and jewelry is held at the Galerie Neumann und Nierendorf (April); he gives Circus performances at the gallery. In Berlin a film on Calder is made as part of the series Artists at Work. In May a Pathé movie "short" is filmed in Calder's Paris studio. In June he sails for New York aboard the De Grasse; on the voyage he meets Louisa Cushing James, a grandniece of William and Henry James. His Circus has more than doubled in size; he gives performances in New York; one, at Aline Bernstein's apartment, is described—and ridiculed—in Thomas Wolfe's novel You Can't Go Home Again. Edward Warburg invites Calder to exhibit two wire sculptures in a group show at the Harvard Society for Contemporary Art, Cambridge, Massachusetts (October–November). Calder shows paintings, wood sculpture, wire sculpture, toys and jewelry at the Fifty-sixth Street Galleries (December). A collection of eighteenth-century mechanical birds in cages is also on view, and these inspire Calder to make his first moving sculpture: wire goldfish bowls in which fish, operated by a crank, swim about.
"So once on board the De Grasse, I started walking the deck. I overtook an elderly man and a young lady. I could only see them from the back, so I reversed my steps the better to see them face on. . . . He was Edward Holton James, my future father-in-law. She was Louisa."

1930

Calder visits Cambridge, Massachusetts, where he exhibits wire sculpture at the Harvard Society for Contemporary Art (January–February) and gives Circus performances for Harvard students. In March he sails for Europe as a passenger on a Spanish freighter. After debarking at Barcelona, he returns to Paris, where he takes a studio at 7 Villa Brune. In the spring he visits southern France and sails to Corsica with a friend in a small sailboat. In Paris his frequent Circus performances bring him into contact with such artists as Léger, Kiesler and Van Doesburg. Louisa James visits Paris during the summer; their courtship continues. In the fall, after a visit to Piet Mondrian's studio, Calder experiments with abstract painting and drawing, then sculpture. He makes Une Boule Noire, une Boule Blanche, a large construction that incorporates the elements of both motion and sound. He is invited to join the Abstraction-Création group, which includes Van Doesburg, Arp, Mondrian, Delaunay, Pevsner, Hélion and others. Calder exhibits at the Salon de l'Áraignée and the Salon des Surindépendants in Paris. Four of his wood sculptures are included in *Painting and Sculpture by Living Americans* at the Museum of Modern Art, New York (December–January 1931). He experiments briefly with stone sculpture and has a number of plaster figures cast in bronze by Valsuani, a foundry located near the Villa Brune studio. In December he returns to the United States to marry Louisa.

"My entrance into the field of abstract art came about as the result of a visit to the studio of Piet Mondrian in Paris in 1930. I was particularly impressed by some rectangles of color he had tacked on his wall in a pattern after his nature. I told him I would like to make them oscillate—he objected. I went home and tried to paint abstractly—but in two weeks I was back again among plastic materials."

1931

On January 17, Calder and Louisa James are married in Concord, Massachusetts. The eve of the wedding Calder gives a Circus performance at the James home. The Calders return to Paris and live in his old studio. His first exhibition of abstract constructions, along with wire portraits and drawings, is held at the Galerie Percier (April–May); the catalogue, titled *Alexander Calder/Volumes-Vecteurs-Densités/Dessins-Portraits*, has a preface by Léger. Calder participates in an Abstraction-Création exhibition at the Porte de Versailles and gives a Circus performance in the exhibition tent. At this time he makes the final figures for the Circus, begins a series of large pen-and-ink circus drawings (completed the following year) and does illustrations for *Fables of Aesop*. The Calders rent a house at 14 rue de la Colonie; they spend the summer in Mallorca and Brittany. In the winter he begins making abstract sculpture with moving parts, operated by electric motors or hand cranks.

"Due to the efforts of some friends in Abstraction-Création, I arranged for a show in the Galerie Percier and Léger wrote the preface. I still had some planks from Villa Brune; we put these on champagne boxes and painted everything white. The objects all ranged around the gallery, one or two were located in the middle, and on the walls overhead were wire portraits. In the window, we had two drawings of the circus."

1932

In February Calder exhibits his motorized and hand-cranked moving sculptures in Paris at the Galerie Vignon; he calls them "mobiles," a term suggested by Marcel Duchamp. At this time Arp proposes the name "stabiles" for the stationary constructions Calder exhibited the previous year. He also exhibits at the Association Artistique "1940" in Paris. His sculpture is included in the permanent collection of a newly founded Museum of New Art in Lodz, Poland. In May the Calders return to the United States, where he exhibits his new moving sculptures at the Julien Levy Gallery, New York (May–June). During the summer he does a series of small circus drawings. In September he and Louisa return to Europe on a Spanish passenger ship. They debark at Barcelona and visit the Mirós on their farm in nearby Montroig, where Calder gives a Circus performance for local farmers and workmen. The Calders then return to their house in Paris,

where he makes the standing mobile *Calderberry Bush*.
At his Julien Levy exhibition Calder told a reporter: "Why must art be static? . . . The next step in sculpture is motion."

1933

Through Miró, Calder is invited to Spain in January: he has an exhibition and gives Circus performances at the University of Madrid and exhibits drawings and sculpture at the Amics de l'Art Nou in Barcelona. In the spring he participates in a group exhibition at the Galerie Pierre, Paris, with Arp, Miró, Pevsner, Hélion and Seligmann. At this time he meets James Johnson Sweeney, the American critic who is to become the leading exponent of his work. He has a one-man exhibition at the Galerie Pierre Colle (May). The Calders return to the United States in June. He is given an exhibition at the Berkshire Museum in Pittsfield, Massachusetts (August). After much searching, they buy an eighteenth-century farmhouse on Painter Hill Road in Roxbury, Connecticut.

". . . we owned our very first house, my first house and I was thirty-five."

1934

In the spring Calder participates in an exhibition sponsored by the City of New York where Alfred H. Barr, Jr., sees and purchases a motorized mobile, *A Universe*, for the Museum of Modern Art, New York. Calder makes a number of Frames (motorized elements set in open frames) and his first outdoor mobile, *Steel Fish*, which he sets up at Roxbury; for the next three years he continues to experiment with large-scale sculpture. In April he has a one-man show at the Pierre Matisse Gallery in New York, where he continues to exhibit until 1943; James Johnson Sweeney writes the catalogue preface. Calder is the only American included in *A Selection of Works by Twentieth-century Artists* at the Renaissance Society of the University of Chicago (June–August). The Calders take up permanent residence in the United States, living in Roxbury summers and spending winters in an apartment at Eighty-sixth Street and Second Avenue in New York. Calder rents small shops nearby—a different one each winter—and converts them into studios.

"These rented shops really worked very well. I would whitewash the lower half of the windows, not to be bothered by onlookers, and if the locale was on the west side of the street, as was often the case, the morning light was fine. I did a lot of work in such places."

1935

Calder's works are exhibited in Chicago, first at the Renaissance Society, University of Chicago (January) and then at the Arts Club (February). At this time he visits Chicago and gives several Circus performances. Returning east by way of Rochester, New York, he is commissioned to make a garden mobile for a private home. The Kunstmuseum of Lucerne, Switzerland, includes his work in the exhibition *Thèse, antithèse, synthèse* (February–March). On April 20 the Calders' first child, Sandra, is born. During the summer he designs mobiles for Martha Graham's ballet *Panorama*, performed at the Bennington School of Dance, Vermont, in August. His first etching, done for a portfolio, *23 Gravures*, edited by Anatole Jakovski, is published in Paris.

"Mrs. [Charlotte] Allen wanted a mobile for her garden. . . . As I

remember, it consisted of some quite heavy iron discs that I found in a blacksmith's shop in Rochester and had them welded to rods progressively getting heavier and heavier."

1936

Calder designs "plastic interludes"—circles and spirals that "perform" on an empty stage, setting the mood for each movement—for Martha Graham's *Horizons*, presented in New York (February–March). He follows this with a mobile set for Erik Satie's symphonic drama *Socrate*, performed at the First Hartford Music Festival, held at the Wadsworth Atheneum, Hartford, Connecticut. His works are exhibited at Vassar College, Poughkeepsie, New York, and at the Pierre Matisse Gallery, New York (February); he is also included in two group shows at the Museum of Modern Art, New York: *Modern Painters and Sculptors as Illustrators* (April–September) and *Fantastic Art, Dada, Surrealism* (December–January 1937).
"I had bought a toy accordion for Louisa, with about eight notes, and she managed to play this. So, I bought one with ivory and 'diamonds' in a hock shop. And she played this even better. Then Paul's birthday arrived and Francine Nelson went all out and got Paul a very fancy accordion. Louisa could play this one even better. So, I got her a better one still. This was a winter of accordion music."

1937

Calder makes his first large-scale stabile, *Whale*. Paul Nelson commissions Calder to design a trophy, executed in stainless steel and wire, for a CBS award. In May the Calders, including Sandra, visit Paris, where they take up temporary quarters in an empty house designed by Nelson. Calder gives Circus performances for his old friends. Through Nelson he meets other architects, Alvar Aalto and, most important, Josep Lluis Sert and Louis Lacasa, designers of the Spanish Pavilion for the Paris World's Fair. They ask Calder to design a fountain displaying mercury from the mines of Almadén—a technical as well as esthetic problem which Calder solves brilliantly. The *Mercury Fountain* is one of the most popular attractions at the Fair. For the summer, the Calders rent a house in Varengeville, Normandy, where Nelson, Sert, Miró, Braque, the critic Herbert Read, the dealer Pierre Loeb and other members of the Paris art community gather. The Calders go to London for the winter and take a flat in Belsize Park. He sets up a studio and gives Circus performances. In December he has an exhibition at the Freddy Mayor Gallery. Other exhibitions: Pierre Matisse Gallery, New York (February–March); *Fantastic Art—Miró and Calder*, Honolulu Academy of Arts (June).
"Léger was at the opening of the Spanish Pavilion and said to me: 'Dans le temps tu étais le Roi du Fil de Fer, mais maintenant tu es le Père Mercure.' ('In the old days you were Wire King, now you are Father Mercury.')"

1938

In February another Calder exhibition is held at the Freddy Mayor Gallery, London. The Calders return to the United States in the spring. He builds a large studio adjoining the farmhouse in Roxbury, and they resume their practice of dividing the year between Connecticut and New York. He is given his first large retrospective exhibition at the George Walter Vincent Smith Art Gallery, Springfield, Massachusetts (November). Included are 67 mobiles, stabiles, wood and wire sculptures, plus 17 drawings and watercolors; James Johnson

Sweeney writes the foreword to the catalogue. For the World's Fair to be held in New York the following year, Calder designs monumental motorized mobiles, but finds no sponsors (years later one of the models served as the basis for *Four Elements*; see 1962). A mobile is included in *Trois siècles d'art aux Etats-Unis* at the Musée du Jeu de Paume, Paris (October); and his drawings are exhibited at the Katharine Kuh Gallery, Chicago.
"Malcolm [Cowley] and I decided we were practically the same age. . . . So, we planned to celebrate together at our house. We went to an Italian bakery in Danbury where they made good bread, and had them make a special cake. It was built like a zoned building, stepped up twice. It was white, with lavender mocha. In mocha it said: FORTY, FIT, FAT, and FARTY . . . This party has always been referred back to as THE birthday party."

1939

The Calders' second daughter, Mary, is born on May 25. The New York Edison Company commissions a water ballet for the fountain of their World's Fair pavilion: Calder "choreographs" a programmed five-minute water display, but the water jets are incorrectly installed and the fountain never functions as intended (see 1954). The Museum of Modern Art, New York, commissions a large mobile, *Lobster Trap and Fish Tail*, for the stairwell of its new building on Fifty-third Street. Calder wins first prize (out of 250 entries) in a Plexiglas sculpture competition sponsored by Röhm & Haas and held at the Museum of Modern Art; the winning design, Calder's first and only effort in this medium, is exhibited at the World's Fair Hall of Industrial Science. His annual exhibition at the Pierre Matisse Gallery is held in May; his work is included in the 1939–40 San Francisco Golden Gate International Exposition.
". . . I proposed [a water ballet like the one done for the Edison Company] to Eero Saarinen for the General Motors Technical Center, near Detroit. This turned out to be the most expensive fountain in captivity, but it really works, I believe, and I have received two or three compliments on it. They still have my rig, but they only show it for important people—so I doubt whether I shall ever see it!"

1940

Calder continues to experiment with large-scale sheet metal sculpture. He exhibits at the Pierre Matisse Gallery, New York (May–June), and has his first exhibition of jewelry at the Marian Willard Gallery, New York (December).
"And now, it was 1940. I had continued to have shows at Pierre Matisse's since 1934, with one or two years out. I'd done such things as The Whale (Museum of Modern Art, New York), The Black Beast, of which I made a copy for Eliot Noyes in New Canaan . . . and The Spherical Triangle, now in Rio. These were fairly large outdoor objects: The Black Beast is eleven feet long and almost nine feet high. They were the forerunners of the big stabiles to come."

1941

Wallace K. Harrison commissions a mobile for the ballroom of the Hotel Avila in Caracas, Venezuela (now in the collection of the Aluminum Company of America, Pittsburgh). Calder gives a private showing of his work at Harrison's home in Huntington, Long Island. Public exhibitions are held at the New Orleans Arts and Crafts Club

(March–April); the Pierre Matisse Gallery (May–June); Design Project, Los Angeles (September–October); and jewelry at the Marian Willard Gallery (December).

"They hung my mobile over the bar in the Hotel Avila, but patrons got drunk looking up at it. Harrison was doing a wing for the Pittsburgh Alcoa building, so he took it back there."

1942

Calder is classified 1-A (top eligibility) by the Army. He is never drafted, but contributes to the war effort by studying civilian camouflage and doing occupational therapy in veterans' hospitals. He and Louisa find old and new friends among the émigré artists who settle in the United States, among them Yves Tanguy and the André Massons. He executes a large standing mobile, *Red Petals*, for the Arts Club of Chicago. His work is included in *Artists for Victory*, an exhibition of contemporary art at the Metropolitan Museum of Art, New York, and he wins fourth prize. He is one of the few Americans represented in the only group exhibition of Surrealist artists held in the United States, *First Papers of Surrealism*, at the former Reid mansion on Madison Avenue, New York (October–November). Other exhibitions: Cincinnati Modern Art Society (April–May); Pierre Matisse Gallery (May–June); Design Project, Los Angeles (September–October); Marian Willard Gallery (December); and the San Francisco Museum of Art.

"Red Petals . . . was made during the war for a little octagonal room lined with rosewood [at the Arts Club of Chicago]. As I become professionally enraged when I see dinky surroundings, I did my best to make this object big and bold—to dwarf these surroundings."

1943

In the spring the Museum of Modern Art schedules a major Calder exhibition to open on September 29. Calder spends much of the year in preparation for the most important exhibition of his work yet to be held. The show is directed by James Johnson Sweeney, who also writes the catalogue; the photographer Herbert Matter assists with the installation. During the exhibition Calder gives Circus performances in the Museum Penthouse, and a film on his work, written and narrated by Agnes Rindge Claflin, is made. The exhibition is such a popular success that it is extended until January 1944. Finding metal increasingly scarce, Calder devises a new form—pieces of carved and sometimes painted wood connected by steel wires—given the name Constellations by Sweeney and Duchamp. In December a jewelry exhibition is held at the Arts Club of Chicago. While Calder is there, most of the Roxbury house is destroyed by fire. Other exhibitions: Pierre Matisse Gallery (May–June); Addison Gallery of American Art, Andover, Massachusetts (June–July).

"[Sweeney] is one of the very rare critics whom I can believe—probably the only one—and his book encouraged me, and many others, to believe I had something!"

1944

The house and studio at Roxbury are rebuilt. Calder experiments with carved and modeled works, executed in plaster and then in bronze; soon this medium is abandoned as too expensive and esthetically somewhat unsatisfactory. Curt Valentin of the Buchholz Gallery (later the Curt Valentin Gallery) becomes Calder's New York dealer. He supports a book project, *Three Young Rats and Other Rhymes*, collected by Sweeney and illustrated by Calder. To coincide with its publication, Valentin holds an exhibition of the original drawings and Calder's new bronzes (November–December). *Three Young Rats* is selected as one of the "Fifty Books of the Year."

"I worked hard at the drawings and repeated many of them several times. Finally we chose the title from one of the rhymes for which I had done the most complicated and successful drawing: Three Young Rats. *. . . Curt exhibited the original drawings when he presented the book to the public in the fall of 1944. As most of the figures are naked, there was one in particular climbing up a chimney that Peggy Guggenheim, in her own manner, discovered as being very obscene."*

1945

Calder begins making mobiles that can be disassembled and mailed in small packets. He draws illustrations for Coleridge's *The Rime of the Ancient Mariner*, published with an essay by Robert Penn Warren the following year. He exhibits his gouaches for the first time at the Samuel M. Kootz Gallery, New York (September), and sculptures at the Buchholz Gallery, New York (November). His father, Alexander Stirling Calder, dies in New York.

"Some architect appealed to me to make one or two very small mobiles to go with the model of a proposed building. . . . These two little objects are the forebears of a line of very small mobiles I occasionally make. I got rather excited making them as small as my so-called clumsy fingers could do them. Then in the fall of 1945, Marcel Duchamp said, 'Yes, let's mail these little objects to Carré, in Paris, and have a show.' So a whole race of objects that were collapsible and could be taken to pieces was born."

1946

Calder produces many gouaches and makes etchings for Eunice Clark's translation of a selection of La Fontaine's *Fables*, published in 1948. Mobiles are used in *Balloons*, a play by Padraic Colum, performed in Boston. A large mobile is commissioned for the Terrace Plaza Hotel (now the Terrace Hilton) in Cincinnati, designed by Gordon Bunshaft of Skidmore, Owings & Merrill. An exhibition of mobiles is held at the Galerie Louis Carré in Paris (October–November); the catalogue, printed by Mourlot, has photographs by Herbert Matter and a preface by Jean-Paul Sartre, who saw an affinity between Calder's sculpture and his own existentialist philosophy. For this exhibition, Calder flies to Paris in June and again in the fall, his first visits to Europe since World War II.

"The show at Carré's opened on October 25, 1946; there were a lot of visitors and even Henri Matisse. The gallery was in the huitième *arrondissement—there are a lot of electric-power users in this section, and from five to six in the afternoon they would turn off the electricity to save coal, as a postwar economy measure. So, we put a candle on the floor under an object with a multitude of small leaves and made it rotate. It was very fine with the shadow going around . . . on the ceiling."*

1947

An exhibition at the Kunsthalle in Berne, Switzerland, includes Calder, Léger and other painters and sculptors (May); it travels to the Stedelijk Museum, Amsterdam (July–August); each museum purchases one of Calder's mobiles. Other exhibitions: The Portland (Oregon) Museum of Art (January); the Buchholz Gallery, New

York (December). He is included in the last major group show of the Surrealist movement, *Le Surréalisme en 1947*, held at the Galerie Maeght, Paris, and does an etching for a book of the same title, published to accompany the exhibition.
When asked what was his connection with the Surrealists, Calder replied, "Very little."

1948

Hans Richter includes two Calder sequences in his Surrealist film *Dreams That Money Can Buy*. Burgess Meredith approaches Calder about a film on his sculpture; Calder suggests that Herbert Matter do the photography for *Works of Calder*, released in 1951. The Calders are invited to Brazil by the architect Henrique Mindlin; they fly to Rio de Janeiro via Mexico, Panama and Trinidad, after leaving their daughters with Calder's sister in California. In Rio an exhibition of his work is held at the Ministerio de Educaçao (September) and then at the Museū de Arte in São Paulo (October–November). Other exhibits of his work are held at the California Palace of the Legion of Honor, San Francisco (October–November) and the Institute of Contemporary Arts, Washington, D.C. He designs a silkscreen-on-canvas "mural scroll"—exhibited the following year—for the wallpaper firm Katzenbach & Warren, New York.
In a statement for the Mural Scrolls *catalogue Calder declared: "I am still very enthusiastic about smearing up somebody's wall."*

1949

International Mobile (twenty feet wide), Calder's largest mobile to date, is designed for the Philadelphia Museum of Art but not accepted for purchase; the mobile eventually goes to the Museum of Fine Arts in Houston. Calder makes two designs, *Splotchy* and *Calder #1*, for wallpaper and coordinated fabrics manufactured by Laverne Originals, New York. He spends much time painting gouaches. His mobiles are used in the ballet *Symphonic Variations*, produced in Rio de Janeiro. He has exhibitions at the Margaret Brown Gallery, Boston (October), and the Buchholz Gallery, New York (November–December), and is featured in *Calder and Sculpture Today* at the Virginia Museum of Fine Arts, Richmond (October).
When installing a mobile in Erwin Laverne's design studio, Calder said, "I'd like to try my hand at doing some wallpapers too."

1950

Calder makes mobiles and other effects for the play *Happy as Larry* by Donagh MacDonagh, produced by Burgess Meredith in New York. With their daughters, the Calders spend the summer in Europe. They visit Paris, the caves of Lascaux, and Brittany. An exhibit of fifty mobiles and stabiles is held at the Galerie Maeght in Paris (June–July), the beginning of a continuing association with this gallery. He designs the cover for *Derrière Le Miroir* (No. 31, July), published by Maeght; it also serves as the poster for his exhibition. The Calders spend August in Finland and Sweden before returning to the United States. The Musée National d'Art Moderne in Paris and the National-museum of Stockholm purchase mobiles. In November *The New York Times* names Calder one of the ten best children's books illustrators of the past fifty years. He has exhibits at Amsterdam's Stedelijk Museum (October), Stockholm's Galerie Blanche (December), the Institute of Contemporary Arts, Washington, D.C., and a major exhibition at the Massachusetts Institute of Technology, Cambridge,

installed by James Johnson Sweeney (December–January 1951); a minor auto accident prevents Calder from actively participating in the M.I.T. exhibition.
"By the spring of 1950, Louisa and I felt the whole family should take a trip to France. Sandra was fifteen then, and Mary eleven."

1951

Calder makes his first Towers, a variety of wall mobile. He exhibits at the Lefevre Galleries, London (January); in Vienna at the Neue Galerie, the Vienna Art Club and the U.S. Information Center; with Miró at the Contemporary Arts Museum, Houston (October–November). He is included in the Seventy-fifth Anniversary Exhibition by seventy-five artists associated with the Art Students League, held at the Metropolitan Museum of Art, New York (February–April). With Willem de Kooning, Stuart Davis, Fritz Glarner and George L. K. Morris, he participates in the symposium "What Abstract Art Means to Me" at the Museum of Modern Art, New York.
On this occasion he said, "That others grasp what I have in mind seems unessential, at least as long as they have something else in theirs."

1952

The year begins with an exhibition of Gongs (sound mobiles) and Towers at the Curt Valentin Gallery, New York (January–February), and at the Margaret Brown Gallery, Boston (March). In the spring Calder travels to Paris to design sets for Henri Pichette's play *Nucléa*, produced by the Théâtre National Populaire. Louisa joins him for the opening, and they visit the André Massons in Aix-en-Provence. They decide to rent a house there for the following year. He is selected for exhibition at the Venice Biennale (installation and catalogue by James Johnson Sweeney) and receives first prize for sculpture. The West German government invites him to tour the country in September, after which the Calders return to the United States. Exhibitions are held at the Galerie Maeght, Paris (November), and the Galerie der Spiegel, Cologne (November–December). He designs an acoustic ceiling for Aula Magna, the auditorium in University City, Caracas, at the request of the architect Carlos Raúl Villanueva; this necessitates close collaboration with the engineering firm Bolt, Bereneck and Newman of Cambridge, Massachusetts.
"[For Nucléa, *Gérard Philippe] wanted an extra stage, two meters above the other, on pipe columns, but I cut it into ribbons and had a semicircular band in the rear of the stage with a ramp sloping down to the footlights and ending with a few steps. At one moment two large panels, 'the clouds,' descended from above, rotating on themselves, displaying white and black sides. I will always remember the lines: 'Nuit et jour.' ('Night and day.') And: 'Jour et nuit.' ('Day and night.')"*

1953

The Calders sail to France on the *Flandre* for a year in Aix-en-Provence. Their first house, "Mas des Roches," has no electricity or water; after some time they move to a better-equipped house, "Malvalat." During this time Calder devotes himself almost entirely to gouaches. He visits an old acquaintance, Jean Davidson, at his home in Saché, on the Indre River near Tours, and in the fall buys "François Premier," an ancient house there, from Davidson. He exhibits thirteen gouaches at the gallery of Christian Zervos in Aix-en-Provence; at the Walker Art Center, Minneapolis (April–May); the Frank

Perls Gallery, Beverly Hills, California (May–June); and with Naum Gabo at the Wadsworth Atheneum, Hartford, Connecticut (October–November). He is awarded a prize at the São Paulo Bienal.

". . . we discovered he [Jean Davidson] in fact owned a house called 'François Premier' with a fantastic cellarlike room with a dirt floor and wine press set in a cavity in the hillside rock. At the time one could barely see anything in there, all doors and windows being plugged with loose stones—a typical French custom when a house is abandoned. I thought to myself: I will make mobiles of cobwebs and propel them with bats."

1954

In January, Calder takes his family to Beirut, where he has been commissioned to make a mobile for the Middle East Airlines office. They tour Lebanon, Syria and Jordan. In the spring they move into the Saché house, remodeled with the help of Davidson; Calder sets up a studio and a *gouacherie* in separate outbuildings. He exhibits gouaches at the offices of Cahiers d'Art in Paris (May); standing mobiles are shown at the Galerie Maeght (October); and Calder presents several performances of the Circus. One of his mobiles is featured at the Milan Triennale in the summer. *Ballet of Seven Sisters*, a programmed fountain based on Calder's ill-fated New York Edison design (see 1939) is installed at Eero Saarinen's General Motors Technical Center in Warren, Michigan. In the late fall the Calders return to the United States. Following Curt Valentin's death, Calder begins his association with the Perls Galleries, New York. At Klaus Perls' suggestion he devises his   **CA**   "signature," for use on metal sculpture. (Note: signed works do not necessarily date from 1954 on; Calder has added his signature to a number of earlier, previously unsigned works.) At the end of the year the Calders depart for India at the invitation of Gira Sarabhai, an architect and designer, daughter of a wealthy industrialist.

". . . I'd brought my pliers with me [to India], and I'd got some metal and wire in Bombay, so I went to work in the [Sarabhais'] garden. Cows were tethered there, and a couple of water buffaloes. . . . I made eleven mobiles and stabiles, and some gold jewelry. We went down to Bombay once or twice . . . and I made a big mobile in a blacksmith shop there. Gira's father, Ambalal, was a little doubtful about my work at first, but he ended up liking it."

1955

The Calders tour India in return for the mobiles which Calder makes on the Sarabhai estate, near Ahmedabad. These are exhibited at a private home in Bombay just before the Calders' departure in March. As promised before Valentin's death, Calder holds an exhibition at the Curt Valentin Gallery, New York; nothing is sold. Recent works are exhibited at the Reid and Lefevre Gallery, London (spring). In *Le Mouvement*, the first exhibition of kinetic art, organized by the Galerie Denise René, Paris (April), Calder is featured as one of the pioneers of motion in art. *A Bestiary*, edited by Richard Wilbur, with illustrations by Calder, is published. He visits Caracas at the invitation of Carlos Raúl Villanueva, who arranges an exhibition at the Museo de Bellas Artes (September–October). He and Louisa return to France; on October 28, Sandra Calder and Jean Davidson are married in Saché, which they make their permanent home. Calder goes to Frankfort to execute a large stabile, *Hextoped*, for the U.S. Consulate. The City of Philadelphia gives him its "Outstanding Citizen" award.

"I knew the head of Amerika Haus in Frankfort, and he introduced me to a bridge builder, Fries. They built the object [Hextoped] for me in two days; it was all ready to be welded, but the Consulate didn't seem to be ready to receive it. So I called Ambassador Conant in Bonn and told him I wanted to put it up and then things began to move. We had to get a Marine sergeant to unlock a door so we could get out the 368—or 386—volts for the welding machine. Then we welded it together in the courtyard of the Consulate."

1956

This is another year of active gouache production. The Calders make a brief trip to the United States, where the Perls Galleries, New York, holds its first Calder exhibition (February–March): they return to Europe in the spring. On October 4, the Calders' first grandchild, Shawn Davidson, is born in Tours, France. Exhibitions: Galleria dell'Obelisco, Rome (March); Galleria del Naviglio, Milan (April); Musée Grimaldi, Antibes (summer); and gouaches at the Galerie Lucie Weil, Paris (autumn).

Calder to Klaus Perls before his first exhibition at the Perls Galleries: "What! You think you can get a thousand dollars for a mobile?"

1957

In the summer the Calders buy "Le Palud," a house in Brittany at the mouth of the Tréguier River. They make a brief trip to Spain. The Kunsthalle in Basel organizes a major exhibition of his work (May–June), and he is the subject, along with Rodin, Brancusi and Gauguin, of an exhibition at the World House Galleries, New York, titled *4 Masters* (March–April).

In his statement for the World House catalogue Calder said: "A long time ago I decided, indeed, I was told that primitive art is better than decadent art. So I decided to remain as primitive as possible, and thus I have avoided mechanization of tools, etc. (in spite of having been trained as an engineer)."

1958

Calder builds a large new studio at Roxbury. He completes three major public commissions: *Whirling Ear* for the Brussels World's Fair; *Spirale* for the UNESCO building in Paris; *.125* for Idlewild International Airport (now Kennedy) in New York. He wins first prize at the Carnegie International Exhibition for *Pittsburgh*, a monumental mobile subsequently purchased and installed at the Greater Pittsburgh Airport. He is included in *Nature in Abstraction* at the Whitney Museum of American Art, New York (January–March). Other exhibitions: large stabiles at the Perls Galleries, New York (February–March); Galerie Blanche, Stockholm.

"When I embarked on stabiles and heavier objects, following Noyes's purchase of The Black Beast, I often worked in several metal shops at the same time. In 1958, I had three metal shops working for me, two in Waterbury and one, ten miles away, in Watertown. I got a sense of being a big businessman as I drove from one to another."

1959

Large stabiles are exhibited at the Galerie Maeght (March–April); Aimé Maeght, the owner, purchases the entire show. In connection with a Calder exhibition at the new Museu de Arte Moderna in Rio de Janeiro (September–October), the Calders go to Brazil; while there, they visit the new capital, Brasilia. He is included in *18 Living*

is organized by the Maison de la Culture in Bourges, France (March–May) and subsequently travels to the Musée des Augustins, Toulouse (September). On the day of the Bourges opening, Calder is made a Commander of the Legion of Honor. He donates a 1953 mobile, *L'Empennage*, to the Fondation Maeght, Saint-Paul-de-Vence, France, which holds a retrospective of his work (April). For his seventieth birthday he has three celebrations: at Saché, Saint-Paul-de-Vence and Ardèche. A large stabile, *Les Trois Pics*, is placed in front of the new railroad station of Grenoble, France, in time for the Winter Olympics. An exhibition featuring a series of standing mobiles titled *Flèches* is held at the Galerie Maeght (October); drawings and gouaches are shown at the Perls Galleries, New York (October–November). Calder's gouaches, mobiles, stabiles and Totems are exhibited and Vilardebo's films about him are shown at the "Art and Culture" festival, Noisy-le-Sec, France (October). Other exhibitions: Dayton's Gallery 12, Minneapolis (April–May), and the Donald Morris Gallery, Detroit (December–January 1969). *Red, Black and Blue*, a motorized mobile commissioned by American Airlines, is installed with Calder's supervision at Love Field, Dallas (it has since been moved to the new Dallas–Fort Worth Airport). Calder authorizes the casting, in limited bronze editions, of a group of his 1944 plasters; the work is done at the Roman Bronze Works, Corona, New York. In December the Calders tour Mexico, where they see *El Sol Rojo* in place at the Aztec Stadium in Mexico City.

"I continued to work in Rome [on Work in Progress*]. . . . Giovanni Carandente was always at my side—at my heels—to draw what he could from me and the others. I made a lot of gouaches for the backdrops. There were people after all—I made some costumes for the bicyclists. About fifteen of these cyclists made gyrating movements on the stage—it was rather difficult to improvise a variety of movements because of the risk of collision. The music [consisted of] little insect cries, amplified."*

1969

Construction is begun on a house adjacent to the new hilltop studio in Saché. The Calders visit the United States in the spring for the installation of two major stabiles: *Gwenfritz* at the Smithsonian Institution in Washington, D.C., and *La Grande Vitesse* in Grand Rapids, Michigan. Exhibitions are held at the Grand Rapids Museum (April) and at Grand Valley State College in Allendale, Michigan (May–June); in June the college awards him an honorary doctorate. While in Michigan, Calder sees for the first time his water ballet at the General Motors Technical Center. On the fiftieth anniversary of his graduation from Stevens Institute of Technology, his Alma Mater awards him the degree of Doctor of Engineering, Honoris Causa. A 1964 stabile, *Three Discs, One Lacking*, is installed in Philadelphia's new Penn Center Plaza. The city of Amboise, France, commissions a stabile which Calder names for the city. He designs stage sets for the ballet *Métaboles*, a production of the Théâtre Français de la Danse at the Odéon, Paris. The Fondation Maeght, Saint-Paul-de-Vence, France, organizes a major retrospective (April–May) for which Calder makes *Morning Cobweb*, a monumental walk-through version of a 1945 stabile, which serves as an entrance to the exhibition. The Maeght exhibition travels to the Louisiana Museum, Humlebaek, Denmark (June–September) and to the Stedelijk Museum, Amsterdam (October–November). *Calder en Venezuela*, an exhibition of some fifty works made during his 1955 visit, is held at the Fundación Eugenio Mendoza, Caracas (July–August). His work is included in a sculpture exhibition in connection with the Fête de l'Humanité, Vincennes, France, in September; he designs a poster for the event. Gouaches are exhibited at the Donald Morris Gallery, Detroit (January–February); standing mobiles at Gimpel Fils, London (February–March). His 1944 sculptures, cast in bronze the previous year, are shown at the Perls Galleries, New York (October–November). The Museum of Modern Art, New York, presents *A Salute to Alexander Calder* (December–February 1970).

As one museum after another organized major exhibitions of his work, Calder observed: ". . . we'll never get out of these retrospectives."

1970

The Calders move into their new house in Saché, but he continues to work in the small studio and in the *gouacherie* next to his old house, "François Premier," using the new studio principally for storage of large works. He executes a mobile as a one-hundredth anniversary gift for Stevens Institute. He designs a terrazzo sidewalk for the Perls Galleries, between Seventy-eighth and Seventy-ninth Streets on Madison Avenue in New York. The Circus, on extended loan, is installed by Calder at the Whitney Museum of American Art, New York. *Peau Rouge, Indiana*, commissioned by the University of Indiana in Bloomington, is installed in front of the new music building. An exhibition of gouaches organized by the Long Beach (California) Museum of Art is shown there (January–February), at the Fine Arts Gallery, San Diego, and in Arizona at the Phoenix Museum of Art. In France an exhibition with Jean Bazaine is held at the Château de Ratilly, Treigny (June–September), and his work is included in *Sculpture in the City*, Reims (June–October). Other exhibitions: Kovler Gallery, Chicago (January–March); recent gouaches and early mobiles at the Perls Galleries, New York (October–November); and a retrospective of works (1961–70) at the Galerie Blanche, Stockholm.

To workmen installing the sidewalk he designed, Calder said: "Don't worry about perfect symmetry—it will look better if it has a few irregularities."

1971

A monumental stabile, *The Halebardeer*, is installed in front of the Opera House in Hanover, Germany. Stabiles and Animobiles, Calder's latest variation on the standing mobile, are exhibited at the Galerie Maeght, Paris (February), and with recent gouaches at the Perls Galleries, New York (October–November). Calder attends the opening of an exhibition of his work at the Musée Toulouse-Lautrec in Albi, France (June–September); the exhibition is subsequently shown at the Maison des Arts et Loisirs, Sochaux, France. The American Academy of Arts and Letters, New York, awards him a Gold Medal for Sculpture and holds an exhibition of his work (May–June). *Calder*, a second study by H. H. Arnason, with photographs by Ugo Mulas, is published. Calder is included in *Sculpture in the Park*, Paramus, New Jersey (June–September). Twenty Aubusson tapestries designed by Calder and executed by Pinton Frères are shown at the Whitney Museum of American Art, New York (October–November); the exhibition travels to numerous American cities. In the late fall Calder visits the campus of Princeton University in New Jersey to see his *Five Discs, One Empty*, recently installed in front of the new art museum. *Fêtes*, a book-length prose poem about Calder by Jacques Prévert, with seven etchings by the artist, is published. Calder designs costumes and sets for *Amériques*, presented by the Ballet-Théâtre Contemporain in Amiens, France. An exhibition of his early works, dating from c. 1927 to 1944, is held at the Taft Museum, Cincinnati (December–January 1972); the Society of the Four Arts, Palm Beach, Florida, presents *Calder/Nevelson/Smith* (March–April). There are exhibitions at the Brook Street Gallery, London (April–May); Galerie d'Art Moderne, Basel (April–June); Studio Marconi, Milan (April–May); Gimpel Fils, London (April–May); John Berggruen Gallery, San Francisco (May–June); Galleria dell'Obelisco, Rome.

Asked about his Animobiles, Calder told a reporter: "I seem to remember animals rather well. I used to draw them in the Central Park Zoo. . . . I draw them on iron and they cut them out with a machine. I don't like to monkey with machines because you have to have the habit of safety."

1972

Calder completes a monumental stabile, *Eagle*, for the Fort Worth (Texas) National Bank. An updated French translation of his autobiography is published by Maeght. Charles Chaboud makes a film titled *Calder un portrait*. Aubusson tapestries designed by Calder for Pinton Frères are exhibited at the Galerie Verrière, Paris (February–March), the Leonard Hutton Galleries, New York (April–May). Calder donates a tapestry design to the Peter Stuyvesant Foundation, Amsterdam, for execution by the Royal Tapestry Weavers, Lesotho, Africa. In connection with the publication of the book *Calder's Circus,* the Whitney Museum of American Art, New York, holds an exhibition of works based on the Circus theme and gives regular showings of the film *Calder's Circus* (April–June); the American Federation of Arts circulates this film, with related exhibition materials organized by the Whitney, to schools, museums and libraries throughout the United States (September–January 1975); the Perls Galleries, New York, exhibits Circus drawings and an early circus oil (October–November). In honor of the artist's forthcoming seventy-fifth birthday the Paris magazine *XXᵉ siècle* publishes *Homage to Alexander Calder*. Mobiles, stabiles and gouaches are shown at the Sala Pelaires, Palma de Mallorca, Spain (September–October); lithographs and gouaches at the Galerie Bollack, Strasbourg. Miró–Calder exhibitions are held at the Fuji Television Company Gallery, Tokyo (November), and at the Galerie Beyeler, Basel (December–January 1973). The Calders and other sponsors of the National Committee for Impeachment take an ad in *The New York Times* (May 31) urging the removal of Richard Nixon from office for his failure to end the Vietnam War.

"I don't have much patriotism, there's nothing to be patriotic about. Trying to get your country to do what you think is right, that's what I would consider patriotism, but other people on the other side of the fence wouldn't."

1973

Galerie Maeght, Paris, exhibits recent mobiles (January); tapestries are shown at the Kunsthalle, Bielefeld, Germany (January–March); other exhibitions are held at the Galerie T. Roussel, Perpignan, France (February–March), and the Sala Gaspar, Barcelona (March–April). The newly opened Zurich branch of Galerie Maeght organizes a retrospective of Calder's work. Mobiles, stabiles and gouaches are exhibited at the Palais des Beaux-Arts, Charleroi, France, in con-

nection with *La Sculpture en plein air* (May–August); a mobile is included in *Le Mouvement*, an exhibition in Dijon, France (June–July), and the mobile, with a selection of lithographs, is then circulated throughout France (1973–74). *Jeune Fille et Sa Suite*, a stabile completed in 1970, is installed at the Michigan Bell Telephone Building in Detroit; the Detroit Institute of Arts holds an exhibition of prints, drawings and illustrated books to coincide with this event (October–November). In October, Calder attends the dedication of *Stegosaurus*, a stabile commissioned for the Alfred E. Burr Mall in Hartford, Connecticut; a small exhibition of drawings and gouaches is held at the University of Hartford, which presents Calder with an honorary degree. In October and November, the Perls Galleries, New York, presents *Calder at 75–Works in Progress:* models of three major stabiles (*Stegosaurus, Flamingo, Four Arches*) and of mobiles commissioned for the National Gallery, Washington, D.C., and for the Philadelphia Federal Reserve Bank. Calder designs a miniature stabile for the Archives of American Art special awards. *Une Floppée de Soleils*, Calder's largest tapestry (eight by twenty feet), is executed by Pinton Frères for IBM, Armonk, New York. Carlos Vilardebo makes his third film on Calder, *Les Gouaches de Sandy*. The Downtown Branch of the Whitney Museum of American Art, New York, presents *3 Sculptors: Calder, Nevelson, David Smith* (December–January 1974). Braniff International Airlines commissions Calder to paint a DC-8 jet. In preparation, he paints eight six-foot scale models in Saché; these are exhibited at the Guggenheim Museum, New York (August–September). The final design is spray-painted on the plane; Calder handpaints details on two of the engine covers at the Braniff hangar in Dallas just before the festive preview flight (October 30–November 2). With Calder, his family and close friends aboard, the plane, named *Flying Colors*, travels from Dallas to Los Angeles, Chicago and New York, where the Calders disembark; the plane continues to Washington, D.C., and Miami, then departs for a South American tour. While in Los Angeles, Calder inspects the site for *Four Arches*, commissioned for the Security Pacific National Bank and installed the following year.

When told that Braniff wanted a Calder-painted jet, he replied, "It might be fun. I'll see what I can come up with."

1974

Exhibitions are held at the Katonah (New York) Gallery (January), the Centre Culturel de Saint-Pierre des Corps, France (April); lithographs and tapestries are shown at the Galerie Jeanne Abeille, Toulouse, France (June), mobiles and stabiles at the Musée Municipal, Cluny, France (June). Calder's roof-painting design for the Kent County Administration Building, located on Calder Plaza with *La Grande Vitesse*, is completed for Festival '74 in Grand Rapids. In July the artist gives a Totem to Saché, where it is installed in the main square. Calder is represented in the Sixth Biennial of Graphic Design in Brno, Czechoslovakia (June–September); in the Agora II exhibition at the Musée de l'Ancienne Douane, Strasbourg, France; and in *Monumenta: Sculpture in Environment*, Newport, Rhode Island (August–October). Perls Galleries, New York, presents Crags (standing mobiles) and Critters (stabiles in human form) in October and November. A Calder Festival is held in Chicago to celebrate the dedication of two major works: *Universe*, a motorized mural for the Sears Tower, and *Flamingo*, a stabile commissioned by the U.S. General Services Administration for Federal Center Plaza, where it stands before a building designed by Mies van der Rohe. Calder attends the dedication ceremonies on October 25, which are preceded by an old-fashioned circus parade inspired by his lifetime interest in circuses. The Museum of Contemporary Art in Chicago holds a large retrospective exhibition (October–December). He is awarded the Grand Prix National des Arts et Lettres by the French Minister of Culture. As a gift for its members, the Archives of American Art publishes *Calder at the Zoo*, a portfolio selected from recently rediscovered zoo drawings, made by Calder in 1925–26 and subsequently misplaced. Mobiles, stabiles, gouaches and lithographs are exhibited at the Galerie Cour Saint Pierre, Geneva (November–January 1975); mobiles and stabiles at the Galerie Denise René-Hans Meyer, Düsseldorf (December–January 1975).

"Most architects and city planners want to put my objects in front of trees or greenery. They make a huge error. My mobiles and stabiles ought to be placed in free spaces, like public squares, or in front of modern buildings, and that is true of all contemporary sculpture."

1975

Crags and Critters are exhibited at the Galerie Maeght, Paris (January). A set of six Aubusson tapestries, designed by Calder and executed by Pinton Frères in a special edition of two hundred to celebrate the American Bicentennial, is exhibited at the Center for the Arts Gallery, Wesleyan University, Middletown, Connecticut (January–March) and subsequently in numerous U.S. cities. The National Collection of Fine Arts, Smithsonian Institution, Washington, D.C., and the Whitney Museum of American Art, New York, co-sponsor a traveling exhibition, *Calder's Circus*, based on the Whitney's 1972 show, to be circulated in the Far East; after a showing at the Bhirasi Institute of Modern Art, Bangkok, Thailand (January–February), the rest of the tour is canceled because of unsettled conditions in Southeast Asia. Hammocks and floor mats, designed by Calder and handwoven by Central American Indians, are exhibited at the Mitchell Sewall Gallery, New York (March–April). The Calders visit Israel for a week in April; he agrees to design a major stabile for Jerusalem, to stand on the northeastern slope of Mount Herzl. In an ad in *The New York Times* (May 15) Calder joins with Marcel Breuer and other artists who worked on the UNESCO building in Paris to protest UNESCO's expulsion of Israel. At the invitation of the French government, *Flying Colors* is exhibited at the Paris Air Show in May; during the show the artist handpaints two of the plane's engine covers, and it is flown over France with the Calders and their guests aboard. Galerie Maeght holds a reception for the artist at which the models for *Flying Colors* are on view. A large retrospective exhibition is organized by the Haus der Kunst, Munich (May–July), and travels to the Kunsthaus, Zurich (August–November). A BMW racing car is painted after a Calder design and competes at Le Mans, France, in June; it is exhibited in Paris at the Louvre (Musée des Arts Décoratifs), shown briefly at the Haus der Kunst retrospective, and after the race installed in the BMW museum in Munich. *Eléments Démontables,* a large mobile commissioned by the Fourth National Bank and

Trust Company of Wichita, Kansas, is installed in a new building designed by Skidmore, Owings & Merrill. Calder receives an Honors Award for *Flamingo* in the Second Biennial Awards Program of the General Services Administration, Washington, D.C. *Laughing Boy*, a plaster head of Sandy, aged twelve, by his father, is rediscoverd and cast in bronze for the Whitney Museum collection at Roman Bronze Works, the foundry used by father and son. In September the stabile *L'Araignée Rouge* is placed at the Rond Point de La Défense Metro station in Paris. As a Bicentennial project, Braniff International commissions Calder to design a new plane, *Flying Colors of the United States*, to serve as flagship of its U.S. fleet; the plane is dedicated in Washington, D.C., on November 17 with the Calders in attendance. He receives the U.N. Peace Medal, and Louisa is awarded the World Federation of United Nations Associations' Woman of the Year Award. The Perls Galleries, New York, presents Calder's *Recent Mobiles and Circus Gouaches* (October–November); at this time the Whitney Museum constructs a large new display case for the Circus and reinstalls the figures under Calder's direction.

Asked how he felt about his Circus some fifty years after he began it, Calder replied, "I'm still very fond of it."

1976

The outdoor standing mobile *Gallows and Lollipops*, 1962, is installed at Yale University, New Haven, Connecticut, in April. To aid the World Federation of United Nations Associations, Calder contributes a lithograph—sold as a limited edition and reproduced on a cacheted envelope accompanying U.N. commemorative stamps. The Greater Philadelphia Cultural Alliance presents a five-day Calder celebration (October). Events include: dedication of the mobile *White Cascade* at the Federal Reserve Bank; premiere of a Calder-inspired ballet, *Under the Sun*, choreographed by Margo Sappington for the Pennsylvania Ballet; a Calder exhibition at the Makler Gallery. The Perls Galleries, New York, exhibits *Works on Paper* by Calder (October-November). *Calder's Universe*, a major retrospective, is held at the Whitney Museum of American Art, New York (October–February 1977), which names Calder its Bicentennial Artist. The show is scheduled to travel to the High Museum of Art in Atlanta, Walker Art Center in Minneapolis, and the Dallas Museum of Fine Arts. A soft-cover edition of this book, published by The Viking Press, serves as catalogue for the exhibition. On October 20, a group of distinguished guests, representing the highest achievements in the fields of the visual arts, literature, music and dance, theater arts and film, attends a special evening at the Museum to honor the Calders.

When asked what was on his mind for the coming years, Calder replied, "I don't plan ahead."

November 11, 1976

Shortly after the first printing of this book and the opening of the Whitney Museum exhibition, Alexander Calder dies in New York.

Author's Bookshelf

The following books, periodicals, exhibition catalogues and other materials were actively used during the preparation of this volume and kept on the bookshelf of the special Calder office in the Whitney Museum through the period of work on the book and exhibition. A number of these publications have bibliographies which may also be consulted, as we have done, for further study of Calder's work. We are particularly indebted to the bibliographies in *Calder/Autobiographie* (no. 1a) and *Alexander Calder* by James Johnson Sweeney (no. 32). "Books," "Periodicals" and "Other" are arranged alphabetically by author or title; in the other sections the entries are chronological.

PUBLICATIONS BY CALDER

BOOKS

1. Calder, Alexander. *Calder: An Autobiography with Pictures.* Foreword by Robert Osborn. New York: Pantheon, 1966, 285 pp. Paperback reprint, Boston: Beacon, 1969. Published in French, *Calder/Autobiographie* (1a). Translated by Jean Davidson. Paris: Maeght, 1972, 209 pp.
The primary source for any study of Calder's life and work. An informal reminiscence, from early childhood to 1966, dictated by the artist to his son-in-law Jean Davidson; illustrated with family photographs and Calder's works in black-and-white and color; includes a short introduction by Calder's close friend the cartoonist Robert Osborn, and a detailed chronology. In the French edition his reminiscences are continued through 1967 and the chronology updated through 1972; photographs of recent works and a very useful bibliography have been added.

STATEMENTS

2. Calder, Alexander. "How Can Art Be Realized," in *Art of This Century*, Peggy Guggenheim, ed. New York: Art of This Century, 1942, p. 96.
Translation of a portion of Calder's statement (in French) for *Art non-figuratif*, a catalogue published by the Abstraction-Création group, Paris, 1932.
3. Calder, Alexander. "Mobiles," in *The Painter's Object*, Myfanwy Evans, ed. London: Gerold Howe, 1937, pp. 62–67.
Calder describes his visit to Mondrian's studio, his sets for Satie's *Socrate* and related mechanized mobiles; includes sketch by Calder of his *Socrate* stage set.
4. "17 Mobiles by Calder," in *Maud and Patrick Morgan / Alexander Calder*, 1943, [n.p.] (see no. 79).
The exhibition notes include a brief account by Calder of his meeting with Mondrian and the origin of his abstract sculpture.
5. Calder, Alexander. "The Ides of Art / 14 Sculptors Write." *The Tiger's Eye* (Westport, Conn.), vol. 1, no. 4 (June 15, 1948), p. 74.
Calder describes his printmaking efforts.
6. Calder, Alexander. Statement in *Calder, Matisse, Matta, Miró: Mural Scrolls.* [New York:] Katzenbach & Warren, 1949, p. 5, with unbound miniature of silkscreen-on-canvas mural designed by Calder for wallpaper manufacturer.
7. Calder, Alexander. "What Abstract Art Means to Me." *Museum of Modern Art Bulletin* (New York), vol. 18, no. 3 (Spring 1951), p. 8.
Text of Calder's statement for a symposium held at MoMA; other participating artists: Willem de Kooning, Stuart Davis, Fritz Glarner and George L. K. Morris.
8. Calder, Alexander. Statement in *Calder, 1955*, p. 3 (see no. 85).
Brief statement (in Spanish), reproduced in Calder's handwriting, about the universe as the inspiration for his work.

INTERVIEWS
(See also "Periodicals," for articles based on interviews with the artist.)

9. Rodman, Selden. *Conversations with Artists.* New York: Devin-Adair, 1957. Introduction by Alexander Eliot. Conversation with Calder, pp. 136–42.
Editor, poet and author of numerous books on art, Rodman visits Calder in his Roxbury studio in 1956; elicits from the artist some uncharacteristically serious comments about his career, his working procedures, and other sculptors, adding his own observations about Calder's "characteristic American traits."
10. Staempfli, George W. "Interview with Alexander Calder." *Quadrum* (Brussels), no. 6, 1959, pp. 9–11. Extract published in *Les Arts plastiques au nouveau siège de l'Unesco*, 1959.
A discussion of *Spirale*, made by Calder for UNESCO in Paris in 1958.
11. Kuh, Katharine. *The Artist's Voice/Talks with Seventeen Artists.* New York and Evanston, Ill.: Harper & Row, 1960, pp. 38–51.
A wide-ranging discussion in the late fifties, touching on all the important aspects of Calder's work in succinct question-and-answer format; brief chronology.

ILLUSTRATED BY THE ARTIST

12. Calder, Alexander. *Animal Sketching.* Pelham, New York: Bridgman Publishers, 1926; 2nd ed., 1941, 62 pp. Paperback reprint, New York: Dover, 1973.
Art instruction book with text and brush drawings by Calder.
13. *Fables of Aesop / According to Sir Roger L'Estrange.* Drawings by Calder. Paris: Harrison of Paris [Monroe Wheeler and Barbara Harrison], 1931, 124 pp. Paperback reprint, New York: Dover, 1967.
14. Sweeney, James Johnson, ed. *Three Young Rats and Other Rhymes.* Introduction by James Johnson Sweeney; drawings by Calder. New York: Curt Valentin, 1944, 130 pp., edition of 760. Reprint, New York: Museum of Modern Art, 1946.
15. Coleridge, Samuel. *The Rime of the Ancient Mariner.* Essay by Robert Penn Warren; drawings by Calder. New York: Reynal and Hitchcock, 1946, 148 pp.
16. La Fontaine, Jean de. *Selected Fables.* Translated by Eunice Clark; etchings by Calder. New York: Braziller, 1948, 88 pp. Paperback reprint, New York: Dover, 1968.
17. Wilbur, Richard, ed. *A Bestiary.* Drawings by Calder. New York: Pantheon Books, 1955, 74 pp.
18. *Calder's Circus.* Text by Cleve Gray. New York: Art in America, 1964, 4 pp. text, 16 prints, unbound, boxed.
Facsimile reproductions (slightly smaller dimensions than originals) of 16 circus drawings which were simultaneously reproduced in an *Art in America* feature article by Cleve Gray (see no. 57); his text is reprinted to introduce the drawings.
19. Elléouët, Yves, ed. *La Proue de la table.* Paris: Le Soleil Noir, 1967, 4 pp., with 7 etchings by Calder; edition of 55.
20. Calder, Alexander, and Prévert, Jacques. *Fêtes.* Paris: Maeght, 1971, 48 pp., unbound, boxed, with 7 embossed etchings by Calder; edition of 200.
21. *Calder at the Zoo.* Introduction by Jean Davidson. Washington, D.C.: Archives of American Art, Smithsonian Institution, 1974, 9 sheets, unbound, in portfolio.
Reproductions of brush drawings, selected from 248 sketches made by Calder at the Bronx and Central Park zoos in New York, 1925–26. The drawings published in *Animal Sketching* (see no. 12) were made at the same time.
22. cummings, e e. *Santa Claus.* French translation by D. Jon Grossman. Paris: Editions de l'Herbe, 1974, 44 pp., unbound, boxed, with 9 etchings by Calder; edition of 175.

BOOKS

ON CALDER

23. Arnason, H. H., and Guerrero, Pedro E. *Calder*. New York: Van Nostrand, 1966, 192 pp.
A critical study by Arnason of the evolution of Calder's sculpture (works in other media not discussed); illustrated with photographs by Guerrero; the detailed chronology is divided into decades.

24. Arnason, H. Harvard, and Mulas, Ugo. *Calder*. New York: Viking, 1971, 216 pp.
A photographic survey of Calder's work made by Mulas during numerous visits with the artist in the sixties. Arnason's introduction documents the artist's career with extensive quotations from Calder's autobiography and other sources; of particular value are excerpts from early catalogues, periodicals and out-of-print books unavailable except in specialized libraries. A useful bibliography.

25. Bellew, Peter. *Calder*. J. Prats Vallès, ed. Barcelona: Ediciones Polígrafa, 1969, 136 pp.
Minimal text in Spanish, English, French and German, with biographical data. Of interest for its photographs by Clovis Prévost, and the juxtaposition of circus photographs with stabiles and mobiles.

26. Bruzeau, Maurice. *Calder à Saché*. Photography by Jacques Masson; design by Charles Feld. Paris: Editions Cercle d'Art, 1975, 198 pp.
The text, with many direct quotations, is based on conversations with Calder in Saché between 1972 and 1974; includes poems by the author, a brief chronology, profuse illustrations (but sketchy captions) of works in all media belonging to Calder, including previously unpublished abstract drawings of 1932.

27. Carandente, Giovanni. *Calder / Mobiles and Stabiles*. New York and Toronto: The New American Library, by arrangement with UNESCO, 1968, 93 pp. Also published in French-English-German-Spanish edition, Lausanne and Paris: Editions Rencontre, 1970, 65 pp. with 24 color slides.
Excellent summary of Calder's career by the Italian museum director and art historian who commissioned Calder's *Work in Progress* for the Rome Opera House, 1968.

28. *Homage to Alexander Calder*. G. di San Lazzaro, ed. Special issue of *XXᵉ siècle* (Paris). Published in English, New York: Tudor, 1972, 107 pp.
Articles by San Lazzaro, Stanley William Hayter, Patrick Waldberg, Alain Jouffroy, Jean Davidson, Gilbert Lascault, Jacques Dupin, Pierre Descargues, Giovanni Carandente, Charles Chaboud, Daniel Lelong, Yvon Taillandier. Of special interest are: Davidson's article on studios used by Calder, from age

nine to the present; general discussions of Calder's work by Descargues and by Lelong; a description of Calder's *Work in Progress* and a discussion of his relationship to kinetic art, both by Carandente. Important catalogue essays by Pascin (1929), Sartre (1946) and Léger (1952) are reprinted, as is a 1959 interview with the artist by Yvon Taillandier. The biographical notes are based on the 1969 Fondation Maeght exhibition catalogue (see no. 99).

29. Lipman, Jean, with Nancy Foote, eds. *Calder's Circus*. New York: E. P. Dutton with Whitney Museum of American Art, 1972, 171 pp.
The central importance of the Circus in Calder's work is documented with Circus figures—photographed for this book by Marvin Schwartz—with stills from the 1961 film *Cirque Calder* (see no. 116) and with reproductions of Circus-related works in the many media used by the artist. Includes an introduction by Jean Lipman, quotations from Calder, a Circus-oriented chronology and a selected bibliography.

30. Mancewicz, Bernice Winslow. *Alexander Calder / A Pictorial Essay*. Grand Rapids, Michigan: William B. Eerdmans, 1969, 64 pp.
Excellent brief summary of Calder's career (with a description of how major stabiles are fabricated), with quotations and chronology; published in conjunction with the installation of *La Grande Vitesse* in Grand Rapids.

31. Ragon, Michel. *Calder / Mobiles and Stabiles*. Petite Encyclopédie de l'Art, no. 87. New York: Tudor, 1967, 62 pp.
Despite the stilted translation, this is an excellent brief summary of Calder's career and style, with an interesting description of Calder's studio by the novelist James Jones.

32. Sweeney, James Johnson. *Alexander Calder*. New York: The Museum of Modern Art, 1951, 80 pp.
Updated edition of the catalogue for the artist's first major museum exhibition in 1943 at MoMA (see no. 80). The first and best critical study of the artist; required reading for anyone interested in Calder's career. Includes excellent documentary material: chronology; lists of exhibitions and of the artist's graphic and theatrical work; bibliography by Bernard Karpel. Limited only by the cutoff date of 1951.

33. ———. "Alexander Calder: Work and Play," in *What Is American in American Art*, Jean Lipman, ed. New York: McGraw-Hill, 1963, pp. 87–93.
Brilliant analysis of the role of play in Calder's oeuvre; originally published in *Art in America*, vol. 44, no. 4 (Winter 1956 / 57), pp. 8–13; also reprinted in anniversary issue of *Art in America*, vol. 51, no. 4 (Aug. 1963), pp. 92–98.

34. ———. *Calder / l'artiste et l'oeuvre*. Archives Maeght, no. 1. Paris: Maeght, 1971, 136 pp.
Sweeney's essay originally appeared in the catalogue for the 1969 Fondation Maeght exhibition (see no. 99).

GENERAL

35. Barr, Alfred H., Jr. *Cubism and Abstract Art*. New York: Museum of Modern Art, 1936, 249 pp. Paperback reprint, 1974.
Book devoted to European artists; passing reference to Calder and influences on his work is interesting because of its early date.

36. Hammacher, A. M. *The Evolution of Modern Sculpture*. New York. Abrams, 1969, 383 pp.
General survey by Dutch art historian; has brief discussion of Calder's work and his relationship to European cultural trends in the 1930s.

37. Lipman, Jean, and Franc, Helen M. *Bright Stars*. Introduction by John I. H. Baur. New York: E. P. Dutton, 1976, 208 pp.
150 works of American art, 1776–1976, are selected for reproduction and commentary; includes three by Calder: *The Brass Family*, *Le Guichet* and *Lobster Trap and Fish Tail*.

38. MacDonagh, Donagh. *Martha Graham: A Biography*. New York: Praeger, 1973, 352 pp.
Detailed account of the two productions, *Panorama* (1935) and *Horizons* (1936), for which Calder designed mobile stage properties.

39. Seuphor, Michel. *Douce province*. Lausanne: Jean Marguerat, 1941, pp. 49–58.
This novel includes a description of Calder, his Paris house and studio, and a night at his Circus in 1932.

40. ———. "Calder," in *The Sculpture of This Century*. New York: George Braziller, 1960, pp. 85–91.
A chapter in this general survey is devoted to Calder; includes interesting account by Ben Nicholson of his first encounter with a Calder mobile.

PERIODICALS

MAGAZINE ARTICLES

41. Andersen, Wayne V. "Calder at the Guggenheim." *Artforum*, vol. 3, no. 6 (March 1965), pp. 37–41.
Review of the 1964 Guggenheim exhibition with discussion of Calder's relation to advanced European art of the 1920s and 1930s.

42. "Calder On-stage." *Newsweek*, March 25, 1968, p. 100.
Account of Calder's *Work in Progress* at the Rome Opera House.

43. "Calder's Kitchen Collection." *Craft Horizons*, Sept./Oct. 1962, pp. 20–23.
Very brief text accompanied by excellent photographs of household objects from Calder's Roxbury house.

44. Canaday, John. "Mobile Visit with Alexander Calder." *The New York Times Magazine*, March 25, 1962, pp. 32–33, 125.
Visit to Roxbury with emphasis on and photos of Calder's household objects.

45. Cate, Curtis. "Calder Made Easy." *Horizon*, vol. 14, no. 1 (Winter 1972), pp. 44–57.
A vivid account of a recent visit to Calder's new house in Saché with an explanation, by the artist, of how a mobile is made; includes 8-page color portfolio of 1970 gouaches.

46. "Close-up—Mobile Maker's Giddy Whirl." *Life*, March 5, 1965, pp. 47–48, 50, 52.
Photographs and lively interview by Jane Howard.

47. Davidson, Jean. "Four Calders." *Art in America*, vol. 50, no. 4 (Winter 1962), pp. 68–73. Family history illustrated with works by Calder, his grandfather, father and daughter.

48–54. *Derrière Le Miroir* (published by Galerie Maeght, Paris; the following issues are devoted to Calder and served as exhibition catalogues; all texts in French).

48. ———, nos. 69–70 (Oct.–Nov. 1954), 10 pp., with cover and 2 illustrations by Calder. Poem by Henri Pichette; essay by Frank Elgar.

49. ———, no. 113 (1959), 26 pp., with sketches by Calder and 2 plates lithographed from his designs. Articles: "Stabiles" by Georges Salles; "Le Luron aux protèges-genoux" by Jean Davidson.

50. ———, no. 156 (Feb. 1966), 32 pp., with cover by Calder, 5 plates lithographed from his gouaches and photographs of Totems and gouaches. "Oiseleur du Fer," poem by Jacques Prévert; critical essay by Meyer Schapiro; "Les Gouaches de Calder" by Nicholas Guppy; excerpt from Calder's autobiography on his Art Students League days.

51. ———, no. 173 (Oct. 1968), 24 pp., with cover by Calder, 6 plates lithographed from his gouaches and photographs of *Flèches*. Articles: "Un géant enfant" by Giovanni Carandente; "Note sur les 'flèches'" by Jacques Dupin.

52. ———, no. 190 (Feb. 1971), 26 pp., with cover by Calder, 3 plates lithographed from his gouaches and photographs of stabiles and Animobiles. "Calder la liberté" by Carlos Franqui.

53. ———, no. 201 (Jan. 1973), 28 pp., with cover by Calder, 4 plates lithographed from his gouaches and photographs of mobiles and stabiles. Articles: "Retour au mobile" by Maurice Besset; "Calder ou le poids de l'air" by André Balthazar.

54. ———, no. 212 (Jan. 1975), 24 pp., with cover by Calder, 6 plates lithographed from his gouaches and photographs of Crags and Critters. "Un tournant chez Calder" by Mario Pedrosa.

55. Devaney, Sally G. "Flying Calder," *The Art Gallery*, Feb. 1974, pp. 16–18, 61, 70.
Calder's *Flying Colors* commission and inaugural flight.

56. [Drexler, Arthur.] "Calder." *Interiors*, vol. 109, no. 5 (Dec. 1949), pp. 80–87.
Cover for this issue designed by Calder; article, with an illustration by the artist, discusses and includes photographs of his 1944 bronzes.

57. Gray, Cleve. "Calder's Circus." *Art in America*, vol. 52, no. 5 (Oct. 1964), pp. 23–48. Prefaced by letter from Miró; includes interview in which Calder comments on his longstanding interest in the circus theme; accompanied by 16-page portfolio of circus drawings of 1931 and 1932. A special dividend is Gray's acute focus on Calder's personality as it emerges during the course of the interview.

58. Gray, Francine du Plessix. "At the Calders'." *House & Garden*, Dec. 1963, pp. 155–159, 189.
Description of Roxbury house with black-and-white and color photographs by Pedro E. Guerrero.

59. Hellman, Geoffrey T. "Calder Revisited." *The New Yorker*, Oct. 22, 1960, pp. 163–64, 167–72, 175–78.
Author discusses the rise in Calder's reputation (and fortune) since they first met in 1940; visit to Roxbury and Segre's Iron Works.

60. Karshan, Donald H. "Graphics '70: Alexander Calder." *Art in America*, vol. 58, no. 3 (May–June 1970), pp. 48–49, with original offset lithograph, *Spirals*, by Calder.

61. Lemon, Richard. "Mobiles: The Soaring Art of Alexander Calder." *Saturday Evening Post*, Feb. 27, 1965, pp. 30–35.
A thorough survey of Calder's career, with many direct quotations; dramatic photographs of the 1964 Guggenheim exhibition.

62. Morgan, Ted. "A Visit to Calder Kingdom," *The New York Times Magazine*, July 8, 1973, pp. 10–11, 29ff.
A portrait of the artist at 75.

63. Osborn, Robert. "Calder's International Monuments." *Art in America*, vol. 57, no. 2 (March–April 1969), pp. 32–49.
Required reading for account of the stabiles and how they are made; includes drawings by Osborn, his interview with the artist, and photographs with descriptions of 21 major stabiles.

64. "Plexiglas Sculpture Prizes Are Awarded." *Pencil Points*, June 1939, pp. 56–57.
Calder wins first prize in competition at MoMA, New York; photograph of winning sculpture (now lost).

65. Rose, Barbara. "Joy, Excitement Keynote Calder's Work." *Canadian Art*, May–June 1965, pp. 30–33.
Review of 1964 Guggenheim exhibition.

66. Russell, John. "Alexander Calder in Saché." *Vogue*, July 1967, pp. 110–15, 119, 121, 130.
Art critic Russell writes about and Lord Snowdon photographs the Calders at their home in France.

67. *Suites*, no. 11 (June 1966), 26 pp. with 3 plates lithographed from Calder's gouaches.
Published by Galerie Krugier & Cie., Geneva, as a catalogue for a retrospective exhibition of Calder's work; photographs of the works and a short text by Giovanni Carandente (stilted English translation).

68. Tuchman, Phyllis. "Alexander Calder's Almadén Mercury Fountain." *Marsyas/Studies in the History of Art*, vol. XVI (1972–73), pp. 97–107.
Scholarly study provides interesting background information on the *Mercury Fountain* and reprints detailed technical description written by Calder in 1938 for M.I.T.'s *Technology Review* and *The Stevens Indicator*, his alma mater's alumni magazine.

69. "A Visit with Calder," *Look*, Dec. 9, 1958, pp. 54–57. Interesting description of how Calder makes a mobile.

NEWSPAPER ARTICLES

70. Campbell, Mary. "The Animobiles Are Here," *Bridgeport Sunday Post*, Dec. 19, 1971. AP review of exhibition at Perls Galleries.

71. Chernow, Burt. "Calder . . . A Hefty Man with the Soul of a Hummingbird." *Fairpress* (Westport, Conn.), Jan. 31, 1973.
Interview with the artist at his Roxbury home.

72. DeLeusse, Claude. "Le Calder Mobile." *Women's Wear Daily*, Oct. 15, 1968.

73. Kempton, Murray. "Mr. Calder Laughs." *New York World-Telegram & Sun*, Nov. 16, 1965.
Account of dedication of *Le Guichet* at Lincoln Center.

74. Knox, Sanka. "Two Stabiles May Stay Put After Move to Harlem." *The New York Times*, Sept. 2, 1967.

75. Root, Waverly. "The Greatest Living American Artist—the Picasso of Iron." *New York Journal-American*, Sept. 9, 1965 (*Los Angeles Times–Washington Post* News Service story).

76. Zimmerman, Diane. "Artist in Perpetual Motion: Calder at 74." *Daily News* (New York), May 24, 1972.

EXHIBITION CATALOGUES

77. Galerie Percier, Paris, April 27–May 9, 1931. *Alexander Calder/Volumes—Vecteurs—*

Densités/Dessins–Portraits, 10 pp. Introduction by Fernand Léger: "Eric Satie illustré par Calder, pourquoi pas?"

78. George Walter Vincent Smith Art Gallery, Springfield, Mass., Nov. 8–27, 1938. *Alexander Calder*, 4 pp. Foreword by James Johnson Sweeney.

79. The Addison Gallery of American Art, Andover, Mass., June 5–July 6, 1943. *Maud and Patrick Morgan/Alexander Calder*, 1 sheet folded. Includes essay "17 Mobiles by Calder."

80. The Museum of Modern Art, New York, Sept. 29, 1943–Jan. 16, 1944. *Alexander Calder*, 64 pp. Text by James Johnson Sweeney; revised in 1951 (see no. 32).

81. Galerie Louis Carré, Paris, Oct. 25–Nov. 16, 1946. *Alexander Calder: Mobiles, stabiles, constellations*, 44 pp. Includes "Les Mobiles de Calder" by Jean-Paul Sartre, according to Calder the best essay ever written about his work. It has been reprinted frequently; the first English translation appeared in *Style en France*, no. 5 (April), 1947, pp. 6–11; it was first published in the U.S. in the Buchholz Gallery catalogue, 1947 (see no. 82).

82. Buchholz Gallery, New York, Dec. 9–27, 1947. *Alexander Calder*, 8 pp. "Calder's Mobiles" by Jean-Paul Sartre; drawing of Calder by Saul Steinberg; photos by Herbert Matter.

83. Buchholz Gallery, New York, Nov. 30–Dec. 17, 1949. *Alexander Calder*, 14 pp. "The Studio of Alexander Calder," a poem by André Masson (translated by Ralph Manheim); sketches of mobiles by Calder.

84. Curt Valentin Gallery, New York, Jan. 15–Feb. 10, 1952. *Alexander Calder/Gongs and Towers*, 12 pp. "Alexander Calder's Mobiles," by James Johnson Sweeney; "Calder," by Fernand Léger (translated by Dolly Chareau); drawings by Calder of objects in exhibition.

85. Museo de Bellas Artes, Caracas. Sept. 2–25, 1955. *Calder*, 12 pp. Introduction by Alejo Carpentier with statement by Calder; biographical notes adapted from James Johnson Sweeney's essay for MoMA catalogue; essays by Jean-Paul Sartre (1946) and Fernand Léger (1952); all texts in Spanish; cover and sketches of objects by Calder.

86. Perls Galleries, New York. March 15–April 9, 1960. *Alexander Calder/"1960,"* 12 pp. Drawings by Calder of works exhibited.

87. Delaware Art Center, Wilmington. Jan. 7–Feb. 19, 1961. *Calder/Alexander Milne, Alexander Stirling, Alexander*, 12 pp. Foreword with brief biographies of each artist by Bruce St. John.

88. Perls Galleries, New York. Feb. 21–April 1, 1961. *Alexander Calder/Joan Miró*, 12 pp. Poem by Miró; drawings by Calder of works exhibited.

89. Lincoln Gallery, London. Nov. 1961. *Calder Gouaches*, 18 pp. Essay by Nicholas Guppy.

90. Tate Gallery, London. July 4–Aug. 12, 1962. *Alexander Calder/Sculpture/Mobiles*, 30 pp. Essay by James Johnson Sweeney.

91. Musée de Rennes, France. Dec. 4, 1962–Jan. 20, 1963. *Alexander Calder/Mobiles/Gouaches/Tapisseries*, 32 pp. Preface by Jean Cassou.

92. Perls Galleries, New York. March 19–April 27, 1963. *Alexander Calder/"1963,"* 8 pp.

93. The Solomon R. Guggenheim Museum, New York. Nov. 1964–Jan. 1965. *Alexander Calder/A Retrospective Exhibition*, 88 pp. Introduction by Thomas M. Messer. Major exhibition of 287 works in all media; valuable bibliography.

94. The Museum of Fine Arts, Houston. Nov. 24–Dec. 13, 1964. *Alexander Calder/Circus Drawings, Wire Sculpture and Toys*, 32 pp. Introduction by James Johnson Sweeney.

95. Musée National d'Art Moderne, Paris. July–Oct. 1965. *Calder*, 56 pp. Preface by Jean Cassou. When the Guggenheim exhibition was shown in Paris, new objects were added and this new catalogue, organized chronologically with documentary photographs, was published.

96. Akademie der Künste, Berlin. May 21–July 16, 1967. *Alexander Calder*, 111 pp. Texts, in German, by Hans Scharoun, Willem Sandberg, Stephan Waetzoldt, Calder, Jean-Paul Sartre, Paul Westheim, Bruno E. Werner (latter two are reprints of reviews of Calder's 1929 Berlin show).

97. Perls Galleries, New York. Nov. 14–Dec. 23, 1967. *Alexander Calder/Early Work—Rediscovered*, 12 pp.

98. Perls Galleries, New York. Oct. 15–Nov. 9, 1968. *Alexander Calder/Space: Drawings 1930–1932, Gouaches 1967–1968*, 16 pp.

99. Fondation Maeght, Saint-Paul-de-Vence, France. April 2–May 31, 1969. *Calder*, 226 pp. Major exhibition of 311 works from 1926 to 1967; works listed by year, many illustrated. Texts in French; of special interest are essay by James Johnson Sweeney commenting on stabiles and later works; an account of *Work in Progress* by Giovanni Carandente; and reprints of important catalogue essays by Sartre (1946) and Léger (1952). Other contributors are Michel Butor, Jean Davidson, Pol Bury, Gabrielle Buffet-Picabia and Francis Miroglio. Complete chronology and reproductions of Calder drawings and letters.

100. Louisiana Museum, Humlebaek, Denmark. June–Sept. 1969. *Louisiana-Revy*, June 1969, 39 pp. This issue of the Louisiana Museum periodical served as a catalogue for the Fondation Maeght exhibition when it was shown in Denmark. Articles by Thomas M. Messer, Jean-Paul Sartre, James Johnson Sweeney, Michel Ragon, Gabrielle Buffet-Picabia, Fernand Léger, Francis Miroglio, Jean Davidson, James Jones, Giovanni Carandente, Gunnar Jespersen, Michel Butor and Calder. Texts in Danish; summaries in German, English and French.

101. Perls Galleries, New York. Oct. 7–Nov. 8, 1969. *Alexander Calder/Bronze Sculptures of 1944*, 20 pp.

102. The Museum of Modern Art, New York. Dec. 1969–Feb. 1970. *A Salute to Alexander Calder*, 31 pp. Introduction by Bernice Rose. Complete presentation of the museum's Calder collection.

103. Long Beach Museum of Art, California. Jan. 11–Feb. 8, 1970. *Calder Gouaches*, 28 pp. Introduction by Wahneta T. Robinson with chronology of major gouache exhibitions.

104. Perls Galleries, New York. Oct. 20–Nov. 28, 1970. *Alexander Calder/Recent Gouaches—Early Mobiles*, 22 pp.

105. Perls Galleries, New York. Oct. 5–Nov. 6, 1971. *Alexander Calder/Animobiles—Recent Gouaches*, 28 pp. Text by Klaus Perls.

106. Taft Museum, Cincinnati, Ohio. Dec. 12, 1971–Jan. 31, 1972. *Early Works: Alexander Calder*, 8 pp. Introduction by Jayne Merkel.

107. Perls Galleries, New York. Oct. 10–Nov. 11, 1972. *Alexander Calder/Oil Paintings*, 28 pp. Excerpt from Calder's autobiography describing his years at New York's Art Students League, where he first studied painting.

108. Perls Galleries, New York. Oct. 15–Nov. 16, 1974. *Crags and Critters of 1974*, 12 pp.

109. Museum of Contemporary Art, Chicago. Oct. 26–Dec. 8, 1974. *Alexander Calder/A Retrospective Exhibition/Work from 1925 to 1974*, 32 pp. "Calder on Balance," by Albert E. Elsen, defines Calder's position in relation to specific sculptural achievements of the twentieth century and notes areas in which Calder has been an innovator.

110. Haus der Kunst, Munich. May 10–July 13, 1975. *Calder*, 140 pp. Large exhibition of 166 works in all media, many illustrated. Introduction by Maurice Besset with chronology; all texts in German.

FILMS

111. *Alexander Calder* (1929). Directed by Dr. Hans Cürlis; filmed by Walter Turck. Part of the series "Artists at Work" produced by the Institute für Kulturforschung, Berlin. Made during Calder's 1929 Berlin visit and exhibition.

112. Pathé movie "short" (1929).
According to the New York *Herald* (Paris edition), May 21, 1929: "Sandy Calder, cartoonist, toymaker and otherwise jack-of-all-trades, reports the completion of his artistic cycle now that he has faced a movie camera. The other day, a host of Pathé people de-

scended upon his studio and 'shot' him before sundown. His comic wood and wire toys also strutted in the glare of the Kleig lights."

113. *Alexander Calder: Sculpture and Constructions* (1944), 10 min. Written and narrated by Agnes Rindge Claflin; filmed by Herbert Matter; produced by the Museum of Modern Art, New York.

Includes a Circus performance, wood and wire sculpture, mobiles in motion; made on occasion of MoMA exhibition, 1943–44.

114. *Dreams That Money Can Buy* (1948), 85 min. Directed and produced by Hans Richter. Sponsored by Peggy Guggenheim's Art of This Century gallery; distributed by McGraw-Hill Films, New York.

This Surrealist film is composed of seven sequences, or "dreams," by Richter, Max Ernst, Marcel Duchamp, Fernand Léger and Calder, who was the subject of two: "Ballet," in which his mobiles and mechanized works are filmed in motion, and "Circus," a brief performance by Calder of some of his Circus figures. A brochure published in 1948 by the original distributor, Films International of America, includes photos, credits and biographical notes on the participating artists; James Johnson Sweeney contributed the brief statement on Calder. (The brochure is on file in the Museum of Modern Art Film Department.)

115. *Works of Calder* (1951), 21 min. Produced and narrated by Burgess Meredith; photographed and directed by Herbert Matter; music by John Cage. The Museum of Modern Art, New York.

A small boy wanders from a windswept beach to Calder's studio where he finds the artist at work. After watching the mobiles for some time, the boy comments that they are "getting all mixed up" in his mind with the images of waves and rustling foliage seen earlier. The images get mixed up in this film, too.

116. *Cirque Calder* (1961), 19 min. By Carlos Vilardebo, Pathé Cinéma, Paris. Available in English: *Calder's Circus* (1963), McGraw-Hill Films, New York.

A wonderful film of Calder performing his Circus, with Louisa at the phonograph, made before a live audience in Calder's house in Saché—his last complete performance.

117. *Alexander Calder: From the Circus to the Moon* (1963), 11 min. By Hans Richter, McGraw-Hill Films, New York.

Inspired by James Johnson Sweeney's notes for Calder's first film with Richter (see no. 114): "From the circus to the moon; Calder has stretched a wire between them. He would dance on it if he could." Richter films Calder at work and play in his Roxbury studio with lively music and some typical Surrealist touches; the brief sequence on the Circus fails to capture the full humor and animation of Calder's performance.

118. *The Great Sail* (1966), 11 min. By Robert Gardner, Phoenix Films, New York.

Calder dons a hard hat to supervise the installation of *La Grande Voile* at the Massachusetts Institute of Technology, spring, 1966. A laborious process is made into a lively film by use of speeded-up photography and the inclusion of snatches of conversation between Calder and the workmen, and comments from passers-by.

119. *Mobiles* (1966), 13 min. By Carlos Vilardebo, Pathé Cinéma, Paris.

Vilardebo returns to Saché to film the Calders in their new house. Louisa gardens, cooks and hooks rugs; in his workshop Sandy, unusually talkative, explains how he makes and balances a mobile; these scenes are interspersed with sequences of mobiles in motion—"it's like looking at an abstract ballet," says Calder.

120. *Alexander Calder: The Creation of a Stabile* (1967), 9 min. Produced by International Nickel Co., New York.

Documents the making of *Man*, a stabile for the World's Fair in Montreal, 1967; shows Calder in his home in Saché, at Etablissements Biémont where the stabile was fabricated, and the stabile in place in Montreal; marred by pretentious narration and trick photography.

121. *Calder un portrait* (1972), 40 min. By Charles Chaboud with Daniel Lelong; music adapted from scores by Edgard Varèse; produced by Aimé Maeght, Paris.

This long film, in French, presents scenes of the Calders in Saché alternating with scenes of the 1969 retrospective at the Fondation Maeght; Etablissements Biémont; *La Grande Vitesse* in Grand Rapids, Michigan; *Man* in Montreal; and excerpts from Vilardebo's *Cirque Calder* (see no. 116). Most interesting are the interviews at the Fondation Maeght in 1969 with Louisa and friends: James Johnson Sweeney, Rufus Stillman, Pol Bury, Eduardo Chillida and Joan Prats.

122. *Les Gouaches de Sandy* (1973), 13 min. By Carlos Vilardebo, Pathé Cinéma, Paris.

Vilardebo's third film of Calder is, like the others, straightforward, unpretentious and thus faithful to the artist's personality and work. He follows the Calders through their daily routine in Saché; the close-ups of Calder in the *gouacherie* and in the large studio are almost as good as being there in person.

OTHER

DOCUMENTS

123. Archives of American Art, Smithsonian Institution, Washington, D.C. *Alexander Calder Papers.* Approximately 2000 items, 1925–62, donated by the artist; available on microfilm in Archives offices in Washington, New York, Boston, Detroit and San Francisco. Most of this collection consists of press clippings, exhibition announcements, letters and photographs. Most valuable is Calder's scrapbook (123a), a large album which he kept from 1927 to 1932, with articles about him and his work from newspapers and periodicals in the U.S., France, Germany and other European countries (the artist subscribed to a clipping service); also exhibition announcements, invitations and reviews. This fascinating record of the formative years of Calder's career —especially valuable for the reproductions of early works (many now lost)—was on loan from the Washington office of the Archives to the Whitney Museum during the preparation of this book.

124. Stevens Institute of Technology, Hoboken, N.J. *Annual Catalogue, 1919–1920.*
List of courses, instructors and curriculum requirements when Calder was a mechanical engineering student at Stevens.

125. ———. *The Link of 1918.*
College yearbook featuring Calder's graduating class (1919); photograph and description of Calder, p. 75.

126. Whitney Museum of American Art, New York. *Artists File, Alexander Calder.* In two sections: (1) miscellaneous correspondence, clippings, exhibition announcements and catalogues, press releases, photographs; (2) documentation of the artist's work in the museum collection, including questionnaires completed by the artist.

ILLUSTRATED BOOKS BY SANDRA CALDER DAVIDSON

127. Davidson, Sandra Calder. *Sylvestre, ou la grenouille de plomb.* Paris: Maeght, 1962, 72 pp., with 4 pp. insert, "A ma fille, quelques grenouilles de plus," by Alexander Calder. Published in English, *Sylvester.* Translated by Alexander Calder, Jean Davidson and Judy Hyun. New York and Chicago: Follett, 1967, 62 pp.
Children's story written and illustrated by Calder's daughter.

128. ———. *Sylvester and the Butterfly Bomb.* Translated by Edite Kroll. Garden City, N.Y.: Doubleday, 1972, 62 pp.
Sequel to *Sylvestre.*

129. ———. *The Turkey and the Eagle. The Great Seal of the United States—an Animal Fable.* New York: Juliette Halioua, 1976, 72 pp.; also issued in a special edition of 500, with a lithograph by the author and a lithograph by Alexander Calder.
Published on the occasion of *Calder's Universe* at the Whitney Museum of American Art.

130. Ironmonger, Ira. *Alligator Smiling in the Sawgrass.* Illustrated by Sandra Davidson. New York: Young Scott Books, 1965, 48 pp.

Who's Who in Calder's World

This is an informal index of people mentioned in this book whose lives have crossed Calder's in some significant way. The identifications that follow each name have been made as minimal as possible; they are simply intended to give the reader an idea of the extraordinary variety of the people in Calder's world. (Numbers in italics refer to illustrations.)

Aalto, Alvar. Architect. 306, 307, 332.
Alberto (Sanchez, Alberto). Sculptor. 28.
Allen, Charlotte. Collector. 331–32.
Anschutz, Thomas. Painter. 10.
Arnason, H. H. Art historian; museum administrator. 337, 338, 342.
Arp, Hans (Jean). Sculptor. 20, 21, 28, 63, 235, 254, 305, 331.

Baker, Josephine. Entertainer. 233, 237, *240, 241,* 330.
Balmer, Clinton. Painter; art instructor. 329.
Barr, Alfred H., Jr. Museum director; art historian. 20, 26, 35, 83, 183, 331, 336, 342.
Baudoin, Pierre. Aubusson tapestry manufacturer. 157, 336.
Baur, John I. H. Museum director; art historian. *130,* 186, 237, 342.
Bazaine, Jean. Painter. 338.
Bazillon, Jacques. Metalworks director. 31, 266, 267.
Beall, Lester. Graphics designer. 38, 39.
Bellew, Peter. Writer. *63,* 342.
Benton, Thomas Hart. Painter. 111, 329.
Bernstein, Aline. Stage costume designer. 60, 61, 330.
Besset, Maurice. Museum director. 343, 344.
Blume, Peter. Painter. 32.
Brancusi, Constantin. Sculptor. 45, 235, *335.*
Braque, Georges. Painter. 332.
Breton, André. Painter. 30.
Breuer, Marcel. Architect. 25, 32, 199, *229,* 306, 340.
Brown, Earle. Composer. 171, *173,* 337.
Bruzeau, Maurice. Writer. 183, 237, 342.
Buffet-Picabia, Gabrielle. Writer. 344.
Bunshaft, Gordon. Architect. 306, 333.
Bury, Pol. Sculptor. 344, 345.
Butler, John. Choreographer. 172, 336.
Butor, Michel. Poet. 336, 344.

Cafritz, Gwendolyn. Collector. 33.
Cage, John. Composer. 345.

Calder, Alexander Milne. Sculptor; grandfather of Alexander Calder. 10, *11,* 185, 329, 336.
Calder, Alexander Stirling. Sculptor; father of Alexander Calder. 10, *12, 13,* 16, 26, 185, 329, 333, 336, 340.
Calder, Louisa James. Wife of Alexander Calder. 6, 13, *15, 16,* 28, 32, 36, 38, 57, 58, 60, 61, 83, *102,* 158, *159, 162,* 172, 199, 207, 208, *209, 210,* 262, 266, 330, 331, 332, 333, 334, 335, 340, 345.
Calder, Nanette Lederer. Painter; mother of Alexander Calder. 10, *13, 14,* 329, 336.
Canaday, John. Art critic. 16, 30, 200, 343.
Carandente, Giovanni. Museum director; art historian. 171, 308, 337, 338, 342, 343, 344.
Carré, Louis. Art dealer. 184, 185, 263.
Cartier-Bresson, Henri. Photographer. 32, 350.
Cassou, Jean. Art critic. 344.
Castiglione, Niccolò. Composer. 171.
Cate, Curtis. Writer. 265, 343.
Chaboud, Charles. Filmmaker. 339, 342, 345.
Chagall, Marc. Painter. 30, *294.*
Chillida, Eduardo. Sculptor. 345.
Claflin, Agnes Rindge. Art historian; museum director. *270,* 333, 345.
Clark, Eunice. Writer. 333, 341.
Clark, Kenneth. Museum director; art historian. 32.
Clementi, Aldo. Composer. 171.
Cocteau, Jean. Artist; writer. 63.
Codyre, Pat. Museum staff member. 83.
Colum, Padraic. Playwright. 171, 333.
Conant, James B. Educator. 335.
Cowley, Malcolm. Literary critic. 332.
cummings, e e. Poet. 133, 341.
Cürlis, Hans. Film producer. *242,* 344.
Cuttoli, Marie. Art dealer; collector. 158.
Cuyler, Alice. Great-aunt of Louisa Calder. *59, 199.*

Dali, Salvador. Painter. 32.
Davidson, Andrea. Daughter of Sandra and Jean Davidson. 13, *16, 17, 83.*
Davidson, Jean. Writer; son-in-law of Alexander Calder. 7, 13, *16, 55,* 81, *106, 114,* 119, *122, 128, 155, 160,* 199, *218,* 334, 335, 337, 341, 342, 343, 344, 345.
Davidson, Jo. Sculptor; father of Jean Davidson. 13.
Davidson, Sandra Calder. Illustrator; daughter of Alexander Calder. 13, *15, 16, 50, 55, 106, 114, 122, 128,* 133, *155, 160, 218,* 331, 332, 334, 335, 345.
Davidson, Shawn. Son of Sandra and Jean Davidson. 13, *16, 47,* 335.
Davis, Stuart. Painter. 334, 341.
de Creeft, José. Sculptor. 183, 221, 233, 330.
de Kooning, Willem. Painter. 334, 341.
Delaunay, Robert. Painter. 331.
de Saint Phalle, Niki. Sculptor. 32.
Descargues, Pierre. Art critic. 263, 342.

de Tomasi, Jane. Sculptor. 12.
Dos Passos, John. Novelist. 32.
Drew, William B. F. Engineer. 19, *90, 117.*
Duchamp, Marcel. Artist. 21, 172, 222, 235, 253, 267–68, 331, 333, 345.
Dudensing, Valentine. Art dealer. 61.
Durante, Jimmy. Comedian. *242.*
Dutilleux, Henri. Composer. 171.

Einstein, Albert. Physicist. 254.
Einstein, William. Painter. 32.
Elléouët, Yves. Writer. 133, 337, 341.
Elsen, Albert. Art historian. 172, 344.
Ernst, Max. Artist. 21, 345.
Evans, Myfanwy. Editor. 341.

Ferrat, Jean. Composer. 171.
Ford, Gerald. President of the United States. 311.
Foujita, Tsugouharu. Artist. 63.
Franck, César. Composer. 171.
Fratellini, Paul and Albert. Circus performers. 60, 63.

Gabo, Naum. Sculptor. 21, 253.
Gaos, José. Commissioner, Spanish Pavilion, Paris World's Fair. 28.
Giacometti, Alberto. Sculptor. 32.
Giedion, Siegfried. Architectural historian. 307.
Gonzalez, Julio. Sculptor. 28.
Goodstadt, George. Lithographer. 135.
Gordon, George. Public relations executive. 187.
Gorky, Arshile. Painter. 32.
Graham, Martha. Dancer; choreographer. 171, 172, 176, 332.
Gray, Cleve. Painter. *52,* 134, 341, 343.
Gray, Francine du Plessix. Writer. 343.
Guéguen, Pierre. Art critic. 47.
Guerrero, Pedro E. Photographer. 337, 342, 352.
Guggenheim, Peggy. Collector. 32, 333, 341.

Halet, Pierre. Choreographer. 171.
Hammacher, A. M. Museum director; art historian. 174, 342.
Harbeck, Mildred. Entrepreneur, decorative arts projects. *61.*
Harrison, Wallace K. Architect. 35, 217, 306, 332, 333.
Hawkins, Frances. Theatrical manager; museum administrator; editor. 39, 209.
Hayes, Kenneth. Banker; brother-in-law of Alexander Calder. 329.
Hayes, Margaret Calder. Sister of Alexander Calder. 13, *14,* 15, *19,* 45, *102, 113, 137,* 200, 207, *211, 213,* 238, 329.
Hayter, Stanley William. Printmaker. 133, 208, 233, 330, 342.
Hazeltine, Louis Alan. Engineer. 19.
Hélion, Jean. Painter. 331.
Hellman, Geoffrey T. Writer. 35, 343.

Hemingway, Ernest. Novelist. 32.
Hepworth, Barbara. Sculptor. 32.
Hirshhorn, Joseph H. Industrialist; collector. *108*.
Horwich, Leonard J. Cattle breeder; collector. *53, 249, 276, 281*.

Jakovski, Anatole. Art critic. 331.
James, Edward Holton. Father of Louisa Calder. 330.
James, Henry. Novelist; great-uncle of Louisa Calder. 13, 330.
James, William. Philosopher; great-uncle of Louisa Calder. 13, 330.
Jewell, Edward Alden. Art critic. 18.
Johnson, Philip. Architect. 306.
Josephson, Matthew. Writer. 28.
Josephy, Robert. Book designer. 61.

Kandinsky, Vassily. Painter. 267.
Karshan, Donald H. Print collector. 135, 343.
Kertész, André. Photographer. 350.
Kiesler, Frederick. Architect; sculptor. 63, 330.
Kiki. Artists' model. *248*.
Kirstein, Lincoln. Director, N.Y.C. Ballet; writer. 32.
Klee, Paul. Painter. 267.
Knapp, Edwin Roe. Engineer. 19.
Knox, Milly and Sandy. Collectors. 61.
Kuh, Katharine. Art dealer; art critic. 18, 25, 184, 254, 263; 264, 341.

Lacasa, Louis. Architect. 332.
Lambert, John. Painter. 13.
Laverne, Erwin. Wallpaper manufacturer. 334.
Lazzini, Joseph. Choreographer. 171.
Le Corbusier (Jeanneret, Charles-Edouard). Architect. 263, 306.
Léger, Fernand. Painter. 20, 21, 28, 30, 40, 63, 112, 172, 235, *243, 270*, 307, 330, 331, 332, 333, 342, 344, 345.
Lelong, Daniel. Art dealer. 26, *280*, 342, 345.
Leskova, Tatiana. Choreographer. 171.
Lipchitz, Jacques. Sculptor. 30.
Lipman, Howard. Stockbroker; collector; executive, art organizations. 6, 7, *162, 212*.
Lipman, Jean. Art editor; writer; collector. 342.
Lloyd, Lallie (Mrs. H. Gates). Museum patron; collector. 258, 276.
Loeb, Pierre. Art dealer. 332.
Luks, George. Painter. 20, 111, 329.

MacDonagh, Donagh. Playwright. 171, *177*, 334, 342.
MacIver, Loren. Painter. 32.
Maderna, Bruno. Composer. 71.
Maeght, Aimé. Art dealer. 335, 336.
Mannes, Marya. Writer. 32.
Masson, André. Painter. 28, 30, 333, 334, 344.

Masson, Diego. Conductor. 171, 337.
Matisse, Henri. Artist. 32.
Matter, Herbert. Photographer. 83, *274*, 333, 344, 345.
McBride, Henry. Art critic. 18.
Meredith, Burgess. Actor; producer. 171, 334, 345.
Messer, Thomas M. Jr. Museum director. 208, *323*, 344.
Mielziner, Jo. Stage designer. 32.
Mies van der Rohe, Ludwig. Architect, 340.
Miller, Arthur. Playwright. 25, 32, 36.
Miller, Dorothy C. Museum curator. 25, *274*.
Miller, Kenneth Hayes. Painter. 20, 111, 329.
Milton, Elizabeth (Mrs. Albert Fink). Collector. 83, *211, 252*.
Mindlin, Henrique. Architect. 334.
Miró, Joan. Painter. 20, 24, *24*, 28, 30, 32, 45, 63, 112, 157, 186, 200, 222, 254, 267, *296–97*, 330, 331, 332, 334, 339, 343, 344.
Miroglio, Francis. Composer. 71, 344.
Molenaar, Toby. Photographer. 350.
Mondrian, Piet. Painter. 20, 21, 32, 63, 83, 112, 113, 235, 253, 254, 263, 330, 331, 341.
Monroe, Marilyn. Actress. 36.
Moore, Henry. Sculptor. 185.
Morath, Inge. Photographer. 350.
Moravia, Alberto. Novelist. 175.
Morgan, Ted. Journalist. 266, 343.
Morris, George L. K. Painter. 333, 341.
Mourlot, Fernand. Lithographer. 135.
Mulas, Ugo. Photographer. 338, 342, 350.
Mulnix, Nancy. Director of city art projects. 186.

Namuth, Hans. Photographer. 350.
Nelson, Paul. Architect. 26, 306, 332.
Nevelson, Louise. Sculptor. 25, 40.
Newman, Muriel Kallis. Collector. *211*.
Newman, Robert B. Acoustical engineer. 184.
Nicholson, Ben. Painter. 261, 342.
Noguchi, Isamu. Sculptor. 36, 38, 61.
Noyes, Eliot. Architect. 306, 307, 308, 332, 335.

Oppenheim, Meret. Artist. 32.
Osborn, Robert. Cartoonist. *17, 29, 184*, 186, 306, 307, 341, 343.
Oswald, Marion. Singer. 30.

Parsons, Betty. Art dealer. 212.
Pascin, Jules. Painter. 63, 234, 330, 342.
Pei, I. M. Architect. 306, 337.
Pemberton, Murdock. Art critic. 111, 221.
Pene du Bois, Guy. Painter. 20, 111, 329.
Perls, Dolly. Art dealer. 31, 81, *92, 104, 105, 109, 209, 272, 278*.
Perls, Klaus. Art dealer. 20, 31, 38, 81, *92, 104, 105, 109*, 187, *209, 272, 278*, 306, 335, 344, 345.
Pevsner, Antoine. Sculptor. 21, 63, 331.
Philippe, Gérard. Actor. 334.

Picasso, Pablo. Artist. 28, 32, 40, 235.
Pichette, Henri. Playwright. 171, *176*, 334, 343.
Piper, John. Painter. 32.
Pollock, Jackson. Painter. 186.
Pompidou, Georges. President of France. 200.
Pond, Cordelia. Museum director. 209.
Poor, Henry Varnum. Painter; ceramic artist. 32.
Prats, Joan. Museum director. *290*, 345.
Prévert, Jacques. Poet. 41, 133, 134, 185, 338, 341, 343.
Prévost, Clovis. Photographer. 342.

Ray, Man. Artist. 63.
Read, Herbert. Art critic. 332.
Réal, Marc. Art director. 59–60.
Rich, Daniel Catton. Museum director. 32.
Richter, Hans. Painter; filmmaker. 21, 334, 345.
Rickey, George. Sculptor. 267.
Robinson, Boardman. Painter. 20, 111, 329.
Rodman, Selden. Poet; art critic. 16, 40, 262, 264, 341.
Root, Waverly. Writer. 45, 46, 343.
Rose, Barbara. Art critic. 40, 41, 343.
Rower, Alexander. Son of Mary and Howard Rower. 13, *15, 16*.
Rower, Holton. Son of Mary and Howard Rower. 13, *16*.
Rower, Howard. Son-in-law of Alexander Calder. 13, *16*, 336.
Rower, Mary Calder. Daughter of Alexander Calder. 13, *16*, 332, 334, 336.
Russell, John. Art critic. 26, 33, 343.

Saarinen, Eero. Architect. 185–86, 306, 332, 335.
Sage, Kay. Painter. 32.
Salemme, Attilio. Painter. 21.
Sandberg, Willem. Poet. 344.
Sarabhai, Ambalal. Industrialist. 335.
Sarabhai, Gira. Architect; designer. 335.
Sartre, Jean-Paul. Philosopher. 32, *104, 105*, 261, 333, 342, 344.
Satie, Erik. Composer. 171, 174, 235, 332, 340, 343.
Schapiro, Meyer. Art historian. 343.
Schmuki, Norbert. Choreographer. 171.
Schwartz, Marvin. Photographer. 57, 342.
Segre, Carmen. Metalworks director. 6, 31, 266, 305, 306, *306, 307*.
Seligmann, Kurt. Painter. 331.
Sert, Josep Lluis (José Luis). Architect. 30, 183–84, *280*, 332.
Seuphor, Michel. Art historian; novelist; artist. 40, 261, 342.
Sexton, Nanette. Photographer; grandniece of Alexander Calder. 350.
Shahn, Ben. Painter. 32.
Shinn, Everett. Painter. 32.
Simonson, Lee. Stage designer. 61.

Sloan, John. Painter. 20, 111, 329.

Smith, David. Sculptor. 36, 40.

Soares, Lota de Macedo. Hostess to the Calders in Brazil, 1948. 207.

Soby, James Thrall. Director, museum programs; collector; art historian. 32, *200, 286.*

Spaeth, Eloise O'Mara. Collector. 267.

Spaeth, Otto. Industrialist; collector. 267.

Spohn, Clay. Painter. 233.

Staempfli, George. Art dealer. 266, 341.

Steichen, Edward. Photographer. 32.

Stein, Leo. Writer; collector. 235.

Steinberg, Saul. Artist. 27, 344.

Stillman, Leslie. Collector. *161, 193, 212, 235.*

Stillman, Rufus. Industrialist; collector. *161, 193, 212,* 235.

Stone, Sacha. Photographer. 234.

Sweeney, James Johnson. Museum director; art critic. 21, 39, 40, 41, 45, 47, 57, 60, 63, 112, 113, 222, *253, 268,* 331, 332, 333, 334, 336, 341, 342, 344, 345.

Taillandier, Yvon. Writer. 342.

Tamayo, Rufino. Painter. 21, 28.

Tanguy, Yves. Painter. 21, 30, 222, 333.

ten Haeff, Ingeborg. Painter; collector. 208, *211, 294.*

Tchelitchew, Pavel. Painter. 32.

Thomson, Virgil. Composer. 32.

Tinguely, Jean. Sculptor. 32.

Urban, Joseph. Stage designer. 183.

Valentin, Curt. Art dealer. 31, *104,* 183, 217, 333, 335.

Van Doesburg, Théo. Painter. 63, 330, 331.

Varèse, Edgard. Composer. 171, *243,* 345.

Vilardebo, Carlos. Filmmaker. 57, 336, 337, 338, 339, 345.

Villanueva, Carlos Raúl. Architect. 184, 334, 335.

Vogelgesang, Sheppard. Stage designer. 183.

von Ripper, Rudolph Charles. Printmaker; jeweler. 133.

Walker, John. Museum director. 32.

Warburg, Edward M. M. Collector; executive, art organizations. *243,* 330.

Warren, Robert Penn. Writer. 333, 341.

Weyhe, Erhardt. Art dealer. *242.*

Wheeler, Monroe. Director, museum exhibitions and publications. 341.

Wilbur, Richard. Poet. 335, 341.

Willard, Marian. Art dealer. 207–208, 332, 333.

Wills, Helen. Tennis player. *243.*

Wolfe, Thomas. Novelist. 61, 330.

Wright, Frank Lloyd. Architect. 35.

Zigrosser, Carl. Museum curator; art critic. 233.

Acknowledgments

TITLE-PAGE DRAWINGS

Illustrations were drawn by Alexander Calder for this book to head the chapters entitled "Toys," "The Circus," "Oil Paintings," "Tapestries and Rugs," "Theatrical Productions," "Innovative Projects," "Household Objects," "Wire Sculpture," and "Mechanized Sculpture."

The sources for illustrations heading the other chapters are:
"Drawings," detail from *Children's Page*, 1943, ink, 22 x 30", collection of the author. "Gouaches," detail from exhibition invitation, Galerie Maeght, Paris, 1968. "Graphic Work," study for cover of *What Is American in American Art*, 1958, gouache, 11 x 11", collection of the author. "Jewelry," detail from exhibition invitation, Perls Galleries, New York, 1966. "Bronzes," *Study for Woman on Cord*, 1944, ink, 22½ x 31", Dr. and Mrs. Arthur E. Kahn, New York. "Wood Sculpture," detail from exhibition catalogue, Curt Valentin Gallery, New York, 1955. "Mobiles," sketch of *.125*, published in *Art in America*, no. 3, 1962. "Stabiles," Tamanoir, 1963, color lithograph, 18⅞ x 25½", Weintraub Gallery, New York.

QUOTATIONS

The source of each quotation in this book is listed below. The page on which the quotation begins appears in italics, followed by the number of the "Author's Bookshelf" entry and page reference(s).
For example: *23*, 1/279 indicates that the source of the quotation beginning on page 23 of this book is "Author's Bookshelf" no. 1—Alexander Calder's *Autobiography with Pictures*, page 279.
   Where more than one quotation occurs on a page, they are listed in sequence. Page numbers are not given for newspaper articles.

PREFACE
7, 1/106

INTRODUCTION
13, 47/72. *16*, 1/36; 44/32; 9/137. *17*, 1/28; 1/26; 1/54–55; 46/50; 24/68. *18*, 11/39; 8/3; 7/8; 71, n.p.; 123a/clipping from *The New York Times*, n.d.; 123a/clipping from *The New York Sun*, May 21, 1932; 124/113. *19*, 125/n.p.; letter from William B. F. Drew to the author, 1974. *20*, 1/71; 1/83; 123a/clipping from *Nord-Sud*, March 1931. *32*, 62/38,40; 46/47; 30/32; 1/118; 1/124; 1/124. *33*, 66/121; 32/70; 7/8; 28/99; 70/n.p.; 72/n.p.; 69/56; 1/149; 76/n.p.; 73/n.p.; 24/204; 59/176. *35*, 63/48; 59/48; 24/205; 61/33; 126/n.p. *36*, 126/n.p.; 72/n.p.; 62/40; in conversation with the author, late 1950s; in conversation with the author, 1960. *38*, 10/10; 1/258; 63/37; 74/n.p. *39*, 1/78; 1/78; 123a/clipping from *Topnotes*, December 28, 1929; quoted in letter from Beverly Lipman to the author, 1975; 33/88. *40*, 65/33; 40/90; 39/53; 33/88; 28/96; 9/136. *41*, 32/7; 65/31; 20/25.

TOYS
45, 9/140; 33/88; 99/10; 32/9; 99/7, 10; 1/80; 75/n.p. *46*, 1/80; 1/84; 123a/n.p. *47*, 77/5; 28/99; 99/10–11.

THE CIRCUS
57, 57/25; 1/73; 11/47; 32/16. *58*, 1/85; 1/115. *59*, 1/130; 136; 1/83. *60*, 1/156–57; 1/153; 1/106–107. *61*, letter from Isamu Noguchi to the author, 1971. *63*, 32/15; in the final paragraph, the discussion of the Circus is essentially the same as in 29/6.

DRAWINGS
81, 57/30; 1/61; 1/61; 21/n.p. *82*, 1/61; 12/43; 12/9; 12/13. *83*, 97/2; 11/39.

OIL PAINTINGS
111, 11/39; 1/61; 1/60; 1/66; 1/67; 1/67; 1/66; 1/85. *112*, 1/92; 1/113.

GOUACHES
119, 1a/189; 45/48; 1/218; 1/214; 1/218; 1/199; 1/234.

GRAPHIC WORK
133, 5/74; 5/74. *134*, 20/9; 20/29; 20/22; 20/22.

TAPESTRIES AND RUGS
157, in conversation with the author, 1974.

THEATRICAL PRODUCTIONS
171, 42/100. *172*, 109/8; 24/29; 79/n.p.; 3/64. *174*, 36/279; 3/64, 67; 42/100.

INNOVATIVE PROJECTS
183, 6/5; 57/27; 123a/clipping from *The New Yorker*, December 7, 1929; 1/102; 1/196. *184*, 1/59; 1/240–41. *185*, 1/189; 1/166; 1/247. *186*, 63/32–33; 1/7. *187*, letter from Calder to George Gordon and Klaus Perls, 1973.

HOUSEHOLD OBJECTS
199, 1/220; 1/136; 1/183; 1/183. *200*, 44/125; 44/125; 44/125.

JEWELRY
207, 1/21; 1/111; 1/116; 28/29; 1/201. *208*, 93/14.

BRONZES
217, 1/196; quoted in letter from Jean Davidson to the author, 1975; 1/196.

WOOD SCULPTURE
221, 3/63; 123a/clipping from *The New Yorker*, February 23, 1929; 123a/clipping from *The New Yorker*, February 23, 1929; 123a/clipping from *New York World*, November 18, 1931; 1/89. *222*, 1/108; 1/179; 24/202.

WIRE SCULPTURE
233, 1/268; 1/72; 1/80; 1/80; 1/86; 123a/clipping from *Art News*, February. 25, 1928. *234*, 123a/clipping from *The New York Times*, March 9, 1928; 1/89, 91; 1/91; 123a/unidentified clipping; 1/98; 28/96; 123a/clipping from *Paris Montparnasse*, June 15, 1929. *235*, 123a/clipping from *Chicago Daily Tribune (Paris edition)*, May 2, 1931; 77/6; 1/118; 1/159. *237*, 37/19; 26/25; the discussion of *The Brass Family* is based on 37/132. *238*, quoted by Margaret Calder Hayes in conversation with the author, 1974.

MECHANIZED SCULPTURE
253, 3/67; 32/25; 1/126. *254*, 126/n.p.; 11/44.

MOBILES
261, 71/n.p.; 82/3–5, 8; 40/85. *262*, 2/96; 1/277. *263*, 11/44; 9/139; 24/201; 28/59; 11/44; 1/198. *264*, 1/214; 11/39; 9/140. *265*, 45/57; 69/56; 1/226. *266*, letter from Jacques Bazillon to the author, 1975; 10/9; 10/9–10; 62/29. *267*, 76/n.p.; 62/32; 69/56; 1/127. *268*, 46/48; 46/50; 7/8; 3/67; 9/142; 63/37.

STABILES
305, 1/130; 1/130; 1/264; 99/44. *306*, 59/177; 63/32. *307*, 1/240; 59/163; 63/33; 63/33, 49. *308*, 63/38; 63/48; 63/48; 63/45; 63/49; 7/8. *310*, quoted by Nancy Mulnix in letter to the author, 1974.

CALDER'S CALENDAR
329, 1/11; 1/21; 1/43; 1/50; 1/54; 1/59; 1/61, 66; 1/71–72. *330*, 1/79; 1/83–84; 1/89, 91; 1/101; 7/8. *331*, 1/118; 123a/clipping from New York *World Telegram*, June 11, 1932; 1/145; 1/156; 1/154. *332*, 1/156; 1/159; 1/168–69; 1/

176; 1/178–79. *333,* quoted in letter from Jean Davidson to the author, 1975; 1/185; 1/184; 1/195; 1/188; 1/189, 194. *334,* in conversation with Klaus Perls, 1975; 6/5; in conversation with Mr. and Mrs. Erwin Laverne, 1949; 1/204; 7/8; 1/209. *335,* 1/220; 59/171; 63/34; in conversation with Klaus Perls, 1956; 24/64; 1/255, 258. *336,* 1/255; 59/167; 1/87; 1/265; 1/265. *337,* 1/271; 1/273; 63/42; 1a/192. *338,* 1a/195; 1a/199; quoted by Klaus Perls, 1970. *339,* 70/n.p.; 62/40; in conversation with Klaus Perls, 1973. *340,* 26/36; in conversation with the author, 1975; in conversation with the author, 1975.

PHOTO CREDITS

Bill Andrews: 196

Archives of American Art, Smithsonian Institution: 33, 34 bottom, 46 top, 46 bottom, 60, 61 bottom, 208 left, 234 top, 234 bottom, 253

E. Irving Blomstrann: 270 left

Lee Boltin: 298 center

A. Dwight Button: 158

John C. Byron: 319 top

Mario Carrieri: 309 bottom

Henri Cartier-Bresson: 36

William Chess: 211 bottom center

Geoffrey Clements: 48 top, 53 top, 124, 137 bottom, 149, 150 bottom, 163, 165, 212 top, 214–15, 222, 223, 229 top right, 239 right, 285, 287, 292 bottom, 300 top

Jean Davidson: 114 bottom right

Everett Studios: 167

Ed Finley: 195 top

Claude Gaspari: 124 top right, 130 top left, 150 top, 218 top left, 267, 279 bottom left, 291 top, 294 bottom left

Paolo Gasparini: 197

George Goodstadt: 135, 152 top right

George Gordon: 186 bottom

Pedro E. Guerrero: 16 bottom, 22–23, 50, 51, 54 bottom, 55, 58 left, 83, 168 top, 168 bottom left, 168 bottom right, 186 top, 200 top left, 201 top right, 201 bottom left, 201 bottom right, 202 bottom left, 204 left, 204 right, 204–205 top, 205 bottom, 227, 230 bottom, 238 bottom, 243 bottom left, 251, 254, 255 top left, 255 right, 258 bottom, 278 bottom left, 312 right, 315 bottom

David Guthrie: 272 right

Haar, Hedrich-Blessing: 259

Hugo P. Herdeg: 193 bottom

William Hill: 325 bottom

Evelyn Hofer: 211 top center

Idaka: 190 left

Léni Iselin: 120

Robert Jaffe: 12 top

Livingston Johns: 303

Magda Jones: 211 top right

Peter A. Juley: 224 top

André Kertész: 59, 61 top

Daniel Keryzaouen: 180 top, 180 bottom, 181

Neil Koppes: 126, 127, 162 bottom left

David Leth: 325 top right

Colin C. McRae: 14 left, 14 center, 102 right, 137 bottom, 210 top right

Richard Marshall: 323 bottom

Herbert Matter: 18, 48 bottom left, 48 bottom right, 49 bottom right, 62, 188, 201 top left, 209 top, 212 bottom right, 228 top left, 228 top right, 228 bottom left, 229 bottom right, 237 right, 238 top left, 243 top left, 250 top, 250 bottom, 263, 271, 274 left, 275 left. 284. 290 right, 312 left

Gwyn Metz: 206 bottom left

Toby Molenaar: 160, 162 top, 162 right

Inge Morath: 159, 307 top

Ugo Mulas: 21, 37 top, 178, 179, 199 bottom, 210 bottom right, 249, 255 bottom left, 257, 266 bottom, 309 top, 313, 315 bottom, 317, 318 bottom

Hans Namuth: 35, 37 bottom, 42–43, 208 bottom

O. E. Nelson: 218 bottom, 242 bottom center

Gordon Parks: 207

Pennsylvania Academy of the Fine Arts: 11 top right

Klaus Perls: 9, 327

Eric Pollitzer: 320 bottom

Ignacy Praszkier: 316 top

David Robbins: 318 top

J. Robert: 290 bottom left

Marvin Schwartz: 63, 64–79

Carmen Segre: 310–11

Nanette Sexton: 211 center left

Rufus Stillman: 15 center, 161, 193 top, 210 bottom left, 212 center right, 308 top, 328

Jerry Thompson: 269

Agnes Varda: 176 bottom, 264 top

Marc Vaux: 212 top left, 236, 237 top

Arthur Vitols: 90 bottom, 100, 102 top, 115 top, 147, 148 bottom, 190 right, 203, 231, 242 right, 246 bottom, 272 left, 274 right, 282 top, 288, 294 right, 314, 321, 324

Ed Webb: 53 right

Leonard Wolfe: 38

Allen Yarinsky: 235

April 1, 1975

Dear Sandy,

We'd like to present our <u>Calder's Universe</u> as the "official" book about you (just as your <u>Autobiography</u> is the official book by you)--this because of the key people involved in your life and work who have collaborated in its production.

You and Louisa first, of course, for working with us all along the way.

Jean Davidson has always, as now again, been generous with help of all kinds, including his permission, with yours, to quote from the <u>Autobiography</u>. Permissions for reproducing works, photos, etc. from Sandra and Mary are also appreciated.

Peggy Hayes, record-keeper of Calder family events, photographs and letters (with focus on her brother!), most generously shared everything for this book.

Klaus and Dolly Perls, as your New York dealers for more than twenty years, have maintained an institutional-type archive of photographs, records, lists of collectors, etc., and made them all available to us. As you know, they worked with us from start to finish.

Daniel Lelong's similar archive, organized for Galerie Maeght, your Paris dealer, was also put at our disposal.

In your autobiography you mention Howard Lipman as your favorite <u>amateur</u>. He is on this list because he shared with me and our editorial group the selection of illustrations. His forty-year interest in your work, based on the conviction that you will always be known as America's greatest artist, qualifies him as the collector best able to check the choice of your work. The selection is the most important aspect of this book, which was planned as a collection in print, to be extended in fact in the Whitney Museum of American Art exhibition.

Finally, we are grateful to your personal and professional friends who talked about you for quotation in my introduction, and to the many others listed in the Acknowledgments page.

I'm detailing all this to ask whether we may preface the book with a page worded just about as I have it here, to recognize our chief collaborators. If so, would you just initial your OK and return this to me?

Best, and love to Louisa,

Jean

Mr. Alexander Calder
Saché 37
Indre et Loire
France

CALDER'S UNIVERSE

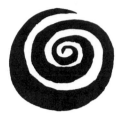

The text of this book has been set in Janson type by The Book Press.
Color separations were made by Capper, Inc.
Ink samples for special flat color sections were supplied by
Calder's lithographer, George Goodstadt, Inc.

The book was printed by Rae Publishing Company, Inc.,
and bound by A. Horowitz & Son.
The typography and design are by Bryan Holme.